The

Demography

of

South Africa

Editorial Advisory Board

A General Demography of Africa

Series Editor: Tukufu Zuberi

THE DEMOGRAPHY OF SOUTH AFRICA
Tukufu Zuberi, Amson Sibanda, and Eric O. Udjo, Eds.

AFRICAN HOUSEHOLDS IN CENSUSES AND SURVEYS
Etienne Van De Walle, Editor

The

Demography

of

South Africa

**Edited by Tukufu Zuberi, Amson Sibanda,
and Eric Udjo**

Statistics
South Africa

M.E.Sharpe
Armonk, New York
London, England

This research was done as part of the collaboration between the African Census
Analysis Project (ACAP) and Statistics South Africa (Stats SA). ACAP is supported by
grants from the Rockefeller Foundation (RF 97013 #21; RF 98014 #22), the Andrew W. Mellon
Foundation, and the Fogarty International Center and the National Institute of Child Health and
Human Development (TW00655-04).

Library of Congress Cataloging-in-Publication Data

The demography of South Africa / edited by Tukufu Zuberi, Amson Sibanda, and
Eric O. Udjo.
    p. cm. — (A general demography of Africa)
Includes bibliographical references and index.
ISBN 0-7656-1563-0 (hardcover : alk. paper)
  1. South Africa—Population—Statistics. 2. Demography—South Africa. I.
Zuberi, Tukufu. II. Sibanda, Amson. III. Udjo, Eric O. IV. Series.
  HB3663.4.A3D46 2005
  304.6'0968—dc22

          2004022249

Table of Contents

List of Tables, Figures, and Appendices   vii

Series Foreword
    Tukufu Zuberi   xvi

Foreword
    Pali J. Lehohla   xix

Introduction
    Tukufu Zuberi, Amson Sibanda, Eric O. Udjo, and
    Martin W. Bangha   xi

1. Population Statistics
    Akil K. Khalfani, Tukufu Zuberi, Sulaiman Bah, and
    Pali J. Lehohla   3

2. Fertility Levels, Differentials, and Trends
    Eric O. Udjo   40

3. Age at First Birth
    Amson Sibanda and Tukufu Zuberi   65

4. An Examination of Recent Census and Survey Data on Mortality
Within the Context of HIV/AIDS
    Eric O. Udjo   90

5. HIV/AIDS in Light of Death Registration Data:
In Search of Elusive Estimates
    Sulaiman Bah   120

6. Parental Survival and Residential Patterns
      Amadou Noumbissi, Ayaga A. Bawah, and Tukufu Zuberi   160

7. Technical Appraisal of Official South African Life Tables
      Sulaiman Bah   181

8. Racial Differences in Household Structure
      Eliya Msiyaphazi Zulu and Amson Sibanda   218

9. Race and Gender Gaps in Education
      Amson Sibanda and Gwendoline Lehloenya   253

10. Migration and Employment
      Tukufu Zuberi and Amson Sibanda   266

About the Editors and Contributors   297
Index   301

List of Tables, Figures, and Appendices

Tables

1.1	Racial Classifications in the Union/Republic of South Africa, 1911–96	11
1.2	South African Population: 1911–96	12
1.3	Percentage of Population Estimated by Method, 1991	16
1.4	Sex Ratio by Estimation Method, 1991	17
1.5	Estimated Undercount by Race, Percent and Year	20
2.1	Brass P/F Ratios Using Hamad's Multipliers Based on Reported Age-Specific Fertility Rates (ASFR), and Average Parities (Parity), and Reported Total Fertility Rates (TFR)	45
2.2	Brass P/F Ratios by Population Group Using Hamad's Multipliers	47
2.3	Current Estimates of Gompertz Parameters, Total Fertility Rates by Population Group	49
2.4	Period Estimates of Gompertz Parameters, Total Fertility Rates, and Mean Age of Fertility Distribution by Population Group	50
2.5	Current Estimates of the Gompertz Parameters and Total Fertility Rates by Province	55
2.6	Estimates of Total Fertility Rates by Population Group in South Africa	58
3.1	Fertility Levels and Trends in South Africa by Race	71
3.2	Mean Age at First Birth, South Africa 1996	72
3.3	Logistic Regression Results (Odds Ratios) for the Effects of Explanatory Variables on the Likelihood of Having a First Birth at Various Ages: All Racial Groups	74
3.4	Logistic Regression Results (Odds Ratios) for the Effects of Explanatory Variables on the Likelihood of Having a First Birth at Various Ages: African Women	78

3.5 Logistic Regression Results (Odds Ratios) for the Effects of
Explanatory Variables on the Likelihood of Having a First Birth
at Various Ages: White Women   81

3.6 Logistic Regression Results (Odds Ratios) for the Effects of
Explanatory Variables on the Likelihood of Having a First Birth
at Various Ages: Colored Women   84

3.7 Logistic Regression Results (Odds Ratios) for the Effects of
Explanatory Variables on the Likelihood of Having a First Birth
at Various Ages: Indian/Asian Women   85

4.1 Reported Life Table Probability of Dying from Birth to Exact
Age x (q_x) from Proportions Dead (D_i) of Children Ever Born
by Population Group   95

4.2 Adult Female Mortality from Reports on Mother Alive Based
on the 1996 Census by Population Group   99

4.3 Adult Male Mortality in South Africa and Lesotho   104

4.4 Estimated Period Parameters of the Female Logit Life Table
by Population Group   105

4.5 Estimated Period Indices of Female Mortality by Population
Group   107

4.6 Estimated Parameters of the Logit Life Table by Province, 1996 110

4.7 Summary Indices of Two-Parameter Female Life Table by
Province, 1996   110

5.1 Comparison of the Death Data from the Population Register
with Those from Stats SA Data for 1996 Base Year   131

5.2 Adjustments of the Population Register Data to Bring Them in
Line with the Data from Stats SA, 1997–2000   133

5.3a Recorded Number of Deaths Due to HIV/AIDS and HIV/AIDS-
Related Causes According to the CDC List, South Africa, 1996   134

5.3b Recorded Number of Deaths Due to AIDS and AIDS-Related
Causes According to the Stats SA List, South Africa 1996   134

5.4a Unadjusted, Adjusted, and "AIDS-Free" Age-Specific Death
Rates (per 10,000) Using the CDC List of AIDS-Related Causes
of Death, South Africa, 1996–2000   135

5.4b Unadjusted, Adjusted, and "AIDS-Free" Age-Specific Death
Rates (per 10,000) Using the Stats SA List of AIDS-Related
Causes of Death, South Africa, 1996–2000   136

5.5a Unadjusted, Adjusted, and "AIDS-Free Age-Specific Percentages,
Using the CDC List of HIV/AIDS-Related Causes of Death,
South Africa, 1996–2000   137

5.5b Unadjusted, Adjusted, and "AIDS-Free" Age-Specific Percentages,
Using the Stats SA List of HIV/AIDS-Related Causes of Death,
South Africa, 1996–2000   138

5.6a   Number of Reported Deaths (over the Period 1993–96) and
        Estimated Deaths (over the period 1997–2000) Due to
        HIV/AIDS and HIV/AIDS-Related Causes (From CDC List)   147
5.6b   Number of Reported Deaths (over the Period 1993–96) and
        Estimated Deaths (over the Period 1997–2000) Due to
        HIV/AIDS and HIV/AIDS-Related Causes (From Stats SA List) 147
5.6c   Number of Reported Deaths Due to Natural Causes by Age
        Group and Sex, 1993–2000   148
5.6d   Total Number of Reported Deaths by Age Group and Sex,
        1993–2000   148
5.6e   Percentage of Reported Natural Deaths (over the Period
        1993–96) and Estimated Percentage of Reported Natural
        Deaths (over the Period 1997–2000) Due to HIV/AIDS and
        HIV/AIDS-Related Causes (From CDC List)   149
5.6f   Percentage of Reported Natural Deaths (over the Period
        1993–96) and Estimated Percentage of Reported Natural
        Deaths (over the Period 1997–2000) Due to HIV/AIDS and
        HIV/AIDS-Related Causes (From Stats SA List)   149
5.6g   Percentage of Reported Total Deaths (over the Period
        1993–96) and Estimated Percentage of Reported Total Deaths
        (over the Period 1997–2000) Due to HIV/AIDS and
        HIV/AIDS-Related Causes (From CDC List)   150
5.6h   Percentage of Reported Total Deaths (over the Period
        1993–96) and Estimated Percentage of Reported Total Deaths
        (over the Period 1997–2000) Due to HIV/AIDS and
        HIV/AIDS-Related Causes (From Stats SA List)   150
5.7a   Leading Underlying Causes of Death Among Males, National
        Sample, 1997–2001   152
5.7b   Leading Underlying Causes of Death Among Females, National
        Sample, 1997–2001   153
6.1   Number of Children Surviving Reported by Mothers Compared
        to Children with Mother Alive, by Racial Group   163
6.2   Proportion of Children with Mother, Father, or Both Parents
        Dead According to Selected Variables (Children Ages 0–14)   167
6.3   Children's Relationship to the Head of Household by Survival
        Status of Parents (children ages 0–14)   171
6.4   Observed Odds that a Child (Female or Male) Residing with His or
        Her Grandparents Resides in a Household Headed by the Couple   172
6.5   Proportion of Children by Household Type and the Survival
        Status of Parents   172
6.6   Children by Household Type and the Survival Status of
        Parents (Odd Ratios)   173

6.7 Multinomial Regression Results Showing the Odds of Either Residing in Single or Extended Households with Unrelated Members Compared with Nuclear Households (Coefficient and Estimated Probabilities) 174

7.1 Trends in Published Life Expectancy at Selected Ages, among the Different Population Groups, Males, South Africa, 1921–94 196

7.2 Trends in Published Life Expectancy at Selected Ages, Among the Different Population Groups, Females, South Africa, 1921–94 197

7.3 Probabilities of Dying Between Age x and $x + n$ by Sex for RSA and Population Group 205

7.4 Probability of Dying Between Age x and $x + n$ Extracted from the South African Life Tables, 1996, for RSA, Provinces, and Urban/Non Urban Areas, Males 206

7.5 Probability of Dying Between Age x and $x + n$ Extracted from the South African Life Tables, 1996, for RSA, Provinces and Urban/Non Urban Areas, Females 206

8.1 Average Household Size by Race, Place of Residence, and Year 225

8.2 Distribution of Household Members by Relationship to Household Head by Race and Year 228

8.3 Type of Household by Race and Year, Whole Country, 1991 (Unweighted) Full Census and 1996 (Weighted) 30 Percent Sample 230

8.4 Type of Household by Race and Year, Rural Areas, 1991 (Unweighted) Full Census and 1996 (Weighted) 30 Percent Sample 232

8.5 Type of Household by Race and Year, Urban Areas, 1991 (Unweighted) Full Census and 1996 (Weighted) 30 Percent Sample 232

8.6 Percentage of Female-Headed Households by Race, Residence, and Year 236

8.7 Logistic Results (Odds Ratios) Predicting the Likelihood That a Woman Is a Head of Household: South Africa, 1996 242

8.8 Logistic Results (Odds Ratios) Predicting the Likelihood That an African Woman Is a Head of Household: South Africa, 1996 247

9.1 Gender Gaps in Primary-School Enrollment: Children Ages 7–18 256

9.2 Gender Gaps in Secondary-School Enrollment: Children Ages 13–24 257

9.3 Gender Gaps in Primary-School Completion: Children Ages 13–20 259

9.4   Gender Gaps in Secondary-School Completion: Children
Ages 18–25   260

9.5   Racial Gaps in Primary-School Enrollment: Children
Ages 7–18   262

9.6   Racial Gaps in Secondary-School Enrollment: Children
Ages 13–24   262

9.7   Racial Gaps in Primary-School Completion: Children
Aged 13–20   263

9.8   Racial Gaps in Secondary-School Completion: Children
Ages 18–25   263

10.1   Sample Distribution of Males Ages 20–55 by Nativity and
Migration Status: South Africa 1996   273

10.2   Odds Ratios from Logistic Regression Models of Employment
for Separate Racial Groups: Foreign-Born Immigrants and
South-African-Born Males, 1996   281

10.3   Odds Ratios from Logistic Regression Models of Employment
for Separate Racial Groups: Foreign-Born Immigrants and
South African-Born Females, 1996   285

10.4   Odds Ratios from Logistic Regression Models of Employment
for South African-Born Internal Migrants and Nonmigrants:
Males, 1996   288

10.5   Odds Ratios from Logistic Regression Models of Employment
for SA-Born Internal Migrants and Nonmigrants: Females,
1996   290

10.6   Odds Ratios from Logistic Regression Models of Employment
for All Racial Groups: South-African-Born Internal Migrants
and Nonmigrants, 1996   292

Figures

1.1   Statistics South Africa's Strategy for Implementing Automatic
Coding of Causes of Death   29

2.1   Trends in Total Fertility Rates by Population Group   53

4.1   Trend in Childhood Mortality by Population Groups   97

4.2   Trend in Adult Female Mortality by Population Group Based
on the 1996 Census   101

4.3   Trend in Childhood Mortality by Province from the 1996 Census   108

4.4   Estimated Female Infant Mortality Rate Per Thousand Live
Births by Province, 1996   109

4.5   HIV Prevalence Among Women Attending Antenatal Clinics
in 2000 and Among Adults 15–49 in 2000   109

5.1a   Comparison of Male Deaths from the Population Register
with Those from Stats SA, South Africa, 1996   131

5.1b Comparison of Female Deaths from the Population Register
with those from Stats SA, South Africa, 1996   132
5.2a Unadjusted Age-Specific Death Rates Among Males,
South Africa, 1996–2000   139
5.2b Adjusted Age-Specific Death Rates Among Males,
South Africa, 1996–2000   139
5.2c "AIDS-Free" Age-Specific Death Rates Among Males
(Maximum List), South Africa, 1996–2000   140
5.3a Unadjusted Age-Specific Death Rates Among Females,
South Africa, 1996–2000   140
5.3b Adjusted Age-Specific Death Rates Among Females, South
Africa, 1996–2000   141
5.3c "AIDS-Free" Age-Specific Death Rates Among Females
(Maximum List), South Africa, 1996–2000   141
5.4a Unadjusted Percentage of Deaths (In Age Range 15–49)
Among Males, South Africa, 1996–2000   142
5.4b Adjusted Percentage of Deaths (In Age Range 15–49) Among
Males, South Africa, 1996–2000   142
5.4c "AIDS-Free" Percentage of Deaths (In Age Range 15–49)
Among Males, South Africa, 1996–2000   143
5.5a Unadjusted Percentage of Deaths (In Age Range 15–49)
Among Females, South Africa, 1996–2000   143
5.5b Adjusted Percentage of Deaths (In Age Range 15–49) Among
Females, South Africa, 1996–2000   144
5.5c "AIDS-Free" Percentage of Deaths (In Age Range 15–49)
Among Females, South Africa, 1996–2000   144
6.1   Proportion of Children with Parent Dead by Age in South Africa 165
6.2   Proportion of Children with Mother Dead by Racial Group   165
6.3   Proportion of Children with Father Dead by Racial Group   166
7.1   Life Table 1(x) Values for White Males, Republic of
South Africa, 1921–85   198
7.2   Life Table 1(x) Values for White Females, Republic of
South Africa, 1921–85   199
7.3   Life Table 1(x) Values for Colored Males, Republic of
South Africa, 1921–85   200
7.4   Life Table 1(x) Values for Colored Females, Republic of
South Africa, 1921–85   201
7.5   Life Table 1(x) Values for Indian/Asian Males, Republic of
South Africa, 19–85   202
7.6   Life Table 1(x) Values for Indian/Asian Females, Republic
of South Africa, 1921–85   203

7.7   South African Life Tables for Males by Population Group,
      1985–94   208
 7.8 South African Life Tables for Females by Population Group,
      1985–94   209
 7.9 South African Life Tables for Males by Province, 1996   210
 7.10 South African Life Tables for Females by Province 1996   211
 8.1 Household Size for Blacks: Percentage of Households by Size
      and Year   226
 8.2 Household Size for Whites: Percentage of Households by Size
      and Year   226
 8.3 Percentage of Children Living with Mothers, South
      Africa, 1996   238
 8.4a Children's Living Arrangements by Mothers' Marital Status:
      Africans   239
 8.4b Children's Living Arrangements by Mothers' Marital Status:
      Colored   239
 8.4c Children's Living Arrangements by Mothers' Marital Status:
      Indians/Asians   240
 8.4d Children's Living Arrangements by Mother's Marital Status:
      Whites   240
10.1 Age Distributions of Males Aged 20–55 by Nativity and
      Migration Status: South Africa, 1996   276
10.2 Age Distributions of Females Aged 20–55 by Nativity and
      Migration Status: South Africa, 1996   276
10.3 Labor Force Participation Rates and Employment Rates for
      Males Aged 20–55 by Migration Status and Nativity: South
      Africa, 1996   277
10.4 Labor Force Participation Rates and Employment Rates for
      Females Aged 20–55 by Migration Status and Nativity: South
      Africa, 1996   277
10.5 Schooling Distributions for Males Aged 20–55 by Migration
      Status and Nativity: South Africa, 1996   279
10.6 Schooling Distributions for Females Aged 20–55 by Migration
      Status and Nativity: South Africa, 1996   279

Appendixes

1.1   Notification/Register of Death/Stillbirth   38
2.1   Fitting the Gompertz Relational Model   61
2.2   Fitting the Relational Gompertz Model to Current Births (F)
      and Children Ever Born (P), 1995: African   62

2.3   Fitting the Relational Gompertz Model to Current Births (F)
        and Children Ever Born (P), 1996: African   62
2.4   Fitting the Relational Gompertz Model to Current Births (F)
        and Children Ever Born (P), 1995: White   63
2.5   Fitting the Relational Gompertz Model to Current Births (F)
        and Children Ever Born (P), 1996: White   63
2.6   Fitting the Relational Gompertz Model to Fertility Reports in
        the 1970 Census: African   64
2.7   Fitting the Relational Gompertz Model to Fertility Reports in
        the 1970 Census: Whites   64
4.1   Trend in Childhood and Adult Female Mortality, African   114
4.2   Trend in Childhood and Adult Female Mortality, Colored   114
4.3   Trend in Childhood and Adult Female Mortality, Indian   115
4.4   Trend in Childhood and Adult Female Mortality, White   115
4.5   Trend in Adult Male Mortality by Population Group Based on
        the 1995 Survey   116
4.6   Trend in Adult Male Mortality by Population Group Based on
        the 1996 Census   116
4.7   Trend in Childhood and Adult Mortality, African   117
4.8   Trend in Childhood and Adult Mortality, Colored   117
4.9   Trend in Childhood and Adult Mortality, Indian   118
4.10   Trend in Childhood and Adult Mortality, White   118
4.11   Estimated Infant Mortality Rate in 1996 and HIV Prevalence
        in 2000 Based on Antenatal Clinics Visits   119
4.12   Estimated Infant Mortality Rate in 1996 and National HIV
        Prevalence among Adults Aged 15–49 in 2000   119
5.1   Conditions Attributable to HIV or Complicated by HIV
        According to the 1993 CDC Definition   157
5.2   Causes of Death that Closely Match Conditions Attributable to
        HIV or Complicated by HIV According to the 1993 CDC
        Definition   158
5.3   List of Causes of Death Often Associated with HIV/AIDS
        According to Stats SA Coding Experience   159
6.1   Proportion of Persons Living in Institutions by Racial Group   179
6.2   Proportion of Persons with Stated Survival Status of Mother
        by Racial Group   179
6.3   Proportion of Persons with Stated Survival Status of
        Father by Racial Group   180

Series Foreword

The performance and prospects of African nations have generated considerable interest in how population dynamics interact with and influence social change in Africa. Yet, very few studies have attempted to provide a general demography of Africa (for notable exceptions, see Brass et al. 1968; National Academy of Sciences 1993, 7 vols.). This is largely because of the paucity and poor quality of available data. In the last thirty years, censuses and surveys have produced data for the study of African demography. These data and increasing scholarly and policy-related interest in African demography have stimulated much research on African population studies (see Zuberi et al. 2003). In response to this interest, this volume, *The Demography of South Africa*, is the first in a series of studies, entitled A General Demography of Africa, that have been carried out under the auspices of the African Census Analysis Project (ACAP).

ACAP is a collaborative initiative between researchers at the University of Pennsylvania and African institutions specializing in demographic data collection, research, and training. This initiative was started as an effort to preserve and to try and maximize the use of African census micro-data for academic and policy-oriented research. Census data are unique in that they provide information at the individual, household, community, and national levels. ACAP has developed a data bank of census data representing each region of sub-Saharan Africa with data that covers the past thirty years.

The African continent consists of fifty-three different countries. In 2000, the nearly 800 million people living in Africa spoke over 2,000 languages and dialects. Between now and the middle of the twenty-first century, African population size is projected to increase from its 2000 level of about 794 million to somewhere between 1.6 billion and 2.3 billion—more than double the current size. Africa's relative proportion of the earth's human population will also rise from its current 13 percent to an astonishing 21 percent by mid-century. These trends represent rough estimates. The general demography of Africa is practically unknown. In general, Africa's demographic history over the past thirty years consists of a vague and impressionistic sketch, which we have accepted as the real demography of Africa. Is it surprising, then, that the demography of Africa should be seen through the prism of the demographic history of Europe, Asia, or Latin America?

For a long time, a lack of data was thought to conceal the true demography of Africa. There has never been a census of all the people residing in Africa at the same time, and where censuses have been taken, they have had different levels of error. In addition to the lack of accurate counts of the number of people in Africa is the lack of population-based estimates of human fertility, mortality, and migration. Tackling population issues in Africa requires a concerted and collaborative effort. The role of high-quality demographic research in providing the empirical bases for strategic interventions is critical.

This multivolume series, A General Demography of Africa, will allow us to take stock of our knowledge of African demography, putting forward a variety of viewpoints on African population and offering a new reading of the demography of Africa. A General Demography of Africa has the advantage of showing the light and shade and openly portraying the differences of opinion that may exist between scholars and African realities.

This multivolume series is a culmination of the efforts made by ACAP over the past ten years not only to preserve African census data and avoid perpetual loss due to poor storage but also to encourage and enhance further analysis of these massive amounts of data. For obvious reasons, census data remain the most important source of population data in Africa that allow policymakers to do more effective work. Effective national vital registration systems do not yet exist for the majority of African nations, and where they exist, they are incomplete. However, considerable efforts over the last two or so decades have enriched the data environment in Africa, and censuses are an important part of this new data regime.

This first volume of A General Demography of Africa, *The Demography of South Africa*, is the result of a collaborative effort between the ACAP and Statistics South Africa (Stats SA). The importance of this volume is highlighted by the fact that, for years, international scholars have not had the opportunity to critically examine issues pertaining to the general demography of South Africa. This has been due to several factors. First, because of the need to maintain international sanctions against various apartheid governments, international scholars in the population field avoided working on the demography of South Africa. Second, the apartheid governments also made sure that international scholars could not effectively analyze demographic issues in South Africa by denying data access to any scholars who might have had any interest.

This book seeks to outline the demographic contours of South Africa. The 1996 South African Population Census is used as the basis for undertaking detailed analyses of fertility, mortality, migration, household structure, education, and employment. Large-scale October Household Surveys and data from a partial vital registration system are also used in conjunction with census data to further understand the relationship between various demographic and economic phenomena.

In 2001, to commemorate Africa Statistics Day in Pretoria, a workshop was organized in collaboration with Stats SA. During the workshop, several members of the South African Development Community Statistics Committee, Stats SA, and other ACAP partners and collaborators discussed several of the chapters included in this volume. We wish to thank all the participants at this workshop for their critical comments on the earlier drafts: L.M. Machirovi, Ana Paula Machedo, Ndiba Kayumba Marcel, Lydia Mohlamme, Jean-Marie Hakizimana, Jacky Galpin, Ilboudo Francois, Harish Bundhoo, Alida Boettcher, Amadou Noumbissi, Liina Kafidi, Laura Ahtime, Melanie du Plessis, Akil Khalfani, Rob Dorrington, Mapitso Lebuso, Risenga Maluleke, Eliya Zulu, Bangha Martin, Hilton Visagie, Ekade Ghalio, Margaret Africa, Pali Lehohla, Lindiwe Makubalo, Sulaiman Bah, and Gugu Gule. We are particularly grateful to Pierre Ngom, Wole Adegboyega, Gobopamang Letamo, and Sangeetha Madhavan for carefully reading selected chapters.

In addition, Pierre Ngom carefully reviewed every chapter. His critical review was invaluable and improved various aspects of the work. Finally, the efforts of Martin W. Bangha in the coordination of the work on this volume and in providing bibliographic assistance were essential in the completion of this project. He carefully assisted at various stages with the formatting and harmonizing of the various chapters. We would like to express our special thanks to Audra Rodgers for her essential administrative support and Timothy Cheney, Mathews Phiri, and Piet Alberts for their help with data programming and manipulation.

We are also grateful to the organizations that provided financial support for the research for this volume: Statistics South Africa, the Population Studies Center at the University of Pennsylvania, the National Institute of Aging (P30 AF12836), Fogarty International Center (TW00004), Rockefeller Foundation (RF 97013 #21; RF 98014 #22), and Andrew W. Mellon Foundation.

Tukufu Zuberi, Series Editor
Lasry Family Professor of Race Relations
University of Pennsylvania
Philadelphia, Pennsylvania

References

Brass, W., A.J. Coale, P. Demeny, D.F. Heisel, F. Lorimer, A. Romaniuk, and E. van de Walle. 1968. *The Demography of Tropical Africa*. Princeton, NJ: Princeton University Press.

National Academy Press. 1993. Population Dynamics of Sub-Saharan Africa: A Series. 7 Vols. Washington, D.C.: National Academy Press.

Zuberi, T., A. Sibanda, A. Bawah, and A. Noumbissi. 2003. "Population and African society." *Annual Review of Sociology* 29: 465–86.

Foreword

The 1996 South African Population Census was the first nationwide enumeration of the people of South Africa following the collapse of apartheid and the beginning of majority rule through democratic elections in 1994. The last nationwide population census prior to the 1996 census was in 1970. Thus, for twenty-six years (1970 to 1996), information on demographic processes (e.g., fertility, mortality, and migration) was based on fragmentary data collected from fragmentary censuses and surveys during that period.

As a consequence, no systematic empirically based literature on demographic processes, socioeconomic factors, and life opportunities in South Africa between 1970 and 1996 exists. The importance of census data for empirically based research and social planning cannot be overemphasized.

The Demography of South Africa presents a unique snapshot of South Africa's history. The book endeavors to capture South Africa's population dynamics in a period that covers the lives of South Africans during and after apartheid. In a way, to borrow the title of Nelson Mandela's autobiography, the "long walk to freedom" will not be easy without a thorough understanding of the demography of South Africa. Understanding the country's past, present, and future population dynamics is central to the fulfillment of the long walk to freedom, equality, democracy, sustainable development, and the fight against today's major challenges, like HIV/AIDS and poverty. In October 1998, Mandela confronted these challenges when he launched the results of the 1996 population census, which forms, by and large, the database for this piece of work.

This book is the first of its kind about postapartheid South Africa's demography. It exploits census information, supplemented by household surveys and vital registration, to gain a better understanding of demographic processes and their interrelationships with socioeconomic phenomena. The book provides insights into the demographic regimes underpinning South Africa's development processes as it charts the country's demographic landscape in the last couple of decades. Additionally, the book reveals the social constructs that have influenced demographic patterns and the practice of official statistics in South Africa.

The work on this volume, which has been led and put together by African scholars and staff of Statistics South Africa, epitomizes a commitment to the ideals of the New Partnership for African Development, which encourages African scholars to understand and use the data.

In the context of the Southern African Development Community Census Project, which remains a focal point for Statistics South Africa, we hope that this book will act as a stimulus for the analysis of the demography of the region. Such an analysis should in turn enhance regional collaboration, as the demographic template in the book could serve as a prototype for gaining insights into the development needs of the region. This book thus serves as a platform for further work. A second work along the lines of this book has been commissioned for the 2001 South Africa Population Census.

This book encourages a multidisciplinary approach in the analysis of population processes and should serve as a guide to students of technical and historical demography. A regional approach in the analysis of population processes will further enhance the capability of African scholars to make positive contributions to Africa and the rest of the world.

I wish to thank all the contributors for their impeccable scholarly work, which has stretched the boundaries of knowledge on the subject of the African continent. I especially wish to thank Tukufu Zuberi and Amson Sibanda of the African Census Analysis Project at the University of Pennsylvania and Eric Udjo of Statistics South Africa.

Pali J. Lehohla
Statistician-General
Statistics South Africa

Introduction

*Tukufu Zuberi, Amson Sibanda, Eric O. Udjo,
and Martin W. Bangha*

The Demography of South Africa provides an analysis of population and society in the Republic of South Africa. The volume presents and examines the demographic contours of postapartheid South Africa. The 1996 South African Population Census is used as the basis for our analysis of fertility, mortality, migration, education, employment, and household structure. These census data are complemented in a few cases by large-scale household surveys and data from a partial vital registration system to further our understanding of the relationship between various demographic, economic, and social phenomena.

The Demography of South Africa offers a unique presentation of the interplay of demographic, social, and economic processes in a society undergoing rapid sociopolitical change as a result of the collapse of apartheid. The demographic behavior of South Africa's various population groups is linked to social, economic, and political inequalities created by policies of separate and unequal development. A comprehensive analysis of the demographic and social processes in South Africa has not been undertaken before. Hence, the timing of this book is critical. This book will be of interest to individuals researching Africa in general and South Africa in particular. The volume provides a general overview of several major demographic processes and trends that affect South Africa.

South Africa has the strongest economy in sub-Saharan Africa. It has been and continues to be a major destination for immigrants from other countries on the continent and Asia. Yet we know very little about its demographic situation and trends. *The Demography of South Africa* is the first book about South Africa to use data from the first postapartheid census.

Organization of the Book

Identifying and tracking demographic trends in South Africa is a unique challenge, given the country's long history of apartheid and the limited availability of demographic information about Africans, Coloreds, and Indians. In effect, the various population groups in South Africa have remained socially apart because of discriminatory laws like the Group Areas Act of 1950 and the Reservation of Separate Amenities Act of 1953 that codified separate racial development and prohibited the social mixing of races. This book sets the stage by providing an overview of the major demographic trends in South Africa. It furnishes a benchmark for discussion of the key policy issues that emerge from studying population and social change in South Africa. Throughout the book, attention is paid to how this use of race and population groups has shaped demographic, social, economic, and family life experiences in South Africa.

We start off with Khalfani et al., who provide a detailed historical overview of the development of the population statistics in South Africa. They take a historical approach in their endeavor to understand the antecedents and the evolution of racial classification in South African censuses from 1911 to 1996. Civil registration and vital statistics systems are examined in conjunction with the nation's population register. The authors use census, archival, statutory, and other governmental data to explain the interrelations of these systems and to analyze the role the system of racial classification plays in population statistics.

In chapter 2, Udjo examines the levels, differentials, and trends in fertility based on a critical analysis of recently available census data in comparison with survey data. He assesses whether or not the fertility inputs in projections of South Africa's population during the apartheid era overestimated fertility. Sibanda and Zuberi further our understanding of the fertility situation in chapter 3 by examining the association between ethnicity, race, and socioeconomic variables and the timing of first birth in South Africa. An examination of these factors lays important groundwork for future research that looks at how women who give birth early are likely to be enmeshed in a social and economic environment that is less than optimal for the growth and development of children and for mothers' reproductive health and social mobility.

In chapter 4, Udjo critically examines various household surveys and census data on mortality to enable the estimation of levels and trends and improve our understanding about mortality variations in the country within the context of HIV/AIDS. It is not possible to ascertain the magnitude of the HIV/AIDS impact based on these surveys and census data alone. However, quantification of deaths due to HIV/AIDS is a crucial issue in South Africa today for obvious reasons.

In chapter 5, Bah reviews options for estimating deaths due to HIV/AIDS using death registration data and highlights the drawbacks and possible sources of error in the different methods employed. The basic question addressed is "How much of the observed increase in deaths between 1997 and 2000 can be accounted for by HIV/AIDS?" Bah looks at three real-life situations with respect to death registration data in South Africa and discusses the estimation of deaths due to HIV/AIDS in these contexts. In the first situation, full national data on causes of death were available for 1996 and death data without cause of death breakdown were available from 1997 to 2000. In the second situation, the same data are available; however, in addition, there is a limited cause breakdown of the death data into natural and unnatural deaths. In the third situation, causes of death data are available based on a sample of all registered deaths from 1997 to 2001.

In chapter 6, Noumbissi et al. examine differences in parental survival and the residential patterns of children. Residential patterns help us to understand the conditions in which children live and the likely impact of the absence of one or both biological parents on their lifetime experiences and achievements. Differentials in parental survival by race and province of residence are examined, and the analysis underscores the important social support role of grandparents in African family systems.

Bah, in chapter 7, reviews the methods used to produce previous life tables and discusses the contextual dynamics underlying them. In the review, he compares the development of life tables in South Africa with parallel developments within the United States, which faced similar circumstances from 1900 to 1970. This study is a contribution to the development of a coherent organizational framework for the production of relevant South African life tables.

In chapter 8, Zulu and Sibanda examine trends, patterns, and differentials in household structure. Household structure is examined from the perspective of extendedness, with a distinction made between the following categories: nuclear, single-parent, extended (direct and composed), single-person households, and unrelated members. South African households are not only a product of existing socioeconomic conditions, but also their form and structure are the outcome of a unique political system and the rise of modern market capitalism, both of which have shaped the society since the end of the nineteenth century. Obviously, racial and ethnic differences in household structure in South Africa have been shaped by the interaction of the social, cultural, economic, and political factors that the country's major racial groups have experienced.

Sibanda and Lehloenya in chapter 9 examine gender, race, and regional gaps in school enrollment and attainment in South Africa. Studying disparities in education is important for several reasons. First, addressing gender, race, and regional gaps in education contributes in many important ways to alleviating social inequalities that impede overall improvements in the quality of life in a society. Second, a major social policy goal of the new South Africa is to close the gaps in employment, housing, health, and other important facets of life that were created by decades of apartheid policies.

In chapter 10, Zuberi and Sibanda examine the interrelationships between migration and employment in the postapartheid labor market. In this analysis, they first compare the labor force outcomes of immigrants to those born in South Africa as a whole, and then compare internal migrants to nonmigrants. Together these chapters provide a picture of the population dynamics underpinning the postapartheid period, and describe *The Demography of South Africa*.

The _____

Demography __

of _____

South Africa __

1. Population Statistics

Akil Kokayi Khalfani, Tukufu Zuberi, Sulaiman Bah, and Pali J. Lehohla

Population statistics measure the changing dynamics of a given population. Births, deaths, migration, the relative population size, composition, and distribution all play key roles in the formation of population statistics. Furthermore, a myriad of social, cultural, political, economic, and ecological factors have an impact on the outcomes of these measures. As we will see, statistical measurements can provide a snapshot of a population at a particular time and place, or a view of a relative population over time. However, these same statistics may say more about the politics, policies, or culture of those who produce and disseminate them than about the population being analyzed. One only has to look at the history of the field of statistics to gain an understanding of the potential dangers of using statistics and various statistical methods to describe and analyze a people (Zuberi 2001a).

Population statistics users consist of policymakers, scholars, businesses, and nongovernmental organizations (NGOs), to name a few. These users attempt to understand patterns or trends either in a segment of or in the total population. These trends may reveal information about various disease regimes (see Udjo and Bah on HIV/AIDS [chapters 4 and 5 in this volume]) or gaps in education (see Sibanda and Lehloenya [chapter 9 in this volume]) in a society. Furthermore, these statistics are often employed by the users to plan for growth or other changes in the composition or dispersal of the population (see Udjo on fertility and Zuberi and Sibanda on migration [chapters 2 and 10, respectively, in this volume]).

Our endeavor here is to examine the systems that provide a foundation for population statistics in South Africa. Population statistics are produced from limited but essential data sources—censuses, civil and vital registration systems (including population registries), and various surveys. We make use of two aspects of South African population statistics—the modern censuses and the civil and vital registration systems (including the population register).[1] The South African government and certain NGOs have conducted numerous surveys, such as the October Household Surveys, and various Demographic and Health Surveys (DHS) and World Fertility Surveys (WFS)-type surveys, to assess the status of the population.[2] Although these types of surveys are important contributors to population statistics, they will not be discussed in this chapter.[3] We divide our examination into two sections. In the first section, we use a historical and sociological approach to look at the system of racial classification in South Africa's censuses from 1911 to 1996. In the second section, we analyze the systems of civil and vital registration used in South Africa.

Racial Classification and the Modern Census

Population enumerations in southern Africa began with the settlement of Dutch colonists at the Cape of Good Hope in 1652 (Zuberi and Khalfani 1999). These enumerations expanded in type and depth over the centuries as the colonists continued to migrate northward, consuming the territory of and impinging upon the rights of indigenous people. The modern census in South Africa began in 1911, after the formation of the Union of South Africa in 1910, and has continued to the present. One fact remains consistent throughout almost 350 years of enumeration in the region: *administrators have racialized every population enumeration in South Africa by subclassifying the population into races.* Thus, population statistics produced from their enumerations reflect the racialized agendas of the various administrations. In this section, we place South Africa's policies of legitimating racial classification in the context of official state policy. We examine the modern systems of racial classification in South African censuses from 1911 to 1996 as part of the state's population statistics program.[4]

The Meaning of Race

Census administrators and scholars have defined the boundaries of race as biological realities. In an important article, South African physical anthropologist Phillip V. Tobias concluded that the "concept of race is valid as long as we are dealing with groups of people; racial features are the average of a large number of individuals' features" (Tobias 1953: 122).[5] From a policy perspective, Census Director C.W. Cousins argued, "One of the most vital questions to be faced in South Africa is whether the white population numerically and otherwise is to hold its own. Distinguished authorities have given a negative reply to the question, and it is clear that the answer, if certainty is possible, can only be secured from the recurring censuses" (Cousins 1923: vi). South African demographers, administrators, and physical anthropologists tended to accept the notion of race. However, unlike the demographers and administrators, anthropologists may not have been directly involved in providing scientific support for the government's racial classification in census enumeration (Tobias 1985; Dubow 1995). As Saul Dubow notes, "because the changed meaning of the term was registered indirectly rather than in an explicit theoretical sense, typological models of racial difference were not consistently dispensed with" (1995:106). We suggest that racial classification in population enumeration is a tradition of convenience, and that this tradition has been used to justify racial stratification.

Racial classification systems assume that race refers to groups of human beings characterized by common anthropometric measurements of skin color, hair type, eye color, or cranium size. When these criteria are not sufficient, common heredity is used as the determinative trait, despite wide ranges of physical traits within the groups. Such topological thinking is static and based on arbitrary categories that depend on the history of social relationships, as opposed to biological relationships (Jackson 2000). This type of thinking characterizes the history of racial classification in racially stratified societies like South Africa, and census-taking is one of the instruments that the South African state used to foster this stratification.

The process of racial classification in South Africa involved at least four facets of government—the legislature, the judiciary, the secretary of Internal Affairs, and the Classification Board. The legislature wrote and revised the statutes that dictated the classification process and standards. Many of these statutes were conflicting, unclear, and/or unspecific. In fact, van Wyk (1984) argues:

> race (color, ethnicity) has had an almost incalculable effect on the law. Adding to the problem is the fact that "racial" provisions are more often than not to be found in obscure, even unlikely, pieces of subordinate legislations. (p. 387)

Later, he continues,

> The conclusion seems to be well founded that a classification in terms of the Population Registration Act may cause a reflection on, but does not itself create or affect, personal status. A person's classification only becomes meaningful in relation to a particular statute. To put it in simple and more concrete terms: *a White person in terms of the Population Registration Act need not be a White person for the purposes of the Immorality Act, the Prohibition of Mixed Marriages Act, or the Group Areas Act.* (p. 400, emphasis added)

Whereas they may have only presented some confusion or frustration for Whites, the classifications affected the life-chances and quality of life for others (Davenport 1991; Pogrund 1990; van Wyk 1984). Where there was great confusion, the legislature sometimes drafted new laws or amendments to existing ones. Possibly understanding the complexity, importance, and confusion surrounding the racial classification process, the legislature gave the secretary of Internal Affairs the authority and responsibility to classify all individuals on the Union's population register.

The judiciary interpreted the various laws related to cases on racial classification brought before them for adjudication. The system of racial classification presented the judiciary with many challenges. However, the legislature established yet another intervening body—the Classification Board (USA 1950b: 283–87)—to review disputes about racial classification. This three-person panel, which included a judge or ex-judge of the South African Supreme Court, or a magistrate, was mandated to hear all requests for reclassification. This formal process allowed that "any person who considers himself aggrieved by his classification by the Director in terms of section *five* and any person who has any objection to the classification of any other person in terms of the said section, may at any time object in writing to the Director against that classification" (USA 1950b: 283 [section 11, subsection 1]).[6] The importance here was that, "The decision as to a person's classification is, under the laws of this country, of cardinal importance to him since it affects his status in practically all fields of life, social, economic and political. An incorrect classification can in all of those fields have devastating effects upon the life of the person concerned" (Van Winsen 1974, as cited in van Wyk 1984: 404).

Racial classifications have developed along the dimensions of physical difference. The racial classification scheme employed in the Republic of South Africa used skin color and ancestry as the criteria. This was problematic in the case of European-origin populations, because, "it would appear that in defining a 'White,' the legislature was faced with the dilemma that descent would obviously not be a proper primary test in view of the fact that many Whites in South Africa are indeed from mixed stock; *appearance and acceptance would remain as the only viable alternatives*" (van Wyk 1984: 406, emphasis added) for determining that someone was "truly" White. "However, to keep the 'lineage' as pure as possible, persons who by their own admission identified themselves as of mixed or Colored descent, were ruled out, while others who could show that both their parents have been classified as White, were ruled in, regardless of the definition" (van Wyk 1984: 406). So theoretically, if a person's grandparent was mixed, but both of his or her parents had been classified as White, then that person (the grandchild) would be classified as White regardless of the other classification requirements. That is, even if the grandchild did not "look" White or was not normally considered to be White, as called for in the statute, she or he would be classified as White. Obviously, the biological ability to reproduce interracially is at odds with the social desire to maintain the boundaries of racial classification. Thus, the system of racial classification has been based on socially accepted or imposed criteria of difference, and biology has been necessarily irrelevant.

Race is an ascribed characteristic and, in theory, racial groups cannot change their racial identities. However, in reality, one racial group may assimilate into another; such has been the case with segments of the Hispanic and Asian populations in the United States (see Barringer, Gardner, and Levin 1993; Ignatiev 1995; McDaniel 1995; Zuberi 2001b). In South Africa, two years after Afrikaners, by way of the National Party, came to power in 1948, the government instituted the formal process for reclassification stated above. A.J. Christopher (1994: 104) notes that in the 1980s many people made use of this reclassification process. The outcome for that decade was that 3,455 Cape Coloreds changed their racial classification to White, and 1,827 Africans changed their racial classification to Colored. Watson poignantly illustrates the nature and problem of the social construction of race and racial classification in South Africa. He argues, "Races and the divisions which exist among them in South Africa reveal the hidden hands of nothing more elemental than the bureaucracy of Pretoria. If this is kept firmly in mind, there is no cause for bewilderment in the facts that brothers and sisters can belong to different *races*, that *White* adults can start life as *Colored* children, that men can live as *Coloreds* but work as *Whites*" (Watson 1970: xiii).

In the discussion about race, another important factor is often neglected, completely forgotten, or thought not to be an issue. Ethnicity should not be confused with race, because race is a distinctly different concept from ethnicity. The two types of group distinctions are used differently in society, especially in racially stratified ones (Hanchard 1994; Wade 1993; Zuberi 2001a). Generally, ethnic identity is a way of distinguishing culturally distinct members within a particular population. Thus, English, Dutch, Germans, French (Huguenots), and Afrikaners are ethnically or nationally different, yet all have been considered White, European, inhabitants, or Christians, within official South African governmental statistics (Zuberi and Khalfani 1999). We can refer to them as European-origin populations (Zuberi 2001a: 106–10).

How race is defined depends on the nature of the state. Racial classification is a social process used to direct social stratification. Thus, racially classifying the population is an effort for or against the processes of racial stratification and domination. If the state advances a policy of racial stratification, the use of race facilitates the administration of racially marginalized populations. Contrarily, if the state advances a policy against racial stratification, then the use of race facilitates the state's fight against racial stratification by providing the empirical data necessary to redress past misdeeds. And, if the state advances a policy against racial distinctions, the use of racialized data becomes part of a process to end the everyday practices of racism, which necessitates race.

European Hegemony

As the European-origin population increased in South Africa, so did its political domination. And, as Europe achieved hegemony throughout the world, South African settlers of European origin became the link between the southern African region and the modern world economy (see Patterson 1975; Ross 1989). The indigenous population was stifled in every way in their attempts at interstate and international commerce and communication (Gerhart 1978). Some scholars describe the situation as a dual economy for the benefit of Europeans (Cell 1982).

The first decade of the twentieth century marked the period that European settlers established dominion over the indigenous inhabitants of South Africa (Thompson 1995: 163–64). Before 1910, southern Africa was composed of various colonies, territories, and protectorates, including the Basutoland, Bechuanaland, Cape of Good Hope, Natal, Orange River Colony or Orange Free State, South West Africa, Swaziland, and Transvaal. Eight years after their successful campaign in the Second Anglo–Boer War, the British government consolidated the Cape of Good Hope, Natal, Orange Free State, and Transvaal colonies under a single authority.[7]

The new state was named the Union of South Africa. The new administration immediately galvanized the former colonial governments' ideologies and policies. Under the auspices of White supremacy, the Union government applied a comprehensive program of racial segregation and discrimination, gained control over the land, and transformed the indigenous inhabitants into wage laborers and land tenants.

The political discourse about race helped forge a common racial identity for the two dominant European ethnic groups—Afrikaner and British. In this discourse, race and ethnicity were seen as distinct realities. Indeed, they served two distinct purposes. Ethnic identity was important during the Afrikaner struggle for national autonomy and hegemony. The Trek Boers were attempting to expand their dominance throughout the southern portion of the African continent. Likewise, the British Empire wanted to continue its efforts at global hegemony, with Cecil John Rhodes striving for a unified Pan Africa under the auspices of the British flag, while simultaneously repressing Afrikaner ambitions to do the same. Hence, wars ensued between the British and the Afrikaner settlers. After the Afrikaners lost the two Anglo–Boer wars, the two groups did not have great affinity or trust for one another. However, they did agree that their survival "depended on the maintenance of white supremacy. On that question no compromise was possible. White must be on top" (Cell 1982: 47). And in that vein, "Generals Botha and Smuts saw Afrikaners and English-speaking whites as flowing together in 'one stream'" (Giliomee 1995: 191).

Between 1910 and 1960, English and Afrikaner political parties maintained a policy of cooperation. However, the English settlers wanted to maintain a formal relationship with the British Empire, while the Afrikaners desired republican independence. In 1961, the Afrikaners realized their republican ambitions when South Africa broke away from the British Commonwealth, forming the Republic of South Africa. The tacit fact here is that in a racially stratified society, the ethnic diversity of the dominant group is unimportant when the issue of racial dominance is afoot. That is, if state policies support racial stratification and domination, ethnic allegiances are necessarily second in the face of racial solidarity.

Racial Classification and the Census, 1911–1996

The modern South African system of racial classification has its roots in the establishment of European political, social, and economic hegemony. Policies of the European-origin population served as the basis for racial identity and the system of apartheid in South Africa in the twentieth century.[8] For example, pass laws were first utilized in the Cape Colony in 1809, and a reserve, or quasi-reserve, system, was initially used in the late eighteenth and early nineteenth centuries to minimize conflicts between Boers on the frontier and various groups of Africans.[9] The first oppressive laws of the Union were designed to benefit European laborers, while segregating and controlling Africans. Examples of these laws are the Mines and Workers Act of 1911, Natives Labour Regulation Act of 1911, Natives Land Act of 1913, and Native Affairs Administration Bill of 1917. The philosophical and policy foundations of European domination crystallized with the passing of apartheid legislation in the 1940s and 1950s.

The first census of the Union of South Africa was conducted in 1911, the year following the establishment of the Union. The two-tier parliamentary government—the House of Assembly and the Senate—passed the Census Act and the 1914 Statistics Act. The Census Act provided for the taking of a quinquennial enumeration of the European population for electoral purposes and a decennial enumeration of the entire population (OCS 1925a). According to section 34:

> The quota of the Union shall be obtained by dividing the total number of European male adults in the Union, as ascertained at the census of nineteen hundred and four, by the total number of members of the House of Assembly as constituted at the establishment of the Union. (USA 1911: 14)

As Director of the Census J.B. Moffat noted, "All that is required for redistribution purposes is the number of European male adults in each Province" (Moffat 1911). Again the enumeration process facilitated racial stratification and in this case gender stratification as well. The census legislators provided a context in which the discourse about racial stratification took place.

Changes in the composition of the population result from a combination of differential fertility, differential mortality, net immigration, and, if race exists, racial classification. In South Africa, racial classification has had a direct impact on the social position of different members of the population. Table 1.1 presents the racial classifications used in the Union/Republic of South Africa censuses from 1911 to 1996. Table 1.2 presents the sizes of these racial groups estimated by the Central Statistical Service (CSS, currently known as Statistics South Africa).

The population enumerations did not take place consistently because of financial problems and the Union's involvement in various wars. The 1914 Statistics Act provided for the

> establishment of the Statistical Council, a body appointed by the Minister of the Interior, consisting of representatives of various Government Departments as well as of members of the public who have been selected because they are eminently qualified to advise the Government on questions connected with the collection of statistics. The object of the advisory agency of the Census Office was to ensure that the various statistical operations were conducted in the best interests of the "public" and that they serve practical purposes and are not merely of an academic nature. (OCS 1925b)

The Office of Census Statistics (OCS) was responsible for collecting and compiling census enumerations and other statistical data. The Statistical Council discussed the census structure and developed the various racial classifications used in the censuses.

The population statistics from the first census of the Union contained data on three major racial classifications: "European or White," "Bantu," and "Mixed and Colored other than Bantu." The census was composed of an extensive set of racial subcategories. The "Bantu" and the "Mixed and Colored other than Bantu" categories were each composed of twenty-three "racial" subclassifications. The extensiveness of these racial classifications illustrates the degree to which the notions of race, nationality, and ethnicity were confounded in the collection of census data. For example, European settlers saw the San and Khoikhoi as being from a different "race" than the Bantu-speaking

Table 1.1

Racial Classifications in the Union/Republic of South Africa, 1911–96[a]

Year	African	Indian/Asian	Colored[e]	European/white
1911	Bantu[d]		Mixed and other colored	European/white
1918[b]				European/white
1921	Native (Bantu)	Asiatic	Mixed and other colored	European
1926[b]				Europeans
1931[b]				European
1936	Natives	Asiatics	Colored	Europeans
1941[b]				European
1946	Natives (Bantu)	Asiatics	Mixed and other colored	European (white)
1951	Natives	Asiatics	Coloreds	Whites
1960	Bantu	Asiatics	Coloreds	Whites
1970	Bantu	Asiatics	Coloreds	Whites
1980	Blacks	Asians	Coloreds	Whites
1985[c]	Blacks	Asians	Coloreds	Whites
1991	Blacks	Asians	Coloreds	Whites
1996[f]	African/Black	Indian/Asian	Colored	White

Source: Official census reports and questionnaires.
Notes:

[a]South Africa became a Republic in 1961.

[b]Census of the European population only.

[c]Household census only.

[d]The Bantu classification consisted of the following subclassifications: Baca, Bachuana, Basuto, Bavenda, Bomvana, Daffir (unspecified), Damara, Fingo, Hlangweni, Ndebele, Northern Rhodesian Tribes, Nyasaland Protectorate Tribes, Other Tribes, Pondo, Pondomise, Portuguese East African Tribes, Southern Rhodesian Tribes, Swazi, Tembu, Tonga (alias for Bagwamba including Tshangana), Xesibe, Xosa, and Zulu.

[e]The Mixed and Colored other than Bantu classification consisted of the following subclassifications: Afghan, American colored, Arabian, Bushman, Chinese, Creole, Egyptian, Griqua, Hottentot, Indian, Koranna-"Hottentot Races," Krooman, Malagasy, Malay (Cape), Mauritian, Mixed, Mozambique, Namaqa-"Hottentot Races," Other, St. Helena, Syrian, West Indian, Zanzibari.

[f]Statistics South Africa collected data for the Griquas separately in 1996, but combined them with the Coloreds in the published tables.

people they encountered in the 1770s. In fact, this distinction continued to be a major issue among physical anthropologists well into the twentieth century (Dubow 1995: 33–65; Tobias 1985).

Several national censuses in the Republic of South Africa included only the European population, or else dropped the race question and predetermined race. The 1918, 1926, 1931, and 1941 censuses were only for the European settler population. For the 1921 census, the enumerators used separate schedules for each racial group. That year, the state determined racial identity for both individuals and households prior to the enumeration.

Part of the confusion surrounding race and racial classification in South

Table 1.2

South African Population: 1911–96

Year	Africans	Indians/ Asians	Coloreds	Europeans	Total
		Racial classifications			
1911[a]	4,019,066		678,146	1,276,242	5,973,454
1921	4,697,813	165,731	545,548	1,519,488	6,928,580
1936	6,596,689	219,691	769,661	2,003,857	9,589,898
1946	7,831,915	285,260	928,484	2,372,690	11,418,349
1951	8,560,083	366,664	1,103,016	2,641,689	12,671,452
1960	10,921,922	477,932	1,510,143	3,078,050	15,988,047
1970	15,339,975	630,372	2,050,699	3,773,282	21,794,328
1980	21,078,600[b]	818,380	2,686,720	5,589,660	30,173,360
1985	24,449,800[b]	821,361	2,832,705	4,568,739	32,672,605
1991	28,397,171[b]	986,620	3,285,718	5,068,110	37,737,619
1996	31,127,631	1,045,596	3,600,446	4,434,697	40,583,573[c]

Sources: Official South African census reports for various years; census micro-data for 1991; and Sadie 1988 for 1980.
Notes:
  [a]In 1911, the Indian/Asian population was included in the Colored population.
  [b]These estimates include numbers from the TBVC (Transkei, Bophuthatswana, Venda, and Ciskei) areas (6,401,390 for 1980; 6,084,400 for 1985; and 6,750,700 for 1991).
  [c]Total includes 375,204 unspecified/others. These are excluded from the calculations in the remaining tables.

Africa is directly related to the established definitions of the various racial groups. In 1950, the legislative basis of apartheid was established. Particularly important for census enumerations were the Population Registration Act and the Group Areas Act. The 1950 Population Registration Act defined a "'colored person' [as] a person who [was] not a white or a native" (USA 1950b: 277). This effort to clarify the racial classification of "Colored" persons led to the conclusion that "some discrepancies are reflected in the . . . Colored and Bantu population figures for certain districts of the Cape Province. *This must be ascribed to apparent erroneous classification*" (RSA 1968: vii; *emphasis added*).

Before 1950, Europeans were defined as White persons who were pure descendants of Europe. From 1950 to 1991, the European population was defined as "Persons who in appearance or who are generally accepted as white persons, but excluding persons who, although in appearance obviously white, are generally accepted as Colored persons" (USA 1950b: 277). The colonial administrations assumed that physical appearance was not enough to make a person White. The social context of being "generally accepted" as White was seen as being more important than physical appearance. Moreover, the effort here was to keep White identity separate from that of other races. Additionally, the definition for White identity was designed to keep Coloreds from "passing" as White or being mistakenly counted as White. This definition for the European classification has always been arbitrary, and illustrates how racial classifications are socially constructed for the benefit of the dominant group.

By the 1960 census, Coloreds were defined as "All persons not included in any of the three [other] groups," including Cape Malays (RSA 1961: v). As previously mentioned, the "Colored" population was particularly difficult to enumerate, because it was composed of many mixed-race persons. Africans were defined as aboriginal races or tribes of Africa and Asians as natives of Asia and their descendants. Historically, the European-dominated colonial administration sought to distinguish between itself, the European-origin population, and others, the African- and Asian-origin populations, along with the mixed or Colored races.

The next major development in the censuses of the Republic occurred at the start of the 1991 census. Just prior to the administration of the 1991 census, the government decided to abandon the collection of race-based data and to repeal the Population Registration Act of 1950 with the enactment of the Population Registration Act Repeal Act of 1991.[10] This change in policy had an impact on the census, vital registration, and other statistics collected and produced by the government. The passing of the act was an effort to appease Africans, trade unions, and others who were the victims of racial discrimination and who wanted to eliminate racial bias. However, the director of the CSS, with the support of some of the leading scholars in the country, decided to collect data on race even though doing so was no longer government policy. The CSS defended its decision to collect racial data on television, in newspapers, and in press releases. They said that the information was needed for demographics and statistical purposes and not political ones. "From a statistical point of view ignoring population group information can do more harm than good. . . . It is not as if population differences will suddenly cease to exist and that the demographic characteristics of all population groups [races] will henceforth be the same" (Bureau for Information 1991). The Bophuthatswana statistics branch made the same argument for its 1991 census (Republic of Bophuthatswana 1991).

The 1996 South African Census Committee decided that the racial classifications for the 1996 census should remain the same as the 1991 census classifications. However, it was decided that the category for Africans would be relabeled "African/Black" instead of just "Black." This was done to distinguish between the Afrikaners and the indigenous Africans, both of whom refer to themselves as Africans (Adegboyega 1995). The other categories were

Indian/Asian, Colored, and White. The decision to maintain these classifications was justified by the claim that most people in the country recognized and understood the categories. Notwithstanding this, Statistics South Africa enumerated the Griquas as a separate racial group, because the group, argued that they did not fit into any of the other racial categories; in the published statistics, however, they were included with the Coloreds.

From 1921 to 1996, the South African government used four broad racial categories in multiracial censuses. The use of these four classifications was determined at a Statistical Council (SC) meeting in November 1921 (SC 1921). One of the council members suggested the use of a fifth classification—Eurafricans. This term had been used earlier in the 1910 Johannesburg municipal census. However, the other council members suggested that a Eurafrican population would be difficult to identify, thus the suggestion was abandoned.

The classifications within these four categories have changed over time, but the attempt has been to classify all individuals into a specific racial group—namely, Africans, Indians/Asians, Coloreds, or Europeans. In some cases, groups within these classifications were officially shifted. For example, Syrians were included under "Asiatics" in 1921 but were switched to "European" thereafter. The most dynamic classification has been the African/Black category. It changed from Bantu to Natives to Bantu to Blacks and finally to African/Black over the course of the twentieth century. The other dynamic aspect to this era was that of the increased use by the state of these socially defined racial classifications to control the nonwhite population in various ways. The legislation that had the greatest effect in this capacity was the Population Registration Act of 1950, which we will discuss below.

A Closer Look at the Last Apartheid Census

The CSS took the last census of the apartheid era in 1991. They enumerated the 1991 Republic of South Africa (RSA) population on a de facto basis. The 1991 census was the first de facto census. All previous censuses were collected on a de jure basis, meaning that RSA citizens as well as foreigners present within the boundaries for more than three months were enumerated. The CSS distributed census questionnaires to the population beforehand and collected completed returns after March 8, 1991. If the respondent was unable to complete the questionnaire or requested assistance in completing the questionnaire, a census enumerator aided in the completion of the form.

Apartheid, as a system, produced extreme levels of residential segregation (Christopher 1992). It was part of a system that disorganized African communities, led to European acquisition and occupation of the land, and led to White control of African labor (Christopher 1983; Magubane 1979: 142–43).

Consequently, by 1991, a comprehensive door-to-door survey was not possible for areas populated by Africans. In fact, the CSS found that "88 areas country-wide . . ." were inaccessible "during the preparations for the enumeration of the census" (RSA 1992b: ix).

The CSS asked the Human Sciences Research Council (HSRC) to estimate the population in these "inaccessible" areas by using a combination of sampling and aerial photographs. The HSRC took a "sample" based on a set of assumptions regarding the number of residents interviewed by a team of eight census enumerators, and inflated the population estimates in accordance with the aerial adjustment factors.[11] The CSS then employed the services of J.L. Sadie and the Bureau of Market Research to produce the estimates for underenumeration. Table 1.3 gives an indication of the extent to which these adjustments affected the published population estimates. The estimates in the table were computed using the 1991 South African census micro-data and the various weights used by the CSS.

The 1991 population census did not successfully enumerate the population. Table 1.3 shows that the CSS enumerated only 64 percent of the total population. Such a large underenumeration reflected the political discontent and opposition of various groups and political organizations to the enumeration, especially the African National Congress (ANC). As late as March 8, 1991, *The Star* newspaper reported, "a stand-off between the African National Congress and the Government over the census continued yesterday, with the ANC sticking to its demand that the R60 million surveys be postponed." In addition to the ANC opposition, *The Star* also reported that there were "reports questioning the fact that members of the public would be asked to state their race—in spite of the announcement that the Population Registration Act was to be scrapped."[12]

The CSS counted only 54 percent of the African population in the 1991 census enumeration. It did a better job counting Coloreds (88 percent), Europeans (89 percent), and Indians/Asians (85 percent). The HSRC estimated about 29 percent of the number of Africans using aerial photographs and survey techniques, but as expected, their estimates negligibly impacted the other three racial groups, 3 percent for Indians/Asians, 1.5 percent for Coloreds, and one hundredth of one percent for Europeans. After the data from the survey and aerial photographs were added, the African population was still thought to be underenumerated by 17 percent, the Indian/Asian population by 12 percent, and the White and Colored populations by 11 percent each (as indicated in Table 1.3).

The apartheid censuses of 1980, 1985, and 1991 all excluded the former homelands—Transkei, Bophuthatswana, Venda, and Ciskei (TBVC). But the CSS made at least one effort to estimate the size of the Republic of South

Table 1.3

Percentage of Population Estimated by Method, 1991

Race	Census	Survey	Aerial	Demo-graphic[a]	All methods	Final estimate	HSRC[b]
Male							
African	52.58	0.69	27.59	19.13	100.00	10,864,932	28.29
Colored	86.82	0.07	1.38	11.73	100.00	1,605,811	1.45
European	88.13	0.00	0.01	11.86	100.00	2,519,833	0.01
Indian/Asian	˙84.07	0.25	2.72	12.96	100.00	488,952	2.97
All	62.91	0.50	19.60	16.99	100.00	15,479,528	20.10
Female							
African	55.05	0.75	29.71	14.49	100.00	10,781,538	30.46
Colored	88.38	0.08	1.55	10.00	100.00	1,679,907	1.63
European	90.28	0.00	0.01	9.71	100.00	2,548,278	0.01
Indian/Asian	85.16	0.24	2.67	11.94	100.00	497,669	2.91
All	65.41	0.54	20.91	13.14	100.00	15,507,392	21.45
All							
African	53.81	0.72	28.65	16.82	100.00	21,646,470	29.37
Colored	87.62	0.08	1.46	10.85	100.00	3,285,718	1.54
European	89.21	0.00	0.01	10.78	100.00	5,068,111	0.01
Indian/Asian	84.62	0.24	2.69	12.44	100.00	986,621	2.94
All	64.16	0.52	20.25	15.06	100.00	30,986,920	20.78

Source: 1991 South African census micro-data. Estimates do not include TBVC (Transkei, Bophuthatswana Venda, and Ciskei), areas.
Notes:
[a]The demographic method represents the estimation for underenumeration.
[b]The Human Sciences Research Council (HSRC) estimated both the survey and aerial methods. By combining the effects of these two methods, the HRSC column illustrates the impact the Council's inflations had on the final population estimates for the 1991 census.

Africa and the TBVC states (RSA 1992a). This effort produced estimates of the size of the population that served as the basis for estimating the level of underenumeration, and also as the basis for the weights used in the micro-data tapes produced by CSS for the 1991 census (see Table 1.2). The Self-Governing Territories (SGT) were not clearly demarcated into Enumeration Areas (RSA 1997). Teams of enumerators were used to "sweep" through these areas without controls of demarcated boundaries or lists.

The method of enumeration had a profound impact on the estimated population. Table 1.4 presents the estimated sex ratio by the method of estimation. Women appear to be overrepresented in the census enumeration. The aerial and survey methods decreased the sex ratio for Africans and Coloreds and increased it for other population groups. That these methods estimated a larger African female population suggested that African males were absent from the areas where the aerial and survey methods were used. This interpretation is consistent with apartheid-imposed patterns of labor and internal migration.

Table 1.4

Sex Ratio by Estimation Method, 1991

Race	Census	Survey	Aerial	Demographic	Estimate
African	95.52	92.09	92.88	132.03	100.77
Colored	98.24	93.08	88.79	117.36	95.59
European	97.62	113.39	100.19	122.14	98.88
Indian/Asian	98.73	103.58	102.07	108.54	98.25
All	96.18	93.05	93.73	129.30	99.82

Source: Table 1.3 in this volume.

The demographic inflation, which estimated the undercount, increased the sex ratio for all population groups, suggesting that males, in general, were underenumerated and that, in particular, African males were considerably underenumerated.

The final estimates of the population sex composition reflect the impact of these inflations. The impact of these changes is most pronounced on the African male population. The sex ratio of the demographic inflation is 132.03, and this indicates a significant inflation of the male population by this method. So significant is the inflation that it produces a deficit of women. While this may reflect the "true" sex ratio of the African population, it also reflects the fact that the African sex ratio is a factor of the inflation methods and not the actual enumeration. The sex ratio for the 1996 census was 92.68 for the entire population. If we compare the sex ratios for the total population for both the 1991 and the 1996 censuses, assuming that the latter is much more representative, as we discuss below, it is clear that the CSS's estimates for the 1991 census do not accurately characterize the size or distribution of the population. In fact, to go from a sex ratio of 99.82 in 1991 to 92.68 in 1996 suggests that men, African men in particular, were unenumerable in 1991 and that the only way to estimate the potential size of their population was through demographic estimation techniques in addition to the enumeration process. These demographic estimations are in no way perfect and potentially overinflated the African male population to justify certain social and political objectives, as has been argued about the use of racial statistics and racial stratification (Zuberi 2000, 2001a).

Transkei, Bophuthatswana, Venda, and Ciskei Censuses of 1980, 1985, and 1991

The Afrikaner constitutions of the Orange Free State, in 1854, and the Transvaal, in 1860, established in law the principle of inequality between

Africans and Europeans in church and state (Thompson 1995: 100–103). When Dr. D.F. Malan led the National Party government to power in 1948, the banner of apartheid was raised high, and the future of the principle of European superiority was legally established. By 1950, the state policy of partition unfolded (Christopher 1994: 66–73). Under the policy of state partition, all Natives in South Africa would become members of an "independent" nation. The objective was to eliminate racial diversity—in particular, to eliminate the African political presence in the most economically well-off areas. These TBVC states served primarily as symbols of domination, as less than 40 percent of the African population lived in the new states by 1951. In 1959, the Promotion of Bantu Self-Government Act created a hierarchy of local governments for the rural reserves. Traditional authorities (such as chiefs and headsmen) assumed power in these "homelands." The South African Native Trust Lands designated certain areas as Native Reserves. With the exception of Ciskei and Transkei, the Native Reserves of Trust Land were grouped together on a linguistic basis and brought under the supervision of the Chief Commissioner. Christopher reports "Census enumerators in the Black states tended to find the characteristics of the dominant group rather than the minority while compiling the census data, thereby statistically reducing the extent of the minority problem" (Christopher 1994: 69). The Republic of South Africa continued these apartheid policies and introduced several consolidation plans that amounted to no more than efforts to resettle African populations without compensation.

The 1970 Bantu Homelands Citizenship Act assigned all Africans to one of the ten homelands that included the four independent states—Transkei, Bophuthatswana, Venda, and Ciskei (TBVC). The Republic of South Africa included six "Self-Governing Territories" (SGT)—Gazankulu, KaNgwane, KwaNdebele, KwaZulu, Lebowa, Qwaqwa—and the Common Area (CA), which included the rest of the country. The Republic established the TBVC states as racial- and ethnic-specific geopolitical units. The populations within the TBVC states and the SGT areas were predominantly African, and they continued to serve as the dominant labor force within the Republic of South Africa. Many of the laborers had temporary residences in South Africa or they commuted to work. The Republic of South Africa granted the TBVC states "independence" in the following years—Transkei in 1976, Bophuthatswana in 1977, Venda in 1979, and Ciskei in 1981.

Transkei, Boputhatswana, and Venda conducted their first population censuses in conjunction with the Republic's 1980 population census. Ciskei's first census was in 1985. The independent statistical offices of the TBVC states conducted the enumerations, but the Republic's statistical department processed the raw data and produced the tabulations. CSS had the physical, personnel, and financial resources to manage this task, but the government also had a vested interest to ensure that the results were favorable to the administration. The tabulated results went back to the individual states, and they, in turn, published them, but not without debate. The census results were used to determine how much money the Republic of South Africa paid these governments from customs revenues. The amount given was determined by the size of the population, so both the Republic and the TBVC states tended to challenge the final results.

In 1985, all four TBVC states conducted population enumerations. The Transkei's census was a de jure estimate of the population and was derived from a sample. The Transkei sample was based on 1,400 aerial photographs. Bophuthatswana and Venda's censuses were modeled after the Republic of South Africa's and, as before, the CSS processed the data and produced the tabulations.

In 1991, the Republic—via the HSRC—monitored the TBVC enumerations. Officials considered the Venda census to be a very accurate enumeration. Ciskei had a 50 percent response rate and used a sample, based on aerial photos of houses in the area, to inflate the population. Data on the racial classifications of the population were collected and tabulated in the censuses for the Republic of South Africa, Bophuthatswana, and Venda.

The Postapartheid Census

In April 1994, South Africa held its first fully democratic elections. Afterward, the Republic of South Africa reincorporated the six SGT and the four TBVC states, and they were integrated into the 1996 census (RSA 1998). In October 1996, the CSS conducted the first census in the Republic of South Africa where the majority of the South African population was not under the oppressive control of a minority population. Either colonial rulers or some form of apartheid government had supervised all previous censuses under a banner of African domination (see Zuberi and Khalfani 1999). These earlier census efforts encountered major problems in enumerating the African population, because the administration either had difficulty accessing African living areas, language barriers were insurmountable, or the European administrators had difficulty distinguishing between various groups of Africans (Zuberi and Khalfani 1999). Table 1.5 presents estimates of underenumeration by race between 1980 and 1996. The 1996 census may be the most complete enumeration ever taken in South Africa.

Compared to the previous censuses, the 1996 population census was a huge success. Stats SA enumerated 93 percent of the population. (In September 1998, the Central Statistical Service [CSS] changed its name to Statistics South

Table 1.5

Estimated Undercount by Race, Percent, and Year

Race	1980*	1985*	1991*	1996
African	22.00	20.40	46.20	10.50
Colored	3.20	3.50	12.40	10.50
European	8.50	5.50	10.80	9.00
Indian/Asian	4.40	6.50	15.40	6.10

Sources: RSA 1992a, 1998; Table 1.3 in this volume.
Note: * The estimate of undercount for these years does not include TBVC areas. All numbers are rounded.

Africa [Stats SA]) Such a large improvement in the enumeration reflected the political success of the reformed South African government and the capable efforts of a reformed statistical department as part of the new administration. Increased support for the enumeration process by South Africans also contributed to the success of the 1996 census. Stats SA counted more than 88 percent of African men and about 90 percent of African women. The Coloreds were counted at about the same rate as Africans, with Indians/Asians being the most completely enumerated racial group (94 percent of men and 95 percent of women); 91 percent of Whites were enumerated.

The Civil, Vital, and Population Registration Systems

The civil registration and vital statistics systems[13] are essential elements in South African population statistics. Here we intend to explore the intricacies of that system from a historical approach, and in doing so, we will call upon our examination of the population registration system in the first part of this chapter. In the South African context, one cannot comprehensively discuss one system without discussing the other.

The Civil Registration and Vital Statistics System Prior to the Population Register

The existence of a civil registration and vital statistics system in South Africa, in a decentralized form, predated the formation of the Union of South Africa in 1910. In fact, colonial registries, journals, and diaries, as well as the Opgaafrols and Monsterrollen van Vrije Lieden (Muster Rolls of Vryliede) served as systems of enumeration and registration of colonial populations from the mid-1600s until the early 1900s (Zuberi and Khalfani 1999). The main purposes of those early systems were to identify taxable and voting populations and population control. Subsequent to the formation of the Union, Act 38 of 1914 established a national statistical office for South Africa. This resulted in the centralization of the collection of vital statistics. However, uniformity in vital registration throughout the Union was only achieved after the Births, Deaths and Marriages Registration Act (Act 17 of 1923) came into effect in 1924. Under Act 17 of 1923, registration of vital events was made compulsory for Africans living in urban areas but was voluntary for Africans/Blacks living in rural areas. This was in line with the Urban Areas Act of 1923. Mamdani argues:

> Section 10 [of the Act] defined the few blacks with legal permission to live in cities and large towns not as having the right to do so, but as exempt from the provisions of the act. For a black person residing in rural areas who wished to move to a city the law prescribed a definite path (1996: 228).

Initially, vital statistics were published only for Whites. In 1937, official vital statistics for Coloreds became available, and a year later they were published for Indians/Asians. During this period, no official vital statistics were produced for Africans.

An African Population Register?

In the 1950s, influx control, a set of laws that monitored and controlled the movements of Africans, became a compulsory policy throughout South Africa (Evans 1997). The Population Registration Act of 1950 was an integral part of this control. It assigned every person an identity number that sealed his or her fate as a South African—either improving or diminishing that individual's life chances. Under the act, there were only three racial classifications: White, Colored, and Native. The latter two were additionally classified according to ethnic group. Oddly missing here is the classification for Asians or Indians. Even though they were not directly pointed out in the act, this group has always been separately classified in the censuses, except for the 1911 census, which obviously predates this act.

The aim of the 1950 act was to make provision for the compilation of a register of the population of the Union, primarily for issuing identity cards. Under the act, anyone whose name was included in the register was assigned an identity number and population group. The register was divided into three parts. One part was for South African citizens, the second part was for permanent residents, and the third part was for temporary residents. The South African Population Register dealt with births, deaths, identities, marriages, divorces, and movements of all South African citizens and permanent residents. Part of the identity number

> was a racial classification: thus 00 meant a white South African, 01 a colored, 02 a Malay, 04 a Chinese, 05 an Asian, down to a 09 for a Nama of South West Africa.

> Two sections, 06 for "Other Asian" and 07 for "Other colored," provided for those who could not be fitted in elsewhere, a sort of miscellaneous of the human race. Those vital two digits were intended to, and did, affect life from birth to death, with every detail specified and fixed by law: in which hospital you could be born; in which suburb you could live. . . . (Pogrund 1990: 79)

Several complicated laws hindered the compilation of vital statistics among Africans. For example, the Native Laws Amendment Act of 1952 mandated that Africans carry reference books (detailed identification books). These reference books consolidated fingerprints, information about the bearer's residency rights in the urban areas, tribal affiliation, employment history, tax payments, and any infractions of urban labor control laws and regulations. These documents were seen as a new type of pass (Mamdani 1996). The reference book was used as a tool of oppression that curtailed African rights. The reference book was also extended to women in the late 1950s. But here it met with much resistance. African women were "unshakably" suspicious of the reference book and quickly learned that the acceptance of it rendered them virtually powerless (Evans 1997). These passes had to be shown when requested by authorities, and failure to do so or a refusal to carry a pass meant imprisonment, a fine, or both. Non-Africans were not subjected to these intense forms of tracking.

In a detailed study of bureaucracy and race during the 1950s, Evans made several interesting observations regarding this system:

> In contrast to the CLB [Central Labour Bureau], the Central Reference Bureau (CRB), established in 1953 in the office of the Under-Secretary for Staff and Administration, performed the more global task of rationalizing and centralizing information on all African individuals. As Ramsey, the first Director of the CRB phrased it, "the Reference Bureau is, after all a reference bureau as well as virtually the Bureau of Census and Statistics for Natives. It should at least control vital statistics and know the number as well as the whereabouts of all adult members of the Native population as required in terms of Section 10(2) of the Population Registration Act, 1950." (1997: 89–90)

The details of the African population were severely underrepresented in the manual South Africa population register (m-SAPR). The systems continued to function in this fashion, more or less, for two decades. The SAPR was computerized in 1972. At that time, only the details of Whites, Coloreds, and Indians/Asians were kept on the new system. This electronic population register (e-SAPR) operated alongside the m-SAPR and did not serve as a replacement for it.

In response to considerable domestic and international protest and sanctions, influx controls were abolished in 1986. The sustained political pressure and resulting economic strain on the country led to additional restrictive laws being abolished (Davenport 1991). Eventually, African data were entered into the e-SAPR in 1986, and Africans were issued uniform identity documents. After 1986, several acts, such as the Population Registration Act of 1991 (Act 114 of 1991) and the Births and Deaths Registration Act, 1992 (Act 51 of 1992), were amended to improve the coverage and content of the population register. The 1991 act abolished the distinction made between persons belonging to different population or racial groups (thereby dropping the population group variable from the population register), and the 1992 act guided the registration of births and deaths throughout South Africa. Act 67 of 1997 and Act 43 of 1998 subsequently amended the latter. Another act that is pertinent to the population register is the Identification Act of 1997 (Act 68 of 1997). This act repealed previous identification acts (Act 72 of 1986, Act 21 of 1991, Act 4 of 1993, and Act 47 of 1995). After the implementation of these various acts and amendments, the population register contained data on individuals in the following categories:

> All children born of South African citizens and permanent residents when the notice of the birth is given within one year after the birth of the child.
> All children born of South African citizens and permanent residents when the notice of the birth is given one year after the birth of the child together with the prescribed requirement for a late registration of birth.
> All South African citizens and permanent residents who upon attainment of the age of 16 applied for and were granted identification cards.
> All South African citizens and permanent residents who die at any age after birth.
> All South African citizens and permanent residents who depart permanently from South Africa.

The population register does not contain data on non-South African citizens who sojourn temporarily in the country, or on South African citizens and permanent residents who died before notice of birth had been given.

The Roles of the Population Register in the Civil Registration and Vital Statistics Systems

The civil registration system is the source for both the population register and the vital statistics system. Because the Department of Home Affairs is responsible for both the population register and the civil registration system, it keeps several databases that relate to different aspects of civil registration records but that are not, strictly speaking, the population register. When the clerks at the various offices of the Department of Home Affairs (DHA) capture the information about a birth, for example, they do so directly into the database at the Nucleus Bureau (the data processing center for the DHA). These transactions are used to update the population register database as well as the birth register. The population register is cumulative, while the vital statistics system is periodic. Details on non-South African citizens or permanent residents could be obtained from the civil registration system but not from the population register. One would say that the vital statistics system was related to the m-SAPR and the different vital registration databases kept by DHA. The e-SAPR hardly fed into vital statistics in the past. Recently, however, the vital statistics system began to include details extracted from the e-SAPR. This complementary system holds the key for the rapid production of vital statistics but is yet to. be fully exploited and analyzed.

The Development of the South African Vital Statistics System

The standing aim in publishing official vital statistics is to report on all vital events that have taken place during the period under consideration. When the completeness of registration of vital events is very low in certain geographic areas of the country or among certain population subgroups within the country, there are different ways of handling the situation. First, these subgroups could be omitted from the vital statistics until the coverage has reached sufficiently high levels. This was the route used in the Union of South Africa during the early stages for developing the vital registration areas. Alternatively, the low reported vital events would be included but commented upon. In the case of South Africa, Stats SA took a combination of both options. The statistical agency published vital statistics exclusively on Whites from 1910 to 1935. As mentioned earlier, in 1937, particulars on Coloreds were included, while those of Indians/Asians were included in 1938.

The CRB was established in the 1950s to serve as a pseudo Bureau of Census and Statistics for Africans. However, there is no evidence that the official national statistical office ever tapped into the resources of the CRB in order to obtain vital statistics data on Africans. Officials used the civil registration forms filed in the Office of the Registrar-General of Births, Marriages and Deaths for Africans prior to 1960. These returns were very meager. From January 1960, the safekeeping of vital registration forms was transferred to the Bantu Reference Bureau falling under the Department of Bantu Administration and Development.

In 1963, the Births and Deaths Registration Act (Act 81) was passed. Under this act, registration of births and deaths for Africans at the district level was to be handled by the Bantu Affairs commissioner, while for all other population groups, it was to be handled by the district registrar. In districts where there were no registrars, the magistrates served as district officers. It was the information that went through the district registrar that formed the mainstream civil registration and vital statistics system. Details of births were kept in the "births register" and those of deaths were kept in the "deaths register." The act made no link between these registers and the population register as outlined in the 1950 act.

Starting in 1968, a separate mortality report was issued for Africans in selected urban magisterial districts. This series continued up to 1977. From 1978, a new series of reports was issued covering deaths of Africans throughout the country. At this stage, the function of civil registration among Africans fell under the jurisdiction of the Department of Co-operation and Development. These series continued up to 1990. For the years 1979 and 1980, information regarding African births was collected and processed. However, due to the underregistration of these births and the high percentage of late registration that occurred, the figures were not published for those years. Subsequently, the collection of information on African births was discontinued in 1981. In July 1989, the collection and processing of information on African births was reinstated. Again, because of continuing problems of incompleteness and lateness, the figures for African births were not published for 1990.

As mentioned earlier, with the enactment of the Population Registration Act Repeal Act of 1991, the population group identifier was dropped from the civil registration system. This affected both the population register and vital statistics. The crucial legal framework for collecting vital statistics for all people living in South Africa is the Births and Deaths Registration Act of 1992 (Act 51 of 1992). This was a logical successor following developments that started in 1985 with the abolition of influx control.

After 1991, vital statistics could no longer be broken up into population groups. The long series of uninterrupted vital statistics for Whites, Coloreds, and Indians/Asians came to an end. With the redrawing of provincial boundaries in 1993 (Act 200 of 1993), geographic breakdown became the primary axis for disaggregating vital statistics.

Operation of the Current System

In South Africa today, the DHA manages vital registration. Informants are required to produce some form of identification at the time of registration of the event. The registration of deaths has changed considerably over time. The old system used two individual forms, a single-page death register (form BI-7) and a single-page medical certificate for deaths and stillbirths (form BI-12). Form BI-7 contained the demographic information about the deceased. Form BI-12 was completed by a medical professional and contained more detailed cause of death information. The causes of death information on the BI-7 sometimes differed from that reported by the physician on the BI-12 form. In the new system, forms BI-7 and BI-12 have been combined into form BI-1663 (see new form, Appendix 1.1).

In the past, different departments used different forms. The DHA mainly used the information on form BI-7. The statistical service relied, primarily, on the causes-of-death information stated by the physician on form BI-12. In this form, the physician was not obliged to state the cause of death if the death was due to unnatural causes. This was done for so-called "practical reasons," as the DHA faced administrative difficulties in following up cases under investigation. This procedure was maintained with regard to the new forms. However, the physician is now required to state if the cause of death is under investigation.

Along with the introduction of the new form, there has been an attempt to increase the accuracy, timing, and completion rate of both birth and death forms. To this end, nurses have been employed to assist in the completion of birth registration forms. Likewise, for the registration of deaths, nurses, undertakers, and pathologists have been sought to aid in the completion of the forms. These individuals are not required to take responsibility for the forms' content.

Efforts to Improve the System During the Second Half of the 1990s

After the 1994 election, the Reconstruction and Development Programme (RDP) became known as the blueprint for the redistribution of resources and services to redress the inequalities of the previous administrations. The time frame for the implementation of the RDP was from 1995 to 2000. The various departments of the new government drafted their own RDP white papers to further the goals of the ANC. The Department of Health, for instance, saw improvement of vital statistics in South Africa as a serious priority in aiding the RDP. "While the Department of Health previously appeared to have re-neged on its public health responsibility and has not engaged in the process, it has now clearly committed itself to improving the situation" (Bradshaw et al. 1998).

The Department of Health established the National Health Information System for South Africa (NHIS/SA) Committee in 1994. The broad objective of the committee was to develop a National Health Information System for South Africa that begins at the local level and feeds into district, provincial, and national levels and includes the private and public sectors. The committee's discussion paper, "Towards a National Policy and Strategy for a National Information System for South Africa," identified birth and death legislation as impeding the successful implementation of the revised health information system. The births and deaths legislation governing vital records needed to be changed if the newly proposed system was to be successful.

The essence of the NHIS/SA principles regarding vital statistics was that their efforts should begin at the local level and feed into the provincial and national levels. The NHIS/SA should incorporate all the former TBVC states as well as the former self-governing territories. The principles stressed the importance of substantial coordination between the relevant role players, namely, DHA and Stats SA. Part of the aim of the information system is to enable the Department of Health to identify and monitor the disparities in health status generated largely by apartheid. NHIS/SA would take into account issues of confidentiality and would endeavor to distribute information quickly to allow decisions to be made and to monitor and evaluate national health policy. Numerous strategies were outlined for carrying out these principles. For vital statistics, four strategies were most relevant. First, information should be developed through a national process involving representatives of provincial and district authorities, community representatives, nongovernmental organizations, scientific communities, and academic institutions. These groups would work together to develop health objectives, health indicators, new data collection forms, health information systems, and the supporting computer and telecommunication methodology and technology. Second, the indicators to be developed should be disaggregated in such a way as to allow for monitoring of apartheid-generated disparities in access to health services. For example, specific levels of breakdown would include race, sex, age, geographic location, and socioeconomic status. Third, information should be disseminated widely to all stakeholders ranging from local authorities to provincial governments. Lastly, NHIS/SA saw its resulting database as an asset to be shared with researchers, whose requests would be cleared through an ethical committee.

Another prominent stakeholder that has emerged during this era could broadly be described as "advocacy groups." In practice, these groups get their message across through one or more of several consultative processes available through cooperative governance. One such mechanism is that instituted by the South African Law Commission (SALC).[14] SALC's main mandate is law reform, to change laws to keep in step with society's changing needs. Any person or body is free to submit proposals to the SALC for the reform of any aspect of South African law. If the proposal warrants law reform, the commission's research staff will prepare a discussion document on the subject. These documents are distributed free of charge, and the public is invited to comment on the proposals they contain. After extensive consultation and debate, a final report is submitted to the Minister of Justice for consideration. As a result, new laws may be enacted or old ones amended. Of interest to the subject of this chapter is the commission's investigation on HIV/AIDS and death registration.

The commission held a workshop on February 7, 1997, entitled "Medical certificates in respect to HIV/AIDS-related deaths." The workshop brought together the Department of Health, Stats SA, a "broad group of researchers," epidemiologists, HIV/AIDS advocacy groups, medical practitioners, lawyers, and human rights activists to debate the issue of a patient's right to privacy with regard to the filling out and processing of the medical certificate with respect to the cause of death. While different views were expressed, in the end, the advocacy groups achieved their aims. The second page of the new death notification form (the "Health page") had the following instruction written on the top: "After completion *seal* to ensure *confidentiality*." Subsequent to the adoption of the new death notification form, other researchers expressed reservations about the usefulness of this approach (Wood and Jewkes 1998). SALC's relationship with vital statistics gives it an open mandate to investigate any aspect of vital statistics for the purpose of legislative reform.

The Stats SA provincial offices agreed to partake in the vital registration process, and consequently, a bimonthly newsletter was started called the *Villages and Townships Vital Statistics Network* (VTVSN). This newsletter is a collaborative venture between the Stats SA subdirectorate of vital statistics and the Stats SA provincial offices. Its stated aim is the improvement of vital registration in villages and townships. The main strategy for accomplishing this was "networking." The Stats SA provincial offices joined the existing vital statistics steering committees in their provinces (comprised of the Department of Health, DHA, and other relevant stakeholders) and took part in their efforts. The officers report their activities in the newsletter, thereby informing members of the wider network the issues addressed and the progress being made.

The Challenges Ahead

Of all the challenges facing the South African vital statistics system, the two most pressing are to improve the coverage of vital events in nonurban areas and to produce timely death statistics for the purpose of monitoring the impact of mortality resulting from HIV/AIDS and other important causes of death. The first concern falls under what Linder (1981) refers to as "relatively intractable problems." These are problems that take a long time to solve and do not have "quick-fix" solutions.

The second problem is solvable, and Stats SA has taken positive steps to do so. One strategy Stats SA is adopting is to use the e-SAPR to produce advance release of death statistics and to use the microfilm of the death notification forms and medical certificates as the primary source for capturing details on causes of death. The captured information will then be processed

Figure 1.1   **Statistics South Africa's Strategy for Implementing Automatic Coding of Causes of Death**

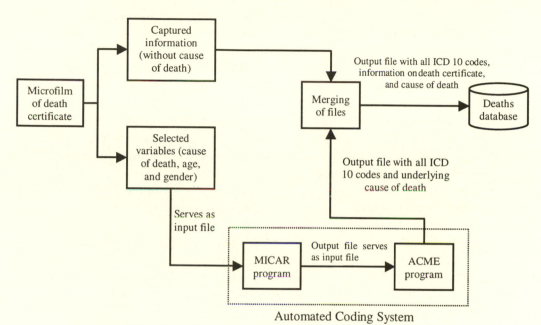

Automated Coding System

Source: Bah 2002.

through a system automatically coding the causes of death. The microfilms are readily available, as is the software. Steps are being taken to interface the automatic coding software with Stats SA's data-capturing system. When the system is fully functional, advance release data could be published within two months after any reference year or month, and cause of death data could be produced one year after the reference year. Figure 1.1 shows the framework designed by Stats SA for the rapid processing of cause-of-death statistics.

Conclusion

Race becomes a fact of identity in racially stratified societies. Even the members of the marginalized racial group feel compelled to maintain the racial classifications. The logic of the racial classification becomes obvious even to these marginalized groups. As mentioned above, the statistics director for Bophuthatswana stated in the 1991 census report that in spite of the negative history of classifying the "four ethnic groups, Whites, Coloreds, Asians and Blacks . . . it does make *demographic sense to retain the classifications . . .* to the extent that one finds more homogeneity within the groupings than differences, and this is crucial to the study of demography amongst other disciplines" (Republic of Bophuthatswana 1991: iv).

Racial classification in South Africa is a perfect example of what Paul Starr (1992) refers to as *legitimate classifications* and *legitimate use* of classifications. According to Starr, governments must determine which classifications will be used in political discourse and administration of the states. Legitimate classifications reflect the government's decisions as to which classifications will be used and which classifications will not be allowed. More than simply a personal choice, classification of social difference by the state is part of how societies socially differentiate. As such, legitimate classifications can fight or aid social stratification. Second, the government must determine when and how legitimate classifications can be used. For example, how will statistical information be organized around them? Legitimate use poses a problem in the political choice of legitimate classifications.

The twentieth century proved to be a tumultuous time for southern Africa, as land continued to be encroached upon and claimed by Europeans. However, it also marks the century in which Africans engaged in armed and other forms of political struggle to regain their land (Gerhart 1978). Toward the end of the twentieth century, Africans regained control in the Republic of South Africa, Namibia, and Zimbabwe.

The history of the development of the South African state and Afrikaner identity played an important role in the development and the composition of the country that is today known as the Republic of South Africa. As one Afrikaner leader noted, "The Afrikaans Language Movement is nothing less than an awakening of our nation to self-awareness and to the vocation of adopting a more worthy position in world civilization."[15] In fact, the Afrikaans Language Movement was to become a major opponent in the struggle against apartheid by the Black Consciousness Movement. Unlike the English-speaking White identity, with its internationalistic identification with European imperialism, Afrikaans and Afrikaner racial identity was based on a specific notion of bringing and developing civilization in South Africa. European origin was equated with civilization, and the new Afrikaner culture was seen as the most recent manifestation of this cultural transformation (Giliomee 1995; Zuberi and Khalfani 1999). Thus, if Afrikaans became the language of the nation, it would also result in a modernization of the population's "self-awareness." This ethnocentric concern with language served as a model for partisan demographic research as well. No single demographer expressed this fact as clearly as J.L. Sadie. In 1949 he wrote:

> In South Africa the outstanding problem, dominating all others, is the relative numbers of the different races constituting the Union's population, and their differential

rates of growth. For in the long run numbers must count. In this connection it is the numerical relation between Europeans and non-Europeans, and in particular between Europeans and Natives, which commands our attention. A complacent attitude towards this problem on the part of the Europeans, who as a minority still rule the country, is, to say the least, irresponsible. (Sadie 1949: 3)

The census has provided social contexts for political discussions about racial categories. The South African state has incorporated official racial classifications into the administration of the state. The colonial governments of the past found it necessary to racially classify the population in order to levy taxes and allocate benefits. The racial classification of the African population facilitated the process of exploiting the colony and transforming indigenous identities to support the colonial process. Administrators and scholars viewed the census as demonstrating South Africa's civilization to the world (see Cousins 1923 and Sadie 1949). Thus, the act of enumeration was an act of defining the colony for the civilized European world. The premodern censuses were key in the colonial process of racializing the identity of the African population.

Official classifications influence personal identities as well as social science research. Given the influence of the government on society, these classifications leave an important imprint on society. The impact of a government classification process is not unique to South Africa. There is abundant evidence around the globe that a government's employment of a racial classification system has an impact on various social and political aspects of that society (Cox 1948; Nascimento and Nascimento 2001; Wade 1993; Zuberi 2001b). But also, official classifications change as a result of changes in the social and political structure. Therefore, there is a symbiotic relationship between the state's efforts to develop and use racial classifications, and the society's use of, adherence to, and development of these classifications.

The official racial classification appears to never change (Starr 1992). Officially, race has been a legitimate classification in colonial and postcolonial South Africa. However, as we have seen in colonial and postcolonial South Africa, the notion of race and racial classification has been dynamic. This dynamism has been part of the political process. Racial classifications helped European colonists identify and label a subordinate population, even though those classifications were arbitrary and unable to systematically group individuals. However, the role of institutions in maintaining and legitimating racial classifications was important to White South African efforts to maintain control and power.

Racial classification of the South African population has been used for political purposes. In particular, apartheid used racial classification to signify African "otherness" and African marginalization. On a broad level, apartheid laws sought to ensure that Whites maintained social, economic, and political control over the country and over Africans. This was deemed necessary, because the African population greatly outnumbered the White citizenry.

Race expresses and symbolizes two different kinds of social things. Race is the outward and visible form of socially salient physical differences; it is also the flag of the population—the sign by which each racial population distinguishes itself from others, the visible mark of its distinctiveness, and a mark that is borne by everything that emanates from the race. Race is the symbol of both stratification and population identity, because both are aspects of society. Thus, racial identity becomes part of a group's collective identity and its sense of history and culture, but *the group transfigured and imagined in the physical form of skin color is what appears as race.* The modern South African census illustrates how important race can be in a political context.

In this chapter, we carefully examined the main contributing factors to population statistics in South Africa—the modern censuses and the civil registration and vital statistics system (including the population register). The census was examined in the context of the state's use of racial classification. The state has racialized all South African enumerations. This racialization was part of the government's system of racial stratification under all previous administrations. Since the 1994 national election and the sweeping victory of the African National Congress, the government has attempted to use racial classification to understand and undo the atrocities of the apartheid era. The ANC-led government instituted the Reconstruction and Development Programme, in 1994, to combat over 300 years of racial oppression. Part of this new program mandated the CSS to monitor the demographic progress of the RDP throughout the country by collecting and publishing relevant statistical data (CSS 1994). To this end, the first postapartheid census successfully challenged the previous administrations' practice of using racial classification as a tool of oppression. This is evidenced by greater overall participation in the enumeration process and is reflected in the increased rate of enumeration of the entire population in the 1996 census.

On a surface level, the South African data sets represent the distribution of the population at different times by age, sex, race, and geographic location. On another level, they reflect a history of governmental policies of racial discrimination in South Africa. We must remember that the purpose of population statistics and their analysis "is the reduction of data. Census or survey micro-data are of such a quantity that analysis is impossible without some process of summarizing the data" (Zuberi 2001a: 101). However, these analyses and reduction processes are not devoid of the cultural, political, or social influences of the collectors and processors of such data (de Graft-Johnson 1988; Zuberi 2001a; Zuberi and Khalfani 1999). Hence, we need to be thoughtful when using or producing such statistics. As in the United States, South Africa "provides an excellent example of how historical origins and race are interrelated in racially stratified societies. Racial data have been used in many ways . . ." however, "[r]racial data are necessary for viewing the effects of racial prejudice . . ." in a society plagued by institutionalized racial stratification and racial discrimination (Zuberi 2001b: 163).

South African civil registration and vital statistics systems and population registers have not been immune from the effects of the government's system of racial classification and segregation. In fact, prior to 1991, the laws that governed the population register had a broad sweeping impact on all population statistics and life chances in the country. Oddly enough, it was the revised version of the same policy that eliminated the use of racial classification in the population register and in the collection of vital statistics data.

The evolution of the civil registration and vital statistics system has been slow and sometimes inefficient. Statistics South Africa has proposed a process (see Figure 1.1) that would aid South Africa in producing timely and more accurate vital statistics. The South African government needs to improve efforts to document vital events in nonurban areas, as well as to expedite the collection of vital data, especially for the monitoring of mortality as a result of HIV/AIDS. Population statistics in South Africa are in a growth period, in terms of scope and intent. The users and the producers of these data will influence this dynamic evolutionary process, and hopefully, these developments will benefit South Africans.

Notes

1. See Zuberi and Khalfani (1999) for a discussion of censuses and other enumerations in southern Africa prior to 1911.

2. See Udjo (chapter 2 of this volume) for a discussion of the October Household Surveys. South Africa also conducted fertility surveys modeled on international Demographic and Health Surveys (DHS) and World Fertility Surveys (WFS).

3. Johan van Zyl (1994) of the Human Sciences Research Council in South Africa presented an unpublished paper at the annual Population Association of America meeting in 1994 that outlined many of the surveys conducted and analyzed by this government organization from 1966 to 1994. See also the South African Data Archive, which is available online at www.nrf.ac.za/sada/.

4. As this volume goes to press, the South African government is preparing to release the results of the 2001 census; hence, the 2001 census results are not incorporated into our analysis.

5. This is the same Philip V. Tobias (1970) who published the landmark study undermining the scientific basis of "claims that races of man have been shown to differ in quantity of brain-substance and especially, of grey matter in the cerebral cortex." However, even at this late date, Tobias maintained a racialized view of human difference.

6. The title of this office was amended from director to secretary by Act 30 of 1960 in the government *Gazette* No. 6402 on April 1, 1960. Section five of the Population Registrations

statute stated that all persons included in the population register will be classified by the secretary of interior, or one of his officers, as either a White person, a Colored person, or a native. The latter two groups were to be further subclassified according to ethnic or other group according to the secretary. The statute further stated that the governor-general could by proclamation add or amend the Colored or native classification as he saw necessary. Lastly, the secretary was empowered with the ability to racially reclassify individuals (after notifying them) he thought were erroneously classified.

7. In addition to the four colonies that composed the Union of South Africa in 1910, Botswana (Bechuanaland Protectorate), Lesotho (Basutoland), Malawi (Nyasaland), Swaziland, Zambia (Northern Rhodesia), and Zimbabwe (Southern Rhodesia) were considered for incorporation into the Union during its formation, as they were either British colonies or protectorates, or territorial possessions of the Cape Colony.

8. As Hermann Giliomee notes, "South Africa's institutionalized racism . . . can best be understood as a product of the Afrikaners' conception of their distinct place in the social structure" (1995: 190).

9. The reserve system consisted of areas on the border of the colonies where Africans resided. These groups of Africans, like the Fingoes, often served as buffers and intermediaries between the European colonists and other groups of Africans (see Zuberi and Khalfani 1999). The reserve system was the precursor to the homeland system later developed by the Nationalist Party.

10. Although the census was administered on March 7, 1991, the Population Registration Act Repeal Act of 1991 did not officially go into effect until June 28, 1991. Therefore, technically and legally, the CSS was still obligated to collect racial data. However, the popular understanding that the Population Registration Act Repeal Act of 1991 was soon to be signed into law created an atmosphere of conflict between the CSS and the various groups opposed to the use and collection of racial data by the government.

11. "The HSRC's field workers and organizers, each with a team of census enumerators, visited the indicated premises and shacks on the ground and ensured that each resident was enumerated. The particulars obtained in this manner were then projected in accordance with the number of dwelling structures to obtain an estimate of inter alia the population number in the specific area. For instance, if the particulars show that for ten dwelling/structures the average occupancy rate is six persons per dwelling, then a hundred dwellings will have an estimated six hundred occupants" (RSA 1992a: ix).

12. There were many news articles on the politics of the 1991 census. For a few additional examples, see the *Transvaler*, February 8, 1991; *The Star*, March 6 and 7, 1991.

13. The civil registration system and the system put in place for generating vital statistics is known as the vital statistics system.

14. "The South African Law Commission was established by the South African Law Commission Act 19 of 1973. . . . The Commission is an advisory body whose aim is the renewal and improvement of the law of South Africa on a continuous basis" (wwwserver.law.wits.ac.za/salc/objects.html).

15. D.F. Malan, cited in Giliomee (1995: 192). Malan, along with General Hertzog, was one of the original Afrikaner nationalists prominent at the beginning of the century.

References

Adegboyega, Wole. 1995. Interview with Akil Kokayi Khalfani, United Nations Population Fund (UNFPA) Census Advisor to the South African Central Statistical Service. December 8.

Bah, Sulaiman. 2002. "Deaths in South Africa that are due to HIV/AIDS and related causes, 1993–2000" (Unpublished document).

Barringer, Herbert, Robert W. Gardner, and Michael J. Levin. 1993. *Asians and Pacific Islanders in the United States.* New York: Russell Sage Foundation.

Bradshaw, D., D. Kielkowski, and F. Sitas. 1998. "New birth and death registration forms: A foundation for the future, a challenge for health workers?" *South African Medical Journal* 88(8): 971–74.

Bureau for Information (BI). 1991. "Statistics on population groups essential." Press release by the News Service, February 6. Pretoria: Central Statistical Service.

Cell, John W. 1982. *The Highest Stage of White Supremacy: The Origins of Segregation in South Africa and the American South.* New York: Cambridge University Press.

Central Statistical Service (CSS). 1994. *Annual Report 1994.* Pretoria: Central Statistical Service.

———. 1997. *Census '96: Preliminary Estimates of the Size of the Population of South Africa.* Pretoria: Central Statistical Service.

Christopher, A.J. 1983. "Official land disposal policies and European settlement in southern Africa, 1860.1960." *Journal of Historical Geography* 4(4): 369–83.

———. 1992. "Segregation levels in South Africa cities, 1911.1985." *The International Journal of African Historical Studies* 25(3): 561–82.

———. 1994. *The Atlas of Apartheid.* London: Routledge.

Cousins, C.W. 1923. Cited in *Census of the Union of South Africa 1921,* Union Government, 15 (1): 11.

Cox, Oliver C. 1948. *Caste, Class, and Race: A Study in Social Dynamics.* New York: Doubleday.

Davenport, T.R.H. 1991. *South Africa: A Modern History,* 4th edition. London: Macmillan Press.

de Graft-Johnson, K.T. 1988. "Demographic data collection in Africa." In *The State of African Demography,* ed. Etienne van de Walle, Patrick O. Ohadike, and Mpembele D. Sala-Diakanda, 13–28. Liège: International Union for the Scientific Study of Population.

Dubow, Saul. 1995. *Scientific Racism in Modern South Africa.* New York: Cambridge University Press.

Evans, I. 1997. *Bureaucracy and Race: Native Administration in South Africa.* Berkeley: University of California Press.

Gerhart, Gail M. 1978. *Black Power in South Africa: The Evolution of an Ideology.* Berkeley: University of California Press.

Giliomee, Hermann. 1995. "The growth of Afrikaner identity." In *Segregation and Apartheid in Twentieth-Century South Africa,* ed. William Beinart and Saul Dubow, 189–205. New York: Routledge.

Hanchard, Michael George. 1994. *Orpheus and Power: The Movimento Negro of Rio de Janeiro and Sao Paulo, Brazil, 1945–1988.* Princeton, NJ: Princeton University Press.

Ignatiev, Noel. 1995. *How the Irish Became White.* New York: Routledge.

Jackson, Fatimah L.C. 2000. "Anthropological measurement: The mismeasure of African Americans." *The Annals of the American Academy of Political and Social Sciences.* 568: 154–71.

Linder, F. 1981. "Problems of improving vital registration systems in developing countries." *International Population Conference, Manila 1981,* Vol. 3. Liège: IUSSP.

Magubane, Bernard Makhosezwe. 1979. *The Political Economy of Race and Class in South Africa.* New York: Monthly Review Press.

Mamdani, M. 1996. *Citizen and Subject: Contemporary Africa and the Legacy of Late Colonialism.* Princeton, NJ: Princeton University Press.

McDaniel, Antonio. 1995. "The dynamic racial composition of the United States." *Dædalus* (winter) 124(1): 179–98.

Moffat, J.B. 1911. Letter to E.D. Durand, Director of the Census Bureau, Department of Commerce and Labour, U.S.A., December 8. Pretoria: RSA State Archives, File No. A1/13 "Permanent Census Office: Views Regarding" in SES A1/5/2.

Nascimento, Abdias do, and Elisa Larkin Nascimento. 2001. "Dance of deception: A reading of race relations in Brazil." In *Beyond Racism: Race and Inequality in Brazil, South Africa, and the United States,* ed. Charles V. Hamilton, Lynn Huntley, Neville Alexander,

Antonio Sérgio Alfredo Guimarães, and Wilmont James, 105–56. Boulder, CO.: Lynne Rienner Publishers .

Office of Census and Statistics (OCS). 1925a. "The Union Census Office: Its organization and methods." Radio broadcast read on A.S. & T. Broadcasting Company Limited in April. Pretoria: Republic of South Africa State Archives, File No. A1/14 "Broadcasting" in SES A1/5/2.

———. 1925b. "The Union Census Office: Its organization and methods (second talk)." Radio broadcast read on A.S. & T. Broadcasting Company Limited in April. Pretoria: RSA State Archives, File No. A1/14 "Broadcasting" in SES A1/5/2.

Patterson, Sheila. 1975. "Some speculations on the status and role of the free people of color in the western Cape." In *Studies in African Social Anthropology,* ed. Meyer Fortes and Sheila Patterson, 159–205. London and New York: Academic Press.

Pogrund, Benjamin. 1990. *How Man Can Die Better: Sobukwe and Apartheid.* London: Peter Halban.

Republic of Bophuthatswana (RB). 1991. *1991 Population Census*: Volume 1, Part 2. Mmabatho: Statistics Branch, Department of Economic, Energy Affairs, Mines & Planning.

Republic of South Africa (RSA). 1961. *Population Census 6th September, 1960: Geographical Distribution of the Population.* Vol. 1. Pretoria: The Government Printer.

———. 1968. *Urban and Rural Population of South Africa: 1904 to 1960.* Report No. 02–02–01. Pretoria: The Government Printer.

———. 1992a. *Population Census 1991: Adjustment for Undercount.* Report No. 03–01–26 (1991). Pretoria: Central Statistical Service.

———. 1992b. *Population Census 1991: Age by Development Region, Statistical Region and District.* Report No. 03–01–03 (1991). Pretoria: Central Statistical Service.

———. 1998. *The People of South Africa: Population Census 1996, Calculating the Undercount in Census '96.* Report No. 03–01–18 (1996). Pretoria: Statistics South Africa.

Ross, Roberts. 1989. "The Cape of Good Hope and the world economy, 1652–1835." In *The Shaping of South African Society, 1652–1840,* ed. Richard Elphick and Hermann Giliomee, 243–80. Middletown, CT: Wesleyan University Press.

Sadie, J.L. 1949. "The political arithmetic of the S.A. population." *Journal of Racial Affairs* 1: 3–8.

———. 1988. *A Reconstruction and Projection of Demographic Movements in the RSA and TBVC Countries.* Pretoria: University of South Africa, Bureau of Market Research. Report No. 148.

Starr, Paul. 1992. "Social categories and claims in the liberal state." *Social Research* 59(2): 263–95.

Statistical Council (SC). 1921. "Minutes of a meeting of the Statistical Council held at Pretoria on Monday the 14th November." State Archives, Transvaal Depot. Ref. No.: SES, 5/10/5.

Statistics South Africa. 2002. *Causes of Death in South Africa, 1997–2001.* Pretoria: Statistics South Africa. Publication No. P0309.2: 33–34.

Thompson, Leonard. 1995. *A History of South Africa*, Revised Edition. New Haven, CT: Yale University Press.

Tobias, Phillip V. 1953. "The problem of race determination: Limiting factors in the identification of the South African races." *Journal of Forensic Medicine* 1(2): 113–23.

———. 1970. "Brain-size, grey matter and race—fact or fiction?" *American Journal of Physical Anthropology* 32: 3.

———. 1985. "History of physical anthropology in southern Africa." *Yearbook of Physical Anthropology* 28: 1–52.

Union of South Africa (USA). 1911. *Statutes of the Union of South Africa, 1910–1911.* Pretoria: The Government Printers.

———. 1950a. *Statutes of the Union of South Africa, 1950.* Pretoria: Parow.

———. 1950b. "Act No. 30 of 1950—Population Registration Act," *Statutes of the Union of South Africa, 1950.* Pretoria: Parow, 275–99.

van Wyk, D.H. 1984. "Race." In *The Law of South Africa,* Vol. 21, ed. W.A. Joubert and T.J. Scott, 385–421. Durban and Pretoria: Butterworth.

van Zyl, Johan. 1994. "History, scope and methodology of fertility and family planning surveys in South Africa." Paper presented at the Population Association of America annual meeting in Miami, May 5–7.

Wade, Peter. 1993. *Blackness and Race Mixture: The Dynamics of Race Identity in Colombia.* Baltimore and London: John Hopkins University Press.

Watson, Graham. 1970. *Passing for White: A Study of Racial Assimilation in a South African School.* London: Tavistock Publications.

Wood, K., and Jewkes, R. 1998. "Opportunities and threats in proposed changes to birth and death registration." *South African Medical Journal* 88(1): 28–29.

Zuberi, Tukufu. 2000. "Deracializing social statistics: Problems in the quantification of race." *The Annals of the American Academy of Political and Social Science* 568: 172–85.

———. 2001a. *Thicker than Blood: How Racial Statistics Lie.* Minneapolis: University of Minnesota Press.

———. 2001b. "The population dynamics of the changing color line." In *Problem of the Century: Racial Stratification in the United States,* ed. Elijah Anderson and Douglas S. Massey, 145–67. New York: Russell Sage Foundation.

Zuberi, Tukufu, and Akil K. Khalfani. 1999. "Racial classification and colonial population enumerations in South Africa." *African Census Analysis Project Working Paper Series #6.* Philadelphia: University of Pennsylvania.

Appendix 1.1   Notification/Register of Death/Stillbirth

REPUBLIC OF SOUTH AFRICA
DEPARTMENT OF HOME AFFAIRS

BI - 1663

NOTIFICATION / REGISTER OF DEATH / STILL BIRTH

in terms of the Births and Deaths Registration Act, 1992 (Act No. 51 of 1992)

Space for Bar Code

* Must be completed in black ink (please tick ✓ where applicable)
* Please refer to instructions

SERIAL No:

FILE No: DATE: A0 1857265

A   PARTICULARS OF DECEASED INDIVIDUAL ☐ / STILLBORN CHILD ☐

Identity number of deceased

Date of death: Y Y Y Y M M D D

Date of birth: Y Y Y Y M M D D

Surname

Age at last birthday: years

Maiden Name (If female)

Sex

Forenames

If death occurred within 24 hours after birth No. of hours alive

MARITAL STATUS OF DECEASED   Single ☐   Civil Marriage ☐   Living as married ☐   Widowed ☐

Religious Law Marriage ☐   Divorced ☐   Customary Marriage ☐

Left thumb print of deceased

PLACE OF BIRTH (municipal district or country if abroad) _____

PLACE OF DEATH (City / Town / Village) _____

PLACE OF REGISTRATION OF DEATH _____

CITIZENSHIP OF DECEASED

B   PARTICULARS OF INFORMANT

Identity number

Initials and Surname

Relationship to deceased   Parent ☐   Spouse ☐   Child ☐   Other kin ☐   Other (specify) ☐

Postal address

Left thumb print of informant

Postal Code   Dialling Code

Was the next of kin of the deceased a smoker* during the past five years?   Yes ☐   No ☐   Refuse to answer ☐   Telephone No.

Date _____   Signature _____

CANCELLED

C   PARTICULARS OF FUNERAL UNDERTAKER

Initials and Surname

Office Stamp of Funeral Undertaker

Designation No.   Place of burial / cremation _____

Date _____   Signature _____

D   CERTIFICATE BY ATTENDING MEDICAL PRACTITIONER / PROFESSIONAL NURSE   Postal Address

I, the undersigned, hereby certify that the deceased named in Section A, to the best of my knowledge and belief, died solely and exclusively due to NATURAL CAUSES specified in Section G ☐

I, the undersigned, am not in the position to certify that the deceased died exclusively due to natural causes ☐

Postal Code

SAMDC / SANC Reg. No.

_____   INITIALS AND SURNAME   _____   SIGNATURE

Date signed: Y Y Y Y M M D D

CERTIFICATE BY DISTRICT SURGEON / FORENSIC PATHOLOGIST

I, the undersigned, hereby certify that a medicolegal post-mortem examination has been conducted on the body of the person whose particulars are given in Section A and that the body is no longer required for the purpose of the Inquest Act, 1959 (Act No. 58 of 1959) and that the cause of death is: Unnatural ☐   Under investigation ☐

Natural (Cause of Death as indicated in Section G) ☐

Postal Address

Initials and Surname

Postal Code

Place of post-mortem _____   Date Y Y Y Y M M D D

Mortuary Reference _____

Signature _____   Date signed Y Y Y Y M M D D

SAMDC Reg. No.

E   FOR OFFICIAL USE ONLY   Initials and Surname of Registrar

Registration of death approved and burial order issued

Office Stamp ▷

Address

Force No. / Designation No.

Persal No.

Date _____   Signature _____

* Someone who smokes tobacco on most days

PARAGON 226639 (H)

NOTIFICATION / REGISTER OF DEATH / STILL BIRTH

BI - 1663
Page 2

INFORMATION FOR MEDICAL AND HEALTH USE ONLY
(After completion *seal* to ensure <u>confidentiality</u>)

Space for Bar Code

SERIAL No:

FILE No: DATE: **A 01857265**

F DEMOGRAPHIC DETAILS

Initials and Surname of deceased

Identity Number

Place of death   1. Hospital: (Inpatient   ER/ Outpatient   DOA   )   2. Nursing Home   3. Home   4. Other (Specify)

FACILITY NAME (If not institution, give street and number)

Usual residential address of deceased #   Suburb

Town / Village

Name of Plot, Farm, etc.   Census Enumerator Area

Street name and number

Magist. Dist.

Deceased's Education (Specify ✓ only highest class completed/achieved)

Postal Code

None	Gr1	Gr2	Gr3	Gr4	Gr5	Gr6	Gr7	Gr8 Form 1	Gr9 Form 2	Gr10 Form 3 NTC1	Gr11 Form 4 NTC2	Gr12 Form 5 NTC3	Univ Tech	CODE

Province

Country

USUAL OCCUPATION OF DECEASED (give type of work done during most of working life. Do not use retired)

TYPE OF BUSINESS/INDUSTRY (e.g. Mining, Farming) refer to instructions

Was the deceased a smoker* five years ago? (✓) :   Yes   Do not know   Not applicable (minor)

G MEDICAL CERTIFICATE OF CAUSE OF DEATH

FOR OFFICE USE ONLY

PART 1. Enter the disease, injuries or complications that caused the death. Do not enter the mode of dying, such as cardiac or respiratory arrest, shock, or heart failure. List only one cause on each line.

Approximate interval between onset and Death (Days/Months/Years)

ICD-10

IMMEDIATE CAUSE (Final disease or condition resulting in death)   a.
Due to (or as a consequence of)

Sequentially list conditions, if any, leading to immediate cause. Enter UNDERLYING CAUSE last (Disease or injury that initiated events resulting in death)   b.
Due to (or as a consequence of)

c.
Due to (or as a consequence of)

d.
Due to (or as a consequence of)

PART 2. Other significant conditions contributing to death but not resulting in the underlying cause given in Part 1.

If a female, was she pregnant 42 days prior to death? (✓) :   Yes   No

If stillborn, please write mass in grams

Do you consider the deceased to be: African   White   Indian   Coloured   Other   (Specify)

Method of ascertainment of cause of death:

1. Autopsy   2. Opinion of attending medical practitioner   3. Opinion of attending medical practitioner on duty

4. Opinion of registered professional nurse   5. Interview of family member

6. Other   (Specify)

Where someone lived on most days   * Someone who smokes tobacco on most days

Source: Statistics South Africa 2002.

2. Fertility Levels, Differentials, and Trends

Eric O. Udjo

The systematic collection of fertility data in South Africa began with the inception of the annual program of October Household Surveys (OHS) by Statistics South Africa in 1994. Since then, regular household surveys have been undertaken. The inclusion of questions on fertility, including birth histories, enables the direct and indirect estimation of current levels and trends in fertility nationally, and in the four main population groups (African, White, Colored, and Indian/Asian). In addition, the inclusion of questions on fertility in the first nationwide population census in October 1996 (1996 South African Population Census) also enables direct and indirect estimation of current levels of fertility in South Africa.

In previous studies, Udjo (1998) utilized the 1995 OHS and the 1996 census to produce estimates of fertility, mortality, and the size of the South African population during the period 1970–96. Since the release of the results of these studies, there has been increasing demand for disaggregated estimates of these demographic indicators for each of the four main population groups. There are various reasons for this, including:

1. In the past, estimates of demographic parameters and population size have traditionally been produced for each of the four main population groups, but national estimates were derived by averaging or summing up the subnational estimates. The argument that has been proffered for this approach is that the country is characterized by different demographic regimes (Sadie 1988), and because it has been racially divided, population estimation has always been done in this way (Simkins 1997, personal communication).

2. The final result from the 1996 census of the population of South Africa (40.6 million) by Statistics South Africa (1999a) was lower than the projected estimate of 42.1 million. The final figure for the size of the White population was also lower than expected (4.4 million instead of a projected figure of 5.3 million, see Statistics South Africa 1999b). Although the estimates of the South African population in the studies by Udjo (1998) did not take into account migration, it was also lower than earlier projections. One of the arguments used to explain the unexpectedly lower population figure is that the fertility of Blacks was overestimated in earlier projections.

In order to address some of the issues raised in the second point above, there is demand for a "four-race" model of fertility, mortality, and migration for population projections in South Africa using recent data.

The objectives of this study are (1) to estimate levels, differentials, and trends in fertility based on a critical analysis of recently available data from Statistics South Africa and (2) to assess whether or not the fertility inputs in projections of South Africa's population during the apartheid era overestimated fertility.

Data

The approach adopted in this study is based on Brass's principle of serendipity: making the most of one's chances or utilizing whatever information is available. In this regard, where possible, this study uses the data on fertility from the 1995, 1997, 1998 OHS and the 1996 census. The 1994 and 1996 OHS are not used: the demographic questions in the 1994 survey were limited compared to the later surveys, while the fertility information in the 1996 OHS could not be analyzed due to the omission of birth order of children during the data processing. As a result, the children could not be uniquely identified and correctly linked to their mothers as in the other surveys. Supplementary analysis was also carried out on the 1970 census and birth registration.

The October Household Surveys

The fertility questions used in the 1995, 1997, and 1998 OHS were broadly similar. However, unlike the 1995 survey, separate questions on births within the last twelve months and children ever born preceded the birth histories in the 1997–98 surveys. Of these surveys, the 1995 round is the most appropriate data set for examining past fertility trends, since its birth histories stretch farther back in time than those of the 1997 and 1998 surveys.

The 1995 survey was carried out on a national sample of 30,000 households drawn from 3,000 enumeration areas, and ten households were selected in each enumeration area. The sample was stratified by province, urban and nonurban areas, and population group and was approximately self-weighting. Hirschowitz and Orkin (1996) provide detailed methodological information regarding the 1995 survey.

The sample size in the 1997 survey was also 30,000 households, but this was reduced to 20,000 households in the 1998 survey. In both cases, the samples were based on the 1996 census enumeration areas. Although they were probability samples, unlike in 1995, the 1997 and 1998 surveys were not self-weighting nationally.

The 1996 Population Census

Following the new political dispensation in South Africa and the first democratic elections of 1994, the first nationwide census since 1970 was carried out in October 1996. The census attempted to canvas all households in the country, but as in other countries, there was a degree of coverage error, which Statistics South Africa, in its final report, estimated as 10.7 percent nationally (Statistics South Africa 1999a).

Censuses do not typically collect birth histories, but the 1996 census household questionnaire included a question for women 12 years and older on the number of children they had ever given birth to. In addition, women were asked how many children they had given birth to in the last twelve months before the census. These questions were the basis of the analysis of fertility from the 1996 census.

The 1970 Census and Birth Registration

Because birth histories become increasingly truncated going back in time, fertility estimations using the method described in the next section could not be carried out for periods before 1980. The 1970 census required African women to report about births during the last twelve months before the census. Women in other population groups were not required to provide this information during the 1970 census. However, for the non-African population (i.e., Colored, Indian/Asian, and White), birth registration information is available for 1970 (see Republic of South Africa 1973). Analysis of fertility for the period 1970 was based on these two sets of information.

Methods

Women outside the reproductive age range of 15 through 49 were excluded from the analysis. Some women reported having had nine births within the last twelve months before the 1996 census. This is not biologically possible at any age (see Bongaarts 1978). Other than multiple births, one should not expect a woman, at any age, to have more than two live births in a given year. No information on multiple births was collected during the 1996 census. As a consequence, and to take sufficient account of multiple births, the analysis of births within the last twelve months in this study utilized a maximum number of six live births. A sensitivity test was performed, however, on all current births reported by women ages 15 to 49 to assess the probable bias arising from this by comparing the results based on different truncation. The results were similar up to a maximum of six births within the last twelve months.

The application of Brass and Coale's (1968) P/F ratio method (or its variants) is a starting point in the analysis of children ever born (P), and births within the last twelve months (current births, F), reported by women of reproductive age during a survey or census because it provides a snapshot assessment of the quality of the data and probable recent trend in fertility.

In the application of the method, the mean parity equivalent, F_i, is estimated using the following equation:

$$F_i = \sum_{j=0}^{i-1} f_j + k_i f_i$$

where f_i is the reported age-specific fertility for a five-year age group, k_i is the multiplying factor that enables the estimation of the additions to mean parity from the specific rates in the current interval to make them comparable (Brass 1996).

The estimated F_is are then compared with reported mean parities P_is. The ratios of P/Fs by age serve as indicators of the consistency and accuracy of the two sets of data. If fertility in a population has not been constant in recent years, it may not be appropriate to estimate the level using the P/F ratio method, but the method could still be used under this circumstance to analyze the trend in fertility. Although Arriaga (1983, 1994) has shown how the P/F ratio method can be used to estimate fertility when fertility has been changing in a population, initial examination of children ever born and current births in this study was based on Brass's method.

The P/F ratio method cannot correct for distortions in reported age patterns of fertility. Other models are required for this purpose. One such model is the relational Gompertz. The relational Gompertz model proposed by Brass (1974, 1981) and developed by Booth (1979) and Zaba (1981) was designed for the evaluation and adjustment of birth distributions derived from reports of births during the last twelve months and children ever born. The model can be fit for detailed analysis of birth histories (see Appendix 2.1 for more details).

The estimation of levels of fertility at different time periods (except 1975) and the smoothing of the age pattern of fertility were based on the relational Gompertz model. As noted above, since birth histories become increasingly truncated going back in time, the model could not be fitted to births prior to 1980 (even in the 1995 survey), because the points were too few. The estimates of fertility for the period 1975 were, therefore, derived by interpolation within the Gompertz parameters, and from total fertility rates using points for which estimates could be made, including those for 1970. At first, a third-degree polynomial interpolation was carried out, but when the results were compared with those derived by linear interpolation, the latter resulted in a better fit to the data. As a consequence, only the results of the linear interpolation are presented.

The analysis of the 1970 and 1996 censuses was based on the unadjusted data. Similarly, the analysis of the household surveys used the unweighted data, but at levels where the data were approximately self-weighting (population group and province).

Current Levels, Differentials, and Trends of Fertility

Application of the P/F Ratio Method

Table·2.1 shows the results of the application of the P/F ratio method to current fertility and children ever born reported in the OHS and the 1996 census using a refined model by Hamad (1982).[1] In all the data sets, the P/F ratios are greater than one (except for women ages 15 through 19 in the 1998 survey). While the P/F ratios increase with the age of the mother in the household surveys data, they decline as the age of the mother increases in the 1996 census data. This is indicative of different patterns of error in the data sets, though in theory this could also be interpreted as indicative of fertility trends (declining fertility in the case of the household surveys, and rising fertility in the case of the 1996 census). Given that the time period between the household surveys and the 1996 census is short (approximately one year), the discrepancies of the age pattern of the P/F ratios derived from the census and surveys are likely attributable to one or a combination of the following:

1. distortion of the current fertility pattern by reporting errors;
2. underreporting of current births by women in the younger age groups; or
3. overreporting of number of children ever born by the older women.

The reports in the data sets on current levels of fertility are suspect, for the following reasons. At face value, the reports suggest that nationally the total fertility rate increased from 2.2 in 1995 to 3.0 in 1996 (a 36 percent increase),

Table 2.1

Brass P/F Ratios Using Hamad's Multipliers Based on Reported Age-Specific Fertility Rates (ASFR), Average Parities (Parity), and Reported Total Fertility Rates (TFR)

Age group	OHS95			1996 Census			OHS97*			OHS98*		
	ASFR	Parity	P/F	ASFR	Parity	P/F	ASFR	Parity	P/F	ASFR	Parity	P/F
15-19	0.041	0.095	1.079	0.047	0.210	1.732	0.023	0.076	1.346	0.049	0.122	0.970
20-24	0.099	0.532	1.091	0.100	0.836	1.547	0.056	0.404	1.429	0.103	0.568	1.018
25-29	0.109	1.246	1.212	0.116	1.631	1.492	0.069	0.962	1.591	0.119	1.290	1.146
30-34	0.089	2.008	1.321	0.115	2.510	1.495	0.077	1.676	1.717	0.110	2.160	1.271
35-39	0.056	2.633	1.410	0.095	3.178	1.442	0.054	2.240	1.727	0.078	2.876	1.330
40-44	0.030	3.028	1.462	0.072	3.719	1.425	0.340	2.646	1.757	0.039	3.415	1.407
45-49	0.014	3.056	1.405	0.057	4.058	1.370	0.015	2.891	1.779	0.012	3.848	1.515
f1/f2	0.411			0.474			0.403			0.477		
m	28.9			28.3			30.8			29.2		
Reported TFR	2.2			3.0			1.6			2.6		

Source: Author's calculations, based on the 1995, 1997, and 1998 October Household Surveys and 1996 census data.
Note: *Since the 1997 and 1998 October Household Surveys were not designed to be self-weighting nationally, it is tricky to derive nationally representative P/F ratios from these two data sets; the figures for these data sets in this table are, therefore, not exactly accurate but indicative.

then declined to a below-replacement level of 1.6 in 1997 (a 47 percent decline), then rose to 2.6 (a 63 percent increase) a year later. Although period total fertility rates could fluctuate from year to year, the magnitude of the reported fluctuations in total fertility rate within such short intervals would be unlikely to occur.

One would also expect some stability in completed family size within a short period. However, the reports indicate that completed family size increased from 3.1 in 1995 to 4.1 in 1996. Again, this is unlikely to occur and is most likely a result of overreporting. It is difficult to assess which of the above factors is largely responsible for the age pattern of the P/Fs without further analysis.

The results of the application of the P/F ratios to the reports by population group in the various data sets are summarized in Table 2.2. Note the similarity between the national P/F ratios (in Table 2.1) and those for Africans for each period. This is because Africans are estimated to comprise over three-quarters of the national population. The P/F ratios are generally above one for each age group and, on average (for the age cohorts), vary from one year to the other within each population group. For each of the population groups, the P/F values for the year 1997 are markedly inconsistent with the values for the other periods. While fertility trends could have implications for P/F ratios, as noted above, it is unlikely that fertility trends explain the period variations in the P/F values by population group. Instead, these are probably a reflection of differences in the quality of the data.

An indication of this data quality problem might be gleaned from the reported total fertility rates for each of the periods. As can be seen from Table 2.2, the reported total fertility rate in 1997 is not consistent with those for the other periods. Among Africans, for example, it is inconceivable that fertility would have declined by more than one child within one year (between 1996 and 1997) and then increased by nearly one child a year later (between 1997 and 1998). Furthermore, among Indians/Asians, the below-replacement reported levels of fertility (less than one in 1997 and 1.8 in 1998) is highly suspect and may be partly attributable to sampling error.

Application of the Relational Gompertz Model to Current Births and Children Ever Born

Further insight into the pattern of fertility was sought by fitting the relational Gompertz model. The results of the application of the relational Gompertz model to births within the last twelve months and children ever born reported by population group in the various data sets are summarized below. For economy of space, Appendices 2.2 through 2.5 show illustrations based only on the 1995 survey and

Table 2.2

Brass P/F Ratios by Population Group Using Hamad's Multipliers

Age	OHS95	Census '96	OHS97	OHS98
African				
15–19	0.94	1.75	1.34	0.95
20–24	1.07	1.58	1.46	1.03
25–29	1.24	1.54	1.61	1.16
30–34	1.39	1.54	1.72	1.31
35–39	1.49	1.48	1.74	1.38
40–44	1.58	1.47	1.79	1.49
45–49	1.49	1.42	1.79	1.61
Average P/F	1.31	1.54	1.63	1.28
Reported total fertility rate	2.3	3.3	1.8	2.7
Colored				
15–19	0.87	1.43	1.25	1.24
20–24	1.03	1.38	1.3	0.94
25–29	1.08	1.34	1.48	1.09
30–34	1.16	1.36	1.69	1.1
35–39	1.22	1.37	1.7	1.12
40–44	1.22	1.41	1.68	1.21
45–49	1.25	1.48	1.9	1.27
Average P/F	1.12	1.4	1.57	1.14
Reported total fertility rate	2.3	2.5	1.3	2.4
Indian/Asian				
15–19	0.97	1.85	0.62	0.66
20–24	1.04	1.44	1.08	1.15
25–29	1.51	1.51	2.26	1.05
30–34	1.51	1.51	2.28	1.51
35–39	1.68	1.48	2.31	1.4
40–44	1.67	1.47	—	1.32
45–49	—	1.46	—	—
Average P/F	1.4	1.53	1.71	1.18
Reported total fertility rate	1.5	2	0.9	1.8
White				
15–19	1.12	2.46	3.34	0.94
20–24	0.97	1.41	1.25	0.94
25 29	1.1	1.41	1.49	1.13
30–34	1.09	1.42	1.72	1.23
35–39	1.15	1.38	1.7	1.23
40–44	1.17	1.34	1.8	1.23
45–49	1.09	1.29	1.67	—
Average P/F	1.1	1.53	1.85	1.12
Reported total fertility rate	1.9	1.9	1.1	1.8

Source: Computed from the 1996 South African Population Census micro-data.

the 1996 census, and only for the African and White populations, because they are by far the most important and contrasting components numerically.

There were differing magnitudes of reporting errors by population group in the reporting of current births and children ever born by women. Although there were differences by population group in the quality of reporting of births at the younger ages, on the whole, for each of the population groups, the reports seemed more reliable for the younger than the older women.

Differences among the population groups in the quality of reporting on births during the 1995 survey include the following:

- Among Indian/Asian and White women in the youngest age group (15 through 29 years), the reporting of births seemed less reliable (probably due to sampling error) than among African and Colored women in the same age group. This was evident from a visual inspection of the points.
- The curving upward of the P points at the oldest age groups among African women indicates underreporting of children ever born at these ages (Appendix 2.2). On the other hand, the curving downward of the P points among non-African women indicates some degree of overstatement of children ever born (Appendix 2.4).
- The F and P points were more dispersed at the oldest ages among White women than women in the other population groups (Appendixes 2.4 and 2.5). This suggests that the quality of the reports was poorer among White women in these age ranges than the corresponding reports of women in the other population groups.
- With regard to the 1996 census, the pattern of errors among the population groups in the reporting of births was similar to that described above among younger women. However, there was a striking similarity among the population groups in the pattern for the oldest age groups—the F and P points curved downward. This suggests that the ages of older women were exaggerated during the 1996 census (see Appendixes 2.4 and 2.5).
- Regarding the other data sets, the points derived from current births showed greater convergence on a straight line in the 1998 OHS than the corresponding points in the 1997 survey among Africans. This suggests that the reports on current births are less reliable in the 1997 survey than in the 1998 survey. In general, among Coloreds, the points derived from current births curved upward after age 35 in the 1997 survey, suggesting substantial underreporting of current births during the survey. However, outliers in the points derived from current births suggest that women ages 35 through 39 also substantially underreported current births during the 1998 survey. The dispersion of the points derived from children ever born among Indian/ Asian women in both data sets could be due to small sample size. With regard to Whites, the points derived from current births and children ever born

Table 2.3

Current Estimates of Gompertz Parameters, Total Fertility Rates by Population Group

	1995	1996	1997	1998
Beta values				
African	0.877	0.809	0.845	0.887
Colored	1.106	1.008	0.868	0.971
Indian/Asian	1.343	1.188	1.068	1.416
White	1.540	1.216	1.254	1.259
Alpha Values				
African	−0.341	−0.275	−0.313	−0.163
Colored	−0.031	−0.048	−0.428	−0.131
Indian/Asian	−0.105	−0.054	−0.296	−0.095
White	−0.018	−0.118	−0.246	−0.107
Total fertility rates				
African	3.6	3.7	3.1	3.5
Colored	2.8	2.8	2.4	2.6
Indian/Asian	2.5	2.7	2.3	2.5
White	2.0	1.9	1.7	1.9
National	3.2	3.2	2.9	3.2

Source: Computed from the 1996 South African Population Census micro-data.

were more dispersed in the 1997 OHS than in the 1998 OHS, which suggests that the quality of the data in the former is poorer than in the latter.

In light of the patterns of error discussed above, a straight line was fitted to the "best" points derived from the application of the model using the group average method in order to estimate the Gompertz parameters. The results are shown in Table 2.3 for the period 1995–98. As seen in the table (bottom panel of Table 2.3), the results indicate that in 1998, total fertility rates were as follows: African (3.5), Colored (2.6), Indian/Asian (2.5), and White (1.9), yielding a national estimate of 3.2. Even after adjustment by fitting the relational Gompertz model, the estimates of total fertility rate based on the 1997 survey appear too low (national: 2.9), as they were inconsistent with the estimates for the other periods. The estimated total fertility rates from the various data sets are, however, consistent with the earlier observation from the results of the P/Fs that current births were underreported during the fieldwork interviews in each of the periods, especially in the household surveys.

Application of the Relational Gompertz Model to the 1995 OHS Birth Histories, 1970 Census, and Birth Registration

Insight into trends in fertility was obtained by fitting the relational Gompertz model to cumulative births for each five-year period before 1995 using the

Table 2.4

Period Estimates of Gompertz Parameters, Total Fertility Rates, and Mean Age of Fertility Distribution by Population Group

	1970	1975	1980	1985	1990	1995
Beta values						
African	0.998	1.033	1.008	0.993	0.953	0.877
Colored	1.109	1.143	1.176	1.036	1.096	1.106
Indian/Asian	1.25	1.197	1.143	1.337	1.032	1.343
White	1.465	1.423	1.38	1.643	1.541	1.54
National			1.062	1.069	0.997	0.975
Alpha values						
African	−0.257	−0.193	−0.128	−0.174	−0.214	−0.341
Colored	−0.111	−0.008	0.095	−0.06	0.021	−0.031
Indian/Asian	−0.223	−0.143	−0.063	0.108	−0.152	−0.105
White	−0.036	−0.081	−0.126	0.114	0.109	−0.018
National			−0.099	−0.101	−0.088	−0.238
Total fertility rates						
African	5.4	5.1	4.7	4.1	3.9	3.6
Colored	5.1	4.2	3.2	3.2	2.9	2.8
Indian/Asian	4.1	3.7	3.2	2.7	2.9	2.5
White	3.1	2.8	2.5	2.2	2.1	2
National	4.9	4.6	4.3	3.5	3.3	3.2
Mean age of fertility						
African	29.8	29.3	29.5	29.9	30.3	30.9
Colored	29.2	28.3	27.9	29.1	28.4	28.2
Indian/Asian	29.4	28.9	28.8	27.6	29.6	28.1
White	28.1	28.3	28.6	27.2	27.4	27.4
National			29.2	29.2	29.3	29.8

	1995	1996	1997	1998		
Unadjusted total fertility rates						
African	2.3	3.3	1.8	2.7		
Colored	2.3	2.5	1.3	2.4		
Indian/Asian	1.5	2.0	0.9	1.8		
White	1.9	1.9	1.1	1.8		
National	2.2	3.0	1.6	2.6		

Source: Computed from the 1996 South African Population Census micro-data.

1995 OHS birth histories. The analysis, however, could not be made for births preceding 1980 because of the truncation of birth histories going back in time. Varying patterns of error by population group were observed in the results. The estimated Gompertz parameters and total fertility rates resulting from the analysis are summarized in Table 2.4.

The results of fitting the model to reported births in the 1970 census data (in the case of Africans) and birth registrations (in the case of Coloreds, Indians/Asians, and Whites) are summarized below. Again, for economy of space, only the results for the African and White populations are shown in Appendixes 2.6 and 2.7.

For each population group, the F points curved downward at the oldest age groups—thus suggesting a pattern of reporting errors in the 1970 census and registration data similar to that found in later surveys. In the case of Africans, the pattern indicates that older women exaggerated current births during the 1970 census as a result of errors in the time location of births (reference period error). With regard to the other population groups, the pattern is indicative of late registration of births occurring in a previous year. Due to biological factors, the number of births to the oldest age groups (if recorded age is correct) is usually small in any human population. But, if not adjusted for, the exaggeration of current births by these women may slightly bias the observed total fertility rate upward.

It was not possible to make any adjustment to the 1970 observed total fertility rate on the basis of the pattern of errors noted above, because the 1970 census and the birth registrations did not include information on children ever born. However, the α and β parameters were estimated from the 1970 census and registration data, taking into consideration the pattern of errors noted above. These estimations are also shown in Table 2.4. The observed total fertility rates in 1970 were 5.4 for Africans, 5.1 for Coloreds, 4.1 for Indians/Asians, and 3.1 for Whites.

Trends and Differentials in the Gompertz Parameters

The estimates of the Gompertz parameters for the period 1970–95 are shown in Table 2.4. The results of the models suggest two patterns of fertility distribution among the four population groups as can been seen from the first panel of the table (the β values). (β is a measure of the pace of childbearing; a value greater than one implies that childbearing is concentrated in a narrow age band). Whereas the spread of the fertility distribution is relatively wide among Africans and Coloreds, it is narrow among Indians/Asians and Whites. The β values among African women show a nearly linear trend. Among White women, the trend was slightly upward after 1980. The trend is not consistent among Colored and Indian/Asian women, with crossovers at some periods.

The β is a measure of the location or timing of childbearing with the standard. Increasing negative α values imply a later onset and late end of childbearing. With regard to the location (or timing) of fertility (second panel of Table 2.4), the estimated α values suggest a late end to childbearing among African women compared with women in the other population groups. This is reflected in the lower α values and, consequently, high model mean ages of the fertility distribution for African women (about thirty years) compared with women in the other population groups (fourth panel of Table 2.4). The results of the model also suggest that reductions in fertility at older ages and a later onset of childbearing each predominated in a different period among Africans and Whites. The pattern is less clear among Colored and Indian/Asian women.

Trends and Differentials in Total Fertility Rates

The third panel of Table 2.4 (illustrated in Figure 2.1) shows trends in total fertility rates resulting from the models. Note that the total fertility rates for 1975 were derived by linear interpolation. As can be seen in Table 2.4 and Figure 2.1, the level of fertility has consistently been highest, not surprisingly, among Africans, and lowest among Whites at any given time period. Coloreds and Indians/Asians have a level in between those of Africans and Whites, although Coloreds have a higher level than Indians/Asians.

The results of the models illustrated in Figure 2.1 show that since 1970 there has been a decline in fertility among the four population groups. In general, there was a more accelerated decline in fertility after 1980 compared to the previous periods, except among Coloreds, who had a steeper decline prior to 1980 than afterward. The accelerated decline after 1980 seems to have been steeper among Africans than among the other population groups. Notably, among Indians/Asians, there was an apparent slight increase in fertility in 1990 and 1996 compared to the levels in 1985 (Tables 2.3 and 2.4). This is not unusual. Total fertility rates can change slightly from year to year, due to tempo changes (i.e., changes in the timing of fertility). For instance, Bongaarts and Feeney (1998) have noted that numbers and rates of birth are depressed during years in which women delay childbearing and inflated in years when childbearing is accelerated.

Time Period Differentials in Age Pattern of Fertility

Changes in the level of fertility over time are the result of shifts in the age pattern and timing of fertility. These shifts can be examined by looking at observed or model age-specific fertility rates. Due to the truncation effect in the analysis of birth histories, it is not possible to obtain a complete picture of time period changes in age patterns of fertility for the seven reproductive age groups from cross-sectional data. For the most current period, reporting errors may distort observed age patterns of fertility. The relational Gompertz model is designed to overcome these problems and hence was used in this study to derive model age patterns of fertility.

Model age-specific fertility rates were estimated for each of the time periods in this study (except 1970) from the estimated Gompertz parameters and

Figure 2.1   **Trends in Total Fertility Rates by Population Group**

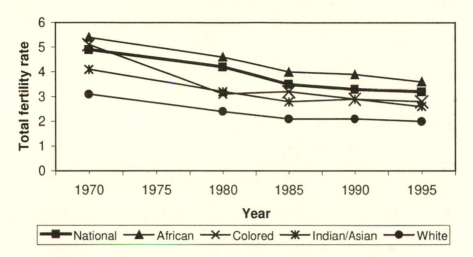

Sources: 1995, 1997, 1998 October Household Surveys; 1970 census; and Republic of South Africa (RSA) 1973.

estimated total fertility rates. For 1970, the model age-specific fertility rates were derived from the estimated Gompertz parameters and observed total fertility rates. Controlling for differences in total fertility rates among the population groups (i.e., total fertility rate = 1), the model age-specific fertility rates indicated three distinct patterns (graphs not shown):

1. somewhat similar age patterns of fertility between 1970 and 1980;
2. divergent age patterns of fertility between 1985 and 1995; and
3. a nearly convergent age pattern of fertility among Indians/Asians and Whites in 1996.

Regional Pattern of Fertility

Estimation of demographic parameters by population group, though desirable in certain respects, is of limited use with regard to targeting of intervention programs and efficient allocation of resources. The direction of differential in demographic parameters (and other statistics) among the population groups in South Africa is predictable, especially given the inequalities perpetuated during the apartheid era. However, resource allocation and intervention programs are not carried out at the population-group level but usually by sectors and spatial units, although a population group may be specifically targeted within the spatial unit. At the subnational level, the first spatial unit in allocation of resources and targeting of intervention programs is regional and, in the South African context, consists of the nine provinces. The provision of demographic information not only at the national level, but at least also at the regional level, enables the identification of spatial risk entities, which may enhance a more spatially efficient allocation of resources. The following section presents the results of the analysis of fertility by province in South Africa based on the 1995 and 1998 October Household Surveys and the 1996 census. (The 1997 survey was excluded from the analysis by province because of its poor quality.)

The fitting of the relational Gompertz model revealed varying degrees of error by province from one data set to the other. In some cases, errors were evident in the reports of the younger women on current births and children ever born.

As can be seen from Table 2.5, with the exception of Northern Cape and Gauteng in 1995, the β values are less than one in each of the provinces. Furthermore, the β values are negative for each of the survey years in all the provinces, with the exception of Northern Cape in 1996 and 1998. The Gompertz parameters thus seem to suggest that the pattern of fertility distribution may be distinct different in Northern Cape compared with the other provinces: they appear to start and terminate childbearing earlier than women in the other provinces.

The estimated total fertility rates suggest that fertility is highest in the Limpopo (4.1) and lowest in Gauteng and Western Cape (2.7). Note, however, that with the exception of Western Cape, the estimates based on the 1996 census are consistently higher than those from the surveys. The differences in the estimates between those derived from the 1996 census on the one hand and those from the household surveys on the other are quite marked, with the exception of KwaZulu-Natal and North West. Given the short interval in the time periods under consideration, it is unlikely that such marked fluctuations in fertility levels are due to a fertility trend but instead are probably an artifact of the data.

Even after adjustments, the "best" estimates based on the 1996 census still overestimate fertility in most of the provinces because of the overreporting of children ever born. The evidence for this was gleaned from the reported mean number of children ever born by age group of women by province for each of the survey years.

In theory, the birth cohorts are not the same for each of the successive survey years, but because the survey years under consideration are one to three years apart, the bulk of the birth cohorts (taking account of mortality) should be largely the same. In view of this, the mean number of children ever born by age of women should not be very different within the period under consider-

Table 2.5

Current Estimates of the Gompertz Parameters and Total Fertility Rates by Province

	1995	1996	1998
Beta values			
Limpopo	0.845	0.876	0.883
Mpumalanga	0.866	0.854	0.861
Eastern Cape	0.917	0.940	0.940
North West	0.864	0.838	0.888
KwaZulu-Natal	0.994	0.894	0.883
Free State	0.864	0.919	0.918
Northern Cape	1.198	1.051	1.027
Gauteng	1.205	0.922	0.979
Western Cape	0.934	0.943	0.967
Alpha values			
Limpopo	−0.346	−0.112	−0.172
Mpumalanga	−0.379	−0.128	−0.175
Eastern Cape	−0.326	−0.224	−0.248
North West	−0.281	−0.199	−0.273
KwaZulu-Natal	−0.311	−0.124	−0.328
Free State	−0.333	−0.224	−0.392
Northern Cape	−0.027	0.002	0.049
Gauteng	−0.183	−0.014	−0.190
Western Cape	−0.199	−0.083	−0.235
Total fertility rates			
Limpopo	4.0	4.6	4.1
Mpumalanga	3.6	4.3	3.7
Eastern Cape	3.5	4.2	3.4
North West	3.3	4.1	3.3
KwaZulu-Natal	3.7	3.9	3.8
Free State	3.4	3.8	3.6
Northern Cape	2.7	3.3	2.8
Gauteng	2.5	2.9	2.7
Western Cape	2.8	2.8	2.7

Source: Computed from the 1996 South African Population Census micro-data.

ation. However, examination of the data revealed a consistently higher reported mean number of children ever born by age of mother in the 1996 census than those reported in the household surveys in each province. This suggests that relative to the household surveys, women overreported children ever born in the 1996 census in each province, thus inflating the "best" estimates of fertility derived from the 1996 census by province.

Conclusion

The results in this study suggest that total fertility rates declined from about 5.4 in 1970 to about 3.7 in 1996 among Africans. Among Coloreds, it declined from about 5.1 to 2.8 during the same period. It fell from about 4.1 to

2.7 among Indians/Asians and from 3.1 to 1.9 among Whites. At the national level, the total fertility rate declined from about 4.9 in 1970 to 3.2 in 1996. One needs to be cautious in comparing the estimates in this study with those from other studies for several reasons. First, there are differences in the methods used in deriving the estimates. Second, the choice of a set of estimates to be used for such comparison is not easy to make because of the wide range of estimates available for the reference period in this study. Third, the reference periods of the estimates in this study differ from some of those in other studies. While the reference period for the estimates in this study is a single-year period, in some cases, studies give estimates for five-year periods. With these caveats, let us take note of some of the estimates given in previous studies.

Regarding the current level of fertility, the following findings are significant. The application of the own-children method to the 10 percent sample of the 1996 census by Sibanda and Zuberi (1999) resulted in the finding of a national total fertility rate (TFR) of 2.8 for 1996. Sibanda and Zuberi's estimate is slightly lower than this author's estimate (3.2) for the same year. Using the reverse-survival technique, the author previously (Udjo 1998) derived a TFR of 2.9 based on children ages birth through 4 and women ages 15 through 49 as reported in the 1996 census, thus corresponding to the year 1994. This is similar to the estimate derived by Sibanda and Zuberi based on children ages birth through 15 and women ages 15 through 49. I argued previously, however, that my estimate based on the reverse-survival method (2.9) appears too low and draws attention to the United Nation's (1983) caution about the use of reverse-survival techniques. The techniques

> are all heavily dependent upon the accuracy of the reported age distribution of the population being studied. Errors in age-reporting or differential completeness of enumeration affecting certain age groups, especially the younger ones, are certain to bias the estimates obtained. Because these deficiencies are all too frequently characteristic of the data sets available, reverse-survival methods are often ineffective in producing reliable fertility estimates.

The preliminary report of the 1998 South Africa Demographic and Health Survey (SADHS) (Department of Health 1999) gives a TFR of 2.9 for 1998. It must be stressed that this figure is the reported TFR as it was directly computed and cannot strictly be compared with the indirectly estimated TFRs. However, this TFR has sometimes been quoted as the current level of fertility in South Africa without adequate caution that the figure has not been adjusted for reporting errors known to be present in birth histories. In view of this, the reported TFR of 2.9 for 1998 should be treated with caution. At the time of the present study, the SADHS data were still unavailable to the public for detailed scrutiny, as the 1996 census data had undergone. This author's estimate of the TFR for 1998, based on Statistics South Africa's data, is 3.2.

Sadie (1988) initially projected, on the basis of estimates, that at the national level TFR in 1995 would be 3.5, but in more recent work (Sadie 1999) estimated a TFR of 3.3 at the national level for the same period. Also, Dorrington et al. (1999) estimated a total fertility rate of 3.2 for the period 1996, on the basis of the Arriaga method. It appears from these examples that there is some reasonable consensus among different researchers in recent studies as to the current (1996–98) level of the TFR in South Africa. One might infer that currently, the TFR could not be lower than 2.8 or higher than 3.3.

With regard to past levels of fertility, Chimere-Dan (1993) reviewed previous estimates of fertility in other studies among the four main population groups in South Africa. These estimates (summarized in Table 2.6), were largely the basis of fertility inputs in various projections of South Africa's population during the apartheid era.

Taking into consideration that the estimates obtained in the present study have been adjusted for errors in the data, and comparing them with those reviewed by Chimere-Dan in Table 2.6, suggests that the fertility of Africans in the 1970s and 1980s was overestimated in some previous studies, while the fertility of the other population groups was slightly underestimated. The lower-than-expected population of South Africa as of October 1996 is partly attributable to overestimation of fertility rates of Africans in the 1970s and 1980s that were included in projections of the population during the apartheid era.

A cohort component rerun of both the national and population-group projections with the new fertility data confirm lower-than-expected 1996 census figures (40.6 million instead of 42 million), especially for the African population (31.1 million instead of 32.1 million). However, the projections also suggest that the 1996 census adjustments for undercount overestimated the country's population, especially for the African population (probably by around 360,000), and underestimated the White population (probably by 100,000).

It would appear that the overestimation of fertility rates of Africans during the apartheid era was, at least in part, the result of the political environment. The absolute and relative size of the African population was a concern in apartheid South Africa. Arising from this concern was the need to demonstrate to the government at the time that the fertility of Africans was very high as a justification for embarking on an intensive family planning program to curb "explosive" population growth among the African population. The following statements appear to support this conclusion. Kuper, with regard to apartheid South Africa, noted

> [T]he racial composition of the Union has altered very little over a period of 40 years: the proportion of Europeans fell from 21.6 percent in 1904 to 20.8 percent in 1946, while the Native percentage increased from 67.4 to 68.5 percent. But the disparity in numbers has widened, from under 2.5 million in 1904 to almost 5.5 million in 1946. (1950: 144)

Table 2.6

Estimates of Total Fertility Rates by Population Group in South Africa

	1970 (1970–75)		1975 (1975–80)		1980 (1980–85)		1985 (1987–89)		1996
African	5.4	(6.3)	5.1	(5.8)	4.7	(5.4)	4.1	(4.6)	3.7
Colored	5.1	(5.2)	4.2	(3.8)	3.2	(3.2)	3.2	(2.9)	2.8
Indian/Asian	4.1	(3.6)	3.7	(2.9)	3.2	(2.7)	2.7	(2.5)	2.7
White	3.1	(2.8)	2.8	(2.2)	2.5	(2.1)	2.2	(1.9)	1.9

Sources: Compiled from Chimere-Dan 1993 (figures in parentheses); 1995 October Household Survey; 1970 census; Republic of South Africa 1973.

On another note, Kuper observed that, "Yet, notwithstanding this lack of reliable data from calculating population trends, the assumed greater rate of increase of the Native population is firmly embedded in the folklore of white South Africa" (1950: 146). On the preservation of "White Civilization," Kuper noted that, *"This is a very real mission of white South Africans"* (1950: 152, emphasis added). According to Kuper, the census was seen as providing documentation of *"black menace"* and that "[E]efforts which have the effect of reducing the morbidity and mortality rates of the Natives would unleash their reproductive capacity, and increase the difficulties of maintaining 'white civilization' in South Africa" (1950: 153, emphasis added).

The intensive family planning program that was advocated decades later may be contextualized against this background. For example, regarding the "Bantu" population, it was argued that, "Like the Colored population, they will remain in the explosive phase of population growth, unless a vigorous family planning program is successfully conducted (Sadie 1970).

There are a number of issues arising from the results of this study, which are pertinent to policy considerations. The early start and late end of child-bearing among African women and in the provinces (except Northern Cape) have health implications, as having children very early (before the age of 20) and too late (after age 34) has a negative effect on the health of the mother and the survival of their offspring.

The current level of fertility, as indicated by the TFR (3.5) among Africans adjusted for mortality (net reproduction rate approximately 1.5) implies that if the current trend continues, the African population will double in about thirty-three years. This has implications for planning with regard to provision of services such as schools, health services, and job creation for the future generation. On the other hand, the below-replacement level of fertility among the White population implies a progressively aging population in proportionate and absolute terms. This also has implications for planning for the future care of this aging segment of the South African population.

Notes

The author gratefully acknowledges the financial support provided by the African Census Analysis Project at the University of Pennsylvania through its fellowship program, and wishes to thank Statistics South Africa for allowing him to utilize the fellowships while in its employ. The author also wishes to thank the Human Sciences Research Council, Pretoria, for permitting him to be away from work to take up a third fellowship from the University of Pennsylvania, only one month after being in its employ, to enable him complete this study. The views expressed in this paper are those of the author and do not necessarily reflect those of Statistics South Africa, the African Census Analysis Project, or the Human Sciences Research Council.

1. Hamad's model reflects more adequately the shape of the fertility curve in the beginning of childbearing. Whereas the Brass fertility polynomial curve rises sharply from an assumed age at the start of childbearing, that of Hamad touches the zero locus tangentially.

References

Arriaga, E.E. 1983. "Estimating fertility from data on children ever born by age of mother." International Research Document, no. 11. Washington, DC: U.S. Bureau of the Census.

———. 1994. "Arriaga technique." In *Population Analysis with Microcomputers,* Vol. 1, Washington DC: U.S. Bureau of the Census, 209–10.

Bongaarts, J. 1978. "A framework for analyzing the proximate determinants of fertility." *Population and Development Review* 4(1): 105–32.

Bongaarts, J., and G. Feeney. 1998. "On the quantum and tempo of fertility." *Population and Development Review* 24(22): 271–91.

Booth, H. 1979. "The estimation of fertility from incomplete cohort data by means of the tansformed Gompertz model." Ph.D. thesis, London School of Hygiene and Tropical Medicine, University of London.

Brass, W. 1974. "Perspectives in population prediction: Illustrated by the statistics of England and Wales." *Journal of the Royal Statistical Society,* series A137, part 4.

———. 1981. "The use of the relational Gompertz model to estimate fertility." *Proceedings of the International Union for the Scientific Study of Population Conference, Manila,* Vol. 3, 345–61. Liège: International Union for the Scientific Study of Population.

———. 1996. "Demographic data analysis in less developed countries: 1946–1996." *Population Studies* 50(3): 451–67.

Brass, W., and A. Coale. 1968. "Methods of analysis and estimation." In *The Demography of Tropical Africa,* ed. W. Brass et al., 88–139. Princeton, NJ: Princeton University Press.

Chimere-Dan, O. 1993. "Racial patterns of fertility decline in South Africa." *Proceedings of the International Union for the Scientific Study of Population Conference, Montreal,* 43–51, Liège: International Union for the Scientific Study of Population.

Department of Health. 1999. *South Africa Demographic and Health Survey 1998: Preliminary Report.* Pretoria: Department of Health.

Dorrington, R., N. Nannan, and D. Bradshaw. 1999. "Current fertility rates in South Africa: 1996 census revisited." Paper presented at the workshop on Phase 2 of Census 1996 Review on behalf of the Statistical Council, Johannesburg, December 3–4.

Hamad, A.M. 1982. "The robustness of the P/F ratio technique for fertility estimation to assumptions and some forms of data errors." Ph.D. thesis, London School of Hygiene and Tropical Medicine, University of London.

Hirschowitz, R., and M. Orkin. 1996. "Living in South Africa: Findings from the October 1995 household survey." Pretoria: Central Statistical Service.

Kuper, L. 1950. "Some demographic aspects of white supremacy in South Africa." *The British Journal of Sociology* 1: 144–53.

Republic of South Africa (RSA). 1973. "Report on births 1964 to 1971, South Africa." Pretoria: Republic of South Africa, Department of Statistics.

Sadie, J.L. 1970. "An evaluation of demographic data pertaining to the non-white population of South Africa." *Economics* 38(2): 171–90.

———. 1988. "A reconstruction and projection of demographic movement in South Africa." Bureau of Market Research, University of South Africa.

———. 1999. "The missing millions." Paper presented to NEDLAC meeting, Johannesburg.

Sibanda, A., and T. Zuberi. 1999. "Contemporary fertility levels and trends in South Africa: Evidence from reconstructed census birth histories." In *The African Population in the 21st Century: Third African Population Conference*, Vol. 1: 79–108. Durban: Union for African Population Studies.

Simkins, C. 1997. "Demographic projections in South Africa." Personal communication.

Statistics South Africa. 1999a. "The people of South Africa, Population Census 1996: Calculating the undercount in Census '96." Pretoria: Statistics South Africa.

———. 1999b. "The people of South Africa, Population Census 1996: Primary tables, the country as a whole." Pretoria: Statistics South Africa,.

Udjo, E.O. 1991. "Fertility levels among Nigeria's Kanuri." *Genus* XLVII(1–2): 163–76.

———. 1996. "Is fertility falling in Zimbabwe?" *Journal of Biosocial Science* 28(1): 25–35.

———. 1998. "Additional evidence regarding fertility and mortality trends in South Africa and implications for population projections." Pretoria: Statistics South Africa.

United Nations. 1983. *Manual X: Indirect Techniques for Demographic Estimation.* New York: United Nations.

Zaba, B. 1981. "Use of the relational Gompertz model in analyzing fertility data collected in retrospective surveys." Centre for Population Studies Working Paper 8: 1–2. London: London School of Hygiene and Tropical Medicine, University of London.

Appendix 2.1   **Fitting the Gompertz Relational Model**

The equation for fitting the Gompertz relational model to current fertility has been given as

$$z(x) - e(x) = \alpha + 0.48(\beta-1)^2 + \beta g(x)$$

where $z(x)$ is

$$-\ln\left[-\ln F_x/F_{(x+5)}\right]$$

where F_x is cumulated age-specific fertility rates up to age x, $e(x)$ and $g(x)$ are tabulated standard values (see Booth 1979), and 0.48 is a constant. Then α and β are parameters for the particular set of fertility rates, respectively, that measure the location (timing) and spread (pace of childbearing) of the fertility distribution. For average number of children ever born (mean parities), $z(i)$ is

$$-\ln\left[-\ln P_i/P_{(i+1)}\right]$$

where P_i is the mean parity in the age group i (see Zaba 1981 and Brass 1974, 1996). Brass (1981), Zaba (1981), and Udjo (1991, 1996), among others, describe the application of the model to birth histories and census data.

Appendix 2.2 **Fitting the Relational Gompertz Model to Current Births (F) and Children Ever Born (P), 1995: African**

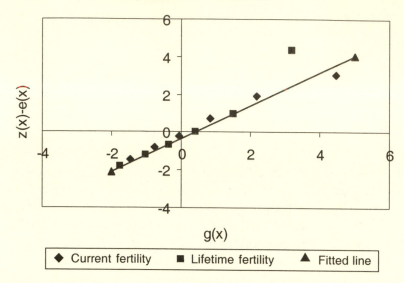

Source: 1996 South African Population Census.

Appendix 2.3 **Fitting the Relational Gompertz Model to Current Births (F) and Children Ever Born (P), 1996: African**

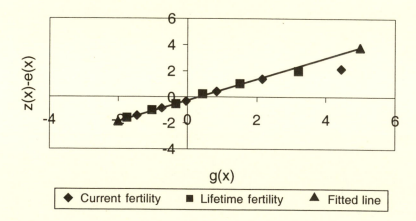

Source: 1996 South African Population Census.

Appendix 2.4 **Fitting the Relational Gompertz Model to Current Births (F) and Children Ever Born (P), 1995: White**

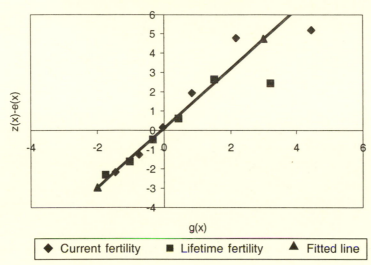

Source: 1995 October Household Survey.

Appendix 2.5 **Fitting the Relational Gompertz Model to Current Births (F) and Children Ever Born (P), 1996: White**

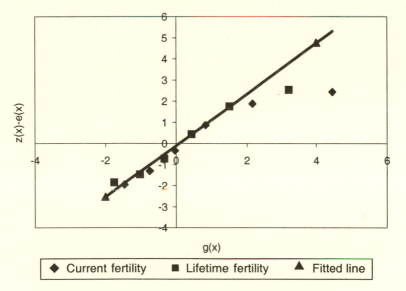

Source: 1995 October Household Survey.

Appendix 2.6 **Fitting the Relational Gompertz Model to Fertility Reports in the 1970 Census: African**

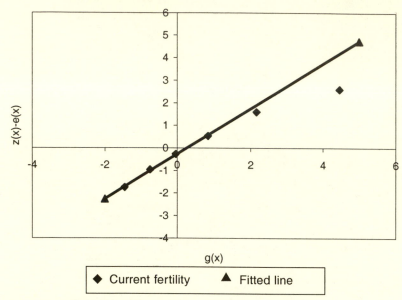

Source: Republic of South Africa 1973.

Appendix 2.7 **Fitting the Relational Gompertz Model to Fertility Reports in the 1970 Census: Whites**

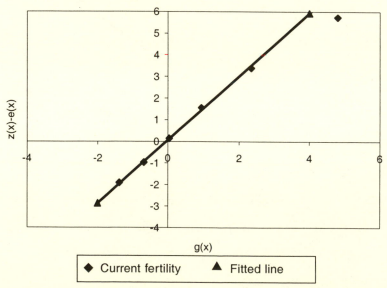

Source: Republic of South Africa 1973.

3. Age at First Birth

Amson Sibanda and Tukufu Zuberi

The transition to motherhood reflects the interaction of biological, cultural, and societal influences. The first birth process is affected by variations in fecundity across individuals and over time for individual women (Rindfuss et al. 1984). Social origins are partly responsible for the transmission of group-specific intergenerational norms and attitudes that affect the timing of first births (Rindfuss and St. John 1983). Socioeconomic processes and religious beliefs also influence individual behavior, thereby contributing to differences in the timing of motherhood and overall fertility between population subgroups (Bledsoe and Cohen 1993; Caldwell and Caldwell 1987; Kiernan and Diamond 1983; McDaniel 1996; Rindfuss et al. 1984). The timing of entry into motherhood is strongly associated with both individual and aggregate levels of fertility. This transition, as well as other adolescent transitions, has broader implications for women's roles outside the home, the health of women and their children, and social institutions (Bongaarts 1999; Cherlin and Riley 1986l; Gage 1998; Menken 1985; Rindfuss et al. 1988; van de Walle 1993).

This chapter examines the association between ethnicity, race, and socioeconomic variables on the timing of first births in South Africa. An examination of these factors should lay an important groundwork for future research into how women who give birth early are more likely to be enmeshed in a social and economic environment that is less optimum for the growth and development of children and for mothers' reproductive health and social mobility. Few studies have examined the nature of this relationship in sub-Saharan Africa.

Race and ethnicity serve as useful variables in identifying relatively homogenous population subgroups with similar beliefs, values, and economic positions. Within the context of reproduction and marriage, these beliefs and values play a significant role in influencing the timing of first births. The relative influence of race and ethnicity on reproductive behavior is also simultaneously the result of socioeconomic status and macro-sociostructural influences (McDaniel 1994, 1996; Morgan et al. 1993; Preston 1974).

Under apartheid, South Africa was arguably the most racially stratified society in the world, with a caste-like social structure. Africans, Coloreds, and Indians/Asians were located at the lower tiers of the apartheid socioeconomic and political structure. Because of discriminatory laws such as the Group Areas Act of 1950 and the Reservation of Separate Amenities Act of 1953 that codified separate racial development and balkanization, and forbade the social mixing of races, the various population groups in South Africa have remained socially apart. Demographic processes in South Africa have been influenced by these processes of racial stratification (Chimere-Dan 1993). Because of its unique history, the timing of first births in South Africa must be analyzed from a perspective of racial stratification (McDaniel 1996). By definition, apartheid rejected racial assimilation. South African demographers tended to view racial differences in demographic outcomes (births or deaths) as a consequence of cultural and racial differences (Sadie 1970, 1971, 1972). Africans were viewed as having pronatalist values that favored large families. By attributing any differences in fertility or mortality simply to racial and cultural differences, this perspective failed to specify the social mechanisms that linked race and racial stratification to fertility or mortality (Forste and Tienda 1996; McDaniel 1996).

Apartheid policies of separate development were designed to ensure marked economic, social, and cultural gaps among the various racial groups in South Africa. In other words, the life experiences of different racial groups (Africans, Whites, Coloreds, Indians/Asians) and the various African ethnic groups have been characterized by different patterns of place of residence, economic success, education, civil liberties, and access to services (Chimere-Dan 1993). Thus, we examine if differences in age at first birth can be associated with differences in socioeconomic status among the various races and ethnic groups. This contention is based on our assumption that socioeconomic status conditions involve many factors that influence the timing of the first birth. Any racial differences that we might pick up are probably the cumulative impact of unequal distribution of resources.

When we focus on the various ethnic groups in South Africa, we should remember that the apartheid policy of creating ethnic-specific homelands for Africans sustained long-standing cultural differences. However, it is equally important to remember that, for most African women, the decision to have a first birth was also influenced by how they perceived their opportunities in the larger society. One cannot ignore the persistent poverty of African women, the majority of whom lived in rural areas (May 1998). Different levels of development also characterized the ten African homelands, with marked inter-homeland inequities in the distribution of goods and services like educational and medical facilities (Case and Deaton 1999; Kaufman 1998).

The decline of fertility in South Africa has shown distinct racial patterns. Although all population groups have experienced substantial fertility declines in the last thirty to fifty years, African birth rates remain higher than those of Coloreds, Indians/Asians, or Whites (Sibanda and Zuberi 1999). Whites have experienced a long and sustained decline in fertility beginning prior to the twentieth century. White fertility declined from a high of seven births per woman in the late nineteenth century to about four births per woman at the turn of the twentieth century. By the mid-1950s, the total fertility rate (TFR) had dropped to about 3.5, and by 1989, some studies indicate that Whites in South Africa had attained below-replacement fertility, with a TFR of 1.9. For Asians, a steady decline in fertility began in the mid-1950s, from a high of about 6.7 births per woman to a low of about 2.5 in the late 1980s. Coloreds also began a steady decline in the 1960s, going from a TFR of 6.5 to about three children per woman on average by the late 1980s. With respect to African fertility, it is estimated that fertility fell from a high of 6.8 to about 4.6 and 3.1 in the late 1980s and mid-1990s (Chimere-Dan 1993; Sibanda and Zuberi 1999).

Data and Methods

Our study uses data from the 10 percent sample of the 1996 South African Population Census. Household and individual data, including age at first birth and other fertility-related data, were obtained for all women aged 12 years and above. We focus on women of ages 15 through 49. In addition to Brass-type questions on children ever born, females ages twelve years and older were also specifically asked the following question: "When was your FIRST child born? (live birth)."

The availability of this question in the 1996 South African census is quite unique, because most African censuses have not normally included such a direct question on age at first birth. Responses to this question are apt to be much more reliable than responses to the question of age at first marriage, because women are more likely to remember the date of such a vital event in their lives. Most researchers have pointed out that the precise dating of age at first marriage is seriously compromised by the fact that marriage is generally regarded as a process and not an event in most African cultures (van de Walle 1993). Although not reported here, the examination of the age at first birth data did not reveal any unusual age heaping patterns. In addition, the data also showed that the timing of the first birth was heavily concentrated at ages 19 to 23 for all racial groups.

We use logistic regression to examine ascribed and achieved factors associated with the timing of motherhood. Logistic regression is used because of the binary nature of the dependent variable, which is that a woman either experienced a first birth or did not (coded as 1 or as 0, respectively).

We considered a number of current demographic and social characteristics measured in the 1996 census to be relevant in the analysis of age at first birth: race, ethnicity, education, rural/urban residence, province, and religion, all of which were coded as a series of dummy variables. These variables were selected for inclusion in the analyses based on both theoretical and empirical indications that they are important predictors of the timing of entry into motherhood (Bledsoe and Cohen 1993; Rindfuss et al. 1988; St. John 1982, Westoff 1992).

Race, ethnicity, and place of residence are social characteristic variables. Race was self-reported, while first language spoken at home was used to capture ethnicity. During apartheid, there were four racial categories in South Africa: Whites, Africans/Blacks, Indians/Asians, and Coloreds. Indians/Asians were South Africans of Asian decent, while Coloreds were South Africans of mixed ancestry. The latter group tended to share the same languages with Whites (i.e., Afrikaans and English). According to Pickel

> this historical development implied for many Colored persons and families primary identification with their European roots to the detriment of their indigenous origins. The distancing from the African heritage matched by aspirations to be accepted into white society was widespread as a mechanism to escape the negative consequences of being classified Colored. Trying to pass for white was an attractive escape mechanism. (1997:78)

Understanding racial classification in South Africa is important, because in some analyses of demographic, health, and epidemiological phenomena, race has been used to show that there is a biological basis behind variations in births, deaths, and health across different racial groups (Ahmad 1993; Cooper and David 1986; Williams et al. 1994; Zuberi 2001). However, advances in biological research have helped us dismiss the "pure" biological reality of race. Thus, most social scientists do recognize that race is a social construct and that "biological" differences between groups alone are not sufficient when explaining some phenomena like fertility, intelligence, or health across population groups. This is because race is confounded with social class, group power, and numerous other factors (Krieger 2000; LaVeist 2000; Preston and Campbell 1993; Stolley 1999). On the other hand, Ngom et al. (1999) contend that in the African context, many researchers have used ethnicity as a cultural marker that supposedly explains differential fertility, mortality, child health, and so on (Caldwell and Caldwell 1987; Calves 1999;

Gage 1998; Lesthaeghe 1989). Most of these studies do not assume that there is any biological basis to ethnicity in Africa.

Because the 1996 South African census did not directly ask for an individual's ethnic background, it is possible that the proxy for ethnicity that we use in this chapter (first language spoken at home) is a dynamic cultural variable. Some individuals may have adopted the most "popular" language spoken in a certain community at the expense of their own "native" language (see Marwick 1978). Children of most immigrant communities are much more prone to adopting the language widely spoken in their neighborhoods as their first language. However, an excellent body of anthropological work in South Africa has continued to demonstrate that there are still important cultural and linguistic differences among the various African ethnic groups (Krige 1968; Kuper 1982; Magubane 1998; Marwick 1978; Preston-Whyte 1978; Schapera 1987). This body of work has primarily focused on issues like religion, marriage practices, political and social organization, and kinship, with very little attention being paid to the timing of the first birth. Thus, this study focuses less on the social distance between the various African groups as measured by such indicators of ethnic identity. Instead, considerable attention is placed on the interaction between social identity and the political environment in which these population groups lived and were allowed to interact with the wider South African community. More importantly, differences in age at first birth can be viewed as a good measure or indicator of social/cultural distance among the various African ethnic groups.

The educational attainment of women at the time of the census will be used in this analysis as a measure of socioeconomic status. It is generally postulated that the timing of the first birth occurs later with increasing education, as education empowers women to modify their reproductive goals and encourages them to use modern contraceptives (Westoff 1992). However, in other situations, the absence of a first birth sometimes explains why women have more education. Education also increases the prospect that women will be gainfully employed, thus placing motherhood and employment in competing roles and affecting the timing of the first birth. Because it is linked with prospects for employment, education is generally used as an indicator of socioeconomic status. Socioeconomic status has repeatedly been shown to have an effect on the probability of having a first birth (Rindfuss et al. 1988). Women of low socioeconomic standing are expected to have a first birth at a younger age than women from higher socioeconomic backgrounds, because they have limited lifetime opportunities that substantially affect the choices they make about the timing of motherhood. If women from a deprived socioeconomic background cannot see any possibility of upward social mobility, they tend to become mothers at younger ages.

Individual or family socioeconomic attributes are not always sufficient when predicting the timing of the first birth. Contextual variables like rural–urban residence and level of regional or community development may influence a woman's decision to have a first birth. In the context of apartheid policies, this distinction is of critical importance, because the opportunities that were available to African women were significantly limited. To capture the potential impact of regional inequalities on individual behavior, we include the provincial dummies in our analysis, as services like family planning were administered through provincial structures (Kaufman 1998). Living in an urban area implies greater exposure to a cosmopolitan culture, better employment and educational opportunities, better health care services, and generally higher expectations to behave in ways perceived to be sophisticated (Pebley et al. 1982).

With regard to religion, we expected Moslems and women who belong to African Independent Churches to have first births at younger ages. Studies have generally shown that high fertility levels are associated with these religions. Because of religious beliefs and religious conservatism, these groups are pronatalist and they tend to restrict women's education and encourage lower age at marriage and minimal use of modern contraception (Gregson et al. 1999; Knodel et al. 1999; Lesthaeghe 1989; van de Walle 1993). In South Africa, religious affiliation is closely associated with race. For example, Pickel (1997) found that most Whites and Coloreds in the Western Cape Province belonged to the Dutch Reformed Church, while a majority of Africans belonged to African Independent Churches.

Results

Fertility estimates calculated from the 1996 census (Table 3.1) show that, to a large extent, fertility levels in South Africa by race mirror the historical patterns noted by other researchers (Chimere-Dan 1993; du Plessis et al. 1991). Africans experience the highest fertility levels, followed by Coloreds, Indians/Asians, and Whites. These differences in fertility levels among the four population groups are partly influenced by the timing of entry into motherhood. Sibanda and Zuberi (1999) and Udjo (1999) have shown that the proportions of women ever married by current age of woman and racial group in South Africa were lowest among African and Colored women. African women have consistently low marriage prevalence at all ages when compared to the other racial groups. On the other hand, the proportion reported as ever married is very high at all ages for Whites and Indians/Asians, indicating that marriage is more universal among these two racial groups.

Table 3.1

Fertility Levels and Trends in South Africa by Race

Year	Africans	Coloreds	Indians/Asians	Whites	National
1981	5.3	5.0	5.1	3.6	4.6
1982	5.7	5.2	5.0	3.7	4.9
1983	5.4	5.2	4.9	3.8	4.7
1984	5.5	5.0	4.7	3.8	4.8
1985	5.2	4.9	4.5	3.7	4.5
1986	5.2	4.8	4.7	3.6	4.5
1987	4.8	4.5	4.0	3.4	4.2
1988	4.6	4.3	4.0	3.2	4.0
1989	4.6	4.4	3.9	3.2	4.0
1990	4.7	4.5	3.8	3.3	4.2
1991	4.5	4.3	3.6	3.1	4.0
1992	4.2	4.1	3.4	3.0	3.7
1993	4.0	3.9	3.2	2.7	3.5
1994	3.6	3.6	2.8	2.6	3.2
1995	3.1	2.9	2.6	2.4	2.8
1996	3.0	3.0	2.5	2.3	2.8

Source: Compiled from Sibanda and Zuberi 1999.

Table 3.2 presents mean ages at first birth for various population subgroups in South Africa. African and White women have the lowest and the highest ages at first birth, respectively (20.3 versus 23.5). Within the African ethnic groups, Swazi, Venda, Ndebele, Northern Sotho, and Tsonga women have mean ages at first birth that are lower than the overall mean for all African women. On the other hand, the difference in the mean age at first birth by place of residence appears to be relatively small, with urban women tending to have their first child at older ages. Lastly, the differences by level of education are not pronounced between uneducated women and those with primary and secondary education. However, it is important to note that simply using the mean age at first birth to examine if there are marked differences in the timing of the first birth can be misleading, because the standard error around this age is quite large. We use multivariate logistic models to predict the likelihood of having a first birth at a specific age while controlling for a number of background factors.

Racial Differences in the Timing of the First Birth

Table 3.3 shows the association between prescribed and achieved characteristics and the likelihood of having a first birth at different ages. Throughout this analysis, we present the odds ratios for each explanatory variable instead

Table 3.2

Mean Age at First Birth, South Africa 1996

Variable	Mean	Standard error	Number of women
Race			
African	20.30	4.16	406,540
Colored	21.07	4.09	54,467
Indian/Asian	22.29	4.19	16,022
White	23.52	4.39	58,157
All women (15–49)	20.80	4.31	535,186
Ethnicity			
Ndebele	20.05	4.05	7,275
Xhosa	20.55	4.21	95,257
Zulu	20.34	4.34	114,659
Northern Sotho	20.03	3.91	46,389
Southern Sotho	20.53	4.17	44,969
Tswana	20.43	4.04	46,661
Swazi	19.30	3.96	12,808
Venda	19.92	3.63	11,717
Tsonga	19.63	3.84	21,228
Place of residence			
Urban	21.19	4.39	318,059
Rural	20.25	4.11	220,755
Education			
None	20.47	4.84	69,366
Primary	20.04	4.14	139,819
Secondary	20.37	3.88	204,319
Postsecondary	22.60	4.32	113,379

Source: Computed from the 1996 South Africa Population Census micro-data.

of presenting the coefficients. An odds ratio of 1.00 implies no difference in the odds of having a first child between categories, while an odds ratio greater than 1.00 indicates an increase in the odds of having a first birth. Lastly, odds ratios below 1.00 indicate a decrease in odds relative to the reference category.

To get better insight into the transition to motherhood in South Africa, we estimate a detailed model in which we control for age at first birth. We restrict our analysis to prescribed variables and a few socioeconomic characteristics, because the timing of some achieved variables is not known. For instance, marital status in 1996 refers to current marital status and not necessarily to the actual marital status of the woman when she had her first child. Therefore, when controlling for age at first birth, we exclude a woman's current marital status from the analysis, because divorced or widowed women could have had their first child at an earlier age, when they were still married or single. We also exclude current employment status, because most formal employment opportunities are generally acquired after attaining a certain age in most societies; therefore, the timing of a first birth can either precede attaining a job or follow later. However, there are some achieved background factors like education, which are generally acquired at certain ages, usually before the onset of reproduction for primary education and, to some extent, for secondary education. In most Western societies, it is expected that a woman will have had a primary education and some high school education before deciding to have a first birth. However, in Africa, there are equally many women who do not even go beyond primary schooling before having a first birth. Despite this shortcoming, education is generally included in models predicting the effects of background factors on the timing of motherhood at various ages (Kiernan and Diamond 1983; Rindfuss et al. 1984, 1988).

When we examine the racial differential in age at first birth, Table 3.3 shows that we have statistically significant differences by race. The table shows that if we only predict the odds of having a first birth at ages seventeen to eighteen, African and Colored women are 2.2 and 2.3 times more likely to have a first birth than White women. These odds ratios are significant at the 0.001 level. Indian/Asian women are also significantly more likely than Whites to have a first birth at these ages. When we look at the odds of having a first child between age 19 and 20, African women still have significantly higher chances than White women. However, between the ages of 21 and 32, the likelihood of becoming a mother becomes significantly lower for African women when compared to the corresponding odds for Whites. Similarly, Coloreds and Indians/Asians are more likely to have a first child below age 22 than Whites. But, between ages 23 and 32, Coloreds also have comparatively lower odds than Whites, while those of Indians/Asians are not significantly different from those of Whites.

In the case of education, women with primary education are only significantly less likely to have a first child than uneducated women at age 17 to 18. But at ages 21 through 22 and 23 through 24, having primary education increases the chance that a woman will have a first child when compared to women with no education. In contrast, women with secondary and postsecondary education have significantly lower odds of becoming mothers at any given age (i.e., between 17 and 32). For example, for a woman with a secondary education, her odds of becoming a parent at age 19 through 20 are only 33 percent of those of a woman with no education. And for women with postsecondary education, the odds are 22 percent of those women with no education. In fact, women with a postsecondary education have less than a third of the odds of uneducated women to have a first child below age 24. This can be associated with the choices women face between caring for children and establishing a career.

The relationship between religion and the timing of motherhood is not

Table 3.3

Logistic Regression Results (Odds Ratios) for the Effects of Explanatory Variables on the Likelihood of Having a First Birth at Various Ages: All Racial Groups

	Odds of having a first birth at age:							
Variable	17–18	19–20	21–22	23–24	25–26	27–28	29–30	31–32
Racial group								
White (reference group)	1.00	1.00	1.00	1.00	1.00	1.00	1.00	1.00
African	2.22***	1.12***	0.79***	0.64***	0.59***	0.54***	0.57***	0.57***
Colored	2.29***	1.51***	1.19***	0.95	0.80***	0.74***	0.68***	0.67***
Indian/Asian	1.43***	1.28***	1.15**	0.97	0.98	1.05	0.80*	1.08
Education								
None (reference group)	1.00	1.00	1.00	1.00	1.00	1.00	1.00	1.00
Primary	0.86***	0.98	1.14***	1.16***	1.07	0.93	0.99	0.92
Secondary	0.34***	0.33***	0.47***	0.63***	0.69***	0.67***	0.79***	0.79***
Postsecondary	NA	0.22***	0.24***	0.32***	0.42***	0.48***	0.69***	0.69***
Religion								
Catholic (reference category)	1.00	1.00	1.00	1.00	1.00	1.00	1.00	1.00
Non Catholic Christian	0.97	0.97	0.96	0.98	1.01	0.99	0.96	0.97
Muslim	0.83***	0.86**	0.89	0.97	1.07	0.84	1.02	0.75*
African Independent Churches	1.18***	1.02	0.96*	0.89***	0.79***	0.79***	0.82***	0.82***
Other religion	0.93*	0.91**	0.86***	0.95	0.86**	0.78***	0.88	0.85
No religion	1.04	0.79***	0.75***	0.67***	0.61***	0.66***	0.69***	0.79***
Residence								
Rural (reference category)	1.00	1.00	1.00	1.00	1.00	1.00	1.00	1.00
Urban	1.39***	1.34***	1.12***	1.01	0.93**	0.93*	0.83***	0.81***
Province								
Gauteng (reference category)	1.00	1.00	1.00	1.00	1.00	1.00	1.00	1.00
Western Cape	0.65***	0.59***	0.63***	0.71***	0.81	0.85***	0.82***	0.87*
Eastern Cape	0.38***	0.47***	0.61***	0.73***	0.74***	0.89**	0.91	0.87*
Northern Cape	0.61***	0.65***	0.80***	1.04	1.01	1.32**	1.04	0.97
Free State	0.55***	0.59***	0.67***	0.75***	0.91**	1.10	0.95	0.88
KwaZulu Natal	0.62***	0.67***	0.79***	0.83***	0.89***	0.97	0.95	0.98
North West	0.70***	0.86***	0.89***	0.89***	0.95	0.89*	0.92	0.86*
Mpumalanga	0.74***	0.81***	0.89***	0.85***	0.84***	0.88**	0.82**	0.77**
Limpopo	0.83***	1.07**	1.19***	1.24***	1.06	1.08	0.87*	0.95
–2 log likelihood	11275.27	9514.56	6223.85	3367.13	1517.65	794.87	318.63	216.76
Degrees of freedom	19	20	20	20	20	20	20	20
N 145,808		157,138	119,447	81,235	53,297	33,657	21,071	13,392

Source: Computed from the 1996 South African census micro-data.
Notes: *p < 0.05; **p < 0.01; ***p < 0.001.

74

well defined (Table 3.3). The odds of having a first birth among non-Catholic Christian women are not significantly different from those of Catholic women at all ages. Muslim women only have significantly lower odds than Catholics at ages 17–18 and 19–20 and beyond that their odds are not correspondingly different from those of Catholics. Probably the interesting religious group to focus on is African Independent Churches, which are quasi-Christian churches. They are mostly composed of Zionist and Apostolic churches, or what are sometimes known as "spirit-type" churches (Gregson et al. 1999). These groups are generally known to exhibit some distinct religious and cultural beliefs like advocating early age at marriage, polygyny, and minimal use of modern contraceptives. For instance, Gregson et al. (1999) found that in rural Zimbabwe, birth rates and infant mortality were higher among women who belong to these spirit-type churches. On the other hand, Sibanda (1994) found slight fertility differentials between Apostolic and Christian women in the city of Chitungwiza, Zimbabwe. Having said this, Table 3.3 shows that women who belong to African Independent Churches are 18 percent more likely than their Catholic counterparts to have a first birth at ages 17–18. At the higher ages (21 and above), they have significantly lower odds than Catholics of having a first birth.

Lastly, Table 3.3 shows the association between place of residence and fertility. Regional differences in the timing of the first birth are usually associated with variations in the spatial distribution of racial/ethnic groups; provision of health, educational, and social services; and jobs. However, a simple place of residence or regional categorization is a crude control for the many differences underlying location-specific attributes. In the case of South Africa, Table 3.3 shows that early childbearing is associated with urban residence. Women living in urban areas were 39, 34, and 12 percent more likely to have a first birth at ages 17–18, 19–20, and 21–22, respectively, when compared to women living in rural areas. However, at the older ages (25 and above), urban women had significantly lower odds of becoming mothers than rural women. Although urban areas are generally endowed with better health and educational services, the higher odds of having a first birth we see at the young ages may be associated with some of the deleterious effects of living in urban environments. Destabilized family structures and a variety of other factors that tend to promote early initiation of sexual intercourse and a breakdown of traditional social controls and cultural practices are generally more common in urban areas (Cobley 1990,; Meekers 1994). For instance, Bledsoe and Cohen (1993) found that in most African countries, young urban women have higher chances of engaging in premarital sexual relations than their rural counterparts. In addition, the effects of urban residence are attenuated by the existence of massive rural–urban migration streams.

Another interesting observation from Table 3.3 is that women who were residing in South Africa's eight other provinces had significantly lower odds of having a first child at most ages when compared to women who were residing in Gauteng, a province that includes the cities of Johannesburg and Pretoria. Although this province happens to be the economic heartland of the country and the wealthiest province, in 1993 its share of the "total national poverty gap was in excess of 10 percent, making it the province with the fourth biggest poverty gap" (Hall and Whiteford 1998: 25). The bulk of this poverty is experienced by Africans, who comprise about 70 percent of the total population of the province. In addition, Gauteng is a major magnet for both uneducated and educated rural migrants looking for work (Crush et al. 1991; Lucas 1987). There is no direct evidence indicating that these factors are behind the relatively higher odds of having a first birth in Gauteng. However, these same factors might be associated with the early timing of the first birth, because disadvantaged women in these groups possibly contribute a disproportionate share of births at young ages.

The only other province with significantly higher odds of having a first birth is the Limpopo Province, particularly for women between ages 19 and 24. This might be associated with extremely high levels of poverty among Africans, who comprise the majority in the province. According to May (1998), poverty is deepest in the Limpopo Province because of the very high levels of poverty in the former homelands of Venda, Gazankulu, and Lebowa, which are part of this province. However, it is important to note that in the case of South Africa, race, place of residence, and socioeconomic status are highly correlated, largely because of the historical policy of separate development and overall economic disenfranchisement of Africans, Coloreds, and Indians/Asians.

Ethnic Differences in the Timing of the First Birth

African Ethnic Groups

In Table 3.4 we present the logistic effects of background factors on the timing of the first birth, focusing only on the various African ethnic groups. The odds of becoming a mother are substantially different among the various ethnic groups in South Africa, even after controlling for some background characteristics. Of all the African ethnic groups in South Africa, Venda women have the highest chances of becoming mothers early compared to Zulu women at all ages. For instance, Venda women are about 2.2 times more likely to have a first child at ages 17–18 and 19–20 than Zulu women. When analyzing patterns of contraceptive use in the former homelands, Kaufman (1998) observed that women who were residing in Venda had the lowest odds of using contraceptives, and these low odds were attributed to the fact that the Venda are generally more pronatalist. Xhosa and Northern Sotho women are also more likely to become mothers at the young ages compared to Zulu women. At the older ages (23 and above), Swazi women and, to some extent, Ndebele women, are the only ones who exhibit lower tendencies to becoming mothers for the first time. On the whole, most ethnic groups exhibit significantly different odds ratios of having a first child in the late teens and early twenties when compared to Zulu women.

The effects of religion on timing of first birth among African women are somewhat intriguing. The chances of having a first birth among Muslims are not significantly different from those of Catholics at almost all ages, even though these two religions are known to have different influences on fertility. Non-Catholic Christian women seem to behave differently from Catholics at ages 21–22 and 23–24, while women who belong to African Independent Churches (mostly Apostolic and Zionists) have significantly higher first birth odds than Catholics below age 20. However, above age 21, their odds become significantly lower than those of Catholics.

Our findings regarding education are consistent with the general findings reported in the literature (Lloyd et al. 2000). Women with secondary and postsecondary education have significantly lower chances of having a first birth than women with no education, at almost all ages. Women with primary education also have lower odds ratios. However, their odds of becoming mothers at ages 21–22 and 23–24 are not significantly different from those of noneducated women. For women with secondary and postsecondary education, the chances of becoming a mother in the late teens and early twenties are particularly low, because women at these ages are more likely to be pursuing careers.

As in the previous analysis of first birth timing by race, the effects of urban residence on the timing of motherhood are positive at the young ages, that is, below age 22. However, the relationship becomes negative and significant above age 25. The provincial variable shows that the odds of having a first birth are still significantly higher among Africans who live in Gauteng province. The limited information available in the 1996 South African Population Census precludes us from exploring the reasons behind these provincial differences. However, we would like to contend that what we seem to be picking up as a provincial differential is probably less important than the social and economic conditions of the neighborhoods and communities in which women live, like crowded living arrangements and the urban squatter environment that is common in African townships.

The persistence of the significance of the ethnic differential suggests that ethnicity may indeed be a proxy for unmeasured social and cultural processes. Future research should attempt to examine data with better measures of cultural, social, and economic processes.

Table 3.4

Logistic Regression Results (Odds Ratios) for the Effects of Explanatory Variables on the Likelihood of Having a First Birth at Various Ages: African Women

	Odds of having a first birth at age:							
Variable	17–18	19–20	21–22	23–24	25–26	27–28	29–30	31–32
African ethnic group								
Zulu (reference group)	1.00	1.00	1.00	1.00	1.00	1.00	1.00	1.00
Ndebele	0.97	0.96	0.97	0.85	0.79**	0.72**	0.80	0.75
Xhosa	1.11**	1.13**	1.11**	1.06*	1.07	0.95	0.98	1.19
Northern Sotho	1.35***	1.35***	1.13***	1.10	1.19**	1.12	0.98	0.99
Southern Sotho	0.99	1.08*	1.11**	1.02	1.03	1.09	0.94	1.25*
Tswana	0.95	1.06	1.10*	1.19	1.16**	1.23**	1.23*	1.33**
Swazi	1.27***	1.06	0.93	0.79***	0.79***	0.70***	0.75*	0.79
Venda	2.18***	2.29***	2.09****	1.95***	1.58****	1.57***	1.76**	1.52*
Tsonga	1.21***	1.21***	0.98	0.86*	0.81**	0.92	0.84	0.99
Education								
None (Reference group)	1.00	1.00	1.00	1.00	1.00	1.00	1.00	1.00
Primary	0.59***	0.83***	0.96	0.96	0.87***	0.86**	0.89*	0.87*
Secondary	0.24***	0.25***	0.34***	0.45***	0.50***	0.54****	0.63***	0.66****
Postsecondary	NA	0.27***	0.24***	0.28***	0.34***	0.44****	0.60***	0.63***
Religion								
Catholic (reference category)	1.00	1.00	1.00	1.00	1.00	1.00	1.00	1.00
Non-Catholic Christian	0.98	0.97	0.94*	0.92**	0.94	0.97	0.85**	0.88
Muslim	1.20	1.11	0.94	0.63	1.34	0.49*	0.67	0.49

African Independent Churches	1.13***	1.01	0.93***	0.85***	0.77***	0.78***	0.83***	0.84***
Other religion	0.96	0.97	0.85**	0.92	0.79***	0.74***	0.89	0.86
No religion	0.99	0.78***	0.73***	0.66***	0.59***	0.65***	0.72***	0.82**
Residence								
Rural (reference category)	1.00	1.00	1.00	1.00	1.00	1.00	1.00	1.00
Urban	1.41***	1.30***	1.09***	1.00	0.92**	0.87***	0.84***	0.79***
Province								
Gauteng (reference category)	1.00	1.00	1.00	1.00	1.00	1.00	1.00	1.00
Western Cape	0.74***	0.57***	0.59***	0.59***	0.68***	0.78**	0.77*	0.95
Eastern Cape	0.32***	0.42***	0.51***	0.62***	0.62***	0.81**	0.89	0.77*
Northern Cape	0.62***	0.59***	0.65***	0.77*	0.73*	1.07	1.19	1.08
Free State	0.52***	0.54***	0.55***	0.65***	0.75***	0.88	0.93	0.74**
KwaZulu-Natal	0.59***	0.65***	0.71***	0.73***	0.77***	0.81***	0.89	0.96
North West	0.69***	0.79***	0.76***	0.68***	0.73***	0.63***	0.78**	0.69***
Mpumalanga	0.62***	0.68***	0.75***	0.75***	0.71***	0.79***	0.83*	0.78*
Northern Province	0.58***	0.73***	0.89***	0.97	0.82**	0.80**	0.79*	0.88
−2 log likelihood	11127.63	7982.15	4730.04	2648.70	1287.84	595.50	224.68	147.19
Degrees of freedom	24	25	25	25	25	25	25	25
N	119,600	122,977	86,785	54,411	33,677	20,606	12,893	8,533

Source: Computed from the 1996 South African Population Census micro-data.
Note: *$p < 0.05$; **$p < 0.01$; ***$p < 0.001$

White Ethnic Groups

In Table 3.5 we present the odds ratios of having a first birth among White women. We have divided the White population into three "ethnic" groups. The first group consists of White women who reported that their first language spoken at home is Afrikaans. Afrikaners are descendents of the early Dutch settlers, who speak Afrikaans as their first language. According to Giliomee, Afrikaner identity is a well-defined feature of South African life, since for most of the twentieth century, Afrikaners "have come to regard 'group-belongingness,' group mobilization and the defense of the group position as positive responses that occur universally" (1995L 190). The second group of Whites in South Africa is of English descent, while the last group consists of other European-origin populations whose first language at home is not Afrikaans or English.

The first two groups first settled in South Africa in the mid-seventeenth and late eighteenth centuries, respectively, and efforts to de-emphasize cultural and political distinctions between them were a common feature of the South African political landscape in the twentieth century (Giliomee 1995; Paden and Soja 1970). In addition, because of their religious beliefs, Afrikaners have been more conservative, to the extent that they have been more puritanical about sexuality and contraception when compared to English-speaking Whites (Caldwell and Caldwell 1993). Thus, these differences make the case for comparing the timing of first births among the White ethnic groups in South Africa interesting.

Although White women in South Africa have close to below replacement fertility, it is not known whether there are any differences in age at first birth between the two main White ethnic groups. According to Caldwell and Caldwell (1993), prior to the 1960s, there were differences in fertility levels between Afrikaners and English South Africans. The fertility of the latter group was close to that of British settlers in the United States and Australia, while Afrikaner fertility was slightly higher. However, since the 1960s, fertility levels between the two groups have converged.

Looking at Table 3.5, it is apparent that Afrikaner women are far more likely to have a first birth at ages 17–18, 19–20, and 21–22 than English-speaking women. This should not be surprising since "the belated fertility decline within the Afrikaner population and the puritan attitudes of its Dutch Reformed Church, were obstacles to the development of a family planning movement" (Caldwell and Caldwell 1993: 233). In addition, this early pattern of first-birth timing is not necessarily due to educational, religious, or place of residence differences between these two groups, as these background factors have been controlled and both groups have generally enjoyed the same socioeconomic

Table 3.5

Logistic Regression Results (Odds Ratios) for the Effects of Explanatory Variables on the Likelihood of Having a First Birth at Various Ages: White Women

Variable	Odds of having a first birth at age:							
	17–18	19–20	21–22	23–24	25–26	27–28	29–30	31–32
White ethnic group								
English (reference group)	1.00	1.00	1.00	1.00	1.00	1.00	1.00	1.00
Afrikaans	1.95***	1.26***	1.24***	1.05	1.05	0.96	0.75***	0.69***
Other whites	0.91	1.03	0.91	0.77	0.90	0.99	0.90	0.85
Education								
None (reference group)	1.00	1.00	1.00	1.00	1.00	1.00	1.00	1.00
Primary	1.50	2.89***	1.63	1.37	1.05	1.54	1.59	1.09
Secondary	0.78***	3.85***	4.39***	3.94***	2.34***	1.61***	1.75***	1.63**
Postsecondary	NA	0.72***	0.81**	0.95	0.98	0.81**	1.29*	1.11
Religion								
Catholic (reference category)	1.00	1.00	1.00	1.00	1.00	1.00	1.00	1.00
Non-Catholic Christian	0.55***	0.79***	0.83***	1.00	1.09	1.12	1.24**	1.38***
Other Religion	1.18	0.83*	0.68***	0.64***	0.65***	0.68***	0.59***	0.72**
Residence								
Rural (reference category)	1.00	1.00	1.00	1.00	1.00	1.00	1.00	1.00
Urban	0.90	0.56***	0.58***	0.55***	0.55***	0.86	0.65***	0.61**
Province								
Gauteng (reference category)	1.00	1.00	1.00	1.00	1.00	1.00	1.00	1.00
Western Cape	0.56***	0.65***	0.66***	0.83***	0.96	0.99	0.82**	0.78**
Eastern Cape	0.89	0.72***	0.90	1.07	0.90	1.28**	0.99	0.84
Free State	0.90	0.92	1.04	0.93	1.27**	1.48***	1.15	0.89
KwaZulu-Natal	1.04	0.94	1.12	1.00	1.02	1.29**	1.03	1.06
North West	0.68***	0.79**	1.01	1.28***	1.49***	1.59***	1.08	1.03
Other Provinces	1.06	1.57***	1.78***	1.51***	1.54***	1.70***	1.06	1.13
−2 log likelihood	371.74	1552.64	1307.54	683.15	297.97	152.62	74.95	52.11
Degrees of freedom	13	14	14	14	14	14	14	14
N	8,529	12,929	14,480	13,707	11,421	8,096	5,065	2,925

Source: Computed from the 1996 South African Population Census micro-data.
Notes: *p < 0.05; **p < 0.01; ***p < 0.001.

and political benefits in South Africa. However, at the older ages, Afrikaner women have significantly lower odds of becoming mothers than English women. On the other hand, women of other European origin are not significantly different from English women. The differences in the timing of motherhood among Afrikaners and English South Africans clearly show that reproductive behaviors among South African Whites have not been homogenous.

However, the education effects for White women depart from those observed among African women. With the exception of women who had their first birth at age 17–18, women with secondary education have significantly higher odds of beginning a family early. For instance, women with secondary education are 4.4 times more likely to have a first child at age 21–22 than uneducated women.

With regard to religion, Table 3.5 shows that the Catholic versus nonCatholic differential is well pronounced below age 22 and above age 29. At younger ages, non-Catholic Christian women are less likely to have a first birth than Catholic women, but at older ages, they tend to have higher first-birth odds. On the other hand, women belonging to other religious groups have significantly lower chances of becoming mothers at all ages when compared to Catholic women. Thus, unlike in the United States, where the Catholic versus non-Catholic fertility differential has diminished (Westoff 1979), religion among Whites in South Africa is significantly associated with the timing of family formation.

Lastly, the patterns of first-birth timing we observe for Whites after controlling for place of residence diverge from the pattern we observe among Africans. Residing in an urban area significantly reduces the odds of having a first child at ages 19 and above. The reason for this sharper rural–urban contrast between Africans and Whites presumably has to do with the fact that a disproportionate number of Whites reside in urban areas, where the timing of family formation competes with many other opportunities like jobs and higher education. With regard to the provincial differential, Whites who live in the second-wealthiest province in the country (Western Cape) have consistently lower odds of becoming mothers than women residing in Gauteng. With the exception of women living in the collapsed category "other provinces," Whites residing in provinces like the Free State and KwaZulu-Natal do not behave differently from women living in Gauteng, except in their late twenties, when their odds of becoming mothers become significantly higher.

Other Ethnic Groups

Table 3.6 shows the association between the timing of the first birth and ascribed and achieved background factors among Colored women. The results indicate that early motherhood seems to be more attractive among women with primary education. For instance, primary educated women are 3.6 times more likely to be mothers than uneducated women at age 17 and 18. These significantly higher odds persist up to age 26. However, when we look at religion, it appears the association between religion and fertility timing is less dramatic. With the exception of first-birth timing at ages 27–28, there are no significant differences in the odds of becoming a mother between Catholics, non-Catholic Christians, and Muslims. Only members of African Independent Churches exhibit significantly lower odds between ages 25 and 30, while women belonging to "other religions" display a fairly consistent pattern of delayed motherhood.

Lastly, Table 3.7 shows the results of logistic regression analyses of the association between the timing of the first birth and background factors among Indian/Asian women. Because less than 3 percent of Indian/Asian women in our sample had no education, we collapsed the "no education" and the "primary education" categories into the "less than secondary education" so as to avoid the problem of small sample size. The results show that postsecondary education makes a substantial contribution to delaying the first birth, while secondary education is associated with significant odds of becoming a mother at ages 23–26 and 29–32. The other background factors like religion and place of residence seem to be of less importance among Indians/Asians.

Conclusion

Physiological factors and a wide array of prescribed and achieved background characteristics affect the timing of the first birth. Our investigation has shown that there are strong associations between the timing of the first birth and race, ethnicity, education, religion, and place of residence in South Africa. The racial differential in the timing of motherhood in South Africa can be traced to racial stratification processes. By controlling for achieved characteristics like education, we only eliminate part of the overall impact of racial stratification on demographic outcomes, because apartheid policies of separate racial development impacted negatively on Africans, Coloreds, and Indians/Asians in terms of equal access to national resources like health care and wealth.

In the case of the African subpopulations, the reasons underlying these strong associations may be attributed to efforts by some of these ethnic groups to maintain their unique cultural identity, which possibly includes differences in the timing of marriage and the onset of reproduction. Thus, individual decision making is shaped by one's social and cultural context. It is also possible that some of these differences may be a consequence of the differential impact of apartheid policies, particularly the provision of economic, health,

Table 3.6

Logistic Regression Results (Odds Ratios) for the Effects of Explanatory Variables on the Likelihood of Having a First Birth at Various Ages: Colored Women

Variable	Odds of having a first birth at age:							
	17–18	19–20	21–22	23–24	25–26	27–28	29–30	31–32
Education								
None (reference group)	1.00	1.00	1.00	1.00	1.00	1.00	1.00	1.00
Primary	3.64***	1.65***	1.54***	1.79***	1.99***	0.75	1.08	1.06
Secondary	0.90	0.68***	1.03	1.37***	1.58***	0.84	1.14	1.15
Postsecondary	NA	0.13***	0.22***	0.42***	0.60***	0.42***	0.59**	1.14
Religion								
Catholic (reference category)	1.00	1.00	1.00	1.00	1.00	1.00	1.00	1.00
Non-Catholic Christian	1.03	0.96	1.03	1.05	0.87	0.76**	0.96	0.99
Muslim	1.01	0.95	0.92	1.08	1.11	0.88	1.01	0.97
African Independent churches	1.09	0.99	0.90	1.07	0.79**	0.76**	0.70**	0.78
Other religion	0.92	0.68***	0.86	0.75*	0.68*	0.61**	0.71	0.85
Residence								
Rural (reference category)	1.00	1.00	1.00	1.00	1.00	1.00	1.00	1.00
Urban	0.86**	1.30***	1.32***	1.20*	1.33**	0.81*	1.25	1.05
Province								
Gauteng (reference category)	1.00	1.00	1.00	1.00	1.00	1.00	1.00	1.00
Western Cape	0.57***	0.56***	0.62***	0.70***	0.67**	0.81	0.83	1.34
Eastern Cape	0.41***	0.43***	0.55***	0.61***	0.59***	0.71	0.68	1.08
Northern Cape	0.49***	0.55***	0.68***	0.99	0.89	1.31	0.88	1.59
Other Provinces	0.66***	0.79*	0.79	1.09	0.88	1.20	0.82	1.73
−2 log likelihood	974.38	1786.51	1133.74	541.45	253.62	96.05	45.79	9.96
Degrees of freedom	11	12	12	12	12	12	12	12
N	13,718	15,908	12,778	8,837	5,503	3,245	2,092	1,300

Source: Computed from the 1996 South African Population Census micro-data.
Note: $*p < 0.05$; $**p < 0.01$; $***p < 0.001$

84

Table 3.7

Logistic Regression Results (Odds Ratios) for the Effects of Explanatory Variables on the Likelihood of Having a First Birth at Various Ages: Indian/Asian Women

Variable	Odds of having a first birth at age:							
	17–18	19–20	21–22	23–24	25–26	27–28	29–30	31–32
Education								
Below secondary (reference group)	1.00	1.00	1.00	1.00	1.00	1.00	1.00	1.00
Secondary	1.29***	1.25	1.29	1.81***	1.69**	1.15	1.66*	1.83*
Postsecondary	NA	0.10***	0.19***	0.31***	0.52***	0.44***	0.76	0.74
Religion								
Hindu (reference category)	1.00	1.00	1.00	1.00	1.00	1.00	1.00	1.00
Muslim	0.92	0.98	1.00	1.14	1.10	0.83	1.04	0.73
Other religion	1.09	0.99	1.02	0.85	1.03	1.39	1.85	1.21
Residence								
Rural (reference category)	1.00	1.00	1.00	1.00	1.00	1.00	1.00	1.00
Urban	0.61*	1.35	1.27	1.14	1.04	1.40	0.90	0.31
Province								
Gauteng (reference category)	1.00	1.00	1.00	1.00	1.00	1.00	1.00	1.00
KwaZulu-Natal	1.34**	1.03	1.04	1.18	1.52**	1.07	0.90	1.03
Other provinces	0.85	0.81	0.93	0.88	1.49*	1.37	1.19	0.92
–2 log likelihood	33.03	984.71	546.83	348.00	106.76	53.73	23.33	23.79
Degrees of freedom	6	7	7	7	7	7	7	7
N	3,088	4,326	4,470	3,583	2,207	1,385	802	497

Source: Computed from the 1996 South African Population Census micro-data.
Notes: *$p < 0.05$; **$p < 0.01$; ***$p < 0.001$

and other essential opportunities, on the various African ethnic groups. In essence, this explanation attributes differential demographic behavior to macro socioeconomic and political structures that affect individual behavior by stratifying groups (McDaniel 1996). In the case of South Africa, these structures amplified the ethnic differential when the apartheid governments created ten ethnically homogenous African homelands, or Bantustans. The creation of ethnically defined homelands like Bophuthatswana (for Tswanas), KwaNdebele (for the Ndebeles), KwaZulu (for the Zulus), Transkei (for Xhosas), Venda (for Vendas), and so on affected these groups in different ways—economic, cultural, or political. In fact, Peires (1995) contends that this divide-and-rule policy of the various apartheid governments engendered conflict between various African groups, thereby creating a heightened sense of ethnic consciousness. Although the massive rural–urban migration processes in South Africa could have possibly undermined the retention of what one might call overt ethnic cultures and what distinguishes them, it is important to note that South Africa's policy of controlled urbanization determined where the various African population groups could live, thereby bolstering ethnic identities even in urban areas (Beinart 1995). However, despite such draconian regulations, most African groups managed to live side by side in many urban areas.

References

Ahmad, W.I.U., ed. 1993. *"Race" and Health in Contemporary Britain.* Milton Keynes: Open University Press.

Beinart, W. 1995. "Chieftaincy and the concept of articulation: South Africa circa 1900–50." In *Segregation and Apartheid in Twentieth-Century South Africa,* ed. W. Beinart and S. Dubow: 176–88. London: Routledge.

Bledsoe, C., and B. Cohen, eds. 1993. *Social Dynamics of Adolescent Fertility in Sub-Saharan Africa.* Washington, DC: National Academy Press.

Bongaarts, J. 1999. "The fertility impact of changes in the timing of childbearing in the developing world." *Population Studies* 53(3): 277–89.

Caldwell, J.C., and P. Caldwell. 1987. "The cultural context of high fertility in sub-Saharan Africa." *Population and Development Review* 13(3): 409–37.

———. 1993. "The South African fertility decline." *Population and Development Review* 19(2): 225–62.

Calves, A.E. 1999. "Marginalization of African single mothers in the marriage market: Evidence from Cameroon." *Population Studies* 53(3): 291–301.

Case, A., and A. Deaton. 1999. "School inputs and educational outcomes in South Africa." *The Quarterly Journal of Economics* CXIV(3): 1047–84.

Cherlin, A., and N. Riley. 1986. Adolescent fertility: an emerging issue in Sub-Saharan Africa. PHN Technical Note 86–23, Washington, DC: The World Bank.

Chimere-Dan, O. 1993. "Population policy in South Africa." *Studies in Family Planning* 24(1): 31–39.

Cobley, A.G. 1990. *Class and Consciousness: The Black Petty Bourgeoisie in South Africa, 1924 to 1950.* New York: Greenwood Press.

Cooper, R.S., and R. David. 1986. "The biological concept of race and its application to public health and epidemiology." *Journal of Health Politics, Policy and Law* 11: 97–116.

Crush, J.S., A. Jeeves, and D. Yudelman. 1991. *South Africa's Labor Empire: A History of Black Migrancy to the Gold Mines.* Boulder, CO: Westview Press and David Philip.

du Plessis, G.E., B.E. Hofmeyer, and W.P. Mostert. 1991. "Fertility differentials in South Africa, 1987–89." In Memorandum to the Director-General of the Department of National Health and Population Development. Pretoria: Human Sciences Research Council.

Forste, R., and M. Tienda. 1996. "What's behind racial and ethnic fertility differentials?" *Population and Development Review* 22. Issue Supplement: Fertility in the United States: New Patterns, New Theories: 109–33.

Gage, A.J. 1998. "Premarital childbearing, unwanted fertility and maternity care in Kenya and Namibia." *Population Studies* 52(1): 21–34.

Giliomee, H. 1995. "The growth of Afrikaner identity." In *Segregation and Apartheid in Twentieth-Century South Africa,* ed. W. Beinart and S. Dubow, 189–205. London: Routledge.

Gregson, S., T. Zhuwau, R.M. Anderson, and S.K. Chandiwana. 1999. "Apostles and Zionists: The influence of religion on demographic change in rural Zimbabwe." *Population Studies* 53(2): 179–93.

Hall, P., and A. Whiteford. 1998. "Poverty gap." In *Service Needs and Provision in Gauteng,* ed. B.M. O'Leary, V. Govind, C.A. Schwabe, and J.M. Taylor, 25–28. Pretoria: Human Sciences Research Council.

Kaufman, C.E. 1998. "Contraceptive use in South Africa under Apartheid." *Demography* 35(4): 421–34.

Kiernan, K., and I. Diamond. 1983. "The age at which childbearing starts—a longitudinal study." *Population Studies* 37: 363–80.

Knodel, J., R.S. Gray, P. Sriwatcharin, and S. Peracca. 1999. "Muslims in Buddhist Thailand." *Population Studies* 53(2): 149–64.

Krieger, N. 2000. "Refiguring 'race': Epidemiology, racialized biology, and biological expressions of race relations." *International Journal of Health Services* 30(1): 211–16.

Krige, E.J. 1968. "Girls' puberty songs and their relation to fertility, health, morality and religion among the Zulu." *Africa* 38(2): 173–97.

Kuper, A. 1982. *Wives for Cattle: Bridewealth and Marriage in Southern Africa.* London: Routledge and Kegan Paul.

LaVeist, T.A. 2000. "On the study of race, racism, and health: A shift from description to Explanation." *International Journal of Health Services* 30(1): 217–19.

Lesthaeghe, R.J., ed. 1989. *Reproduction and Social Organization in Sub-Saharan Africa.* Berkeley: University of California Press.

Lloyd, C., C.E. Kaufman, and P. Hewett. 2000. "The spread of primary schooling in Sub-Saharan Africa: Implications for fertility change." *Population and Development Review* 26(3): 483–515.

Lucas, R. 1987. "Emigration to South Africa's mines." *The American Economic Review* 77(3): 313–30.

Magubane, P. 1998. *Vanishing Cultures of South Africa: Changing Customs in a Changing World.* New York: Rizzoli International.

Marwick, M. 1978. "Household composition and marriage in a Witwatersrand African Township." In *Social System and Tradition in Southern Africa, Essays in Honour of Eileen Krige,* ed. J. Argyle and E. Preston-Whyte, 36–54. Cape Town: Oxford University Press.

May, J., ed. 1998. *Poverty and Inequality in South Africa, Summary Report.* Durban: Praxis.

McDaniel, A. 1994. "Historical racial differences in living arrangements of children." *Journal of Family History* 19(1): 57–77.

———. 1996. "Fertility and racial stratification." *Population and Development Review* 22, Issue Supplement: Fertility in the United States: New Patterns, New Theories: 134–50.

Meekers, D. 1994. "Sexual initiation and premarital childbearing in Sub-Saharan Africa." *Population Studies* 48(1): 47–64.

Menken, J. 1985. "Age and fertility: How late can you wait?" *Demography* 22: 469–83.

Morgan, S.P., A. McDaniel, A. Miller, and S.H. Preston. 1993. "Racial differences in household and family structure at the turn of the century." *American Journal of Sociology* 98(4): 798–828.

Ngom, P., I. Sarr, and A. Gaye. 1999. "Ethnic diversity and assimilation in Senegal: Evidence from the 1988 census." Paper presented at Third African Population Conference, Durban: December 6–10.

Paden, J.N., and E.W. Soja. 1970. *The African Experience*, Vol. II: Syllabus. Evanston, IL: Northwestern University Press.

Pebley, A.R., J.B. Casterline, and J. Trussell. 1982. "Age at first birth in 19 countries." *International Family Planning Perspectives* 8(1): 2–7.

Peires, J.B. 1995. "Ethnicity and pseudo-ethnicity in the Ciskei." In *Segregation and Apartheid in Twentieth-Century South Africa,* ed. W. Beinart and S. Dubow, 256–84. London: Routledge.

Pickel, B. 1997. *Coloured Ethnicity and Identity: A Case Study in the Former Coloured Areas in the Western Cape/ South Africa.* Hamburg: Lit Verlag.

Preston, S.H. 1974. "Differential fertility, unwanted fertility, and racial trends in occupational Achievement." *American Sociological Review* 39(4): 492–506.

Preston, S.H., and C. Campbell. 1993. "Differential fertility and the distribution of traits: The case of IQ." *American Journal of Sociology* 98(5): 997–1019.

Preston-Whyte, E. 1978. "Families without marriage: A Zulu case study." In *Social System and Tradition in Southern Africa: Essays in Honour of Eileen Krige,* ed. J. Argyle and E. Preston-Whyte, 55–85. Cape Town: Oxford University Press.

Rindfuss, R.R., and C. St. John. 1983. "Social determinants of age at first birth." *Journal of Marriage and the Family* 45: 553–65.

Rindfuss, R.R, S.P. Morgan, and C.G. Swicegood. 1984. "The transition to motherhood: The intersection of structural and temporal dimensions." *American Sociological Review* 49(3): 359–72.

———. 1988. *First Births in America: Changes in the Timing of Parenthood.* Berkeley: University of California Press.

Sadie, J.L. 1970. "An evaluation of demographic data pertaining to the non-white population of South Africa." *South African Journal of Economics* 38(2): 171–91.

———. 1971. "Population and economic development in South Africa." *South African Journal of Economics* 39(3): 205–22.

———. 1972. "The costs of population growth in South Africa." *South African Journal of Economics* 40(2): 107–18.

Schapera, I. 1987. "Kinship and marriage among the Tswana." In *African Systems of Kinship and Marriage,* ed. A.R. Radcliffe-Brown and D. Forde, 140–65. London: Kegan Paul International.

Sibanda, A. 1994. "Socio-economic and cultural differentials in fertility in Zimbabwe." In *The Demography of Zimbabwe: Some Research Findings,* ed. W. Muhwava. Harare: Earthware Publishing Services.

Sibanda, A., and T. Zuberi. 1999. "Contemporary fertility levels and trends in South Africa: Evidence from reconstructed census birth histories." In *The African Population in the 21st Century: Third African Population Conference*, Vol. 1, 79–108. Durban: Union for African Population Studies,

St. John, C. 1982. "Race differences in age at first birth and the pace of subsequent fertility: Implications for the minority group hypothesis." *Demography,* 19(3): 301–14.

Stolley, P.D. 1999. "Race in epidemiology." *International Journal of Health Services* 29(4): 905–10.

Udjo, E.O. 1999. "Recent evidence of differentials in marital patterns in South Africa." Paper presented at the Demographic Association of Southern Africa Annual Conference, Saldanha Bay, July 5–7.

van de Walle, E. 1993. "Recent trends in marriage ages." In *Demographic Change in Sub-Saharan Africa,* ed. Karen A. Foote, Kenneth H. Hill, and Linda G. Martin, 117–52. Panel on Population Dynamics of SubSaharan Africa, Committee on Population, National Research Council. Washington, DC: National Academy Press.

Westoff, C.J. 1979. "The end of 'Catholic' fertility." *Demography* 16: 209–17.

———. 1992. "Age at marriage, age at first birth and fertility in Africa." World Bank Technical Paper Number 169. Washington, DC: The World Bank.

Williams, D.R., R. Lavizzo-Mourey, and R.C. Warren. 1994. "The concept of race and health status in America." *Public Health Reports* 109: 26–41.

Zuberi, T. 2001. *Thicker than Blood: How Racial Statistics Lie.* Minneapolis, MN: University of Minnesota Press.

4. An Examination of Recent Census and Survey Data on Mortality Within the Context of HIV/AIDS

Eric O. Udjo

As in many less developed countries, surveys and censuses are the primary sources of information on mortality in South Africa in the absence of complete coverage of vital registration. However, prior to 1994, there was no systematic effort to collect mortality data on a national scale in surveys and censuses in the country. Hitherto, mortality estimates were based on fragmentary data, and the estimation methods and quality of the data were largely unclear. Consequently, and with the HIV/AIDS epidemic, estimates of mortality for South Africa vary, and often by a large margin.

Similar to fertility, the systematic collection of mortality data in South Africa began with the annual program of October Household Surveys (OHS) launched by Statistics South Africa in 1994. The mortality questions (including birth histories) in the household surveys enable the direct and indirect estimation of mortality levels nationally, and by the four main population groups. In addition, the questions on mortality in the population census of October 1996 (Census '96) enable indirect estimation of levels of and trends in mortality in South Africa.

Childhood mortality is a sensitive indicator of the general welfare of any population. It is also an indicator of the health status and level of socioeconomic development of any population.

Adult mortality impacts the labor force and the general welfare of the population. The ability of any population to produce goods and services for sustenance and development is partly dependent on the quality of its labor force. Quality in this regard includes, among other things, skills, training, and experience acquired over time through formal education and the work environment. To ensure that the labor force has the necessary skills, various sectors of the population make large investments in education, starting from childhood. The investments (often long-term) in education and training could erode if mortality is high in adult life (when the skills are needed).

Because some skills are highly specialized, scarce, and not easily replaceable, government policy is usually to reduce mortality and, subsequently, to maintain a low level of mortality. The study of levels and trends in mortality in a population is therefore of critical importance to a government as an indicator of the changing health status and welfare of its citizenry, and as a basis for formulating appropriate policies to preserve its human resources for social and economic development.

This chapter critically examines the 1995 and 1998 OHS and 1996 census data on childhood and adult mortality in South Africa and attempts to estimate levels and trends of mortality so as to improve our knowledge about variations in the country within the context of HIV/AIDS.

Data and Methods

The analysis in this chapter is based on three data sets collected by Statistics South Africa—the 1995 and 1998 OHS and the full count of the 1996 population census. Although the 1994 household survey data were available, the demographic questions were more limited than in the 1995 survey. The 1997 survey was of poor quality in comparison with the 1995 and 1998 surveys (see chapter 2 on fertility in this volume). The 1995 survey was therefore a more appropriate data set for examining past trends, while the 1998 survey was more appropriate for examining more recent trends. This is because the mortality derived from the former stretches farther back in time, while the mortality from the latter is for a relatively more recent period. For ease of interpretation, the results of the analysis by population are presented only for the 1995 survey and the 1996 census, while the results of the analysis by region of residence are presented for the 1998 survey and the 1996 census.

The 1995 and 1998 October Household Surveys

Childhood mortality can be estimated directly from birth histories, depending on the quality of the birth history reports. The 1995 and 1998 household surveys in South Africa were carried out on a national sample of 30,000 households. In each case, the sample was stratified by province, urban and nonurban areas, and population group. The 1995 survey was approximately self-weighting nationally, while the 1998 survey was not self-weighting nationally, but roughly self-weighting at other levels, including the regional (provincial) level. (See Hirschowitz and Orkin [1996] for details regarding the design of the October Household Surveys.) The 1995 and 1998 surveys collected birth histories from women less than 55 years of age at the time of the survey. Direct estimates of childhood mortality were calculated using the birth histories.

The 1996 Population Census

Censuses do not collect birth histories. However, the household questionnaire used in the South African population census of October 1996 included questions on past and current births and number of children surviving. The tabulation of the responses to these questions by five-year age groups of women in the reproductive age group enables indirect estimation of childhood mortality. The 1996 census has an advantage over the household surveys in the sense that sampling issues do not arise (except in the estimation of undercount). Statistics South Africa (1998) gives details regarding the design and execution of the 1996 census.

Childhood Mortality

Given the dates of births of children, the dates of death of those dead, and the survey date, it is possible to calculate the proportion of children dying at different age intervals, and hence the life table probabilities of dying and surviving at specific ages. This procedure was widely applied to World Fertility Survey birth history data (Rutstein 1983). The procedure can be applied using statistical software. In my analysis I used the SPSS survival procedure. This procedure was applied in the present study to obtain direct estimates of childhood mortality from the 1995 and 1998 birth histories.

Direct estimates of childhood mortality are vulnerable to certain kinds of errors, such as dating errors and the selective omission of dead children. The accuracy of the survival functions are dependent on the accurate reporting of dates of birth and dates of death of the children. The survival functions may also be biased by large-scale omission of dead children (see Udjo [1987] for details). Although there is no systematic way of estimating the time location of the survival functions obtained directly from birth histories, experience with time location of childhood mortality indirectly estimated suggests that the survival functions would relate to approximately one to fifteen years before the survey.

Brass (1971) developed a model for estimating life table survival probabilities from birth to certain exact ages among children from information on proportions dead among children ever born reported by women of reproductive age. The equation developed by Brass for converting the proportions dead among children ever born into life table probabilities of survival is

$$q_x = D_i k_i$$

where q_x is the probability of dying between birth and exact age x, D_i is the proportion dead of children ever born to women in age group i, and k_i is a multiplier that adjusts for nonmortality factors determining the value of D_i.

Using several data sets from different countries collected in the World Fertility Surveys, Fernandez (1985, 1989) showed that the Brass method overestimates mortality of children born to younger mothers. Fernandez thus developed a set of coefficients for adjusting the estimates derived from the Brass method. The q_xs presented in this study were estimated using the refinement by Fernandez.

The estimated q_xs were converted into α values (level of childhood mortality) using Brass's (1971) logit system, while the reference period of the levels was estimated using Brass's later (1985) method.

The possible biases that may affect the estimates include the following:

(a) Selective omissions of dead children: If parity is understated, it seems probable that dead children would be more likely to be understated, and hence, there would be a downward bias in the estimates of childhood mortality.

(b) The sensitivity of estimates to the assumed age pattern of mortality embodied in the standard life table chosen for converting the q_xs into α values (see Udjo [1987] for details).

Adult Mortality from Orphanhood Reports

Adult mortality among females and males can be indirectly estimated based on two separate orphanhood questions—whether or not a person's mother is alive and whether or not a person's father is still alive (at the time of a census or survey). The question regarding the survivorship of mothers is used for the estimation of maternal orphanhood, while paternal orphanhood is estimated from the question regarding the survivorship of fathers. Both questions were included in the 1995 and 1998 surveys and the 1996 census questionnaires.

The method developed by Brass (1971) for translating the proportions of persons with a surviving parent into probabilities of survival from a base age B to age $B+N$ is based on the following equation:

$$l_{B+N}/l_B = W_N \left(_5P_{N-5} \right) + _5P_N \left(1 - W_N \right)$$

where l_{B+N}/l_B is the probability of surviving from a base age B to $B+N$, and N is the central age between two adjacent five-year age groups; $_5P_{N-5}$ is the proportion in the age group $N-5$ to N having a surviving parent; $_5P_N$ is the proportion in the age group N to $N+5$ having a surviving parent; and W_N is a weighting factor, which depends on N and the location of childbearing, represented by the mean age of childbearing, M.

The survival probability values are translated into levels of adult mortality, α, using Brass's logit system (Brass and Bamgboye 1981). The time locations of each of the α values are estimated using the method developed by Bamgboye (1982) and Brass and Bamgboye (1981).

Certain weaknesses of the orphanhood method need to be highlighted. First, the mortality experience of nonparents or of parents without a surviving child is not represented in orphanhood information (Hill 1977; United Nations 1983). Second, the estimates derived from the youngest age groups tend to be unusable due to the adoption effect (Udjo 1998). Third, paternal orphanhood estimates are not particularly robust (Brass 1971).

Life Tables

Two-parameter life tables were constructed on the basis of the estimated childhood and orphanhood estimates for specific time periods using the Brass logit system; α and β in the two-parameter system define the general level and the relationship between childhood and adult mortality in a population, respectively. The procedure for splicing the childhood and adult mortality estimates to enable the derivation of the two parameters are described by Udjo (1991).

Results

Childhood Mortality by Population Group

To arrive at an estimate of the level of child mortality in South Africa, this author began by estimating childhood mortality levels directly using the 1995 OHS. However, the estimates obtained using these surveys are unreliable. An examination of the quality of the data seems to indicate that women omitted a large proportion of dead children during the survey. This was evident from the improbably low level of childhood mortality. For example, the reported total mortality in the first five years of life, q_5, was about ten per thousand among Africans and Coloreds, and less than four per thousand among

Table 4.1

Reported Life Table Probability of Dying from Birth to Exact Age x (q_x) from Proportions Dead (D_i) of Children Ever Born by Population Group

Age of mothers	15–19	20–24	25–29	30–34	35–39	40–44	45–49
African							
D_i	0.087	0.077	0.083	0.096	0.115	0.140	0.168
Age x	1	2	3	5	10	15	20
q_x	0.060	0.069	0.082	0.101	0.121	0.139	0.167
Alpha	−0.382	−0.500	−0.486	−0.444	−0.440	−0.399	−0.348
Date	94.6	93.0	91.1	88.8	86.4	83.6	80.2
$p_2/p_3 = 0.520$							
$m = 28.2$							
Colored							
D_i	0.066	0.050	0.050	0.055	0.066	0.087	0.110
Age x	1	2	3	5	10	15	20
q_x	0.045	0.043	0.049	0.058	0.071	0.089	0.113
Alpha	−0.533	−0.744	−0.759	−0.742	−0.734	−0.650	−0.575
Date	94.7	93.0	91.1	88.9	86.4	83.6	80.3
$p_2/p_3 = 0.518$							
$m = 29.8$							
Indian/Asian							
D_i	0.055	0.037	0.028	0.028	0.031	0.037	0.048
Age x	1	2	3	5	10	15	20
q_x	0.047	0.036	0.030	0.032	0.034	0.038	0.050
Alpha	−0.636	−0.929	−1.080	−1.108	−1.117	−1.103	−1.017
Date	95.0	93.8	92.0	89.9	87.5	84.9	81.8
$p_2/p_3 = 0.391$							
$m = 30.0$							
White							
D_i	0.088	0.035	0.026	0.025	0.028	0.031	0.038
Age x	1	2	3	5	10	15	20
q_x	0.079	0.035	0.028	0.030	0.031	0.032	0.040
Alpha	−0.361	−0.941	−1.117	−1.145	−1.167	−1.192	−1.134
Date	95.1	94.1	92.3	90.3	87.9	85.4	82.4
$p_2/p_3 = 0.350$							
$m = 31.0$							

Source: 1996 South African Population Census

Indians/Asians, and Whites. Hence, the results presented in this chapter are from indirect estimates.

Table 4.1 shows the life table probabilities of dying, q_x, derived from proportions dead, Di, of children ever born reported by women in the 1996 census. There is no obvious indication from the table of omission of dead children by African and Colored women. The q_x values show the expected rise with the age of children. Among Indian/Asian and White women, on the other hand, the

q_x values decrease with age up to age 5 and increases very gradually afterward. The slow increase in the q_x values after age 5 among Indian/Asian children is indicative of errors in the reporting of dead children by older mothers.

The q_1 values, which indicate the level of mortality in the first year of life, range from a high of seventy-nine per thousand among White children to a low of forty-five per thousand among Colored children. The corresponding high mortality value for White children is surprising. Given the magnitude of the effects of racial inequality on children's health in South Africa (Burgard 2002), it is very unlikely that mortality in infancy is currently higher among White children than among Colored or African children. As expected, the implied levels (α values) suggest that there are large disparities in childhood mortality across racial lines, with Africans and Coloreds fairing poorly when compared with Indians/Asians and Whites.

With the exception of the most current period, the α values among Africans seem to suggest that childhood mortality among Africans is roughly twice the level among Coloreds and nearly three times the level among Indians/Asians and Whites. These disparities may be confounded by errors in the reporting of dead children among the different population groups. The disparities might also be viewed within the context of different levels of fertility among the population groups. Africans and Coloreds have a higher level of fertility than Indians/Asians and Whites. Studies have shown that there is a relationship between fertility and child survival (Udjo 1996, 1997a). On the one hand, various factors related to reproductive behaviors (such as maternal age, parity, and birth interval) are linked to child survival. On the other hand, fertility may be a volitional or nonvolitional response to child survival.

Child Mortality Trends

To get a better understanding of mortality levels in South Africa, Figure 4.1 graphs the α values shown in Table 4.1. The trends indicate a modest decline up to 1992 and a rise since 1994 in childhood mortality among the four population groups. However, the apparent pace of the rise among White children is highly suspect. At face value, and based on a one-parameter logit system, it implies a reduction in life expectancy at birth of about eighteen years within three years (1992–95). Furthermore, it implies a higher level of mortality among White compared to African children in recent years.

There are a number of theoretical explanations for the apparent rapid rise in mortality among White children and to a lesser extent among Indian/Asian children. First, this could be due to an overreporting of dead children.

Figure 4.1   **Trend in Childhood Mortality by Population Groups**

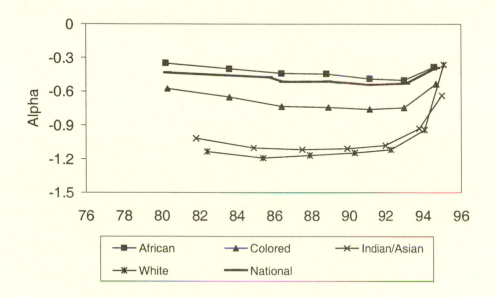

Source: 1996 South African Population Census.

Younger women could have included stillbirths in their reports on children ever born. If stillbirths are reported as live births and subsequently reported as dead children, this increases the proportions dead among children ever born, thereby exaggerating the level of childhood mortality in recent years. If this was the case, there is no apparent explanation for why White women ages 15 to 19 reported more stillbirths during the 1996 census than in previous surveys. Second, the preliminary report on the 1998 South Africa Demographic and Health Survey observed a similar trend in childhood mortality (Department of Health 1999). The report contends that it is likely that the upward trend in childhood mortality in recent years is "associated with the HIV/AIDS epidemic that is currently underway in South Africa." If that were the case, one would expect, on the basis of available evidence on HIV/AIDS prevalence, that the trend would be more marked among African than among White or Indian/Asian children, because HIV/AIDS prevalence is reported to be higher among Africans (Shisana and Simbayi 2002). Figure 4.1, however, shows the contrary. Lastly, this trend could be due to the progressive underreporting of dead children by older mothers. However, the levels of mortality recorded up to about 1992 among White children appear probable, and hence, this explanation is unlikely.

Given these issues, it is difficult to draw conclusions about the factors responsible for the rising trends in childhood mortality in recent years. A combination of factors may be at play and these need to be investigated by further research.

Adult Mortality by Population Group

Levels and Trends in Adult Female Mortality

The maternal orphanhood method is applied to the reports from females about mother's survival status in order to determine trends in female mortality. The reason for preferring the analysis based on female respondents is as follows. According to Blacker (1977), males have a tendency to exaggerate their ages, and because the proportions with mother alive fall rapidly with increasing age of respondents, any exaggeration of reported ages implies that the proportions with living mothers would be biased upward. Table 4.2 shows the proportions with mother alive fall with increasing age of respondents for all population groups in the 1996 census.

The adult female mortality levels obtained from the results based on the 1995 OHS were erratic (graph not shown) compared with those based on the 1996 census. The 1996 census suggests a sharp decline in adult female mortality in the 1980s (Figure 4.2), with three distinct patterns: a moderate level among Africans and Coloreds; a low level among Whites; and an earlier intermediate level (between those of Africans and Whites), but a more recent low level among Indians/Asians (Table 4.2).

Internal and External Consistency of the Levels and Trends in Adult Female Mortality

The magnitude of the improvement in adult female mortality implied by the life expectancies after age 15 (e_{15}) in the 1980s is doubtful in its accuracy, especially among Indians/Asians and Whites. Consider the following examples based on the 1995 survey:

1. Between 1981 and 1985 e_{15} apparently increased from 49.7 years to 59.2 years among Indian/Asian female adults (i.e., a gain of nearly ten years in less than five years).
2. Among adult White females, e_{15} also increased from 56 years to 64.3 years between 1984 and 1988 (a gain of more than eight years in less than five years).
3. In less than two years (1985–87), e_{15} also increased by over four years among Colored female adults.

Table 4.2

Adult Female Mortality from Reports on Mother Alive Based on the 1996 Census by Population Group

Age of respondents	10–14	15–19	20–24	25–29	30–34	35–39	40–44
African							
Proportion with mother alive	0.969	0.950	0.912	0.856	0.783	0.699	0.598
Central age	15	20	25	30	35	40	45
Age 25+N	40	45	50	55	60	65	70
l_{25+N}/l_{25}	0.965	0.947	0.914	0.864	0.797	0.714	0.609
−Apha	0.889	0.869	0.783	0.701	0.651	0.648	0.666
Implied e_{15}*	57.0	56.7	55.5	54.3	53.6	53.5	53.8
Years before census	6.1	7.8	9.4	10.8	12.1	12.9	13.0
Date	89.9	88.2	86.6	85.2	83.9	83.1	83.0
$M = 28.2$							
Colored							
Proportion with mother alive	0.971	0.949	0.904	0.844	0.761	0.669	0.556
Central age	15	20	25	30	35	40	45
Age 25+N	40	45	50	55	60	65	70
l_{25+N}/l_{25}	0.969	0.952	0.916	0.869	0.796	0.715	0.606
−Apha	0.953	0.925	0.793	0.728	0.647	0.652	0.660
Implied e_{15}*	57.9	57.5	55.7	54.7	53.5	53.6	53.7
Years before census	5.8	7.5	9.1	10.5	11.8	12.8	14.1
Date	90.2	88.5	86.9	85.5	84.2	83.2	81.9
$M = 29.8$							
Indian/Asian							
Proportion with mother alive	0.984	0.971	0.943	0.891	0.802	0.692	0.559

Central age	15	20	25	30	35	40	45
Age 25+N	40	45	50	55	60	65	70
l_{25+N}/l_{25}	0.983	0.974	0.954	0.919	0.845	0.749	0.616
–Alpha	1.274	1.247	1.136	1.016	0.834	0.747	0.684
Implied e_{15}*	61.8	61.5	60.2	58.7	56.3	55.0	54.1
Years before census	5.8	7.4	8.9	10.2	11.5	12.5	14.1
Date	90.2	88.6	87.1	85.8	84.5	83.5	81.9
$M = 29.9$							
White							
Proportion with mother alive	0.986	0.976	0.956	0.926	0.878	0.809	0.708
Central age	15	20	25	30	35	40	45
Age 25+N	40	45	50	55	60	65	70
l_{25+N}/l_{25}	0.983	0.973	0.953	0.923	0.876	0.802	0.691
–Alpha	1.282	1.230	1.125	1.046	0.974	0.914	0.866
Implied e_{15}*	61.9	61.3	60.1	59.1	58.2	57.4	—
Years before census	6.2	7.9	9.4	10.8	11.8	12.4	—
Date	89.8	88.1	86.6	85.2	84.2	83.6	—
$M = 26.9$							

Source: Computed from the 1996 South African Population Census microdata.

Note: *e_{15} is based on a one-parameter logit system and is therefore only roughly indicative. It is more appropriate to estimate life expectancies based on a two-parameter system as in Table 4.7.

Figure 4.2   **Trend in Adult Female Mortality (Female Respondents) by Population Group Based on the 1996 Census**

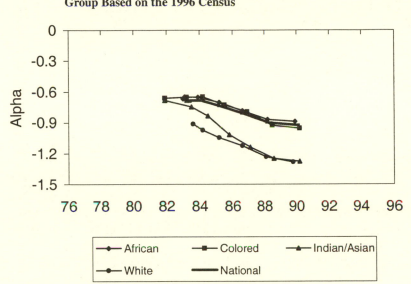

Source: 1996 South African Population Census.

As a further means of evaluating the consistency of the levels and trends, they were combined with those for childhood mortality in each population group (see Appendices 4.1–4.4).

Africans

Between 1984 and 1990, the trend among Africans in adult female mortality derived from the 1996 census was steeper than that derived from the 1995 survey. It is probable that the steeper trend derived from the former is due to underreporting of dead mothers by younger persons. In general, the trend based on the 1995 survey was similar to the trend in childhood mortality derived from the 1996 census. Both the 1995 survey and the 1996 census suggest that, among Africans, adult female mortality is relatively lower than childhood mortality.

Coloreds

The decline in adult female mortality derived from the 1996 census among Coloreds was broadly similar to the decline in childhood mortality during the period 1982–85, but thereafter, the apparent decline was steeper in adult females than in childhood mortality. The steeper decline in the more recent period in adult female mortality is probably due to the same reasons noted for Africans. It appears that the 1995 survey exaggerated the decline in adult female mortality among Coloreds.

Indians/Asians

The trend in adult female mortality among Indians/Asians prior to 1985 derived from the 1995 survey was consistent with that derived from the 1996 census but showed a steeper trend than for childhood mortality. Why this would be the case is rather puzzling. Furthermore, while the 1995 survey indicated rising adult female mortality after 1985, the 1996 census indicated the opposite. This is unusual, given the findings from various studies on mortality trends throughout the world.

Child survival is usually sensitive to socioeconomic conditions and health intervention programs in a population. Though controversial, the impact of the malaria eradication program and socioeconomic development on the general mortality level and childhood mortality, in particular, in Sri Lanka is well documented (see Frederickson 1960; Gray 1974; Meegama 1969; Newman 1970). Changes in maternal and child mortality in a ten-year period attributable to health and nutritional interventions in some Gambian villages are other examples of the sensitivity of child survival to health intervention programs (see Lamb et al. 1984). During the 1950s and 1970s in the more developed countries, the United Nations (1982) observed that generally, the greatest declines in mortality were in the youngest age groups. In view of these findings, and because health intervention programs usually tend to focus more on children than adults, the steep decline in adult female compared to childhood mortality among South African Indians/Asians is rather peculiar.

Whites

The 1995 survey and the 1996 census suggest a sharp decline in adult female mortality among Whites between 1983 and 1985. The 1996 census, for example (though less marked than the 1995 survey), suggests a gain in e_{15} of nearly two years in about one and a half years. The accuracy of a gain of such magnitude is doubtful.

Levels and Trends in Adult Male Mortality by Population Group

Both the 1995 OHS and the 1996 census indicate somewhat similar differences in the levels of adult male mortality among the population groups (see Appendices 4.5 and 4.6). Not surprisingly, the reported levels are highest among Africans and least among Whites. While the trends derived from the 1996 census indicated a decline in mortality in the 1980s among all population groups, those derived from the 1995 survey indicated an increase in mortality in the 1980s among Africans and Coloreds. In a study estimating the levels and trends of adult male mortality at the national level, Udjo (1997a) drew attention to two explanations proffered for the high level and rising trend in adult male mortality—violence and HIV/AIDS. The first reported HIV/AIDS case in South Africa was in 1981. Given the epidemiology of the virus, especially with regard to the incubation period, it is doubtful whether HIV/AIDS would have had a substantial impact on adult male mortality as far back as the early 1980s in the country. The rising trend in adult male mortality among Africans and Coloreds derived from the 1995 survey is probably due to overreporting (by the younger respondents) of fathers as dead when in fact they were alive.

Internal and External Consistency of the Levels and Trends in Adult Male Mortality

The reported levels of adult male mortality in the population groups appear too high. At face value, implied life expectancies after age 15 (e_{15}s) derived from the 1996 census give the impression that the level of adult male mortality among Africans in the 1980s was similar to the level among adult males in Lesotho in the 1960s (Table 4.3). This is unlikely, though Timeaus (2001), commenting on these results in a workshop, argues that Lesotho was probably safer in the 1960s than South Africa in the 1980s. The implied life expectancies after age 15 derived from the 1995 survey showed similar levels.

As a further means of evaluating the reports of living fathers in the 1996 census, the levels and trends derived from the 1996 census were compared with the levels and trends in childhood and adult female mortality in each population group (see Appendices 4.7–4.10).

The levels for adult male mortality were much higher than those for child and adult female mortality. The levels for adult males *should* be higher than those for adult females; however, the disparity between the two is probably exaggerated due to errors in reports on the survivorship of parents. Reporting errors in the survivorship of parents appear to result in overreports of maternal survival and underreports of paternal survival. In the case of the survivorship of mothers, the errors appear to be largely due to the "adoption effect," which is common in survivorship reports in African censuses and surveys. In the South African context, Mandela has noted that "In African culture. . . We do not make the same distinctions among relations practiced by Whites. We have no half-brothers or half-sisters. My mother's sister is my mother; my uncle's son is my brother; *my brother's child is my son, my daughter*" (1994: 9, emphasis added).

Table 4.3

Adult Male Mortality in South Africa and Lesotho

South Africa
African

Year	1989.9	1986.7	1984.6	1982.4	1980.8
−Alpha	0.159	0.142	0.098	0.047	0.068
Implied e_{15}	45.7	45.4	44.7	43.9	44.2

Colored

Year	1989.1	1987.1	1985.1	1983.1	1981.7
−Alpha	0.491	0.424	0.339	0.250	0.220
Implied e_{15}	51.1	50.0	48.6	47.2	46.7

Indian/Asian

Year	1989.6	1987.7	1985.9	1984.0	1982.6
−Alpha	0.693	0.612	0.491	0.358	0.259
Implied e_{15}	54.2	53.0	51.0	48.9	47.3

White

Year	1988.9	1987.0	1985.3	1983.7	1982.5
−Alpha	0.879	0.795	0.702	0.590	0.493
Implied e_{15}	56.9	55.7	54.3	52.6	51.1

Lesotho

Year		1969	1967.1	1965.2
−Alpha		0.067	0.081	0.098
Implied e_{15}		44.3	44.6	44.8

Sources: For South Africa: 1996 South African Population Census; for Lesotho: I. Timaeus, "Mortality in Lesotho: A study of levels, trends, and differentials based on retrospective survey data." *World Fertility Survey Scientific Reports*, no. 59 (1984).

Regarding the survivorship of fathers, the errors may be due to the "absentee effect" (i.e., a father was alive at the time of the census/survey but was reported as dead either because the respondent had never seen him or because he had not actively played the role of a father). While the adoption effect biases maternal orphanhood estimates downward, the "absentee effect" biases paternal orphanhood estimates upward. This may have contributed to the exaggeration of the disparities in the paternal and maternal orphanhood estimates. The next section integrates the childhood and orphanhood estimates by means of life tables. The life table is one way of summarizing the mortality experience of a cohort (Preston et al. 2001). The parameters used in generating the life tables presented below were derived from the results of the analysis presented above.

Female Life Tables by Population Group

The weakness of one-parameter life tables (i.e., life tables based solely on either childhood or adult mortality) has long been recognized (see Blacker 1977).

Table 4.4

Estimated Period Parameters of the Female Logit Life Table by Population Group

	Year						
	1996	1995	1990	1985	1980	1975	1970
African							
−Alpha	0.676	0.676	0.675	0.614	0.554	0.493	0.432
Beta	0.777	0.777	0.823	0.824	0.827	0.828	0.831
Colored							
−Alpha	0.791	0.791	0.793	0.727	0.660	0.594	0.528
Beta	0.966	0.966	1.040	1.039	1.039	1.038	1.038
Indian/Asian							
−Alpha	0.853	0.853	0.830	0.799	0.769	0.738	0.707
Beta	1.034	1.034	1.025	1.025	1.026	1.025	1.025
White							
−Alpha	1.190	1.190	1.222	1.192	1.162	1.132	1.102
Beta	0.972	0.972	1.076	1.076	1.076	1.076	1.076

Sources: 1995 October Household Survey, 1996 South African Population Census.

According to Brass, "a single parameter is not normally enough to describe the variation in mortality that is found in different populations" (1971). In view of this, it is now common practice to construct life tables based on two parameters using the Brass logit system. Three- and four- parameter models have also been developed as a result of the rather poor fit of a two-parameter model at certain ages in some populations. However, these have not been as widely applied as the two-parameter models in mortality analysis. The female life tables described in the next section using the Brass two-parameter logit system are based on the more reliable parts of the data as noted in the analysis above.

The child survival question in the 1996 census was not split by sex. A splitting factor of $\alpha = 0.18$ was applied to separate the estimates of childhood mortality by sex among Africans, Coloreds, and Indians/Asians (see Udjo 1995 for details). In the case of Whites, a splitting factor of $\alpha = 0.288$ was used. This is based on the male–female difference in e_0 of eight years estimated for Europe in 1998 by the Population Reference Bureau (PRB 1998). The estimated parameters of the logit system for quinquennial periods for females are shown in Table 4.4, and the resulting life tables are summarized in Table 4.5 (see Udjo 1991, 1995 for details of the procedure). Because of the poor quality of the data, meaningful life tables could not be constructed for males.

The results presented in Table 4.4 reinforce some of the observations from the previous section, such as a moderate level of mortality among African and Colored females, a low level of mortality among White females, and an intermediate level among Indian/Asian females. High female childhood mortality relative to adult female mortality among Africans, and a similar pattern among Coloreds up to 1990 (β values are less than 1) are also observed. Indians/ Asians and Whites also have low female childhood mortality relative to adult female mortality. Lastly, a similar pattern exists among Coloreds after 1990 (β values are greater than 1) as well.

Table 4.5 suggests that mortality in the first five years of life ($_5q_0$) among females in the population groups has increased slightly in recent years, except among Indians/Asians. The estimated infant mortality rates in 1996 range between seventeen per thousand female live births (among Whites) and fifty-two per thousand female live births (among Africans). According to the results of the models, although White females have a higher life expectancy at birth compared to the other population groups, they had the least gain in life expectancy at birth over the years.

Regional Patterns of Female Mortality

Using the methods described above, the patterns of female mortality were also examined by province by combining the information from the 1996 census with that from the 1998 OHS. The highlights of the results are given below.

The childhood mortality levels derived from the 1998 OHS are consistently lower than those derived from the 1996 census in each province. This is probably due to higher levels of underreporting of childhood deaths in the 1998 OHS. It could also be due to larger scale reporting of stillbirths as live births in the 1996 census.

Two distinct patterns emerge from the estimates derived from the 1996 census. First, the Eastern Cape Province appears to have the highest level of childhood mortality over time, while the Western Cape has the lowest. Second, childhood mortality levels appear to have been on the increase in all provinces since the 1990s (see Figure 4.3). With the exception of Mpumalanga and KwaZulu-Natal, this trend was also evident from the 1998 survey (graph not shown).

Regarding female adult mortality, both the 1996 census and 1998 OHS gave somewhat similar results on a substantial number of data points. By definition, the 1998 survey provides more current information; hence we will examine only the results derived from this data set.

Similar to the trend in childhood mortality, the results suggest that the level of adult female mortality has also been rising since the 1990s in most provinces except Gauteng, Eastern Cape, and Northern Cape. An overall picture of current levels of female mortality in the provinces was obtained by combining the childhood and adult female mortality information from the 1996 census and 1998 survey, respectively, based on the most recent data

Table 4.5

Estimated Period Indices of Female Mortality by Population Group

Year	1996	1995	1990	1985	1980	1975	1970
African							
$_1q_0$	0.052	0.052	0.048	0.054	0.060	0.067	0.074
$_4q_1$	0.037	0.037	0.037	0.041	0.046	0.052	0.058
$_5q_0$	0.086	0.086	0.081	0.091	0.101	0.113	0.125
e_{15}	56.8	56.8	56.2	55.3	54.3	53.3	52.3
q_0	64.6	64.6	64.3	62.7	61.0	59.3	57.5
Colored							
$_1q_0$	0.029	0.029	0.025	0.029	0.033	0.037	0.042
$_4q_1$	0.028	0.028	0.026	0.030	0.034	0.039	0.044
$_5q_0$	0.055	0.055	0.050	0.057	0.065	0.073	0.083
e_{15}	56.0	56.0	55.2	54.3	53.3	52.2	51.2
e_0	66.2	66.2	65.8	64.3	62.8	61.1	59.5
Indian/Asian							
$_1q_0$	0.029	0.029	0.031	0.033	0.035	0.037	0.039
$_4q_1$	0.021	0.021	0.023	0.024	0.025	0.027	0.029
$_5q_0$	0.050	0.050	0.052	0.056	0.059	0.062	0.066
e_{15}	56.1	56.1	55.9	55.3	55.0	54.6	54.1
e_0	67.1	67.1	66.7	66.0	65.3	64.6	63.9
White							
$_1q_0$	0.017	0.017	0.013	0.014	0.015	0.016	0.017
$_4q_1$	0.011	0.011	0.010	0.011	0.012	0.012	0.013
$_5q_0$	0.028	0.028	0.023	0.025	0.026	0.028	0.029
e_{15}	61.1	61.1	60.4	60.1	59.7	59.4	59.0
e_0	73.7	73.7	73.4	72.9	72.5	72.0	71.5
National							
$_1q_0$	0.051	0.051	0.050	0.055	0.061	0.067	0.073
$_4q_1$	0.037	0.037	0.039	0.043	0.047	0.052	0.057
$_5q_0$	0.084	0.084	0.086	0.094	0.103	0.113	0.123
e_{15}	56.6	56.6	55.6	54.8	54.0	53.2	52.4
e_0	64.5	64.5	63.4	62.0	60.6	59.1	57.6

Sources: Computed from 1995 October Household Survey, 1996 South African Population Census. National level estimates compiled from Udjo 1998.

points (except for Limpopo and Northern Cape, in the case of adult female mortality). For these two provinces, other data points were used because of the unlikely levels of adult female mortality implied by the most recent data points. This procedure enabled the construction of two-parameter logit life tables for the female population in each province.

The estimated parameters and summary indices of the logit life tables are shown in Tables 4.6 and 4.7. Figure 4.4 illustrates the implied infant mortality rates. The graph suggests that the Eastern Cape and the Free State currently

Figure 4.3   **Trend in Childhood Mortality by Province from the 1996 Census**

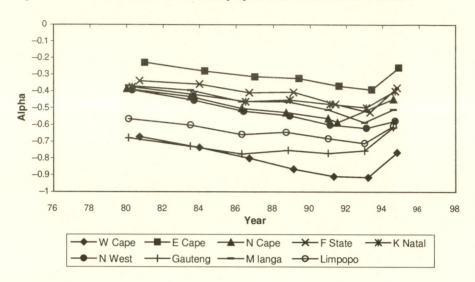

Source: 1996 South African Population Census.

have the highest female infant mortality rates (eighty-three and sixty-four per thousand, respectively). The Western Cape has the lowest level (thirty per thousand). Thus, there appears to be a large disparity in infant mortality levels by province in South Africa.

Discussion

In the absence of complete coverage of vital registration, larger problems are often encountered in the estimation of mortality than in fertility estimation from censuses and surveys in sub-Saharan Africa. The analysis in this study highlights this general problem. Omission of dead children in the report on survivorship of children tends to be greater than omission of births, because usually there is greater unwillingness to talk about the dead. Estimates of childhood mortality derived directly from the birth histories of the 1995 survey compared with those indirectly estimated from the 1996 census suggest that the unwillingness to talk about the dead was more marked in the 1995 survey than in the 1996 census.

In the present study, varying degrees of error in the reporting of dead children may have confounded disparities in childhood mortality levels across population groups and provinces. Varying degrees of the "adoption effect" may also have confounded these results. The paternal orphanhood reports were largely unusable, perhaps due to the father "absentee effect." In view of

Figure 4.4   **Estimated Female Infant Mortality Rate per Thousand Live Births by Province, 1996**

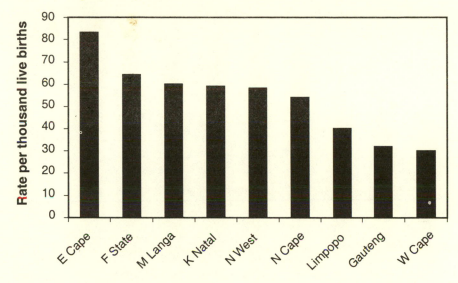

Sources: 1996 South African Population Census; 1998 October Household Survey.

Figure 4.5   **HIV Prevalence Among Women Attending Antenatal Clinics in 2000 and Among Adults 15–49 in 2000**

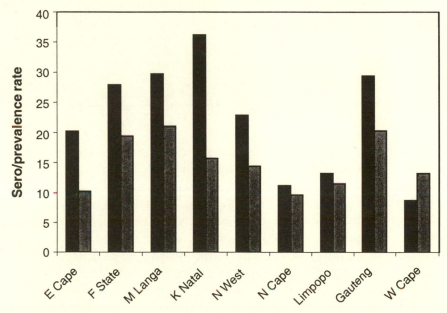

Sources: Department of Health 1999; Shisana and Simbayi 2002.

Table 4.6

Estimated Parameters of the Logit Life Table by Province, 1996

	α	β
Western Cape	−0.794	0.950
Eastern Cape	−0.532	0.673
Northern Cape	−0.553	0.880
Free State	−0.590	0.751
KwaZulu-Natal	−0.612	0.773
North West	−0.650	0.743
Gauteng	−0.879	0.830
Mpumalanga	−0.609	0.767
Limpopo	−0.764	0.833

Sources: 1996 South African Population Census, 1998 October Household Survey.

Table 4.7

Summary Indices of Two-Parameter Female Life Table by Province, 1996

	$_1q_0$	$_4q_1$	$_5q_0$	e_{15}	e_0
Western Cape	0.030	0.028	0.056	56.3	66.4
Eastern Cape	0.083	0.049	0.126	56.4	61.2
Northern Cape	0.054	0.045	0.095	53.6	60.8
Free State	0.064	0.044	0.104	56.0	62.4
KwaZulu-Natal	0.059	0.042	0.097	56.0	63.0
North West	0.058	0.039	0.094	57.0	64.1
Gauteng	0.032	0.025	0.055	59.0	69.0
Mpumalanga	0.060	0.042	0.098	56.0	63.0
Limpopo	0.040	0.031	0.068	57.3	66.4

Sources: 1996 South African Population Census, 1998 October Household Survey.

this, the estimates presented in this study are to be regarded as roughly indicative of levels and trends in mortality in South Africa.

In spite of these concerns, a number of tentative statements can be made from the results of this study. First, childhood mortality among Africans is probably twice the level found among other population groups. Among other factors, the disparity in childhood mortality should also be viewed within the context of the different levels of fertility among the population groups. Second, even after adjusting for atypical levels of childhood mortality among the younger women (ages 15 to 29), it appears that childhood mortality levels have increased in recent years across all population groups. Without providing strong evidence, a number of discussions adduce the rising trend (in recent years) to HIV/AIDS. Presumably, a large proportion of infant deaths due to AIDS would have resulted from mother-to-child transmission. If that was the case, the childhood mortality pattern by population group as well as by region should be similar to that of HIV/AIDS prevalence if other factors were not at play. As can be seen from a rough comparison, the infant mortality rate and HIV prevalence by region have different patterns (see Figures 4.4 and 4.5). Furthermore, the correlation is very weak ($r = 0.318$, in the case of infant mortality and HIV prevalence among women attending antenatal clinics; $r = -0.140$ in the case of infant mortality and adult HIV prevalence). Also, without controlling for other factors, antenatal sero-prevalence suggests that only about 10 percent of the differences in infant mortality in the provinces are explained by differences in HIV prevalence in the provinces (see r^2 values in Appendices 4.11 and 4.12). These rough comparisons and simple linear regressions suggest that other factors may also be at play in the rise in infant mortality rates in recent years and that this area requires further research. Third, adult female mortality is higher among Africans and Coloreds compared to the other population groups. The disparity may be connected with fertility variables among the population groups. Pregnancy-related deaths are a major component of adult female mortality in many parts of sub-Saharan Africa. Besides health services factors like the differential uptake of antenatal care, the impact of teenage pregnancy and parity on maternal mortality and other aspects of adult female mortality across the population groups need to be investigated. At the regional level, adult female mortality levels appear to have increased in the 1990s.

Deducing from the large population group and regional disparities in the levels of mortality, Africans and those living in provinces such as the Eastern Cape and the Free State are the most vulnerable. Interventions to reduce disparities in mortality in the population groups and across regions should therefore focus on these areas. There is uncertainty regarding the levels of adult male mortality, and further research is needed in this regard.

Note

The author gratefully acknowledges the financial support provided by the African Census Analysis Project at the University of Pennsylvania through its fellowship program and wishes to thank Statistics South Africa for allowing the author to utilize the fellowships while in its employ. The author also wishes to thank the Human Sciences Research Council, Pretoria, for permitting him to be away from work to take up a third fellowship from the University of Pennsylvania, only one month after being in its employ, to enable him to complete this study. The views expressed in this paper are those of this author and do not necessarily reflect those of Statistics South Africa, the African Census Analysis Project, or the Human Sciences Research Council.

References

Bamgboye, E.A. 1982. "The time location of reports of survivorship: Estimates for maternal and paternal orphanhood and the ever-widowed." Ph.D. thesis, Faculty of Medicine, University of London (London School of Hygiene and Tropical Medicine).

Blacker, J.G.C. 1977. "The estimation of adult mortality in Africa from data on orphanhood." *Population Studies* 31(1): 107–28.

Blacker, J., A.G. Hill, and I. Timaeus. 1985. "Age patterns of mortality in Africa: An examination of recent evidence." Paper presented at the IUSSP conference, Florence.

Brass, W. 1971. "Methods for estimating fertility and mortality from limited and defective data." Occasional Publication of the laboratory for Population Statistics, The University of North Carolina at Chapel Hill.

———. 1985. "Advances in methods for estimating fertility and mortality from limited and defective data." Occasional Publication, Center for Population Studies, London School of Hygiene and Tropical Medicine.

Brass, W., and E.A. Bamgboye. 1981. "The time location of reports of survivorship: Estimates for maternal and paternal orphanhood and the ever-widowed." Centre for Population Studies Working Paper No. 81–1, London School of Hygiene and Tropical Medicine.

Burgard, S. 2002. "Does race matter? Children's height in Brazil and South Africa." *Demography* 39(4): 763–90.

Department of Health. 1999. *South Africa Demographic and Health Survey, 1998: Preliminary Report*. Pretoria: Department of Health.

Fernandez, C.R.E. 1985. "The influence of differentials in child mortality by age of mother, birth order and birth spacing on indirect estimation methods." Ph.D. thesis, Faculty of Medicine, University of London (London School of Hygiene and Tropical Medicine).

———. 1989. "The effects of maternal age, birth order and birth spacing on indirect estimation of child mortality." In *Proceedings of the International Population Conference New Delhi*. Liege: IUSSP, Vol. 2, 65-86.

Frederickson, H. 1960. "Malaria control and population pressure in Ceylon." *Public Health Reports* 76(8): 659–63.

Gray, R.H. 1974. "The decline of mortality in Ceylon and the demographic effects of malaria control." *Population Studies* 28(2): 205–29.

Hill, K. 1977. "Estimating adult mortality levels from information on widowhood." *Population Studies* 31: 75–84.

Hirschowitz, R., and M. Orkin. 1996. *Living in South Africa: Selected Findings of the 1995 October Household Survey*. Pretoria: Central Statistics Service (Statistics South Africa).

Lamb, W.H., F.A. Ford, C.M. Lamb, and R.G. Whitehead. 1984. "Changes in maternal and child mortality rates in three isolated Gambian villages over ten years." *The Lancet* (October) 20: 912–13.

Mandela, N.R. 1994. *The Long Walk to Freedom*. Transvaal, South Africa: Macdonald Purnell.

Meegama, S.A. 1969. "Malaria eradication and its effects on mortality levels." *Population Studies* 23(2): 305–6.

Newman, P. 1970. "Malaria control and population growth." *Journal of Development Studies* 6 (2): 133–58.

Population Reference Bureau. 1998. *World Population Data Sheet*. Washington DC: Population Reference Bureau.

Preston, S.H., P. Heuveline, and M. Guillot. 2001. *Demography: Measuring and Modeling Population Processes*. Oxford: Blackwell.

Rutstein, S.O. 1983. "Infant and child mortality: Levels, trends and demographic differentials." *World Fertility Survey Comparative Studies*, no. 24. Voorburg: International Statistical Institute.

Shisana, O., and L. Simbayi. 2002. "South African national HIV prevalence, behavioural risks and mass media household survey 2002." In *Nelson Mandela/HSRC Study of HIV/AIDS*, Cape Town: Human Sciences Research Council.

Statistics South Africa. 1998. *The People of South Africa Population Census, 1996: The Count and How It Was Done*. Pretoria: Statistics South Africa.

Timaeus, I. 1984. "Mortality in Lesotho: A study of levels, trends and differentials based on retrospective survey data." *World Fertility Survey Scientific Reports*, no. 59.

———. 2001. "Comment on Udjo's four-race model of mortality in South Africa." Fourth African Census Analysis Project (ACAP) Workshop, Dakar, Senegal, January 15–17.

Udjo, E.O. 1987. "Levels and trends in infant and child mortality among some Kanuri of northeast Nigeria." *Journal of Tropical Pediatrics* 33(1): 43–47.

———. 1991. "Adult mortality from information on orphanhood and widowhood among Nigeria's Kanuri." *Journal of Biosocial Science* 23(2): 155–65.

———. 1995. "Childhood and adult mortality patterns in Botswana." In *1991 Population and Housing Census Dissemination Seminar*, 131–43. Republic of Botswana: Central Statistics Office.

———. 1996. "Child survival, health and family planning interventions and fertility in Zimbabwe." In *Child Survival Health and Family Planning Programmes and Fertility*, 1–96. New York: United Nations.

———. 1997a. *Fertility and Mortality Trends in South Africa: The Evidence from the 1995 October Household Survey, and Implications on Population Projections*. Pretoria: Statistics South Africa.

———. 1997b. "The effect of child survival on fertility in Zimbabwe: A micro-macro levels analysis." *Journal of Tropical Pediatrics* 43(5): 255–66.

———. 1998. *Additional Evidence Regarding Fertility and Mortality Trends in South Africa and Implications for Population Projections*. Pretoria: Statistics South Africa.

———. 1999. "Recent evidence of levels, trends and differentials in fertility in South Africa." Paper presented at the workshop on Fertility in Southern Africa, School of Oriental and African Studies, University of London, September 22–24.

United Nations. 1982. *Levels and Trends of Mortality Since 1950*. New York: United Nations.

———. 1983. *Manual X: Indirect Techniques for Demographic Estimation*. New York: United Nations.

Appendix 4.1   **Trend in Childhood and Adult Female Mortality, African**

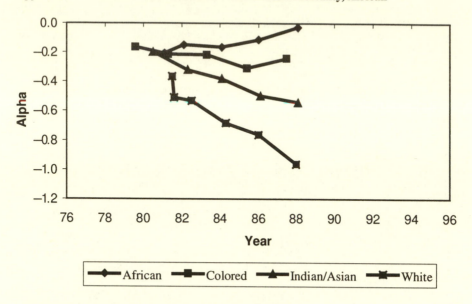

Sources: 1995 October Household Survey and 1996 census.

Appendix 4.2   **Trend in Childhood and Adult Female Mortality, Colored**

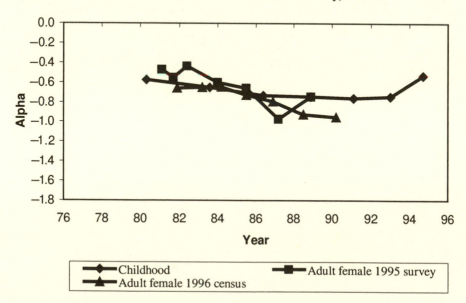

Sources: 1995 October Household Survey and 1996 census.

Appendix 4.3   **Trend in Childhood and Adult Female Mortality, Indian**

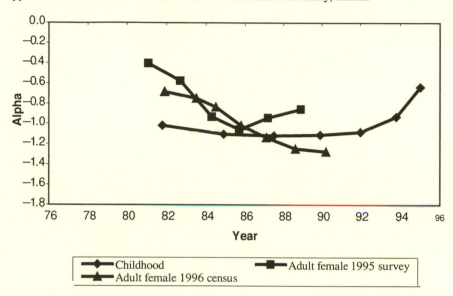

Sources: 1995 October Household Survey and 1996 census.

Appendix 4.4   **Trend in Childhood and Adult Female Mortality, White**

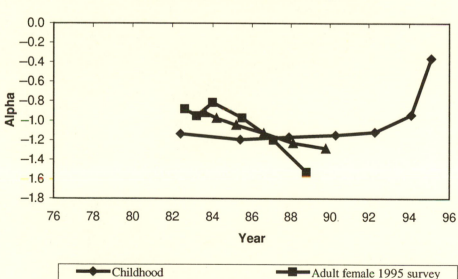

Sources: 1995 October Household Survey and 1996 census.

Appendix 4.5   **Trend in Adult Male Mortality by Population Group Based on the
1995 Survey**

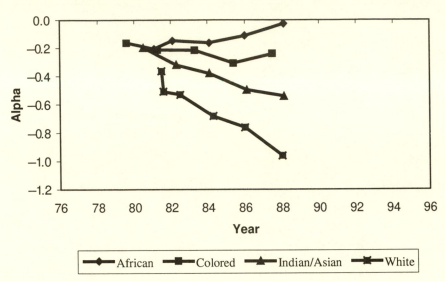

Source: 1995 October Household Survey.

Appendix 4.6   **Trend in Adult Male Mortality by Population Group Based on the
1996 Census**

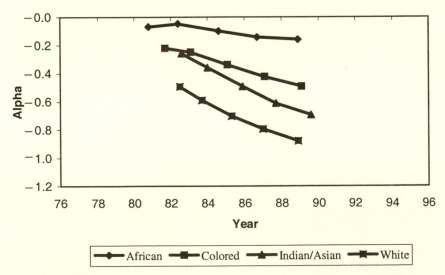

Source: 1996 South African Census.

Appendix 4.7   **Trend in Childhood and Adult Mortality, African**

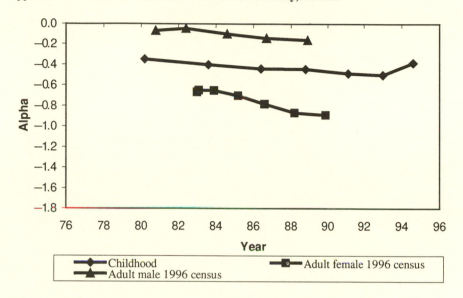

Source: 1996 South African Census.

Appendix 4.8   **Trend in Childhood and Adult Mortality, Colored**

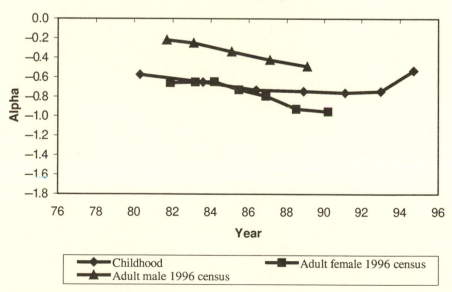

Source: 1996 South African Census.

Appendix 4.9   **Trend in Childhood and Adult Mortality, Indian**

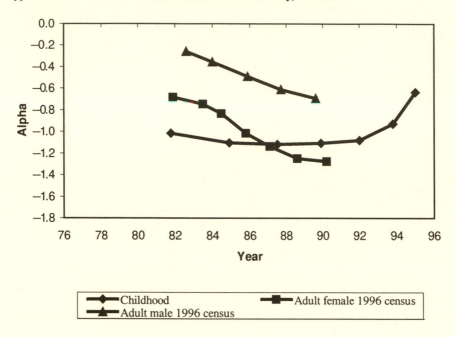

Source: 1996 South African Census.

Appendix 4.10   **Trend in Childhood and Adult Mortality, White**

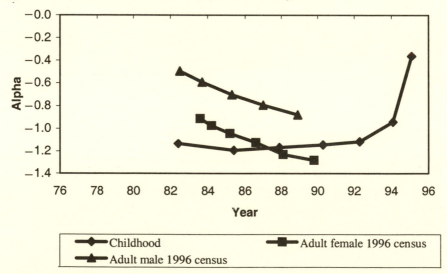

Source: 1996 South African Census.

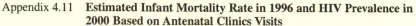

Appendix 4.11   **Estimated Infant Mortality Rate in 1996 and HIV Prevalence in 2000 Based on Antenatal Clinics Visits**

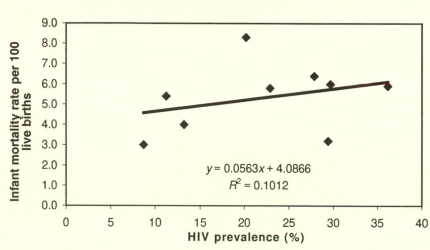

Sources: 1996 South African Census; 1998 October Household Survey; Department of Health 1999.

Appendix 4.12   **Estimated Infant Mortality Rate in 1996 and National HIV Prevalence among Adults Aged 15–49 in 2000**

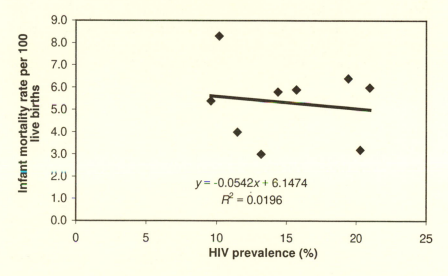

Sources: 1996 South African Census; 1998 October Household Survey; Shisana and Simbayi 2002.

5. HIV/AIDS in Light of Death Registration Data

In Search of Elusive Estimates

Sulaiman Bah

Rather than viewing vital registration data as being dichotomous (available or not available), it is best to view them as being continuous and improving incrementally. At any point in time, a combination of factors, ranging from the degree of completeness to the quality of the data and the kind of data available, determines how the vital registration data can shed light on specific causes of death, in particular, HIV/AIDS. Quantification of deaths due to HIV/AIDS is a crucial issue in South Africa today. The basic question we address in this chapter is, How much of the observed increase in deaths between 1997 and 2000 can be accounted for by HIV/AIDS? Our answer involves looking at three real-life situations with respect to death registration data in South Africa and discussing the estimation of deaths due to HIV/AIDS in those contexts. In the first situation, full national data on causes of death were available for 1996, and death data without cause of death breakdown were available from 1997 to 2000. In the second situation, the same data were available; however, in addition, there was a limited cause breakdown of the death data into natural and unnatural deaths. In the third situation, causes of death data were available based on a sample of all registered deaths from 1997 to 2001. What are some of the options for estimating deaths due to HIV/AIDS in these three different situations? What are the drawbacks and possible sources of error in the different methods employed? We will address these methodological issues below.

The Production of Death Registration Data

The basic source of data for official death statistics is the death notification form and its accompanying medical certificate. A minimal set of information from these forms is captured at the offices of the Department of Home Affairs (DHA), and this information is subsequently transferred to the population register, which is updated daily. After information from the death notification forms has been captured, the forms are sent to the headquarters of the DHA in Pretoria for microfilming and verification. In the old system (pre-2002), hard copies of the forms were sent to Statistics South Africa (Stats SA) for processing only after the microfilming and verification were completed. Under this arrangement, the detailed death data published by Stats SA lagged considerably behind the deaths data on the population register. Hence, by early 2002, the latest year for which cause-of-death data were available for South Africa was 1996. This process of acquiring death registration forms from the DHA was drastically revised in 2002. Under the new arrangement, the DHA would send Stats SA rolls of microfilm containing the forms, and Stats SA would scan the images and print copies of the death notification form (without waiting for the verified hard copies). In this way, Stats SA saved processing time and was able to publish in December 2002 cause-of-death data based on a 15 percent sample of rolls of microfilm prepared between January 1997 and April 2002.

The two sets of national death data available in South Africa are (a) detailed death data extracted from the death notification forms and their accompanying medical certificate with respect to death (captured at Stats SA) and (b) the minimum set of information from these forms (captured at the offices of the DHA), which is subsequently transferred to the population register (with daily updating), but only for those with identity numbers.

Premises Underlying the Methods Used

The methods used in situations one and two, where current data on causes of death are unavailable, but data on overall mortality and older data on causes of death are available, are based on two premises. The first premise is that there is inherent regularity in patterns and trends in causes of death that could be exploited. This premise is supported by three explanations. First, in the absence of sudden epidemic outbreaks, there is a relation between the number of deaths due to specific causes from one year to the next. Second, cause-of-death structures change regularly (either rapidly or slowly) over time rather than suddenly. Third, because of the phenomenon of competing risks, reduction due to deaths by one cause or group of causes of deaths are accompanied by a rise in another cause or group of causes of deaths. Examples of a few demographic studies on trends in causes of death can be found in the works of Preston (1972), for European and "overseas European" populations, and of Palloni and Wyrick (1981), for Latin America. Examples of exploitation of the regularity in the change in cause-of-death structure can be found in the works of Lopez and Hull (1983), Hakulinen et al. (1986), and Murray and Lopez (1994). As part of this exploitation, it is possible to use trend data to make short-term projections regarding causes of death. While these observations hold largely true in the short run, they cannot be used as the basis for making long-term projections. Studies on time series of causes of death have shown that, in many instances, deaths due to specific causes (those easily responsive to interventions) have manifested reversals in their trends in the long run.

The second basic premise is that with two or more interrelated sets of information or sources of data, it is possible to impose "checks and balances" in the analysis to arrive at meaningful conclusions. As the research problem and the available data vary widely, there is no standardized way of imposing these checks and balances. In this case, we adopt a two-step procedure for using the two interrelated data sets. Our first step is to validate the "new" population register data (DHA data), and our second step is to standardize it to the full death data set (Stats SA data) for the same reference year (1996). The validation will help establish the viability of the DHA data for further analysis, while the standardization will help make the two data sets comparable. Once comparison factors for 1996 have been obtained for any reference group, they can be applied to the 1997 to 2000 data set from the population register to get standardized values for the same reference groups.

Hence, values of Stats SA registered deaths in the age group i, D_i^{st}, for year t, $D_i^{st,t}$, are estimated as follows:

$$D_i^{st,t} = D_i^{pr,t} * g_i^{1996}$$

where, g_i^{1996} is the age-specific ratio of deaths in the Stats SA data to that in the population register for the 1996 base year; $D_i^{pr,t}$ is the total number of deaths in the age group i for year t, as obtained from the population register. With this standardization, it would be possible to compare Stats SA data for 1996 (or even from 1990 to 1996) with the adjusted DHA data from 1997 to 2000.

Estimating Deaths Due to HIV/AIDS Using Death Data and Limited Data on Causes of Death

The methodological core for handling situations one and two is based on the approach of grouping and projecting. The practice of grouping discrete categories to form a broader group is a common practice in demography. This is done not only for reasons of parsimony, but also for the purpose of minimizing the effect of misreporting (with the assumption that the misreported event would still lie within the broader group). For the years for which we have detailed data on causes of death (1996 and earlier), we group together all causes of death that are coded as HIV/AIDS and all those that may be associated with HIV/AIDS to form the group of HIV/AIDS and possible HIV/AIDS-related causes of deaths (ARC). The grouped causes of death (for only 1996 or for the available years) are then used to make short-term projections for the years for which detailed data on causes of death are not yet available (1997–2000).

There are two difficulties faced in this grouping exercise. The first difficulty is agreeing on which causes of death comprise these "possible HIV/AIDS-related causes of death." The second is determining what proportion of these causes of death are actually due to HIV/AIDS. The first problem is much easier to solve than the second one. However, even in this case, the solution is not straightforward. Even though there are several clinical definitions of AIDS in Africa (for example, the Bangui major/minor criteria, the Bangui scoring system, the WHO clinical definition, the Lesbordes scoring system, and the Pallangyo definition), most or all of them were developed to help clinicians rapidly diagnose HIV/AIDS as the cause of death (Bélec et al. 1994). Some of the definitions use diagnostic criteria such as weight loss or chronic fatigue, which are not written in the death notification forms as "causes of death." Therefore, once the underlying cause of death has been written and coded, the opportunity to use diagnostic information is lost. However, in the case where multiple causes of death have been listed, the diagnostic information is retrievable to a large extent. In the case of South Africa, the data available up to 1996 were all coded based on the concept of identifying the single underlying cause of death obtained from either the list of causes on the death notification forms or from the underlying cause as stated by the physician. Under these circumstances, decisions have to be made as to how to arrive at a list to use for defining "possible HIV/AIDS-related causes of death." An existing list could be used, or one could be developed. The scientific basis for using a validated list is much stronger than using a list that is yet to be tested and validated.

One established list for identifying causes of death associated with HIV is that based on the Center for Disease Control and Prevention's (CDC) 1993 definition of HIV/AIDS. That definition categorizes adolescents and adults as asymptomatic (category A), symptomatic with conditions attributable to HIV (category B), and true AIDS (category C) (Beers and Berkow 1999). The list is reproduced with permission in Appendix 5.1. The conditions in categories

B and C and the causes of death that closely match those conditions are listed in Appendix 5.2. While the CDC list is very comprehensive, one major problem is its failure to include respiratory tuberculosis and pulmonary tuberculosis. In South Africa there is evidence suggesting that some amount of TB mortality is attributable to HIV/AIDS (Wilkinson and Davies 1997). In a national study of TB mortality and HIV/AIDS, Kleinschmidt singled out the two provinces of KwaZulu-Natal and North West and made the following observations about them:

> The very sharp increases of more than 250 percent in registered TB mortality among younger women in these two provinces would be consistent with an increase in AIDS mortality, with TB falsely recorded on death certificates. (Kleinschmidt 1999: 272)

For this study, the decision was finally made to use two lists for identifying causes of deaths that could be related to HIV/AIDS. One is strictly based on the CDC 1993 definition (shortened as CDC list) and one is based on South African coding experience (shortened as SA list). Senior coders of causes of deaths at Stats SA compiled a list of causes of death that were most often written on the notification of death forms in cases where HIV was involved. The list, given in Appendix 5.3, was verified using the CDC list and the list of causes that emerged from the CDC study "Surveillance for AIDS-defining opportunistic illnesses, 1992–1997" (Jones et al. 1999). Most of the causes in the SA list occurred either in the CDC list or in the CDC surveillance study. Roughly speaking, the CDC list would provide minimum estimates, while the SA list would provide maximum estimates. Leaving aside deaths that are ill-defined and unspecified, one can hypothesize that actual deaths due to HIV/AIDS would be lower than the maximum estimates because a certain percentage of deaths classified as due to these HIV/AIDS-related causes may in fact not be due to HIV/AIDS.

After having formed a subgroup of causes due to and related to HIV/AIDS, we could then proceed to project deaths either with the assistance of an AIDS model (situation one) or without such a model (situation two). These two situations are further elaborated upon in the following sections.

Situation One: Underlying Causes of Death Data for 1996 and from 1997 to 2000

For 1996, death data were available from both Stats SA and the population register. For subsequent years (1997–2000), only death data from the population register were available. In this situation, we adopted the procedure of first using the 1996 death data from Stats SA to break down age and sex among the HIV/AIDS and HIV/AIDS-related causes of deaths. Next, we used the age and sex breakdown in the number of HIV/AIDS and HIV/AIDS-related deaths to estimate such deaths over the period 1997–2000. There were many approaches we could have used. For this case, we chose the approach of estimating the rate of growth of HIV/AIDS cases from the seroprevalence survey data and applied the same rate of growth to the HIV/AIDS and HIV/AIDS-related deaths for 1996. We use the AIDS projection spreadsheet (AIDSproj) from the Futures Group International to obtain estimates of AIDS cases from the seroprevalence data. The model works by fitting a gamma curve on seroprevalence data for as many years as available and making adjustments to infer prevalence for the general population. Details on how this was applied on South African data can be found in Stats SA (2001a). Hence, values of $D^i(x, x+n)$ for the year t, $D_t^i(x, x+n)$, are estimated as follows:

$$D_t^i(x, x+n) = D_{1996}^i(x, x+n)e^{r(t-1996)}$$

where r is the rate of growth of AIDS cases between 1996 and 2000, as obtained from the growth in the number of estimated AIDS cases obtained from AIDSproj.

While this method can yield an estimate of the number of deaths due to HIV/AIDS and HIV/AIDS-related causes, the figures can also be used another way, paying less attention to the absolute numbers and more to their relative effect. Because Stats SA (2001b) had reported on the increase in mortality (bulge) in the adult ages and speculation had emerged about the contribution of deaths due to HIV/AIDS to the observed increases, an attempt could be made to "explain away" the bulge. According to this logic, if HIV/AIDS is fully responsible for the bulge, then its removal should flatten out the curve. Failure of the curve to flatten suggests one of two things: either there are other causes of death contributing to the bulge (countering the claims of "alarmists") or the estimates of deaths due to HIV/AIDS underestimate the true amount of HIV/AIDS and HIV/AIDS-related deaths (proving that the "alarmists" were realists and casting doubt on the methods used to arrive at the estimates).

To estimate deaths due to HIV/AIDS, three sets of age-specific rates and ratios were computed. The first set is for the unadjusted population register (PR) data for the period 1996 to 2000 (PR1), the second is the adjusted PR data for the same set of years (PR2), and the last is the adjusted PR data from which estimated deaths due to HIV/AIDS and all possible HIV/AIDS-related causes have been removed (PR3).

Situation Two: Underlying Causes of Death Data for 1996 and from 1997 to 2000, with Breakdown into Natural and Unnatural Causes of Death

In this second situation (faced from late 2001 to early 2002), underlying cause-of-death data were available for 1996, as in situation one above, but death data from the population register (1997–2000) could further be broken down into natural and unnatural deaths. After having standardized the population register data as outlined above, our first step was to separate unnatural from natural deaths. The natural deaths for the 1990–96 Stats SA data were then separated into HIV/AIDS and other possible HIV/AIDS-related causes and other natural deaths. These numbers were used to make estimates of such deaths in the 1997–2000 adjusted DHA data. Further details are given in the subsections following.

Separating Unnatural Causes of Death from Natural Causes of Death in the DHA Data

Separation of the DHA data into unnatural causes of death and natural deaths was done for several reasons. First, this permits study of the trend in unnatural causes of death and allows us to see to what extent these deaths contribute to the trend in mortality. Second, the unnatural causes of deaths allow for the clear identification of deaths not related to HIV/AIDS. Last, the natural causes of death provide the maximum number of deaths related to HIV/AIDS.

The separation turns out to be relatively simple, if one exploits a slight "twist" in legislation and turns it into a statistical advantage. The Births and Deaths Registration Act, No. 51 of 1992, did not require physicians to state the cause of death if it was due to unnatural causes. This makes the DHA data fairly precise in recording unnatural causes of death, because deaths due to such causes were only recorded as "unnatural causes" or one of its limited variants. In the coding for unnatural causes of deaths, only the following variants (in English and Afrikaans) were considered: "unnatural," "unnatural cause," "unnatural causes," "unnatural death," "onnatuurlike," "onnatuurlik," "onnatuurlike oorsake," "onnatuurlike oosaak," and "onnatuurlike dood." These terms were included on the vast majority of the forms in which unnatural deaths were recorded.

Making Short-Term Projection of Deaths Related to HIV/AIDS

In line with our first basic premise, we fit a parametric function on the reported deaths due to HIV/AIDS and ARC for the years between 1990 and

1996. The parameters of the function were estimated and used to make short-term projections from 1997 to 2000. In line with our second basic premise (i.e., imposing checks and balances), we ensured that the projected deaths due to HIV/AIDS and ARC did not exceed the number of deaths due to natural causes. This was done for ages 15 to 49. This age range was practical for several reasons: the population register data were more useful for ages above 15 than below; for higher ages (e.g., above 60), possible HIV/AIDS-related deaths might have ceased to be HIV/AIDS-related; and these were the working ages for which deaths had more serious economic implications than for outside these ranges.

In mathematical symbols, what we were doing at this third step is as follows. The function fitted to the age-specific deaths due to HIV/AIDS and ARC is of the form

$$y_i = \sum_{j=0}^{n} a_{ij} x^j,$$

while the one fitted to the total deaths in the age group 15–49 is of the form $x' = t' - 1996$

$$y = \sum_{j=0}^{n} a_j x^j$$

where i stands for five-year age groups ($i = 1$ stands for 15–19, $i = 2$ stands for 20–24, etc.), a_{ij} are parameters to be estimated ($j = 0, 1, 2, \ldots n$), and

x is time in years, measured as $x = t - t_0$ where, $1990 < t \leq 1996$ and $t_0 = t_{min} - 1$.

The first estimate of age-specific deaths due to HIV/AIDS and HIV/AIDS-related causes is given by

$$\hat{D}_i^{AIDS} = \sum_{j=0}^{n} \hat{a}_{ij} x'^j$$

where, $\hat{a}_{ij}$ is the estimated parameters and x' is given as $x' = t' - 1996$, where $1996 < t' \leq 2000$.

Similarly, the estimated number of deaths due to HIV/AIDS and HIV/AIDS-related causes in the age group 15–49 is given by

$$\hat{D}^{AIDS} = \sum_{j=0}^{n} \hat{a}_j x'^j$$

where $\hat{a}_j$ is the estimated parameter. In the case where polynomials used in fitting the totals were of different degrees from those used in fitting the sub-components (the five age groups within the 15 to 45 age range), the estimated number of deaths obtained from the subcomponents would not necessarily add up to that obtained from the independent total. In such a case, estimates would need to be revised to reconcile the totals. However, in a case where the polynomial of the same degree consistently fit all the age groups as well as the total, such an adjustment would not be necessary. Another kind of adjustment would be necessary though. This is described in the next subsection.

Using Ex-Post Projections to Adjust Ex-Ante Ones

While it is acceptable to use polynomial functions to make short-term projections, it is preferable that the polynomial function be fitted on a large number of data points before using the parameter estimates to make projections. In some cases (as in this one), increasing the observation points is not a feasible option for various reasons. Death data for the whole of South Africa are only available since the 1994 data set. While the inclusion of the 1993 data set would not cause much distortion, the death data for the early 1990s would need to be adjusted before being used in conjunction with the post-1994 data set to form a consistent time series.

As an alternative to increasing the number of observation points, a strategy of ex-post/ex-ante projection can be gainfully put to use (Ostrom 1990). For the projection period, 1997–2000, one has the recorded number of natural deaths but not the deaths due to HIV/AIDS and ARC. The polynomial models can be fit to the number of natural deaths (1993–96), and projections of these numbers can be compared with the ex-post recorded numbers of natural deaths. The ratios of the two numbers would provide adjustment factors with which to adjust the ex-ante estimates of deaths due to HIV/AIDS and ARC.

The first estimate of the age-specific deaths due to HIV/AIDS and HIV/AIDS-related causes would then be revised as follows:

$$D_i^{AIDS} = \frac{\hat{D}_i^{AIDS}}{c_i}$$

where $c_i = \dfrac{\hat{D}_i^N}{D_i^N}$, $\hat{D}_i^N$ is the estimated number of natural deaths, and D_i^N is the recorded number of natural deaths (adjusted only for missing IDs).

Computing Different Age-Specific Percentages of Deaths

After having separated out total registered deaths into natural and unnatural deaths and, subsequently, the natural deaths into deaths due to HIV/AIDS and ARC and other natural deaths, the following age-specific percentages are computed:

$$p_{1i} = \frac{D_i^{UN}}{D_i} \cdot 100$$

where D_i^{UN} is the number of deaths due to unnatural causes in age group i, and D_i is the total number of deaths occurring in the same age group;

$$p_{2i} = \frac{D_i^{N}}{D_i} \cdot 100$$

where D_i^{N} is the number of deaths due to natural causes in age group i, and

$$(D_i^{N} = D_i - D_i^{UN})$$

$$p_{3i} = \frac{D_i^{AIDS}}{D_i^{N}} \cdot 100$$

where D_i^{AIDS} is the adjusted number of deaths due to HIV/AIDS and ARC in age group i; and

$$p_{4i} = \frac{D_i^{AIDS}}{D_i} \cdot 100$$

All these percentages measure different effects. The first one, p_{1i}, measures the contribution of deaths due to unnatural causes among total registered deaths in each age group. The second one, p_{2i}, measures the contribution of deaths due to natural causes among total deaths in each age group. The third one, p_{3i}, measures the contribution of deaths due to HIV/AIDS and ARC to total natural registered deaths in each age group. The last, p_{4i}, measures the contribution of deaths due to HIV/AIDS and ARC to total registered deaths due to unnatural causes in each age group. As an illustration of the difference between two of these measures, in a situation where deaths due to unnatural causes are much higher than natural deaths, and deaths due to HIV/AIDS and ARC are high, p_{3i} may be high but lower than p_{4i}. If, on the other hand, deaths due to unnatural causes are much lower than natural deaths, but deaths due to HIV/AIDS and ARC are high, then p_{3i} would be close to p_{4i}, and both measures would be high.

Situation Three: Underlying and Multiple Causes of Death Data from 1997 to 2001, Based on a Sample of All Registered Deaths

In contrast to the situations described above, situation three is based on the processing of a 15 percent sample of all rolls of microfilm of death certificates prepared between January 1997 and April 2002. In all, 1,872 rolls were prepared and 281 rolls selected by systematic random sampling after stratifying by year of preparation of rolls. For each selected roll of microfilm, all the death notification forms contained in it were printed, coded for both underlying and multiple causes of death, and captured. From the captured data, causes of death can be grouped as required, and desired percentages can be computed.

Results

Results from Situation One

As mentioned earlier, while for 1996 death data are available from both Stats SA and the population register, for subsequent years only death data from the population register are available. A comparison of the Stats SA and the PR data for the base year 1996 is shown in Table 5.1, and the age-specific numbers of deaths in the table have been plotted in Figures 5.1a and 5.1b for males and females, respectively.

The figures show three features. First, for age groups above 15 to 19, the patterns of the two data sets are similar. Second, for all the age groups, the PR data are consistently lower than those of Stats SA data. Last, for ages below 15, the PR data are considerably lower than those of Stats SA data. The ratio of the Stats SA to the PR data was computed for all age groups. These ratios were used to adjust the PR data to the level of Stats SA data for the period 1997–2000, as shown in Table 5.2.

The adjusted figures show male deaths increasing from 203,861 in 1997 to 281,917 in 2000, and female deaths increasing from 157,868 to 249,242 over the same period.

The age breakdown of HIV/AIDS deaths and all possible HIV/AIDS-related deaths recorded in 1996 and the estimates for 1997 to 2000 are shown in Table 5.3a for males and females, respectively, using the CDC list, and in Table 5.3b for males and females, respectively, using the Stats SA list. The

Table 5.1

Comparison of the Death Data from the Population Register with Those from Stats SA Data for 1996 Base Year

Age in Years $(x, x+n)$	Male			Female		
	Population register	Stats SA data	Ratio Stats SA to DHA $g_{1996}(x, \backslash x + n)$	Population register	Stats SA data	Ratio Stats SA to DHA $g_{1996}(x,x + n)$
0–4	1,797	17,292	9.6227	1,610	15,320	9.5155
5–9	449	1,816	4.0445	299	1,282	4.2876
10–14	335	1,602	4.7821	237	1,156	4.8776
15–19	1,801	4,334	2.4064	795	2,455	3.0881
20–24	6,750	9,347	1.3847	3,369	4,910	1.4574
25–29	8,950	11,477	1.2823	4,895	6,213	1.2693
30–34	9,812	12,709	1.2953	5,265	6,549	1.2439
35–39	9,442	11,953	1.2659	5,037	6,296	1.2500
40–44	9,822	12,328	1.2551	5,023	6,234	1.2411
45–49	10,428	12,895	1.2366	5,323	6,364	1.1956
50–54	10,170	12,366	1.2159	5,260	6,451	1.2264
55–59	11,179	13,715	1.2269	7,215	8,523	1.1813
60–64	9,994	12,084	1.2091	8,292	9,891	1.1928
65–69	11,813	13,942	1.1802	10,152	12,023	1.1843
70–74	10,491	12,274	1.1700	8,877	10,543	1.1877
75–79	10,347	11,837	1.1440	11,294	13,365	1.1834
80–84	6,367	7,376	1.1585	8,153	9,761	1.1972
85+	5,504	6,443	1.1706	10,688	12,750	1.1929

Source: Statistics South Africa database.

Figure 5.1a **Comparison of Male Deaths from the Population Register with Those from Stats SA, South Africa, 1996**

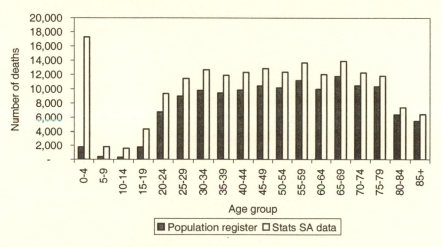

Source: Statistics South Africa database.

Figure 5.1b   **Comparison of Female Deaths from the Population Register with Those from Stats SA, South Africa, 1996**

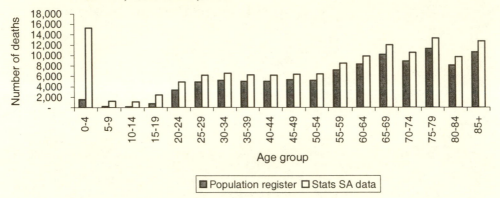

Source: Statistics South Africa database.

use of HIV/AIDS-related deaths figures allows for the misreporting of deaths due to HIV/AIDS and acts to provide a safe upper limit for such deaths. The figures may overestimate deaths due to HIV/AIDS in the higher ages (above 50) but remain closer to the true level for deaths in the adult ages 15 to 49.

The tables show estimated deaths among males that were due to HIV/AIDS and all possible HIV/AIDS-related causes, based on the CDC list, increasing from 5,553 in 1996 to 20,007 in 2000, and among females from 6,159 in 1996 to 28,552 in 2000. When the Stats SA list is used, the figures show an increase for males from 12,231 in 1996 to 44,067 in 2000. For females, the corresponding estimated increase was from 9,197 in 1996 to 42,636 in 2000. For the broad age range 15 to 49 considered, the highest numbers of estimated HIV/AIDS deaths occured in the age group 30 to 44 among males and 25–39 among females.

Age-specific death rates and percentages of deaths were then computed for three sets of data, PR1, PR2, and PR3. These results are shown in Tables 5.4a to 5.5b and illustrated in Figures 5.2a to 5.5c.

When the PR data are analyzed as reported, the log of the age-specific death rates in Figure 5.2a exhibits two features. The log rates show a rapid rate of increase in mortality from ages 15 to 19 to ages 20 to 24. This rapid increase is present in all the data years. From ages 25 to 29 to ages 40 to 44, the mortality levels increase with time, but the rate of increase is not drastic. With the adjustment of the PR data, the first feature (regarding age groups 15 t019 and 20 to 24) becomes less pronounced, while the second feature remains. As all the deaths due to HIV/AIDS and all possible HIV/AIDS-related causes are removed, Figure 5.2c shows that the curves are largely flattened. However, a small bulge remains that can be translated to indicate some increase in mortality in the ages over 30, from 1997 to 2000.

Table 5.2

Adjustments of the Population Register Data to Bring Them in Line with the Data from Stats SA, 1997–2000

Age group $(x, x + n)$	1996 adjustment ratio $g_{1996}(x, x + n)$	1997	1998	1999	2000
Males					
0–4	9.623	21,170	25,510	30,004	41,330
5–9	4.045	2,313	2,888	3,656	4,437
10–14	4.782	2,004	2,965	3,706	4,218
15–19	2.406	4,312	4,697	5,747	5,860
20–24	1.385	9,624	9,911	10,201	10,028
25–29	1.282	12,903	15,098	16,674	17,907
30–34	1.295	14,199	17,099	19,992	22,565
35–39	1.266	14,006	16,929	19,506	22,191
40–44	1.255	13,764	16,159	18,115	20,380
45–49	1.237	14,315	16,336	17,793	19,158
50–54	1.216	13,176	14,927	16,308	18,122
55–59	1.227	14,991	16,374	17,057	16,947
60–64	1.209	13,137	14,459	15,286	17,174
65–69	1.180	14,375	15,359	15,153	14,935
70–74	1.170	12,900	14,600	15,193	15,803
75+	1.155	26,672	29,123	29,233	30,865
Total		203,861	232,433	253,625	281,917
Females					
0–4	9.516	18,279	21,676	28,537	37,957
5–9	4.288	1,616	2,337	3,134	3,790
10–14	4.878	1,546	2,019	2,785	3,351
15–19	3.088	2,600	3,283	4,441	5,142
20–24	1.457	6,009	7,156	8,791	10,110
25–29	1.269	8,171	10,751	13,976	17,438
30–34	1.244	8,047	10,664	13,992	17,922
35–39	1.250	7,748	9,908	12,543	15,748
40–44	1.241	7,309	9,035	10,471	12,842
45–49	1.196	7,086	8,443	9,744	10,984
50–54	1.226	7,205	8,239	9,185	10,758
55 59	1.181	8,962	9,861	10,028	10,274
60–64	1.193	10,903	11,677	12,027	13,585
65–69	1.184	12,795	14,347	14,724	14,621
70–74	1.188	11,716	13,777	14,783	17,189
75+	1.191	37,874	43,056	43,649	47,531
Total		157,868	186,229	212,811	249,242

Source: Computation based on Statistics South Africa database.

Table 5.3a

Recorded Number of Deaths Due to HIV/AIDS and HIV/AIDS-Related Causes According to the CDC List, South Africa, 1996

| Age group | Estimated AIDS and AIDS-related deaths | | | Recorded causes of deaths for 1996 r (exp) = 0.320437 | | | |
	Pure AIDS	AIDS related	Total	1997	1998	1999	2000
Males							
15–19	14	74	88	121	167	230	317
20–24	167	181	348	479	661	910	1,254
25–29	526	402	928	1,279	1,761	2,427	3,344
30–34	704	568	1,272	1,752	2,414	3,326	4,583
35–39	578	548	1,126	1,551	2,137	2,945	4,057
40–44	456	578	1,034	1,425	1,963	2,704	3,725
45–49	263	494	757	1,043	1,437	1,980	2,727
15–49	2,708	2,845	5,553	7,651	10,540	14,522	20,007
Females							
15–19	107	130	237	348	510	749	1,099
20–24	541	398	939	1,378	2,022	2,967	4,353
25–29	734	587	1,321	1,938	2,844	4,174	6,124
30–34	653	570	1,223	1,795	2,633	3,864	5,670
35–39	447	581	1,028	1,508	2,213	3,248	4,766
40–44	235	527	762	1,118	1,641	2,407	3,533
45–49	136	513	649	952	1,397	2,050	3,009
15–49	2,853	3,306	6,159	9,037	13,261	19,459	28,552

Source: Computation based on Statistics South Africa database.

Table 5.3b

Recorded Number of Deaths Due to AIDS and AIDS-Related Causes According to the Stats SA List, South Africa, 1996

| Age group | Estimated AIDS and AIDS-related deaths | | | Recorded causes of deaths for 1996 r (exp) = 0.320437 | | | |
	Pure AIDS	AIDS related	Total	1997	1998	1999	2000
Males							
15–19	14	227	241	332	457	630	868
20–24	167	561	728	1,003	1,382	1,904	2,623
25–29	526	1,170	1,696	2,337	3,219	4,435	6,111
30–34	704	1,796	2,500	3,444	4,745	6,538	9,007
35–39	578	1,902	2,480	3,417	4,707	6,486	8,935
40–44	456	1,893	2,349	3,236	4,459	6,143	8,463
45–49	263	1,974	2,237	3,082	4,246	5,850	8,060
15–49	2,708	9,523	12,231	16,851	23,216	31,986	44,067
Females							
15–19	107	348	455	668	980	1,438	2,109
20–24	541	927	1,468	2,154	3,161	4,638	6,805
25–29	734	1,215	1,949	2,860	4,196	6,158	9,035
30–34	653	1,229	1,882	2,762	4,052	5,946	8,725
35–39	447	1,030	1,477	2,167	3,180	4,666	6,847
40–44	235	862	1,097	1,610	2,362	3,466	5,086
45–49	136	733	869	1,275	1,871	2,745	4,029
15–49	2,853	6,344	9,197	13,495	19,802	29,057	42,636

Source: Computation based on Statistics South Africa database.

Table 5.4a

Unadjusted, Adjusted, and "AIDS-Free" Age-Specific Death Rates (per 10,000) Using the CDC List of HIV/AIDS-Related Causes of Death, South Africa, 1996–2000

	1996			1997			1998			1999			2000		
	PR1	PR2	PR3	PR1	PR2	PR3	PR1	PR2	PR3	PR1	PR2	PR3	PR1	PR2	PR3
Males															
15–19	8.7	21.0	20.6	8.5	20.4	19.8	9.0	21.7	20.9	10.8	26.0	24.9	10.8	25.9	24.5
20–24	34.8	48.2	46.4	35.6	49.3	46.9	36.4	50.4	47.1	37.2	51.5	46.9	36.2	50.2	43.9
25–29	53.4	68.5	62.9	58.8	75.4	68.0	67.5	86.5	76.4	73.1	93.7	80.1	77.0	98.7	80.3
30–34	66.5	86.1	77.5	73.0	94.6	82.9	86.6	112.2	96.4	99.9	129.3	107.8	111.2	144.1	114.8
35–39	72.8	92.2	83.5	84.0	106.4	94.6	100.2	126.8	110.8	113.9	144.2	122.4	128.0	162.1	132.5
40–44	94.9	119.1	109.1	102.7	128.9	115.5	117.0	146.8	129.0	127.4	159.9	136.1	139.4	175.0	143.0
45–49	127.5	157.6	148.4	137.5	170.0	157.6	152.5	188.6	172.0	161.7	200.0	177.7	169.7	209.8	180.0
Females															
15–19	3.7	11.5	10.4	3.9	11.9	10.3	4.8	14.7	12.4	6.3	19.6	16.3	7.2	22.3	17.5
20–24	16.1	23.5	19.0	19.7	28.7	22.1	23.4	34.1	24.5	28.6	41.7	27.6	32.8	47.8	27.2
25–29	27.2	34.5	27.2	34.9	44.3	33.8	44.8	56.9	41.8	56.9	72.2	50.6	69.3	88.0	57.1
30–34	32.5	40.4	32.9	39.2	48.8	37.9	51.1	63.6	47.9	66.0	82.1	59.4	83.3	103.6	70.8
35–39	36.7	45.8	38.4	43.9	54.9	44.2	54.6	68.3	53.0	67.4	84.2	62.4	82.5	103.1	71.9
40–44	45.3	56.2	49.3	51.2	63.5	53.8	61.1	75.8	62.0	68.4	84.8	65.3	81.0	100.6	72.9
45–49	61.7	73.7	66.2	65.8	78.7	68.1	75.3	90.0	75.1	83.5	99.8	78.8	90.5	108.1	78.5

Source: Computation based on Statistics South Africa database.

Key:

PR1 = Rates computed using unadjusted data from the population register.

PR2 = Rates computed using adjusted data from the population register.

PR3 = Adjusted rates from which AIDS and AIDS-related deaths have been removed.

Table 5.4b

Unadjusted, Adjusted, and "AIDS-Free" Age-Specific Death Rates (per 10,000) Using the Stats SA List of AIDS-Related Causes of Death, South Africa, 1996–2000

	1996			1997			1998			1999			2000		
	PR1	PR2	PR3	PR1	PR2	PR3	PR1	PR2	PR3	PR1	PR2	PR3	PR1	PR2	PR3
Males															
15–19	8.7	21.0	19.8	8.5	20.4	18.8	9.0	21.7	19.6	10.8	26.0	23.1	10.8	25.9	22.1
20–24	34.8	48.2	44.4	35.6	49.3	44.2	36.4	50.4	43.4	37.2	51.5	41.9	36.2	50.2	37.0
25–29	53.4	68.5	58.4	58.8	75.4	61.8	67.5	86.5	68.1	73.1	93.7	68.8	77.0	98.7	65.0
30–34	66.5	86.1	69.2	73.0	94.6	71.7	86.6	112.2	81.1	99.9	129.3	87.0	111.2	144.1	86.6
35–39	72.8	92.2	73.1	84.0	106.4	80.4	100.2	126.8	91.5	113.9	144.2	96.2	128.0	162.1	96.8
40–44	94.9	119.1	96.4	102.7	128.9	98.6	117.0	146.8	106.3	127.4	159.9	105.7	139.4	175.0	102.3
45–49	127.5	157.6	130.3	137.5	170.0	133.4	152.5	188.6	139.6	161.7	200.0	134.2	169.7	209.8	121.6
Females															
15–19	3.7	11.5	9.3	3.9	11.9	8.8	4.8	14.7	10.3	6.3	19.6	13.2	7.2	22.3	13.1
20–24	16.1	23.5	16.5	19.7	28.7	18.4	23.4	34.1	19.0	28.6	41.7	19.7	32.8	47.8	15.6
25–29	27.2	34.5	23.7	34.9	44.3	28.8	44.8	56.9	34.7	56.9	72.2	40.4	69.3	88.0	42.4
30–34	32.5	40.4	28.8	39.2	48.8	32.0	51.1	63.6	39.4	66.0	82.1	47.2	83.3	103.6	53.2
35–39	36.7	45.8	35.1	43.9	54.9	39.5	54.6	68.3	46.4	67.4	84.2	52.9	82.5	103.1	58.3
40–44	45.3	56.2	46.3	51.2	63.5	49.5	61.1	75.8	56.0	68.4	84.8	56.8	81.0	100.6	60.7
45–49	61.7	73.7	63.6	65.8	78.7	64.6	75.3	90.0	70.1	83.5	99.8	71.7	90.5	108.1	68.5

Source: Computation based on Statistics South Africa database.

Key:
  PR1 = Rates computed using unadjusted data from the population register.
  PR2 = Rates computed using adjusted data from the population register.
  PR3 = Adjusted rates from which AIDS and AIDS-related deaths have been removed.

Table 5.5a

Unadjusted, Adjusted, and "AIDS-Free" Age-specific Percentages, Using the CDC List of HIV/AIDS-Related Causes of Death, South Africa, 1996–2000

	1996			1997			1998			1999			2000		
	PR1	PR2	PR3	PR1	PR2	PR3	PR1	PR2	PR3	PR1	PR2	PR3	PR1	PR2	PR3
Males															
15–19	3.2	5.8	5.7	2.8	5.2	5.0	2.7	4.9	4.7	2.9	5.3	5.1	2.7	5.0	4.7
20–24	11.8	12.5	12.0	11.0	11.6	11.0	9.7	10.3	9.6	8.9	9.4	8.6	8.0	8.5	7.4
25–29	15.7	15.3	14.1	15.9	15.5	14.0	16.0	15.7	13.9	15.8	15.4	13.2	15.5	15.2	12.3
30–34	17.2	16.9	15.2	17.3	17.1	15.0	18.0	17.8	15.3	18.7	18.5	15.4	19.3	19.1	15.2
35–39	16.6	15.9	14.4	17.5	16.9	15.0	18.2	17.6	15.4	18.7	18.1	15.3	19.4	18.8	15.4
40–44	17.2	16.4	15.1	17.3	16.6	14.8	17.5	16.8	14.8	17.5	16.8	14.3	18.0	17.3	14.1
45–49	18.3	17.2	16.2	18.3	17.2	16.0	18.0	17.0	15.5	17.5	16.5	14.6	17.2	16.2	13.9
Females															
15–19	2.7	6.3	5.7	2.3	5.5	4.8	2.3	5.5	4.7	2.6	6.0	5.0	2.4	5.7	4.5
20–24	11.3	12.6	10.2	11.5	12.8	9.9	10.8	12.1	8.7	10.7	11.9	7.9	10.1	11.2	6.4
25–29	16.5	15.9	12.5	17.9	17.4	13.3	18.7	18.1	13.3	19.5	18.9	13.3	19.9	19.3	12.5
30–34	17.7	16.8	13.6	18.0	17.1	13.3	18.9	18.0	13.6	20.0	18.9	13.7	20.9	19.9	13.6
35–39	17.0	16.1	13.5	17.3	16.5	13.3	17.5	16.7	13.0	17.8	17.0	12.6	18.3	17.5	12.2
40–44	16.9	16.0	14.0	16.4	15.6	13.2	16.1	15.3	12.5	15.0	14.2	10.9	15.0	14.2	10.3
45–49	17.9	16.3	14.6	16.5	15.1	13.1	15.6	14.3	11.9	14.5	13.2	10.4	13.3	12.2	8.8

Source: Computation based on Statistics South Africa database.

Key:

PR1 = Rates computed using unadjusted data from the population register.

PR2 = Rates computed using adjusted data from the population register.

PR3 = Adjusted rates from which AIDS and AIDS-related deaths have been removed.

Table 5.5b

Unadjusted, Adjusted, and "AIDS-Free" Age-Specific Percentages, Using the Stats SA List of HIV/AIDS-Related Causes of Death, South Africa, 1996–2000

	1996			1997			1998			1999			2000		
	PR1	PR2	PR3	PR1	PR2	PR3	PR1	PR2	PR3	PR1	PR2	PR3	PR1	PR2	PR3
Males															
15–19	3.2	5.8	5.5	2.8	5.2	4.8	2.7	4.9	4.4	2.9	5.3	4.7	2.7	5.0	4.2
20–24	11.8	12.5	11.5	11.0	11.6	10.4	9.7	10.3	8.9	8.9	9.4	7.7	8.0	8.5	6.3
25–29	15.7	15.3	13.0	15.9	15.5	12.7	16.0	15.7	12.3	15.8	15.4	11.3	15.5	15.2	10.0
30–34	17.2	16.9	13.6	17.3	17.1	12.9	18.0	17.8	12.8	18.7	18.5	12.5	19.3	19.1	11.5
35–39	16.6	15.9	12.6	17.5	16.9	12.7	18.2	17.6	12.7	18.7	18.1	12.1	19.4	18.8	11.2
40–44	17.2	16.4	13.3	17.3	16.6	12.7	17.5	16.8	12.2	17.5	16.8	11.1	18.0	17.3	10.1
45–49	18.3	17.2	14.2	18.3	17.2	13.5	18.0	17.0	12.6	17.5	16.5	11.1	17.2	16.2	9.4
Females															
15–19	2.7	6.3	5.1	2.3	5.5	4.1	2.3	5.5	3.9	2.6	6.0	4.1	2.4	5.7	3.4
20–24	11.3	12.6	8.8	11.5	12.8	8.2	10.8	12.1	6.7	10.7	11.9	5.6	10.1	11.2	3.7
25–29	16.5	15.9	10.9	17.9	17.4	11.3	18.7	18.1	11.1	19.5	18.9	10.6	19.9	19.3	9.3
30–34	17.7	16.8	12.0	18.0	17.1	11.3	18.9	18.0	11.2	20.0	18.9	10.9	20.9	19.9	10.2
35–39	17.0	16.1	12.3	17.3	16.5	11.9	17.5	16.7	11.4	17.8	17.0	10.7	18.3	17.5	9.9
40–44	16.9	16.0	13.2	16.4	15.6	12.1	16.1	15.3	11.3	15.0	14.2	9.5	15.0	14.2	8.6
45–49	17.9	16.3	14.1	16.5	15.1	12.4	15.6	14.3	11.1	14.5	13.2	9.5	13.3	12.2	7.7

Source: Computation based on Statistics South Africa database.
Key:
   PR1 = Rates computed using unadjusted data from the population register.
   PR2 = Rates computed using adjusted data from the population register.
   PR3 = Adjusted rates from which AIDS and AIDS-related deaths have been removed.

Figure 5.2a   **Unadjusted Age-Specific Death Rates Among Males, South Africa, 1996–2000**

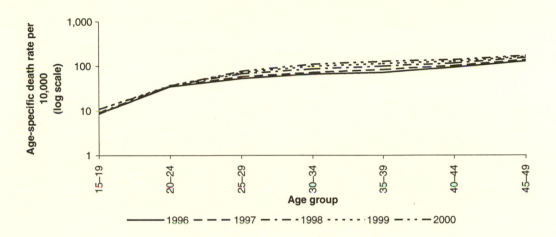

Source: Computation based on Statistics South Africa database.

Figure 5.2b   **Adjusted Age-Specific Death Rates Among Males, South Africa, 1996–2000**

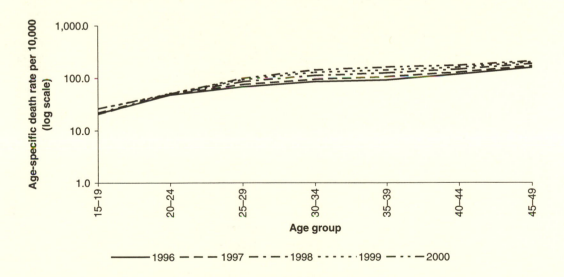

Source: Computation based on Statistics South Africa database.

Figure 5.2c **"AIDS-Free" Age-Specific Death Rates Among Males (maximum list), South Africa, 1996–2000**

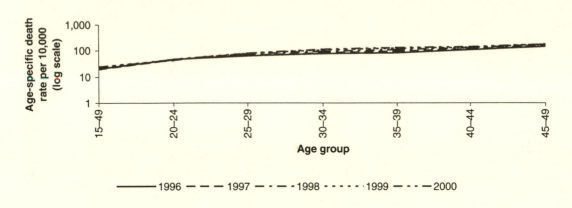

Source: Computation based on regrouped Statistics South Africa database.

Figure 5.3a **Unadjusted Age-Specific Death Rates Among Females, South Africa, 1996–2000**

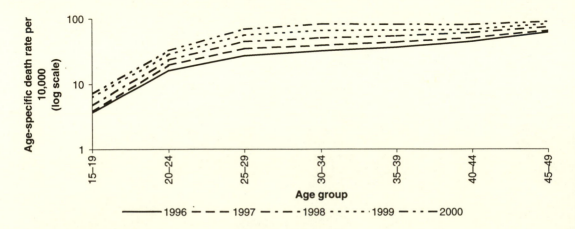

Source: Computation based on Statistics South Africa database.

Figure 5.3b   **Adjusted Age-Specific Death Rates Among Females, South Africa, 1996–2000**

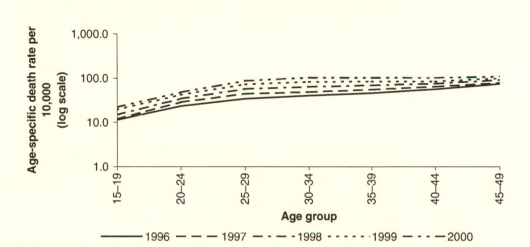

Source: Computation based on Statistics South Africa database.

Figure 5.3c   **"AIDS-Free" Age-Specific Death Rates Among Females (Maximum List)**
South Africa, 1996–2000

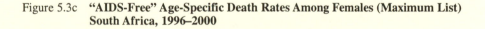
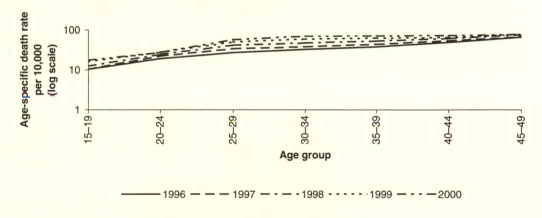

Source: Computation based on regrouped Statistics South Africa data.

Figure 5.4a   **Unadjusted Percentage of Deaths (in Age Range 15–49) Among Males, South Africa, 1996–2000**

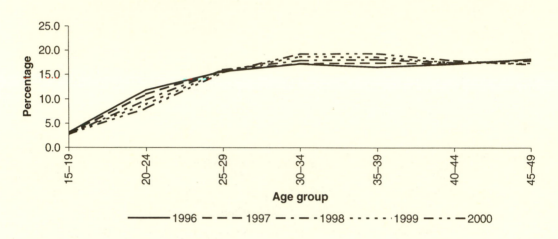

Source: Computation based on Statistics South Africa database.

Figure 5.4b   **Adjusted Percentage of Deaths (in Age Range 15–49) Among Males, South Africa, 1996–2000**

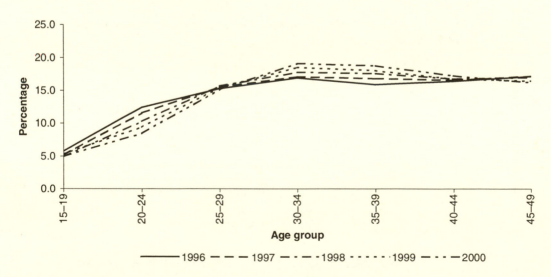

Source: Computation based on Statistics South Africa database.

Figure 5.4c   **"AIDS-Free" Percentage of Deaths (in Age Range 15–49) Among Males, South Africa, 1996–2000**

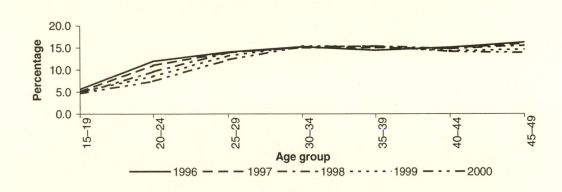
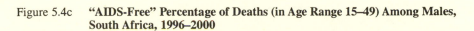

Source: Computation based on regrouped Statistics South Africa data.

Figure 5.5a   **Unadjusted Percentage of Deaths (in Age Range 15–49) Among Females, South Africa, 1996–2000**

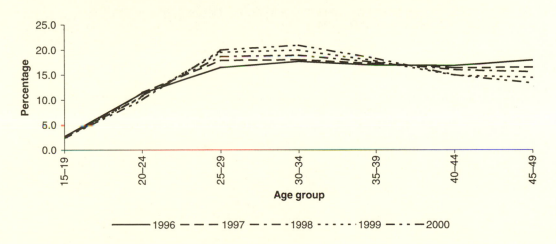
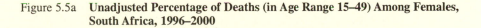

Source: Computation based on Statistics South Africa database.

Figure 5.5b   **Adjusted Percentage of Deaths (in Age Range 15–49) Among Females, South Africa, 1996–2000**

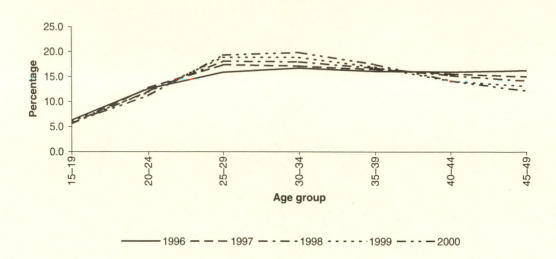

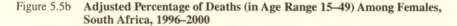

Source: Computation based on Statistics South Africa database.

Figure 5.5c   **"AIDS-Free" Percentage of Deaths (in Age Range 15–49) Among Females, South Africa, 1996–2000**

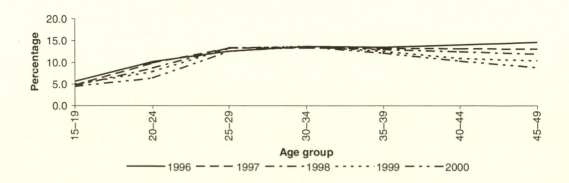

Source: Computation based on regrouped Statistics South Africa data.

For females, the unadjusted log rates exhibit features similar to those found for males. One difference is that there is a rapid increase in mortality levels over the years. The increase in levels is highest over the age range 15–19 to 20–24, followed by the age range 20–24 to 25–29. As in the case of males, the adjusted rates reduce the pronouncement of the rate of increase in mortality for the age range 15–19 to 20–24. Unlike males, the log rates show an appreciable increase for ages below 20–24. For ages beyond 20–24, the log rates over time exhibit a funnel shape, with the width of the curves tunneling down with increase in age. Also unlike males, Figure 5.3c does not show any disappearance of the bulge, but rather its persistence, even after the removal of deaths due to HIV/AIDS and all possible HIV/AIDS-related causes. The effect of the bulge is most evident in the middle adult ages between 25 and 34 years.

The age-specific percentages of deaths are shown in Figures 5.4a to 5.4c for males and in Figures 5.5a to 5.5c for females. The unadjusted percentages of deaths among males, as shown in Figure 5.4a, exhibit three features. Between age groups 15–19 and 25–29, the percentages cluster but tend to decrease with time. Between age groups 25–29 and 40–44, the age-specific percentages of deaths increase with time. Between age groups 40–44 and 45–49, the percentages of deaths cluster together, with a tendency to decrease with time. The adjusted percentages in Figure 5.4b exhibit these same features, but they become clearer and more distinct. In effect, there is a relative shift in deaths from the young adult ages (under 30 years) to the middle adult ages (between 30 and 44 years). With the removal of deaths due to HIV/AIDS and all possible HIV/AIDS-related causes, Figure 5.4c shows that the above-mentioned features are attenuated. The proportions decrease over time over almost all the ages, with the exception of the age ranges 30–34 to 35–39.

As in the case of males, the unadjusted percentages of deaths among females, as shown in Figure 5.5a, also exhibit three features, but in a different form. From age ranges 15–19 to 20–24, the curves cluster, while from 20–24 to 35–39 they increase with time, and for ages 35–39 to 45–49 they decrease with time. However, with the adjusted percentages, Figure 5.5b shows that for the age ranges 15–19 to 20–24, the percentages cluster and tend to decrease with time. With the removal of deaths due to HIV/AIDS and all possible HIV/AIDS-related causes, Figure 5.5c shows similar features to males (in Figure 5.4c), but with wider dispersion in the curves.

Results from Situation Two

The results of estimates of deaths due to HIV/AIDS and HIV/AIDS-related causes are shown in Table 5.6a, for groupings based on the CDC list, and in

Table 5.6b, for groupings based on the Stats SA list. For both these tables, the figures from 1993 to 1996 are based on actual data. These data points form the bases for the short-term projection for 1997 to 2000, using a second-degree polynomial function. The first estimates from these projections are revised using the ex-post/ex-ante method that makes use of the relationship between the number of natural deaths as obtained from population register data and estimates of the number of natural deaths obtained from fitting the polynomial function to natural death data from 1993 to 1996. The number of natural deaths and the total number of deaths are given in Tables 5.6c and 5.6d. As done above, for 1993 to 1996, the data are based on the actual published figures, while for 1997 to 2000, they are based on adjustment of the population register (for missing IDs).

The estimate of number of deaths due to HIV/AIDS and HIV/AIDS-related causes is used to compute percentages of natural deaths (shown in Tables 5.6e and 5.6f) and total deaths (shown in Tables 5.6g and 5.6h).

Table 5.6e shows that, as a percentage of natural deaths, the number of deaths due to HIV/AIDS and ARC (based on the CDC list) in the age group 15–49 has been increasing steadily for both males and females. For males it increased from 7.1 percent in 1993 to 14.4 percent in 1996 to an estimated 16 percent in 2000. For females the increase was higher. The number increased from about 11 percent in 1993 to 20.3 percent in 1996 to an estimated 22.6 percent in 2000. So, for either males or females, deaths due to HIV/AIDS and ARC in the age group 15–49 by the year 2000 made up less than a quarter of all natural deaths within that broad age range. With regard to specific five-year age groups, for males, deaths due to HIV/AIDS and ARC accounted for less than 25 percent of all natural deaths within any given age group during 1996 and during 2000. For females in 1996, deaths due to HIV/AIDS and ARC accounted maximally for over 25 percent of all natural deaths in two age groups (20–24 and 25–29). By 2000, the numbers of such age groups are estimated to have increased to three (20–24, 25–29, and 30–34).

Table 5.6f shows that, as a percentage of natural deaths, the number of deaths due to HIV/AIDS and ARC (based on the Stats SA list) in the age group 15–49 has been increasing rapidly for both males and females. For males, it increased from 19.2 percent in 1993 to 31.7 percent in 1996 to an estimated 35.5 percent in 2000. For females, the increase was also rapid. It increased from about 17 percent in 1993 to 30.3 percent in 1996 to an estimated 35 percent in 2000. So, for either males or females, by the year 2000, deaths due to HIV/AIDS and ARC in the age group 15–49 were estimated at slightly less than 36 percent of all natural deaths within that broad age range. With regard to age groups, for males, deaths due to HIV/AIDS and ARC accounted for more than 25 percent of all natural deaths within all but two age

Table 5.6a

Number of Reported Deaths (over the period 1993–96) and Estimated Deaths (over the period 1997–2000) Due to HIV/AIDS and HIV/AIDS-Related Causes (from CDC list)

Age group	1993	1994	1995	1996	1997	1998	1999	2000
Males
15–19	62	48	84	88	98	134	194	205
20–24	96	137	246	348	372	476	526	515
25–29	205	364	606	928	1,134	1,546	1,836	2,063
30–34	259	476	797	1,272	1,560	2,065	2,612	3,036
35–39	271	444	769	1,126	1,436	1,909	2,373	2,800
40–44	261	400	629	1,034	1,367	1,863	2,347	2,858
45–49	233	301	524	757	940	1,188	1,397	1,592
Total	1,387	2,170	3,655	5,553	6,908	9,182	11,285	13,069
Females
15–19	102	110	188	237	264	388	554	672
20–24	177	329	593	939	1,206	1,554	2,019	2,392
25–29	208	422	819	1,321	1,909	2,667	3,638	4,678
30–34	266	395	793	1,223	1,627	2,329	3,185	4,203
35–39	253	403	627	1,028	1,428	1,985	2,681	3,569
40–44	256	380	547	762	947	1,207	1,456	1,811
45–49	253	337	495	649	763	955	1,136	1,313
Total	1,515	2,376	4,062	6,159	8,145	11,087	14,667	18,638

Source: Computation based on Statistics South Africa database.

Table 5.6b

Number of Reported Deaths (over the period 1993–96) and Estimated Deaths (over the period 1997–2000) Due to HIV/AIDS and HIV/AIDS-Related Causes (from Stats SA list)

Age group	1993	1994	1995	1996	1997	1998	1999	2000
Males
15–19	142	138	196	241	266	367	536	566
20–24	252	317	473	728	803	1,068	1,222	1,232
25–29	442	697	1,068	1,696	2,107	2,932	3,546	4,049
30–34	622	972	1,508	2,500	3,136	4,252	5,490	6,491
35–39	738	1,023	1,600	2,480	3,271	4,512	5,789	7,020
40–44	795	1,077	1,658	2,349	2,902	3,743	4,529	5,349
45–49	764	1,026	1,623	2,237	2,633	3,201	3,650	4,058
Total	3,755	5,250	8,126	12,231	15,118	20,076	24,762	28,766
Females
15–19	189	232	386	455	466	634	840	957
20–24	343	531	944	1,468	1,900	2,466	3,227	3,850
25–29	389	639	1,234	1,949	2,837	3,991	5,478	7,086
30–34	418	645	1,235	1,882	2,459	3,477	4,712	6,175
35–39	366	527	914	1,477	2,106	2,967	4,048	5,430
40–44	347	469	758	1,097	1,460	1,960	2,467	3,178
45–49	293	407	601	869	1,081	1,427	1,771	2,121
Total	2,345	3,450	6,072	9,197	12,310	16,923	22,544	28,798

Source: Computation based on regrouped Statistics South Africa data.

Table 5.6c

Number of Reported Deaths Due to Natural Causes by Age Group and Sex, 1993–2000

Age group	1993	1994	1995	1996	1997	1998	1999	2000
Males
15–19	859	699	899	1,013	1,113	1,551	2,313	2,497
20–24	1,199	1,182	1,508	2,145	2,325	3,103	3,587	3,658
25–29	1,710	1,929	2,779	4,041	5,004	6,997	8,543	9,856
30–34	2,422	2,819	4,058	6,100	7,514	10,115	13,056	15,475
35–39	3,450	3,777	5,286	6,986	8,610	11,344	14,141	16,830
40–44	4,542	4,957	6,659	8,345	9,690	12,009	14,173	16,481
45–49	5,376	5,845	7,969	9,935	11,108	13,100	14,691	16,192
Total	19,558	21,208	29,158	38,565	45,364	58,220	70,504	80,989
Females
15–19	987	884	1,227	1,472	1,613	2,402	3,493	4,334
20–24	1,240	1,471	2,424	3,537	4,542	5,894	7,740	9,283
25–29	1,524	1,941	3,101	4,627	6,536	9,087	12,422	16,056
30–34	1,941	2,232	3,513	5,065	6,488	9,156	12,463	16,444
35–39	2,210	2,654	3,547	4,947	6,364	8,414	11,008	14,350
40–44	2,806	3,249	4,015	5,186	6,214	7,813	9,405	11,743
45–49	3,051	3,506	4,539	5,560	6,238	7,591	8,863	10,134
Total	13,759	15,937	22,366	30,394	37,996	50,357	65,394	82,343

Source: Computation based on regrouped Statistics South Africa data.

Table 5.6d

Total Number of Reported Deaths by Age Group and Sex, 1993–2000

Age group	1993	1994	1995	1996	1997	1998	1999	2000
Males
15–19	3,195	3,077	3,995	4,334	4,289	4,580	5,490	5,607
20–24	5,960	6,332	8,256	9,347	9,500	9,299	9,245	8,943
25–29	6,626	7,296	9,637	11,477	12,681	14,308	15,218	15,872
30–34	6,767	7,411	10,128	12,709	13,930	16,284	18,593	20,696
35–39	6,998	7,267	9,944	11,953	13,857	16,496	18,739	20,986
40–44	7,067	7,723	10,183	12,328	13,694	15,961	17,684	19,717
45–49	7,007	7,954	10,721	12,895	14,299	16,193	17,534	18,728
Total	43,620	47,060	62,864	75,043	82,250	93,120	102,503	110,549
Females
15–19	1,604	1,514	2,079	2,455	2,602	3,332	4,559	5,275
20–24	2,109	2,469	3,666	4,910	6,079	7,260	8,953	10,286
25–29	2,530	3,023	4,499	6,213	8,090	10,550	13,817	17,244
30–34	2,868	3,276	4,821	6,549	8,017	10,608	13,827	17,603
35–39	3,024	3,521	4,674	6,296	7,710	9,767	12,238	15,360
40–44	3,419	3,971	4,927	6,234	7,258	8,896	10,264	12,587
45–49	3,533	4,004	5,212	6,364	7,066	8,371	9,614	10,832
Total	19,087	21,778	29,878	39,021	46,821	58,784	73,273	89,185

Source: Computed from the 1996 South Africa Population Census micro–data.

Table 5.6e

Percentage of Reported Natural Deaths (over the period 1993–96) and Estimated Percentage of Reported Natural Deaths (over the period 1997–2000) Due to HIV/AIDS and HIV/AIDS-Related Causes (from CDC list)

Age group	1993	1994	1995	1996	1997	1998	1999	2000
Males								
15–19	7.22	6.87	9.34	8.69	8.83	8.63	8.40	8.19
20–24.	8.01	11.59	16.31	16.22	16.02	15.34	14.67	14.08
25–29	11.99	18.87	21.81	22.96	22.66	22.09	21.49	20.94
30–34	10.69	16.89	19.64	20.85	20.76	20.42	20.01	19.62
35–39	7.86	11.76	14.55	16.12	16.68	16.83	16.78	16.64
40–44	5.75	8.07	9.45	12.39	14.11	15.51	16.56	17.34
45–49	4.33	5.15	6.58	7.62	8.46	9.07	9.51	9.83
Total	7.09	10.23	12.54	14.40	15.23	15.77	16.01	16.14
Females								
15–19	10.33	12.44	15.32	16.10	16.34	16.16	15.85	15.52
20–24	14.27	22.37	24.46	26.55	26.56	26.37	26.08	25.77
25–29	13.65	21.74	26.41	28.55	29.21	29.35	29.28	29.13
30–34	13.70	17.70	22.57	24.15	25.08	25.43	25.55	25.56
35–39	11.45	15.18	17.68	20.78	22.45	23.60	24.35	24.87
40–44	9.12	11.70	13.62	14.69	15.24	15.45	15.48	15.42
45–49	8.29	9.61	10.91	11.67	12.23	12.59	12.81	12.96
Total	11.01	14.91	18.16	20.26	21.44	22.02	22.43	22.64

Source: Computation based on regrouped Statistics South Africa data.

Table 5.6f

Percentage of Reported Natural Deaths (over the period 1993–96) and Estimated Percentage of Reported Natural Deaths (over the period 1997–2000) Due to HIV/AIDS and HIV/AIDS-Related Causes (from Stats SA list)

Age group	1993	1994	1995	1996	1997	1998	1999	2000
Males								
15–19	16.53	19.74	21.80	23.79	23.94	23.65	23.18	22.68
20–24	21.02	26.82	31.37	33.94	34.52	34.42	34.08	33.68
25–29	25.85	36.13	38.43	41.97	42.10	41.91	41.51	41.08
30–34	25.68	34.48	37.16	40.98	41.74	42.04	42.05	41.94
35–39	21.39	27.08	30.27	35.50	37.99	39.77	40.94	41.71
40–44	17.50	21.73	24.90	28.15	29.95	31.17	31.95	32.45
45–49	14.21	17.55	20.37	22.52	23.71	24.43	24.84	25.06
Total	19.20	24.75	27.87	31.72	33.33	34.48	35.12	35.52
Females								
15–19	19.15	26.24	31.46	30.91	28.91	26.39	24.06	22.08
20–24	27.66	36.10	38.94	41.50	41.83	41.85	41.69	41.48
25–29	25.52	32.92	39.79	42.12	43.41	43.92	44.10	44.14
30–34	21.54	28.90	35.16	37.16	37.91	37.98	37.81	37.55
35–39	16.56	19.86	25.77	29.86	33.09	35.27	36.77	37.84
40–44	12.37	14.44	18.88	21.15	23.49	25.09	26.23	27.06
45–49	9.60	11.61	13.24	15.63	17.34	18.80	19.98	20.93
Total	17.04	21.65	27.15	30.26	32.40	33.61	34.47	34.97

Source: Computation based on regrouped Statistics South Africa data.

Table 5.6g

Percentage of Reported Total Deaths (over the period 1993–96) and Estimated Percentage of Reported Total Deaths (over the period 1997–2000) Due to HIV/AIDS and HIV/AIDS-Related Causes (from CDC list)

Age group	1993	1994	1995	1996	1997	1998	1999	2000
Males								
15–19	1.94	1.56	2.10	2.03	2.29	2.92	3.54	3.65
20–24	1.61	2.16	2.98	3.72	3.92	5.12	5.69	5.76
25–29	3.09	4.99	6.29	8.09	8.94	10.80	12.06	13.00
30–34	3.83	6.42	7.87	10.01	11.20	12.68	14.05	14.67
35–39	3.87	6.11	7.73	9.42	10.37	11.58	12.66	13.34
40–44	3.69	5.18	6.18	8.39	9.98	11.67	13.27	14.50
45–49	3.33	3.78	4.89	5.87	6.57	7.34	7.97	8.50
Total	3.18	4.61	5.81	7.40	8.40	9.86	11.01	11.82
Females								
15–19	6.36	7.27	9.04	9.65	10.13	11.65	12.14	12.75
20–24	8.39	13.33	16.18	19.12	19.85	21.41	22.55	23.26
25–29	8.22	13.96	18.20	21.26	23.60	25.28	26.33	27.13
30–34	9.27	12.06	16.45	18.67	20.30	21.95	23.03	23.88
35–39	8.37	11.45	13.41	16.33	18.53	20.33	21.91	23.23
40–44	7.49	9.57	11.10	12.22	13.05	13.57	14.19	14.39
45–49	7.16	8.42	9.50	10.20	10.80	11.41	11.81	12.12
Total	7.94	10.91	13.60	15.78	17.40	18.86	20.02	20.90

Source: Computation based on regrouped Statistics South Africa data.

Table 5.6h

Percentage of Reported Total Deaths (over the period 1993–96) and Estimated Percentage of Reported Total Deaths (over the period 1997–2000) Due to HIV/AIDS and HIV/AIDS-Related Causes (from Stats SA list)

Age group	1993	1994	1995	1996	1997	1998	1999	2000
Males								
15–19	4.44	4.48	4.91	5.56	6.21	8.01	9.77	10.10
20–24	4.23	5.01	5.73	7.79	8.45	11.49	13.22	13.78
25–29	6.67	9.55	11.08	14.78	16.61	20.49	23.30	25.51
30–34	9.19	13.12	14.89	19.67	22.51	26.11	29.53	31.36
35–39	10.55	14.08	16.09	20.75	23.60	27.35	30.89	33.45
40–44	11.25	13.95	16.28	19.05	21.19	23.45	25.61	27.13
45–49	10.90	12.90	15.14	17.35	18.42	19.77	20.81	21.67
Total	8.61	11.16	12.93	16.30	18.38	21.56	24.16	26.02
Females								
15–19	11.78	15.32	18.57	18.53	17.93	19.03	18.43	18.14
20–24	16.26	21.51	25.75	29.90	31.26	33.97	36.04	37.43
25–29	15.38	21.14	27.43	31.37	35.07	37.83	39.65	41.10
30–34	14.57	19.69	25.62	28.74	30.68	32.78	34.08	35.08
35–39	12.10	14.97	19.55	23.46	27.31	30.38	33.08	35.35
40–44	10.15	11.81	15.38	17.60	20.11	22.03	24.04	25.25
45–49	8.29	10.16	11.53	13.65	15.30	17.05	18.42	19.58
Total	12.29	15.84	20.32	23.57	26.29	28.79	30.77	32.29

Source: Computation based on regrouped Statistics South Africa data.

groups during 1996. By 2000, the proportions were estimated to have risen to more than 40 percent in two out of seven age groups. For females, in 1996, deaths due to HIV/AIDS and ARC accounted for more than 25 percent of all natural deaths in all but two age groups. It was estimated that HIV/AIDS and ARC deaths would continue to account for more than 25 percent of all natural deaths in all but two age groups by 2000. Tables 5.6g and 5.6h show that as a percentage of total deaths, the number of deaths due to HIV/AIDS and ARC based on the Stats SA list and the CDC list are basically in the same direction as those estimated using the natural deaths.

Results from Situation Three

The results of the national sample data on registered causes of death have been published by Stats SA (2002b). Tables 5.7a and 5.7b are two extracts from the published tables. The tables show the top 90 percent leading under- lying causes of death among males and females in the total national sample.

From the published data, it can be seen that deaths due to HIV/AIDS ranked fourth (6.5 percent) among males and first among females (8.5 percent), when all the sample data are considered. For males, the other HIV/AIDS-related causes of death appearing among these leading causes were tuberculosis (9.1 percent), influenza and pneumonia (5.8 percent), and intestinal infections (3.1 percent). In total, these causes easily comprise 24.5 percent of all male deaths in the sample. For females, the other HIV/AIDS-related causes of death appearing among these leading causes were influ- enza and pneumonia (6.9 percent), tuberculosis (6.7 percent), and intestinal infections (4.1 percent). In total, these causes easily comprise 26.2 percent of all female deaths in the sample.

Discussion

In a study on deaths due to HIV/AIDS in Africa, the following observation was made:

> In Africa, the direct enumeration of AIDS deaths from civil registers is also prob- lematic because death registration is often incomplete and declared causes usually unreliable. (Pictet et al. 1998: 2217–18)

To some extent this is true in South Africa. However, partly because of the existence of the population register and the national identification system, registration of vital events is high in urban areas, especially among adults (who have been accustomed to carrying identity documents). In addition, con-

Table 5.7a

Leading Underlying Causes of Death Among Males, National Sample, 1997–2001

Short name for the subgroup of causes of death	ICD–10 codes	Total sample N	Total sample %	1997 N	1997 %	1998 N	1998 %	1999 N	1999 %	2000 N	2000 %	2001 N	2001 %
Total	All codes	150,969	100.0	26,249	100.0	30,218	100.0	32,489	100.0	28,136	100.0	33,877	100.0
Unspecified unnatural causes	Y10–Y34	23,549	15.6	5,457	20.8	5,530	18.3	4,908	15.1	3,555	12.6	4,099	12.1
Tuberculosis	A15–A19	13,712	9.1	1,978	7.5	2,465	8.2	2,833	8.7	2,743	9.7	3,693	10.9
Ill-defined causes of mortality	R95–R99	12,353	8.2	2,242	8.5	2,506	8.3	2,448	7.5	2,237	8.0	2,920	8.6
HIV disease	B20–B24	9,793	6.5	1,016	3.9	1,588	5.3	2,333	7.2	2,267	8.1	2,589	7.6
Influenza and pneumonia	J10–J18	8,740	5.8	1,068	4.1	1,550	5.1	1,775	5.5	1,923	6.8	2,424	7.2
Cerebrovascular disease	I60–I69	7,423	4.9	1,323	5.0	1,430	4.7	1,664	5.1	1,376	4.9	1,630	4.8
Other forms of heart disease	I30–I52	7,221	4.8	1,408	5.4	1,526	5.0	1,523	4.7	1,277	4.5	1,487	4.4
Ischemic heart disease	I20–I25	6,123	4.1	1,083	4.1	1,195	4.0	1,399	4.3	1,106	3.9	1,340	4.0
Chronic lower resp. diseases	J40–J47	5,761	3.8	956	3.6	1,191	3.9	1,259	3.9	1,070	3.8	1,285	3.8
General symptom and signs	R50–R69	4,809	3.2	959	3.7	1,077	3.6	960	3.0	785	2.8	1,028	3.0
Intestinal infectious diseases	A00–A09	4,741	3.1	730	2.8	981	3.2	974	3.0	1,010	3.6	1,046	3.1
Cancer of dig. sys.	C15–C26	4,177	2.8	836	3.2	848	2.8	920	2.8	706	2.5	867	2.6
Diabetes mellitus	E10–E14	2,943	1.9	536	2.0	584	1.9	634	2.0	535	1.9	654	1.9
Cancer of resp. sys.	C30–C39	2,779	1.8	517	2.0	541	1.8	650	2.0	497	1.8	574	1.7
Disease of liver	K70–K77	2,317	1.5	436	1.7	479	1.6	520	1.6	382	1.4	500	1.5
Hypertensive diseases	I10–I15	2,196	1.5	398	1.5	419	1.4	480	1.5	394	1.4	505	1.5
Assault	X85–Y09	1,943	1.3	163	0.6	274	0.9	596	1.8	465	1.7	445	1.3
Other land transp. accident	V80–V89	1,898	1.3	202	0.8	331	1.1	540	1.7	370	1.3	455	1.3
Renal failure	N17–N19	1,737	1.2	303	1.2	336	1.1	376	1.2	305	1.1	417	1.2
Other bacterial diseases	A30–A49	1,630	1.1	288	1.1	304	1.0	331	1.0	301	1.1	406	1.2
Malnutrition	E40–E46	1,482	1.0	273	1.0	362	1.2	316	1.0	304	1.1	227	0.7
Cancer of male gen.	C60–C63	1,424	0.9	246	0.9	251	0.8	321	1.0	278	1.0	328	1.0
Episodic and paroxysmal disorders	G40–G47	1,288	0.9	230	0.9	203	0.7	286	0.9	270	1.0	299	0.9
Inflam. diseases CNS	G00–G09	1,273	0.8	181	0.7	239	0.8	267	0.8	247	0.9	339	1.0
Resp. and cardiovasc. disorders (perinatal)	P20–P29	1,154	0.8	265	1.0	266	0.9	225	0.7	219	0.8	179	0.5
Pulmonary heart diseases	I26–I28	1,039	0.7	175	0.7	202	0.7	220	0.7	203	0.7	239	0.7
Other diseases of resp. system	J95–J99	990	0.7	144	0.5	201	0.7	162	0.5	213	0.8	270	0.8
Cancer of ill-defined	C76–C80	941	0.6	158	0.6	197	0.7	213	0.7	168	0.6	205	0.6
Diseases of esophagus, stomach	K20–K31	896	0.6	152	0.6	182	0.6	175	0.5	190	0.7	197	0.6
Perinatal disorders	P90–P96	816	0.5	144	0.5	224	0.7	164	0.5	149	0.5	135	0.4
All other causes	The remainder	13,821	9.2	2,382	9.1	2,736	9.1	3,017	9.3	2,591	9.2	3,095	9.1

Source: Statistics South Africa 2002b.

152

Table 5.7b

Leading Underlying Causes of Death Among Females, National Sample, 1997–2001

Short name for the subgroup of causes of death	ICD-10 codes	Total sample N	%	1997 N	%	1998 N	%	1999 N	%	2000 N	%	2001 N	%
Total	All codes	128,612	100.0	20,692	100.0	24,638	100.0	27,231	100.0	25,111	100.0	30,940	100.0
HIV disease	B20–B24	10,886	8.5	1,154	5.6	1,684	6.8	2,478	9.1	2,535	10.1	3,035	9.8
Ill-defined causes of mortality	R95–R99	10,551	8.2	1,810	8.7	2,090	8.5	2,001	7.3	1,990	7.9	2,660	8.6
Cerebrovascular disease	I60–I69	9,763	7.6	1,642	7.9	1,841	7.5	2,087	7.7	1,914	7.6	2,279	7.4
Influenza and pneumonia	J10–J18	8,932	6.9	1,058	5.1	1,442	5.9	1,801	6.6	1,933	7.7	2,698	8.7
Tuberculosis	A15–A19	8,635	6.7	1,076	5.2	1,424	5.8	1,724	6.3	1,819	7.2	2,592	8.4
Other forms of heart disease	I30–I52	8,613	6.7	1,543	7.5	1,738	7.1	1,861	6.8	1,562	6.2	1,909	6.2
General symptom and signs	R50–R69	7,453	5.8	1,318	6.4	1,635	6.6	1,445	5.3	1,356	5.4	1,699	5.5
Unspecified unnatural causes	Y10–Y34	7,179	5.6	1,707	8.2	1,695	6.9	1,542	5.7	1,036	4.1	1,199	3.9
Intestinal infectious diseases	A00–A09	5,219	4.1	753	3.6	1,046	4.2	1,038	3.8	1,126	4.5	1,256	4.1
Diabetes mellitus	E10–E14	4,690	3.6	798	3.9	867	3.5	1,006	3.7	930	3.7	1,089	3.5
Ischemic heart disease	I20–I25	4,549	3.5	677	3.3	902	3.7	1,071	3.9	862	3.4	1,037	3.4
Chronic lower resp. diseases	J40–J47	3,933	3.1	678	3.3	818	3.3	800	2.9	741	3.0	896	2.9
Hypertensive diseases	I10–I15	3,574	2.8	573	2.8	636	2.6	781	2.9	720	2.9	864	2.8
Cancer of dig. sys.	C15–C26	2,763	2.1	492	2.4	563	2.3	639	2.3	492	2.0	577	1.9
Cancer of fem. gen.	C51–C58	2,325	1.8	453	2.2	460	1.9	503	1.8	418	1.7	491	1.6
Other bacterial diseases	A30–A49	1,857	1.4	328	1.6	336	1.4	374	1.4	335	1.3	484	1.6
Renal failure	N17–N19	1,658	1.3	314	1.5	298	1.2	348	1.3	286	1.1	412	1.3
Cancer of breast	C50	1,501	1.2	258	1.2	292	1.2	353	1.3	259	1.0	339	1.1
Disease of liver	K70–K77	1,310	1.0	243	1.2	276	1.1	275	1.0	221	0.9	295	1.0
Malnutrition	E40–E46	1,256	1.0	230	1.1	301	1.2	289	1.1	240	1.0	196	0.6
Inflam. diseases CNS	G00–G09	1,159	0.9	133	0.6	198	0.8	255	0.9	253	1.0	320	1.0
Pulmonary heart diseases	I26–I28	1,051	0.8	158	0.8	196	0.8	228	0.8	219	0.9	250	0.8
Cancer of resp. sys.	C30–C39	1,028	0.8	182	0.9	210	0.9	227	0.8	177	0.7	232	0.7
Resp. and cardiovasc. disorders (perinatal)	P20–P29	962	0.7	239	1.2	206	0.8	170	0.6	179	0.7	168	0.5
Cancer of ill-defined	C76–C80	942	0.7	171	0.8	177	0.7	205	0.8	185	0.7	204	0.7
Other diseases of resp. system	J95–J99	843	0.7	115	0.6	170	0.7	153	0.6	173	0.7	232	0.7
Perinatal disorders	P90–P96	747	0.6	124	0.6	205	0.8	162	0.6	142	0.6	114	0.4
Other land transp. accident	V80–V89	741	0.6	97	0.5	132	0.5	209	0.8	135	0.5	168	0.5
Diseases of esophagus, stomach	K20–K31	735	0.6	98	0.5	123	0.5	164	0.6	152	0.6	198	0.6
Other acute lower resp. infections	J20–J22	702	0.5	106	0.5	140	0.6	167	0.6	119	0.5	170	0.5
Episodic and paroxysmal disorders	G40–G47	687	0.5	95	0.5	124	0.5	158	0.6	152	0.6	158	0.5
Aplastic and other anemias	D60–D64	679	0.5	95	0.5	145	0.6	135	0.5	130	0.5	174	0.6
All other causes	The remainder	11,689	9.1	1,974	9.5	2,268	9.2	2,582	9.5	2,320	9.2	2,545	8.2

Source: Statistics South Africa 2002b.

certed efforts made since 1995 to improve the coverage of birth and death registration had an effect on improving registration in the nonurban areas over the period from 1996 to 2000.

In the face of the challenge of incomplete registration and misreporting of HIV/AIDS as the cause of death, various ingenious methods have been devised using the administrative system (surrounding death and burial) to estimate the number of deaths due to HIV/AIDS. In one study in Brazzaville, Congo, conducted in 1996, researchers undertook a morgue-based study to assess the contribution of HIV/AIDS to general mortality. Over a period of thirty consecutive days, assessment was made of the causes of death for all bodies delivered to the morgues of Brazzaville (where all corpses must be taken, as per the legal requirements of the country, before they can be buried). The specially trained medical doctors questioned the next of kin on the clinical signs and symptoms preceding the death and on the circumstances of death. The bodies were examined for signs of HIV/AIDS based on the WHO definition, and admission records of the deceased were collected and checked. The study found that the leading cause of death among adults (over 15) was HIV/AIDS, accounting for 25.1 percent of all deaths. The other leading causes of deaths were cardiovascular disease (a natural cause of death), accounting for 15.4 percent of all deaths, and external causes of death (unnatural causes), accounting for 9.9 percent of all deaths (Pictet et al. 1998).

This chapter has reported on three separate methods used to try to estimate the number of deaths due to HIV/AIDS in South Africa. Two of the methods were analytic, while the third method was based on an actual sample. In a way, the data from the sample (upon hindsight) provides a benchmark against which to assess the validity of the two analytic methods. What the sample study has shown is that HIV/AIDS has become the leading cause of death in South Africa. However, giving a precise estimate of deaths due to HIV/AIDS is rather elusive when using death registration data alone. One reason for this is the misreporting of deaths due to HIV/AIDS. Trying to group the different causes of death to arrive at HIV/AIDS-related causes of death is helpful to some extent. If we take tuberculosis as an example, it is clearly associated with HIV/AIDS in many instances. However, the fact remains that there are some TB deaths that are genuine TB deaths and not HIV-related. The same goes for the other related causes. One difficult area that has not been considered is the issue of the "ill-defined" causes of death—the causes of death that are stated as "natural causes" and "heart failure." Once HIV/AIDS has been misreported as TB, it could also be misreported as a "natural cause." There is a need to work on finding out the causes of death that hide under "ill-defined" causes.

In situations where cause-of-death data are not available for the immediate past, the methods used in situations one and two above could be helpful. However, it is necessary to guard against the weaknesses of these methods and against jumping to conclusions. In the first method, justification has to be provided for using AIDSProj as opposed to other programs/software for making HIV/AIDS projections. Because the underlying growth rates used in the first method are derived from the HIV/AIDS deaths obtained via AIDSProj, if that software underestimated deaths due to HIV/AIDS, then their mathematical elimination would not lead to the flattening of the curve as desired. In the first as well as second methods, the grouping of the deaths does not take into account the "ill-defined" causes of death, which could lead to some underestimation. In the second method, a polynomial regression based on few data points might give reliable estimates. Lastly, the ex-post/ex-ante adjustment, while logical, might not adequately capture the changing relationship between deaths due to HIV/AIDS and natural deaths.

Conclusion

Death registration data, when reasonably complete, can adequately show recent increases in mortality. With deaths broken down by natural and unnatural deaths, we can start identifying the areas where mortality increases are a problem. With breakdown by cause of death, we can identify a bit more clearly the leading causes of death contributing to the rise in mortality. However, in the context of misreporting of causes of death, we cannot expect the cause-of-death data themselves to provide accurate estimates of the number of deaths due to HIV/AIDS. Some additional modeling is needed for more precision in the estimates. With the availability of multiple causes of death data, we hope to make some progress toward achieving this goal. However, any differences in estimates should not detract from the fact that HIV/AIDS has become South Africa's biggest health problem in the twenty-first century. With a redoubling of efforts, it is hoped that some gains can be made toward combating this biggest source of premature mortality.

References

Beers, M., and R. Berkow, eds. 1999. *The Merck Manual of Diagnosis and Therapy.* Whitehouse Station, NJ: Merck Research Laboratories.

Bélec, L., T. Brogan, F. Kéou, and A. Georges. 1994. "Surveillance of Acquired Immunodeficiency Syndrome in Africa." *Epidemiologic Reviews* 16(2): 403–17.

Hakulinen, T., H. Hansluwka, A.D. Lopez, and T. Nakada. 1986. "Estimation of global mortality pattern by cause of death." In *New Developments in the Analysis of Morality and Causes of Death,* ed. H. Hansluwka et al. Bangkok: Amarin Press.

Jones, J., D. Hanson, M. Dworkin, D. Alderton, P. Fleming, J. Kaplan, J. Ward. 1999. "Surveillance for AIDS-defining opportunistic illnesses, 1992–1997." In *CDC Surveillance Summaries,* April 16. *Morbidity and Mortality Weekly Report* (48) No. SS-2: 1–22.

Kleinschmidt, I. 1999. "South African tuberculosis mortality data—showing the first sign of the AIDS epidemic?" *South African Medical Journal* 89(3): 269–73.

Lopez, A.D., and T.H. Hull. 1983. "A note on estimating the cause of death structure in high mortality populations." *Population Bulletin of United Nations* No. 14: 1982.

Murray, C., and A. Lopez. 1994. "Global and regional causes-of-death patterns in 1990." *Bulletin of the World Health Organization* 72: 447–80.

Ostrom, C. 1990. *Time Series Analysis Regression Techniques.* Newbury Park, CA: Sage.

Palloni, A., and R. Wyrick. 1981. "Mortality decline in Latin America: Changes in the structure of causes of death, 1950–1975." *Social Biology* 28(3–4): 187–216.

Pictet, G., S. Le Coeur, P. M'Pelé, N. Brouard, and M. Lallemant. 1998. "Contribution of AIDS to the general mortality in Central Africa: Evidence from a morgue-based study in Brazzaville, Congo." *AIDS* 12: 2217–23.

Preston, S. 1972. "Influence of cause of death structure on age patterns of mortality." In *Population Dynamics,* ed. T.N.E. Greville. New York: Academic Press.

Statistics South Africa (Stats SA). 1999. *Villages and Townships Vital Statistics Network (VTVSN).* Issue No. 10, July/August. Pretoria: Stats SA.

———. 2001a. "Mid-year Estimates, 2001" (Statistical release P0302). Pretoria: Stats SA.

———. 2001b. "Advance release of recorded deaths, 1997–2000" (Statistical release 0309.1). Pretoria: Stats SA.

———. 2002a. "Deaths in South Africa that are due to HIV/AIDS and related causes, 1993–2000." Unpublished discussion document. Pretoria: Stats SA.

———. 2002b. "Causes of deaths in South Africa, 1997–2001: Advance release of recorded causes of death" (Statistical release P0309.2). Pretoria: Stats SA.

Wilkinson, D., and G. Davies. 1997. "The increasing burden of tuberculosis in rural South Africa: Impact of the HIV epidemic." *South African Medical Journal* 87: 447–50.

Appendix 5.1

Conditions Attributable to HIV or Complicated by HIV According to the 1993 CDC Definition

Conditions attributable to HIV or complicated by HIV (category B)
    Bacillary angiomatosis
    Candidiasis, oropharyngeal (thrush)
    Candidiasis, vulvovaginal; persistent, frequent, or poorly responsive to therapy
    Cervical dysplasia (moderate or severe)/cervical carcinoma in situ
    Constitutional symptoms, such as fever (38.5° C or diarrhea lasting >1 mo
    Hairy leukoplakia, oral
    Herpes zoster (shingles), involving at least two distinct episodes or more than one dermatome
    Idiopathic thrombocytopenic purpura
    Listeriosis
    Pelvic inflammatory disease, particularly if complicated by tubo-ovarian abscess
    Peripheral neuropathy
AIDS-indicator conditions (category C)
    Candidiasis of bronchi, trachea, or lungs
    Candidiasis, esophageal
    Cervical cancer, invasive
    Coccidioidomycosis, disseminated or extrapulmonary
    Cryptococcosis, extrapulmonary
    Cryptosporidiosis, chronic intestinal (>1 mo duration)
    Cytomegalovirus disease (other than liver, spleen, or nodes)
    Cytomegalovirus retinitis (with loss of vision)
    Encephalopathy, HIV-related
    Herpes simplex: chronic ulcer(s) (1 mo duration); bronchitis, pneumonitis, or esophagitis
    Histoplasmosis, disseminated or extrapulmonary
    Isosporiasis, chronic intestinal (>1 mo duration)
    Kaposi's sarcoma
    Lymphoma, Burkett's (or equivalent term)
    Lymphoma, immunoblastic (or equivalent term)
    Lymphoma, primary, of brain
    Mycobacterium avium complex or *M. kansasii,* disseminated or extrapulmonary
    M. tuberculosis, any site (pulmonary or extrapulmonary)
    Mycobacterium, other species or unidentified species, disseminated or extrapulmonary
    Pneumocystis carinii pneumonia
    Pneumonia, recurrent
    Progressive multifocal leukoencephalopathy
    Salmonella septicemia, recurrent
    Taxoplasmosis of brain
    Wasting syndrome due to HIV

Source: Reproduced with permission from *The Merck Manual of Diagnosis and Therapy,* Edition 17, p. 1313, edited by Mark H. Beers and Robert Berkow. Copyright 1999 by Merck & Co., Inc., Whitehouse Station, NJ.

Appendix 5.2

Causes of Death that Closely Match Conditions Attributable to HIV or Complicated by HIV According to the 1993 CDC Definition

	ICD-10 code	ICD-9 code
Other congenital malformations of skin	Q82	757
Candidiasis	B37	112
Candidiasis	B37	112
Noninflammatory cervix/cervical carcinoma in situ	N87/D06	622/233
Other noninfective gastroenteritis and colitis	K52	558
Lip disease	K13	528
Herpes zoster (shingles)	B02	53
Purpura and other hemorrhagic disease	D69	287
Listeriosis	A32	27
Pelvic inflammation	N73/N70	614
Other polyneuropathies	G62	357
Candidiasis	B37	112
Candidiasis	B37	112
Cervix cancer	C53	180
Coccidioidomycosis	B38	114
Cryptococcosis	B45	117
Protozoal intestinal disease	A07	7
Cytomegaloviral disease	B25	78
Cytomegaloviral disease	H30/B25	363/078
Encephalopathy	G93/B22	348/209
Herpes viral (herpes simplex) infections/other disorders of skin and subcutaneous tissue, not elsewhere classified/bronchitis, not specified as acute or chronic/pneumonia, organism unspecified	B00/L98/ J40/J18	054/709/ 490/486
Histoplasmosis	B39	115
Protozoal intestinal disease	A07	7
Kaposi's sarcoma	C46	173
Diffuse non-Hodgkin's lymphoma	C83	200
Diffuse non-Hodgkin's lymphoma	C83	200
Other and unspecified types of non-Hodgkin's lymphoma	C85	202
Infection due to other mycobacteria	A31	31
Miliary tuberculosis	A19	18
Infection due to other mycobacteria	A31	31
Pneumocystosis	B59	136
Pneumonia, organism unspecified	J18	486
Creutzfeldt–Jakob disease	A81	46
Other salmonella infections	A02	3
Toxoplasmosis	B58	130
Human immunodeficiency virus (HIV) disease resulting in other specified diseases	B22/R64	209/799

Source: Statistics South Africa categorization of codes.

Appendix 5.3

List of Causes of Death Often Associated with HIV/AIDS According to Stats SA Coding Experience

	ICD-10 code	ICD-9 code
A. Deaths due to HIV/AIDS		
Human immunodeficiency virus (HIV) disease resulting in infectious and parasitic diseases	B20	209
Human immunodeficiency virus (HIV) disease resulting in malignant neoplasms	B21	209
Human immunodeficiency virus (HIV) disease resulting in other specified diseases	B22	209
Human immunodeficiency virus (HIV) disease resulting in other conditions	B23	209
Unspecified human immunodeficiency virus (HIV) disease	B24	209
B. Causes of deaths closely associated with HIV/AIDS		
Diarrhea and gastroenteritis of presumed infectious origin	A09	9
Respiratory tuberculosis	A16	11
Zoster (herpes zoster)	B02	53
Cytomegaloviral disease (CMV disease)	B25	78
Cryptococcosis meningitis	B45	117
Meningitis	G03	322
Pneumocystosis	B59	136
Pneumonia candidiasis	B37	112
Kaposi's sarcoma	C46	173
Lymphoma	C83/C85	200/202
Purpura and other hemorrhagic conditions	D69	287
Metabolic disorders	E70-E88	270:277
Lymphoadenopathy	R59	785
Septicemia	A41	38
Anemia	D64	285

Source: Statistics South Africa regrouping.

6. Parental Survival and Residential Patterns

Amadou Noumbissi, Ayaga A. Bawah, and Tukufu Zuberi

The current HIV/AIDS epidemic in sub-Saharan Africa is likely to have unanticipated consequences on household and family structure. The majority of HIV/AIDS cases are found among the most productive segment of the population, between the ages of 20 and 40 (Quinn 2001). The concentration of HIV/AIDS deaths in this age group has significant consequences for the family, because most people in this group are bearing and raising young children. When parents of young children die, their grandparents and other relatives often care for them. Thus, the HIV/AIDS epidemic results in an increased burden for the extended family that has to care for orphans. Africa may also witness an increase in the number of households headed by children as a result of the scourge of HIV/AIDS. The residential patterns of children are influenced by the survival of their parents as well as by cultural and socioeconomic practices, such as child fosterage (McDaniel and Zulu 1996). Parental survival has a direct impact on the nature of extended family relationships.

The proportion of individuals without a surviving parent is becoming an important social problem in the southern African region. According to Hunter and Williamson (1999, 2000), the proportion of children less than 15 years of age with at least one parent deceased in South Africa increased from 4.3 to 5.0 percent between 1990 and 1995. By 2000, this proportion had jumped to 9.1 percent. Abandoned to themselves as the traditional safety net becomes overwhelmed (Foster 2000), and in the absence of adequate support, children may be forced to drop out of school or be compelled to work in order to survive, often ending up in the streets. An increase in the number of orphans is likely to worsen biases introduced by child "adoption" effects when studying child health and survival (Lloyd and Desai 1992). The capacity of the extended family, especially grandparents, to care for orphans may be exceeded with the rapid increase in the number of young orphans who need care.

In this chapter, we focus on residential patterns of individuals in South Africa according to the survival status of their parents using 1996 census micro-data. First we describe the data used in the analysis, next we discuss reporting of parental survival in these data, followed by a discussion of residential patterns and parental survival status. Finally, we provide a multivariate analysis of the correlates of children's living arrangements.

Data and Methods

Information on the survival status of parents together with individual, household, and community characteristics available in most African censuses give us the leverage to examine levels, differentials, and spatial variations of parental survival and its effects on the living arrangements of their children over time. Because of a lack of data for estimating adult mortality in Africa, the focus of past research using parental survival data has almost exclusively centered on the estimation of levels, trends, and patterns of adult mortality using indirect methods (Brass and Hill 1973; Hill and Trussell 1977; Timaeus 1992, 1993; Bah 1999). Little attention has been paid to the living arrangements of children who report the death of one or both of their parents in Africa.

While we acknowledge that knowing the levels and trends of adult mortality is important, potentially large-scale orphaning because of increases in adult mortality deserves considerable attention. This is especially critical to policy formulation with respect to strengthening or establishing structures to accommodate the increasing needs of children without parents. For instance, knowing which segments or subgroups of the population have the highest proportions of children without surviving parents allows for the maximization of policies by targeting resources to those areas or subgroups that will be in dire need of them.

The data for this paper come from a 30 percent sample of the 1996 South African Population Census micro-data. In most African censuses, questions are asked about the survival status of parents of household members, that is, whether the member's biological mother or father is alive or not. South Africa introduced this question in its census for the first time in 1996. Brass and Hill (1973), Hill and Trussell (1977), and Timaeus (1992) established equations that transform proportions of children with living parents into adult probabilities of survival. The assumption underlying this methodology is that every person knows his or her biological mother and father and will be able to report accurately on their survival status. In the case of census data, the household head is the respondent. Because the household head may not necessarily know or remember accurately all information related to each household member, his or her responses may be a source of error.

Although the question on parental survival status specifically refers to biological parents, a false answer may be stated if the child is adopted or fostered or if the parental survival status is unknown. Persons living in institutions and the homeless were not asked this question; therefore, these people will be excluded from our analysis. We do not expect the exclusion of this population to bias our analysis in any way, since only 2,470 homeless out of 9,059,571 (0.0003 percent) households were surveyed (Statistics South Africa 1998). The institutional population constitutes less than 3 percent of the total population and is mostly made up of White and Colored children who are probably in boarding schools, and also by elderly Whites living in homes for the aged (see Appendix 6.1). There are also some individuals for whom information on the survival status of their parents is unknown (about 1 percent of mothers and 3 percent of fathers). The numbers of these persons vary appreciably by racial group (see Appendixes 6.2 and 6.3). The graphs show that unknown survival status of parents is highest among Africans and lowest among Indians/Asians. For instance, about 3.8 percent of African children ages birth to 14 were reported as having fathers with an unknown survival status, and 1 percent lived in households where the head did not know the survival status of the childs' mothers.

Results

In order to verify the magnitude of the issue of child fosterage, we compared the number of surviving children reported to all women, regardless of age, to the number of people in the population with a surviving mother (see Table 6.1). Table 6.1 presents the numbers of surviving children reported by women ages twelve and above and those of children with reported surviving mother alive. Preston notes that these two numbers should be equal in a closed population or if migration is negligible (Brass 1975; Preston cited in UN 1983, UN 1985). The likely errors move in opposite directions: a tendency to underreport children by mothers will lower the number of surviving children, and failure to correctly report a dead mother will increase the number of people with a surviving mother.

As can be observed from Table 6.1, the proportion of children reporting a surviving mother is slightly higher than the number of surviving children reported by mothers. This is particularly the case for the African population and "others," where the difference between the numbers of surviving children

Table 6.1

Number of Children Surviving Reported by Mothers Compared to Children with Mother Alive, by Racial Group

Racial group	Surviving children reported by women (1)	Surviving mother reported by children (2)	Difference (2)/(1)
African	21,393,296	24,034,437	1.123
Colored	2,545,262	2,690,577	1.057
Indian/Asian	713,752	775,608	1.087
White	2,863,454	2,990,304	1.044
Others	185,053	258,656	1.398
All	27,700,817	30,749,583	1.110

Source: Computed from the 1996 South African Population Census micro-data.

reported and those with a surviving mother alive are, respectively, about 12 and 40 percent higher. The difference is relatively smaller for the other population groups, especially for the White population, for which the difference in the two numbers is only about 4 percent. This inconsistency, especially among Africans, might be caused by the underreporting of the number of children by mothers, especially children who are not living with their mothers and oldest children who may have already left the parental home. It might also be due to the presence in the country of persons whose mothers are living abroad or have not been captured in the census.

To determine the extent of the association between the race of parents (as well as other factors such as sex, place, and region of residence) and the residential patterns of children, we first used simple percentages, odds, and odds ratios to examine the level of the associations at the bivariate level. Subsequently, we estimated a multinomial logit model with residential type as a dependent variable to see if the observed relationships at the bivariate level persist. We identified five household types, drawing on the works of Morgan et al. (1993), McDaniel (1994), McDaniel and Morgan (1996), and Gage, Sommerfelt, and Piani (1996). The five household types identified are (1) single-person, (2) nuclear,[1] (3) nuclear-augmented, (4) extended, and (5) extended augmented. These terms are defined below. We postulated that orphans are more likely to live in extended households. Because the dependent variable has more than two categories, in our multivariate analysis we used a multinomial logit model, which is better suited for such a situation (Long 1997; Allison 1999).

The outcome variable of interest is the survival status of the parent—mother-only dead, father-only dead, or both parents alive or dead. The other independent variables controlled for in the model are age of the child, his or her race, and place and province of residence.

Age Pattern of Reported Parental Death

The proportion of children reporting a dead parent should increase with age, because as children grow older they are more likely to have a dead parent. However, there may be heterogeneity in the survival status of parents by population groups and gender because of differential access to health and economic resources and also because of biological differences, especially related to the sexes. For instance, some researchers observe higher male mortality at older ages (Elo and Preston 1992, 1996; Smith and Kington 1997). In Figure 6.1, we present the proportion of children with reported parent(s) dead by age and parental sex. The proportion of children reporting both parents dead increases with age. However, differences exist between reported mother-only dead and father-only dead. At all ages, the proportion of children reporting their fathers dead is higher than the proportion of children reporting their mothers dead. While about 40 percent of persons aged 40 years reported the death of their fathers only, less than 10 percent of persons of the same age reported the death of their mothers only.

These large differences are not simple cultural or data artifacts but are the result of both higher male mortality and differences in the age at childbearing between men and women.

Differentials in Reported Parental Death

The differences in the patterns by age are even more apparent when presented by racial groups. While it is clear that the White population has a survival advantage compared to other racial groups for males and females, distinct patterns by the sex of the parents also exist (Figures 6.2 and 6.3). For instance, up to and between the ages of 45–49, African children have the highest proportion of their fathers reported dead, followed by Colored and Indians/Asians, who appear to have identical levels (Figure 6.3). On the other hand, differences in the reported death status of mothers for African, Colored, and Indian/Asian children are less obvious (Figure 6.2). African children seem to have a lower proportion of mothers reported dead than Colored and Indian/Asian children before age 30. Even more curious is the fact that beyond age 55, mothers of African children seem to be dead at lower rates than Whites. This apparent survival advantage to African mothers is probably a result of poor data quality, as shown in Table 6.1.

Given the differences observed above, we examined further the reported death status of parents by sex, place, and region of residence. Results are presented in Table 6.2. We also included in this analysis the percentage of individuals with unknown parental survival status by race and place and province of residence.

Figure 6.1 **Proportion of Children with Parent Dead by Age in South Africa**

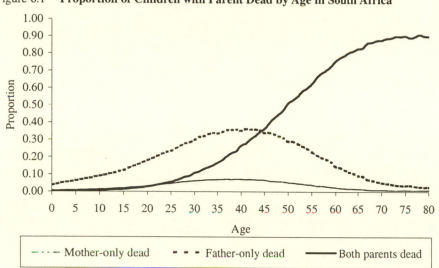

Source: Computed from the 1966 South African Population Census micro-data.

Figure 6.2 **Proportion of Children with Mother Dead by Racial Group**

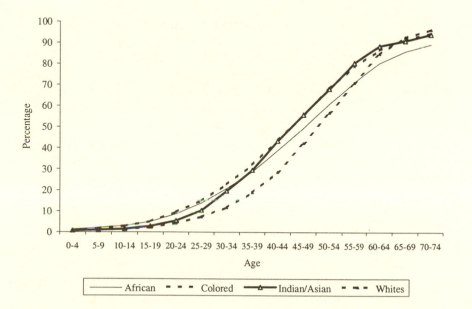

Source: Computed from the 1966 South African Population Census micro-data.

Figure 6.3   **Proportion of Children with Father Dead by Racial Group**

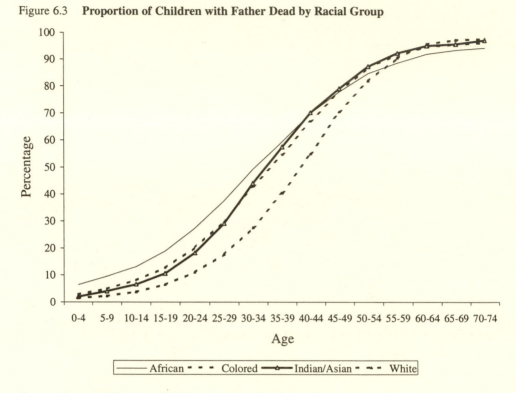

Source: Computed from the 1966 South African Population Census micro-data.

The results provide an interesting picture of differences in the levels of reported parental survival in the country, both by race and province or place of residence, an issue clearly of policy relevance when it comes to figuring out which subgroups and provinces need more attention in terms of health interventions. For instance, about 10 percent of all children ages birth through 14 have at least one parent reported dead (summation of both parents dead, father-only dead, and mother-only dead for the whole country). There are, however, marked differences by the sex of the parent. For instance, while only about 2 percent of the children in that age range reportedly lost their mother, almost 9 percent of them reported a dead father, whatever the survival status of the other parent. However, only about 1 percent of children ages birth through 14 reported no surviving parent. A relatively high proportion of children did not know the survival status of their parents. Overall, about 4 percent of children ages 14 or less were in this situation, and this proportion varied by racial group and place and province of residence.

After excluding these children with unknown survival status of parents, we suspected that the marked differences between the percentages of children with

Table 6.2

Proportion of Children with Mother, Father, or Both Parents Dead According to Selected Variables (children ages 0–14)

	Both dead	Mother-only dead	Father-only dead	Both alive	One unknown	Total
Racial Group						
African	0.009	0.012	0.085	0.855	0.040	1.00
Colored	0.005	0.013	0.045	0.917	0.020	1.00
Indian/Asian	0.004	0.007	0.037	0.936	0.016	1.00
White	0.003	0.007	0.023	0.940	0.027	1.00
Residence						
Rural	0.007	0.011	0.063	0.887	0.033	1.00
Urban	0.008	0.012	0.087	0.852	0.041	1.00
Province						
Western Cape	0.004	0.010	0.046	0.918	0.022	1.00
Eastern Cape	0.009	0.013	0.104	0.845	0.029	1.00
Northern Cape	0.006	0.015	0.052	0.898	0.029	1.00
Free State	0.008	0.014	0.078	0.861	0.040	1.00
KwaZulu-Natal	0.009	0.012	0.078	0.874	0.026	1.00
North West	0.007	0.012	0.068	0.859	0.055	1.00
Gauteng	0.007	0.009	0.058	0.889	0.037	1.00
Mpumalanga	0.007	0.012	0.054	0.893	0.034	1.00
Limpopo	0.007	0.010	0.090	0.829	0.064	1.00
South Africa	0.008	0.012	0.076	0.867	0.037	1.00

Source: Computed from the 1996 South African Population Census micro-data.

father and mother dead are not only the result of cultural differences or practices; they are also likely the result of higher male mortality levels in the country. These differences are even more striking when we break them down by race and province of residence. For example, while only about 3 percent of White children between the ages of birth and 14 have lost at least one parent, the corresponding figure for the African population is 11 percent. In terms of distribution by sex, about 1 percent of White children ages birth to 14 report dead mothers and about 1.2 percent of African children in the same age range report dead mothers. The corresponding figures for children reporting dead fathers are 2.3 percent for Whites and 8.5 percent for Africans. Also, while about 1 percent of African children in the same age range are reported to have lost both parents, about 0.3 percent of White children within those ages report both parents dead.

Oddly, rural areas have lower levels of paternal and maternal deaths compared to the urban areas. Similarly, the levels of parental survival differ by province. For example, while about 1.3 percent of mothers of children ages birth through 14 and 10.4 percent of fathers in the same age range have been reported dead in the Eastern Cape, only 1.0 percent of mothers and 4.6 percent of fathers of children in that age range are reported to have died in the Western Cape. With the exception of Limpopo Province, where the level of paternal deaths seems high, while maternal deaths are relatively low, and Northern Cape, with the opposite situation, results from the rest of the provinces suggest that where the survival status of mothers is high, then so is the survival status of fathers. Western Cape appears to have the highest level of both maternal and paternal survival status. On the other hand, the Eastern Cape, Free State, and KwaZulu-Natal provinces report the highest level of parental loss compared to the rest of the provinces, with the Eastern Cape experiencing the highest levels. These provinces are also among the provinces with the highest numbers of children with unknown survival status of their parents.

It is important to note that the provinces with the highest level of reported paternal deaths coincide with the provinces where the former homelands and Bantustan were located. The areas surrounding Lesotho in the Eastern Cape, KwaZulu-Natal, Free State, Limpopo, and North West provinces, which were part of the former homelands, have the highest proportions of children without a surviving father. The reasons for this observation need to be investigated further. Note that a similar pattern is not observed for mothers.

Residential Patterns and Parental Survival

An essential dimension of household and family structure is the residential patterns of the population, for in many ways, family experiences are dramatically influenced by residential situations. The living arrangements of children are influenced by the marital conditions of their parents, parental survival status, number of children in the household, and patterns of fosterage and other forms of extended family arrangements. African residential patterns are complex. This is especially likely to be the case for South Africa, which is a multiracial society where the types and structures of households are not only determined by current socioeconomic factors but may also be the result of the past political system of apartheid that has shaped South African society (see Zulu and Sibanda, chapter 8 of this volume). The conquest of the country by European populations and the development of capitalism, along with labor force migration and the implementation of the apartheid regime allowing the creation of homelands with restrictive influx control policies, have affected the residential patterns of African, Colored, and Indian/Asian populations. Also, the high level of male migration from rural to urban and mining areas has affected marriage patterns in South Africa, explaining, at least partially, the high number of never-married and out-of-wedlock births (Sibanda and Zuberi 1999).

Various types of residential patterns can be identified in terms of the types of living arrangements found in African households. A household is conventionally defined as a group of people who live together and share common cooking arrangements. These people may or may not necessarily be related. In the 1996 South African Population Census, a household was defined as consisting "of a person or a group of persons, who occupy a common dwelling (or part of it) for at least four days a week and who provide themselves jointly with food and other essentials for living" (Statistics South Africa 1998). In other words, they live together as a unit. Therefore, people who occupy the same dwelling unit, but who do not share food or other essentials, are enumerated as belonging to separate households.

Our interest here is to examine how the residential patterns of children are affected by the survival status of their parents. Thus, we are interested in the composition of the households. In classifying households, different authors have provided slightly different classifications. For instance, Gage, Sommerfelt, and Piani (1996) classified households, on the basis of Demographic Health Survey (DHS) data, broadly as two main types: elementary and extended. They further subcategorized elementary household structures as (1) single-parent households consisting of a head and his or her biological children, without spouses or other persons; (2) nuclear households consisting of a head and his or her spouse and their biological or adopted children, without other persons; and (3) polygynous households, where there is a head and more than one spouse and their biological children. They subcategorized extended households as two groups: three-generational and laterally extended households. They defined three-generational households to include those in which parents and parents-in-law of the head live, or to include the head and his or her grandchildren, with at least one biological child of the head and/or spouse present. Laterally extended households, according to their classification, are those that are composed of the head, his or her siblings, and other relatives or nonrelatives.

Following the methodology of Morgan et al. (1993), McDaniel (1994), and McDaniel and Morgan (1996), who have examined historical living arrangements in the United States, we use the relationships of members of households to the head of the household, along with the number of persons in the household, to classify households into five broad, mutually exclusive categories that essentially capture the different classifications proposed by Gage, Sommerfelt, and Piani (1996). We do not distinguish polygynous households in our classification, because the South African census did not provide information on polygyny. Thus, we distinguish the following household types: (1) single-person (an individual who lives alone); (2) nuclear (household head and/or spouse, and biological or adopted children); (3) nuclear augmented (nuclear household plus nonrelatives); (4) extended (nuclear household plus other relatives); and (5) extended augmented (extended household plus nonrelatives). It should be noted that single-person households in a real sense are also nuclear; however, for the purpose of our analysis, we isolated these in order to have an idea of the proportion of persons in South Africa who live alone.

To understand the dynamics within various household types enumerated above, we first examined the relationship of the various household members to the head. In other words, we were interested in knowing whether individuals live in households headed by themselves, their spouses, their children, relatives, or others with whom they may not be biologically related. We also examined how the survival status of parents affects this relationship. We distinguished between situations with a father-only dead, mother-only dead, and both dead or alive because of the implications of each on children's well-being. Table 6.3 shows that, in South Africa, a relatively small percentage of children live with a nonrelative (about 1 percent overall). This proportion does not vary significantly with the reported survival status of the parent. However, a large proportion of children live with their grandparents (26.4 percent). This proportion increases when children lose either one or both of the parents. For example, about 34 percent of children whose father and mother are both reported dead live with their grandparents. Almost the same proportion of children whose mothers alone are reported dead are living with their grandparents. When both parents are alive, a high proportion of children ages birth through 14 are reported to reside with their grandparents—about 25 percent. This finding supports the idea that child fosterage is very high in South Africa.

Another interesting observation is that a relatively high proportion of young persons who have reported parental deaths reside with their siblings (see Table 6.3). More than 10 percent of children below age 15 who reported the loss of both parents reside with their siblings versus only 2 percent when both parents are reported alive, about 5 percent when only the father is reported dead, and more than 6 percent when only the mother is reported dead. Also, as expected, when one of the parents dies, children are more likely to be living with the other surviving parent. However, this is more likely to be the case when the father dies as compared to when the mother dies (56 percent versus 47 percent).

In Table 6.4, we present simple odds to show whether children who live with their grandparents are more likely to live with their grandmothers or grandfathers. The results suggest that the majority of children living with their grandparents reside in households headed by women, whatever the survival status of their parents, implying that grandchildren often live with their grandmothers. The likelihood of children living with their grandmothers is even higher when the father is reported dead and the mother alive.

In Table 6.5, we present the percentage of individuals living in different

Table 6.3

Children's Relationship to the Head of Household by Survival Status of Parents (Children Ages 0–14)

Survival status of parents	Head	Spouse	Son/ daughter	Brother/ sister	Father/ mother	Grand- child	Other relative	Non- related	Not stated	Total
Both dead	1.56	1.80	31.86	10.76	0.22	33.51	8.92	2.43	8.94	100
Mother-only dead	0.57	0.62	47.28	6.43	0.18	32.73	6.66	1.60	3.93	100
Father-only dead	0.41	0.54	56.42	4.65	0.18	29.67	3.94	1.04	3.16	100
Both alive	0.22	0.39	65.10	2.00	0.10	25.27	2.76	0.91	3.25	100
One unknown	0.26	0.48	42.93	2.31	0.09	41.08	4.35	3.40	5.08	100
South Africa	0.25	0.41	63.15	2.34	0.11	26.35	3.00	1.04	3.36	100

Source: Computed from the 1996 South African Population Census micro-data.

Table 6.4

Observed Odds that a Child (Female or Male) Residing with His or Her Grandparents Resides in a Household Headed by the Couple

Survival status of parents	Household headed by				
	Grandmother (1)	Grandfather (2)	Both Grandparents (3)	Odds ratios (1)/(2)	Odds ratios (3)/(2)
Both dead	1.71	0.10	0.39	17.58	4.03
Mother-only dead	1.33	0.16	0.41	8.35	2.60
Father-only dead	2.77	0.07	0.25	40.31	3.65
Both alive	1.18	0.08	0.62	14.08	7.37
One unknown	1.68	0.08	0.43	21.37	5.46
South Africa	1.26	0.09	0.57	14.26	6.39

Source: Computed from the 1996 South African Population Census micro-data.
Note: The odds values (o) are calculated for each cell as: o = proportion/(1 – proportion).

Table 6.5

Proportion of Children by Household Type and the Survival Status of Parents

Survival status of parents	Single	Nuclear	Nuclear augmented	Extended	Extended augmented	Total N
Both dead	0.28	21.51	5.20	55.92	17.08	100.0
Mother-only dead	0.11	29.53	4.41	50.54	15.41	100.0
Father-only dead	0.07	34.33	3.59	48.55	13.46	100.0
Both alive	0.03	45.91	4.45	36.91	12.69	100.0
One unknown	0.05	29.69	5.53	49.27	15.46	100.0
South Africa	0.04	44.07	4.43	38.55	12.92	100.0

Source: Computed from the 1996 South African Population Census micro-data.

household types and the reported survival status of their parents. It appears that the death of a mother tends to determine more where a child is likely to reside than the death of a father. For instance, when the mother is reported dead and the father is believed to be alive, about 30 percent of the children live in nuclear households. This means that these children are either living with their fathers or are adopted. On the other hand, when the father is reported dead and the mother is still alive, about 34 percent of the children either live with their mother or are adopted. This also suggests that when the mother is reported dead and the father alive, children are more likely to be fostered, with either relatives or nonrelatives, as opposed to when the father is thought to be dead and the mother is alive. When both parents are reported dead, children are more likely to live with their relatives than to live with nonrelatives, as expected. However, a surprising 22 percent of children are

Table 6.6

Children by Household Type and the Survival Status of Parents (Odds Ratios)

Survival status of parents	Single	Nuclear	Nuclear augmented	Extended	Extended augmented
Both dead	9.22	0.32	1.18	2.17	1.42
Mother-only dead	3.48	0.49	0.99	1.75	1.25
Father-only dead	2.21	0.62	0.80	1.61	1.07
Both alive	1.00	1.00	1.00	1.00	1.00
One unknown	1.50	0.50	1.26	1.66	1.26
South Africa	1.20	0.93	0.99	1.07	1.02

Source: Computed from the 1996 South African Population Census micro-data.

reported to be living in nuclear households even when both parents are dead, which suggests that these children have been adopted.

Very few children reside alone: the proportion of children residing alone rises from almost 0 percent when both parents are alive to about 0.3 percent when both parents are dead (odds ratio 9) and 0.1 percent when the mother only is dead (odds ratio 2) (see Tables 6.5 and 6.6).

Multivariate Analysis

Given the observed relationships at the bivariate level, we estimated a multinomial logit model in order to examine whether some of the observed relationships at the bivariate level persist when we control for background factors such as race, place of residence, and province of residence. For the multivariate analysis, we limited our analysis to children below 15 years of age, because our interest is in estimating where children are more likely to live when either one or both parents are believed to be dead. Therefore, the dependent variable in the model is the type of household in which the child resides. We excluded from the analysis cases where the status of the household type is not specified. Table 6.7 presents results of the analysis.

As noted earlier, we expected more children to live in nuclear households as opposed to either being alone or living in augmented households. However, as was observed at the bivariate level, results of the multinomial regression suggest that the death of the mother is more likely to affect this pattern than is the death of the father. For instance, when the mother only is dead, the odds that a child will reside in a single-parent household or live alone rather than live in nuclear households is about five times the odds for the reference category (both parents alive). On the other hand, when the father is dead, the odds of a child living in a single rather than a nuclear household are about 2.5

Table 6.7

Multinomial Regression Results Showing the Odds of Either Residing in Extended, Single, or Households with Unrelated Members Compared with Nuclear Households

Variable	Single versus nucleated	Extended versus nucleated	Augmented versus nucleated
Intercept	0.002***	0.888***	0.343***
Survival status			
Mother only	5.191*	2.042***	1.734***
Father only	2.570***	1.575***	1.245***
Both dead	18.141***	2.992***	2.648***
Both alive	1.000	1.000	1.000
Racial group			
White	0.383*	0.205***	0.531***
Colored	0.628	0.853***	1.133***
Asian	0.358	0.559	0.266***
Africans	1.000	1.000	1.000
Place of residence			
Rural	1.412***	1.091***	1.210***
Urban	1.000	1.000	1.000
Province			
Eastern Cape	1.338***	1.457***	1.251***
Free State	0.926	1.001***	0.657***
KwaZulu-Natal	0.762***	1.219***	2.006***
Mpumalanga	1.170	1.089***	1.125
North West	1.157	1.364***	1.417***
Northern Cape	1.332	1.459***	1.365***
Limpopo	1.350***	1.235***	0.866***
Western Cape	0.659**	0.993***	0.919***
Gauteng	1.000	1.000	1.000

Source: Computed from the 1996 South African Population Census micro-data.
Notes: *$p < 0.5$; **$p < 0.01$; ***$p < 0.001$.

times higher than when both parents are alive. A similar pattern is observed when we compare the odds of living in extended households to those of living in nuclear households. That means children are more likely to live in extended households with nonrelated members rather than in nuclear households when one of the parents is dead.

The odds that White children reside in single, extended, or augmented households rather than in nuclear households range from about one-fifth to one-half the odds for the African population, indicating that White children are more likely to reside in nuclear households as compared to African children. A similar pattern is observed for the Indian/Asian population, but children of Coloreds are more likely to reside in nonrelated households rather than in nuclear households.

With regard to place of residence, the odds that children in rural areas will reside in single, extended, or augmented households rather than in nuclear households are higher than the odds for those residing in urban areas, after controlling for the survival status of the parents and other variables, such as race and province of residence. This is consistent with what we would expect to happen as societies move from traditional, rural areas to more urban ones. With increasing rates of urbanization, the nuclear family tends to grow (Caldwell 1977). There are also significant provincial differences, probably resulting from noncontrolled interaction effects between province, racial group, and place of residence. For example, while children in the Western Cape are most likely to reside in nuclear households, children in the Eastern Cape, Northern Cape, and North West provinces are more likely to reside in extended households as compared to the reference category (Gauteng). The odds of children residing alone are higher in the Eastern Cape, the Limpopo Province, and the Northern Cape, compared to those in Guateng, controlling for other selected variables.

Conclusions

This chapter uses the information on the survival status of parents to study the residential patterns of individuals in South Africa. Survival status of parents has so far been used mainly for estimating adult mortality in Africa. We demonstrate that this information, along with the information about individual, household, and community characteristics available in most African censuses, has allowed us to examine the levels, differentials, and spatial variation of parental survival as well as their effects on the living arrangements of individuals.

We first examined the reported parental survival status of children, results of which suggest that about 10 percent of all children between the ages of birth and 14 have lost at least one parent. The interesting observation is the huge differences in reported parental survival by sex of the parent. While only 2 percent of the children reported having lost a mother, 9 percent reported the loss of the father, an observation that is consistent with suggestions in the literature of South Africa that men are "missing," a phenomenon attributed in the past to higher male mortality resulting from occupational hazards such as mining, and more recently attributed to HIV/AIDS. Large differentials exist by race, with a larger percentage of parents reported dead in the African population than in other population groups, especially Whites. Again, this might be due to the fact that Africans are more prone to occupational hazards, but it is also an indication that they are disadvantaged in terms of receiving adequate health care and other social support systems as a result of the policies of apartheid (Moerdijk 1981; Burgard 2002). We also found considerable differences in parental survival by province of residence, with the Eastern Cape, Free State, KwaZulu-Natal, and Limpopo Province having the highest reported deaths of parents compared with the rest of the provinces. A majority of the former TBVC states were located in these provinces, and these provinces would have suffered most from the regional inequalities produced by apartheid.

Residential patterns speak to the conditions under which children live, which, as we know, not only affect children psychologically, but also affect the resources available to them. Therefore, we examined the impact of parental survival on the residential patterns of children. Both bivariate and multivariate examinations revealed interesting findings. For instance, results showed that few children reside with nonrelatives, which does not seem to vary with their parental status. Overall, close to equal proportions of children live in nuclear as in extended households, but White children are more likely to live in nuclear households than the other population groups. However, we observe that a large proportion of children tend to live with their grandparents, and the percentage of this population increases with the death of at least one parent. This finding emphasizes the role of the extended family, especially the social-support role of the grandparents, in African family systems (Baker-Aggarwal, van de Walle, and Mokomane 2001).

Also, as expected, when one parent dies, his or her children are likely to continue to reside with the other surviving parent. However, an interesting observation is that this is more likely when the father is dead as opposed to when the mother is dead, indicating that mothers are more likely to be main caregivers than fathers. Thus, when the mother of a child dies, children are more likely to live with their grandparents than when the father dies.

Note

1. A nuclear household is considered to be a husband and/or wife and children (including adopted and/or fostered children and stepchildren).

References

Allison, D. Paul. 1999. *Logistic Regression Using the SAS System, Theory and Application.* Cary, NC: SAS Institute Inc.

Bah, Sulaiman. 1999. "Diagnostic tests on assessing the quality of maternal orphanhood data from the 1996 South African census and implications for the indirect estimation of adult mortality." Discussion Paper 99–5. London, ON: University of Western Ontario.

Baker-Aggarwal, Ria, Etienne van de Walle, and Zitha Mokomane. 2001. "Extramarital child-bearing and the residence of children in Botswana." Unpublished manuscript. Philadelphia: Population Studies Center, University of Pennsylvania.

Brass, William. 1975. *Methods of Estimating Fertility and Mortality from Limited and Defective Data*. Chapel Hill, NC: Laboratories for Population Statistics, University of North Carolina.

Brass, William, and K. Hill. 1973. *Estimating Adult Mortality from Orphanhood*, Vol. 3, 111–23. Congrès de Liège: International Union of the Scientific Study of Population (IUSSP).

Burgard, Sarah. 2002. "Does race matter? Children's height in Brazil and South Africa." *Demography* 39(4): 763–90.

Caldwell, J.C. 1977. "The economic rationality of high fertility: An investigation illustrated with Nigerian survey data." *Population Studies* 31(1): 5–28.

Elo, I.T., and S.H. Preston. 1992. "Effects of early-life conditions on adult mortality: A review." *Population Index* 58(2): 186–212.

———. 1996. "Educational differences in mortality." *Social Science and Medicine* 42(1): 47–57.

Foster, G. 2000. "The capacity of the extended family net for orphans in Africa." *Psychology, Health and Medicine* 5(1): 55–62.

Gage, Anastasia J., A. Elisabeth Sommerfelt, and Andrea L. Piani. 1996. *Household Structure, Socioeconomic Level, and Child Health in Sub-Saharan Africa*. DHS Analytical Reports no. 1. Calverton, MD: Macro International Inc.

Hill, K., and J. Trussell. 1977. "Further developments in indirect mortality estimation." *Population Studies* 31(2): 313–34.

Hunter, S., and J. Williamson. 1999. *Children on the Brink, Strategies to Support Children Isolated by HIV/AIDS*. Washington, DC: The Synergy Project of TvT Associates, Inc. HIV-AIDS Division of the U.S. Agency for International Development (USAID).

———. 2000. *Children on the Brink, Updated Estimates and Recommendations for Intervention*. Washington, DC: The Synergy Project of TvT Associates, Inc. HIV-AIDS Division of USAID.

Lloyd, C.B., and S. Desai. 1992. "Children's living arrangements in developing countries." *Population Research and Policy Review* 11: 193–216.

Long, J. Scott. 1997. *Regression Models for Categorical and Limited Dependent Variables*. Thousand Oaks, CA: Sage.

McDaniel, A. 1994. "Historical racial differences in living arrangements of children." *Journal of Family History* 1 (19): 57–77.

McDaniel, Antonio, and S. Philip Morgan. 1996. "Racial differences in mother–child co-residence in the past." *Journal of Marriage and the Family* 58: 1011–17.

McDaniel, Antonio, and Eliya Zulu. 1996. "Mothers, fathers, and children: Regional patterns in child–parent residence in sub-Saharan Africa." *African Population Studies* 11: 1–28.

Moerdijk, Donald. 1981. *Anti-development: South Africa and Its Bantustans*. Paris: The UNESCO Press.

Morgan, S. Philip, Antonio McDaniel, Andrew T. Miller, and Samuel Preston. 1993. "Racial differences in household and family structure at the turn of century." *American Journal of Sociology* 98(4): 798–828.

Quinn, C. Thomas. 2001. "AIDS in Africa: A retrospective." *Bulletin of the World Health Organization* 79(12).

Sibanda, A., and T. Zuberi. 1999. "Contemporary fertility levels and trends in South Africa: Evidence from reconstructed census birth histories." In *The African Population in the 21st Century: Third African Population Conference*, vol. 1, 79–108. Durban: Union for African Population Studies.

Smith, J., and R. Kington. 1997. "Demographic and economic correlates of health in old age." *Demography* 34(1):159–70.

Statistics South Africa. 1998. *The People of South Africa: Population Census, 1996, The Count and How It Was Done*. Report no. 03–01–17(1996). Pretoria: Statistics South Africa.

Timaeus, Ian M. 1992. "Estimation of mortality paternal orphanhood: A reassessment and new approach." *Population Bulletin of the United Nations* 33.

————. 1993. "Adult mortality." In *Demographic Change in Sub-Saharan Africa*, 218–55. Washington, DC: National Research Council, National Academic Press.

United Nations. 1983. *Manual X: Indirect Techniques for Demographic Estimation*. New York: United Nations.

————. 1985. *Socioeconomic Differentials in Child Mortality in Developing Countries*. ST/ESA/SER. A/97. New York: United Nations.

Appendix 6.1 **Proportion of Persons Living in Institutions by Racial Group**

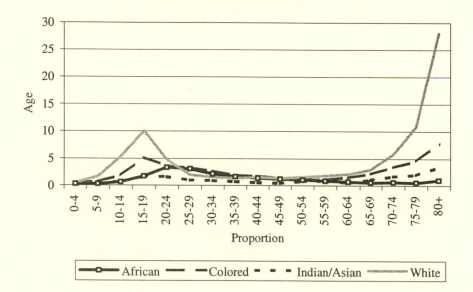

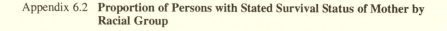

Source: Computed from the 1996 South African Population Census micro-data.

Appendix 6.2 **Proportion of Persons with Stated Survival Status of Mother by Racial Group**

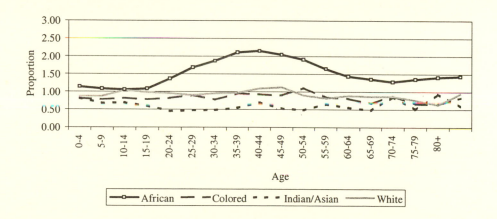

Source: Computed from the 1996 South African Population Census micro-data.

Appendix 6.3 **Proportion of Persons with Stated Survival Status of Father by Racial Group**

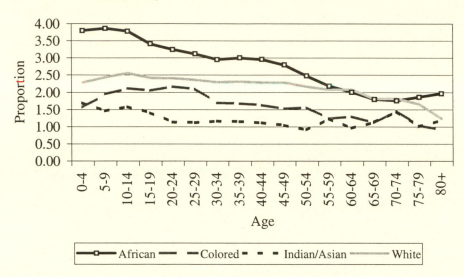

Source: Computed from the 1996 South African Population Census micro-data.

7. Technical Appraisal of Official South African Life Tables

Sulaiman Bah

In the years prior to 1985, national life tables published by Statistics South Africa (Stats SA) were based on registered deaths and were disaggregated according to population group and gender. The disaggregation in the life tables by population group was done only for Whites, Indians/Asians, and Coloreds. No life tables were produced for South Africa as a whole or for subnational geographic areas. The assumption underlying the construction of these life tables was that death registration was complete in these population groups. The life tables were then computed using the direct approach. For Africans, death registration was considered grossly incomplete, and hence life tables for this major population group were not published. Since the repeal of the Population Registration Act of 1950 in 1991, registered deaths are no longer available by population group. This makes 1990 the last year for which registered deaths are available by population group. As such, no life tables were published for the 1991 census year. After 1991, the civil registration/vital statistics (CR/VS) system continued functioning, but its potential for producing life tables needed to be reassessed. During this post-1991 period, several forces have had a simultaneous impact on the CR/VS system. First, a high level of underregistration in nonurban areas has been persistent. Second, since the second half of the 1990s, there has been an ongoing concerted effort to improve vital registration throughout the country. Last, there has been evidence of a decline in fertility and an increase in mortality in recent years. Against this background, South Africa conducted a census in 1996 covering the whole country, including Transkei, Bophuthatswana, Venda, and Ciskei—the former TBVC states.

The major challenge facing the statistics agency was how to produce life tables for the post-1985 period. Several questions arose. First, could the values in the older life tables be used as standards against which to judge future ones? Second, to what extent could the post-1985 life tables build on the pre-1985 ones? Last, in response to the new South African reality, what added dimensions should future South African life tables include? The tools and the organizational framework used in producing South African life tables in the past would need careful study to assess their appropriateness in these new circumstances. This chapter reviews the methods used in producing those life tables and discusses the contextual dynamics underlying them. However, these questions and concerns cannot be adequately answered if confined only to the developments within South Africa. We also review parallel developments taking place within another country facing similar circumstances: the United States from 1900 to 1970. It is hoped that the findings of this study will contribute to the development of a coherent organizational framework for the production of relevant South African life tables.

Development of Life Tables in the United States, 1900–70

Obtaining the Basic Inputs for Constructing Life Tables

In the United States, the development of a civil registration system was a long process. As there were many scattered collection points, a practical solution to the problem of developing a national data set for civil registration was the registration area concept, first proposed in 1880:

> The basic concept of the registration area is that separate sub-national areas, in which civil registration is complete, can be joined to create a total area for more comprehensive statistics for national purposes. The objectives are to coordinate information from many reporting systems and to work to develop and improve other subsystems until they can enter the system. Eventually all subsystems will be incorporated. In the beginning, a registration area will contain a small proportion of the population but as the area expands the proportion will increase until the entire population is included. The area will produce reliable and accurate data for the population it represents and at the same time be a sound statistical base for other national estimates. (Lunde 1980: 7)

This national registration system started off with the identification of states that had functioning vital registration systems and registered higher percentages of vital events than other states. These states comprised what was referred to as "original registration states." They were ten states (mostly in the northeast of the United States) and the District of Columbia (Glover 1921). These states became part of the Death-Registration Areas (DRA). Following on the DRA concept, the Birth-Registration Areas (BRA) were organized in 1915 and initially consisted of the ten original registration states and the District of Columbia. As other states improved their registration of vital events, they were included in the vital registration areas. Between 1916 and 1932, states were progressively added to both the BRAs and DRAs, and the whole process was completed in 1933, with the addition of Texas (National Office of Vital Statistics 1950).

Estimation of the Completeness of Birth and Death Registration

As the number of births is used in calculating life table measures for the younger ages (under age three), the estimate of completeness of birth registration is necessary for calculating accurate life tables. The assessment of the completeness of birth registration in the United States has been carried out through several exercises and projects. Tests were carried out in 1940, 1950, and 1969–70. The tests provided correction factors for those years and the factors for other years, were obtained by either interpolation or extrapolation (Robinson et al. 1993). These estimates, particularly those for non-Whites, are continuously improved as better evidence comes along. For example, prior to the 1940 test, the percentage of completeness of birth registration for 1929 was estimated at 93.5 percent for Whites and 88.1 percent for non-Whites. After the test, these were reduced to 91.3 percent and 78 percent for Whites and non-Whites respectively (Whelpton 1950). As another example, prior to the 1969–70 test, it was assumed that registration of births was complete and, as such, corrections for underregistration had been discontinued by the Bureau of the Census since 1959. Hence, the following statement: "In the preparation of the 1959–61 decennial life tables no allowance was made for possible incompleteness in the enumeration of the population in registration of births or deaths" (Greville 1967: 2).

However, the 1969–70 data resulted in the revision of the pre-1970 estimates (Coale and Rives 1973). After the results of the 1980 census, the Bureau of the Census undertook several projects evaluating the accuracy of the 1940 birth registration test. The investigations concluded that the 1940 test appeared to underestimate the completeness of the registration of Black births (Himes and Clogg 1992). As expressed by Preston et al.: "The bureau now believes that African American births were not as severely underregistered in the period 1935–1939 as it thought earlier and therefore that less correction for birth under registration was required" (1998: 14).

Strategic Technical Decisions Made When Preparing Life Tables

The construction of U.S. life tables fell within the ambit of the "the life table program." The work output of this program has been summarized as follows:

> Three series of life tables are prepared by the National Center for Health Statistics—complete, provisional abridged, and final abridged. The complete life tables for the U.S. population contain life table values for single years of age. They are based on decennial census data and deaths for a 3-year period around the census year and have been prepared since 1900. The provisional abridged life tables contain values by 5-year age groups and are based on 10-percent sample of deaths. The final abridged life tables . . . also contain values by 5-year age groups but are based on a complete count on all reported deaths. (NCHS 1992: 1)

The first set of complete life tables was for 1900–2. In 1921, a unique set of life tables was prepared for the period 1901–1910. The life tables were based on reported deaths and the mean population for the entire ten-year period. The abridged life tables were started in 1945, and the provisional life tables began in 1958.

Strategic technical decisions were made about three aspects of constructing life tables: methods, data adjustment issues, and publication (number of life tables, breakdowns to be included, and frequency of publishing). In the following sections, we cite cases where different strategic technical decisions were made regarding the construction of U.S. life tables over the decades.

The existing methods could be applied or modified as warranted. Two examples are given below:

> In deciding the method to be used for the construction of life tables for the United States various methods were studied closely, and the one set forth by Mr George King . . . was adopted with some modifications. (Foudray 1923: 10)

The general method proposed by T. Greville (1967) was used in preparing the decennial life tables for 1939–41 and in constructing life tables for 1949–52. Since 1953, a modified Greville method has been used for preparing all subsequent life tables.

As many censuses are often not 100 percent accurate, informed decisions need to be made as to whether any adjustments should be made on the census data before using them for life table construction and, if so, which adjustments should be made. Two common problems with the census data are: a) age misreporting and b) differential underenumeration. The general underlying principle is to make minimum adjustments to the census data.

In preparing life tables for 1910 (and earlier), age heaping was observed at ages of death that were multiples of five, and mortality rates in the advanced ages were found to be irregular. In this regard, the following remarks were made:

> While adjustments in such cases are necessary, all irregularities in the figures in these life tables have not been removed by smoothing processes. This policy was adopted in order to avoid the possible elimination of small but characteristic variations in mortality. (Glover 1921: 18)

In the 1960 census, there was substantial evidence of overreporting of 1900 as the year of birth among non-Whites. As a result, the population was redistributed by age between 55 and 64 before construction of life tables was begun. For the 1970 census, no adjustment was made in the underlying census data for misreporting of age. However, the adjusted 1970 census data were used to prepare the decennial life tables for 1969–71 instead of the "official" 1970 census figures (NCHS 1975). Beginning with 1970, the deaths of non-residents of the United States have been excluded from the life table statistics (NCHS 1992).

Different strategic decisions were made regarding different age segments. In calculating mortality rates for those under age 2, the 1901 to 1910 life tables used enumerated populations and reported deaths instead of birth registrations, as the reported number of births was found to be too small (Glover 1921). As birth statistics improved, they were used in calculating the denominators of the mortality rates at ages under 2 instead of population figures. In the 1959–61 life tables and earlier, approximate methods were used to derive death rates for ages 85 and over. In the life tables for 1969–71, the interpolation and graduation formula of de Beers was used for obtaining values of deaths and population for ages 90–94. From the life tables of 1979–81 onward, mortality rates at ages 95 and over were based on the experience of the Medicare program and values at ages 85–94 were adjusted to provide a smooth transition between the rates based on registered deaths and those based on Medicare.

The contents of these life tables have changed over time as warranted. In the abridged life tables for the various states for the period 1919–20, life tables, by sex, were constructed separately for Whites and for African Americans but not for the aggregate. For 1939, abridged life tables were published for the first time, showing urban and rural breakdowns by race. The urban areas were subdivided into two groups: cities with populations of 100,000 or more and other urban areas (Bureau of the Census 1943). When the definition of urban and rural was changed in the 1960 census, in ways that were not compatible with the classification used in vital statistics, the breakdown in the life tables was changed correspondingly. For the decennial life tables prepared for 1959–61, complete life tables were published for the first time, showing breakdown by metropolitan and nonmetropolitan areas (NCHS 1967). Beginning with 1960, the abridged life tables have included selected life table functions for single years of age. These values were obtained by interpolation of the values in the abridged life tables (National Office of Vital Statistics 1964).

In comparing a series of life tables over time, qualifying statements are often made with regard to comparability of older life tables with earlier ones.

The following remarks were made in connection with comparison of five decennial life tables covering the period 1900–1951:

> In using these tables it must be remembered that values for earlier periods are not strictly comparable with those for later periods. The number of Death-registration States limited the area covered at each period, and values for periods prior to 1929–1931 do not cover the entire continental United States. Neither does the values for the periods prior to 1949–1951 cover all nonwhites, but are limited to . . . [African Americans] only. It should be remembered, also, that there has been progressive improvement in the completeness of death reporting during this period. (Sirken and Carlson 1954: 6)

Once intercensal population estimates have been revised, the published life tables for those intercensal years are also revised, as in the following case:

> Life table values shown in this section differ from those shown for 1959, because the previous estimates of the 1959 population have now been revised on the basis of the latest estimates for 1959, which take into account the 1960 census enumeration. (National Office of Vital Statistics 1963: 5)

For example, the life tables for the years 1961–69 were revised using the U.S. decennial life tables for 1959–61 as the standard. Likewise, the life tables for the years 1971–79 were revised using the U.S. decennial life tables for 1969–71 as the standard (NCHS 1992).

South African Life Tables, 1921–85

During the period 1920–85, official life tables were published for the following census years: 1921, 1926, 1936, 1946, 1951, 1960, 1970, 1980, and 1985. The breakdown in these life tables was only by population group and sex. The first two sets of life tables were published only for Whites. Life tables of Coloreds were added beginning with the 1936 census year, and life tables for Indians/Asians were added beginning with the 1946 census year. No life tables were produced for the whole of South Africa (in the earlier years, the Union of South Africa). The earlier life table reports had only complete life tables, while the latter ones had both abridged and complete life tables. The basic methodology used in all the life tables from 1921 to 1985 was built on that used for developing the 1921 life tables. Over the years, slight modifications were made in the core methodology as warranted or as newer techniques were developed. The methodology was more clearly outlined in the pre-1970 life tables than in those for 1970 and beyond. In general, different methods were used for different specific age segments. These age segments roughly referred to infancy, childhood, postchildhood, and the last years of life.

For estimating mortality in infancy and childhood, the method used attempted to relate the number of deaths to the appropriate cohort exposed to the risk of dying during that period. This was the hardest part to estimate correctly. The methods used were continuously improved with time. The methods used in the 1921 and 1926 life tables differed from the ones used in the 1936 and 1946 life table reports. Of these different methods, the one with the theory that was most established in the literature was the one used in the life tables constructed for 1946 and 1951. The theory underlying the method is outlined in London (1988), and it formed the basis for the construction of the U.S. life tables as well. According to this method, q_x can be estimated as

$$q_x = 1 - \frac{P_x^{z+1}}{E_x^Z} \frac{E_{x+1}^Z}{P_x^z}$$

where

E_x^Z represents those attaining age x during calendar year z,

E_{x+1}^Z represents those attaining age $x + 1$ during calendar year z,

P_x^z represents those aged x at the beginning of the calendar year z, and

P_x^{z+1} represents those aged x at the end of the calendar year z.

In the 1946 and 1951 life table reports, this formula was used only for the age 0. For ages 1 to 5, the formula used is similar to that used in producing life tables for England and Wales. The formula for the probability of dying between exact ages x, q_x is given below:

$$q_x = \frac{D_x^{y,y+2}}{\left(\begin{array}{c} \frac{1}{8}(B_1^{y-3} + 3B_2^{y-3} + 5B_3^{y-3} + 7B_4^{y-3}) + B^{y-2,y-1} \\ + \frac{1}{8}(7B_1^y + 5B_2^y + 3B_3^y + B_4^y) - D_{x-2}^{y-2,y} - D_{x-1}^{y-1,y+1} \end{array} \right)}$$

where

$D_x^{k,k+n}$ represents the number of deaths at age x during the period k to $k + n$,

B_i^k represents the number of births in year k, during quarter i, and

$B^{k,k+n}$ represents the number of births during the period k to $k + n$.

In constructing the life tables for 1970, 1980, and 1985, special techniques were also used for obtaining q_x values in childhood and infancy. However, the explanation of the techniques used in constructing these life tables was less precise than that of the older life tables. For example, all that was said about calculating q_0 was the following:

> Age 0 was calculated by relating deaths to the appropriate base number in each birth cohort. (Central Statistical Service 1987: ix)

Similarly, for ages 1–7, the technique used was described as:

> The q_x values were then graduated by means of a moving average. (Central Statistical Service 1987: ix)

For the postinfancy ages (6 and over), the first step used in obtaining mortality rates was to group the population and the deaths into unconventional five-year age groups (for example, 9–13, 14–18, etc.), in order to minimize the problem of digit preference for ages ending in zero or five. Subsequently, as in the case of the U.S. life tables, different methods of interpolation and graduation were applied to different age segments.

For the age ranges over 6 (11 to 96 in the 1921 and 1926 life tables; 11 to 101 in the 1936 life tables; 11 to 86 in the 1946 life tables), the population and death data were first grouped into five-year age groups and then interpolated and graduated. A two-step process was followed. First, King's formula was used to obtain central (pivotal) values of the five-year age group. The formula is given by:

$$U_{x+2} = .2w_x - .008\Delta^2 w_{x-5}$$

where

U_{x+2} is the population or deaths at age $x + 2$ and

w_x is the sum of the five values of the population or deaths for ages x to $x + 4$.

The central death rate, m_x was then calculated, and q_x was obtained using the following formula:

$$q_x = \frac{2m_x}{2 + m_x}$$

This method has been used in all the life tables since 1921. The second step was to interpolate between these pivotal values for single-year values of q_x. Here, the methods were continuously improved as better methods became available. For the life tables up to 1936, these values were obtained by oscillatory interpolation of the function $\log (q_x + 0.1)$. For the 1946 life tables, the Karup-King formula and a slight modification of it were used for ages below 21, and the Jenkins fifth-difference modified oscillatory interpolation formula was used for ages 21 to 86. For the 1951 life tables, the Jenkins formula was used throughout; the Jenkins reproducing formula was used for ages below 20, and the Jenkins nonreproducing formula was used for ages above 20. For the 1970, 1980, and 1985 life tables, the Beers nonreproducing formula was used for interpolating between 8 and 27, and the Jenkins modified formula was used for interpolating between ages 28 and 83. In passing, it must be noted that in preparing the 1939–41 life tables for the United States, the Jenkins formula was also used, but for ages 32 upward.

For the end-of-life ages, the methods employed were improved over time as well. For the 1921 life tables, an assumption was made that q_x would attain unity before age 101 and then a graphical method was used to obtain q_x for the ages 91 to 101. For the 1926 life tables, a function was used to relate survivorship at two adjacent ages with survivorship at two fixed ages. For the 1936 life tables, the Newton–Sheppard formula of adjusted differences was used for ages 91 to 101. For the 1946 life tables, two strategies were used. For population groups for which the Makeham curve fitted well (Whites), it was used to obtain q_x values. For other population groups, the life tables were arbitrarily closed at 105 for males and 106 for females. For the 1951 life tables, the method opted for in obtaining q_x values for ages over 80 was the one proposed by Greville in preparing U.S. life tables for 1939–41. For the life tables for 1970 and beyond, the Beers six-term fifth difference formula was used to derive q_x values for ages over 83.

South African Life Tables from 1985 to 1994 and 1996

In trying to produce life tables for post-1985 South Africa, the situation faced by the statistical agency after the 1996 census was as follows:

- Provincial boundaries in 1996 were different from what they were in the late 1980s and early 1990s.
- Vital statistics after 1990 could not allow for the breakdown of the data into population groups.
- The 1991 census did not cover the whole of the "new South Africa" as the 1996 census did.

- life tables were needed by population group, by province, and for South Africa as a whole (national).

Strategic decisions needed to be made as to how to proceed. Out of the different available options, the following decisions were made:

- Only the 1996 census would be used.
- The data on survivorship of kin available from the 1996 census would be used to produce retrospective life tables for the 1980s, for the various population groups. During the 1980s, HIV/AIDS had not become a major problem, and hence, life tables for that era would provide a pre-AIDS baseline.
- The 1996 registered deaths would be used to produce life tables for the geographic areas. As 1996 falls within the period that HIV/AIDS has been emerging as a public health problem, the 1996 life table would reflect this issue. Furthermore, as death registration was incomplete, especially in the nonurban areas, the reported deaths would have to be corrected for incompleteness before using them for constructing life tables.

Once these decisions had been made, the choice of methods available became limited.

Data from the 1996 census on survivorship of children ("children ever born" and "children alive") allowed for the estimation of childhood mortality, and data on survivorship of parents ("father alive" and "mother alive") allowed for the estimation of adult mortality. These two sets of estimates were linked using a graduation formula, and these values served as the input into life table construction. However, since the death of children or that of parents refers to some event in the past, the life tables also referred to some time in the past. Appropriate techniques were used to adjust life tables so they referred to a fixed date or to a range of dates. Following is a summary of life table construction methods from questions on survivorship of kin. Further details can be found in United Nations (1983).

In constructing the South African life tables for population groups, the specific formulae used were as follows:

$$q(x) = k(i)\,D(i)$$

where

$q(x)$ is the probability of dying between birth and age x,

$D(i)$ is the proportion of children dead among those ever borne by women in age group i (beginning at age group 15–19), and

$$k(i) = a(i) + b(i) * \frac{P(1)}{P(2)} + c(i) * \frac{P(2)}{P(3)}$$

$P(1)/P(2)$ and $P(2)/P(3)$ are parity ratios and are used as indicators of fertility.

This method of obtaining $q(x)$ values is generally referred to as the Trussell variant of the Brass method. The formulas allow for the duration of exposure to the risk of dying. This duration of exposure is related to the age of the woman and the timing of childbearing.

For estimating adult mortality, the variant used was that of Timaeus (1992). In that variant, the conditional probability of males surviving from one adult age to another was given as

$$l(35 + n) / l(35) = \beta_0(n) + \beta_1(n) \bar{M} + \beta_2(n)_5 S_{n-5} + \beta_3(n)_5 S_n$$

The conditional probability of females surviving from one adult age to another is given as

$$l(25 + n) / l(25) = \beta_0(n) + \beta_1(n) \bar{M} + \beta_2(n)_5 S_{n-5}$$

where $_5S_n$ is the proportion of respondents in a five-year age group, n to $n + 4$, with living fathers (in the case of estimating male adult mortality) or living mothers (in the case of estimating female adult mortality). $\bar{M}$ is the mean age at childbearing, and $b_0, b_1, b_2,$ and b_3 are regression coefficients. In order to link the childhood and the adult mortality estimates, the Brass logit model was used, and the iterative method suggested in United Nations (1983) was employed.

However, in trying to apply these methods, two problems were encountered: one pertaining to childhood mortality and the other to adult mortality. The 1996 census could not allow for the reported children dead to be broken down by gender. Thus, the total mortality had to be first estimated, after which additional assumptions were made on how to separate this mortality into its gender components. As outlined in Statistics SA (2000), starting off with the expression for combining male life table survivors, $l^m(x)$, with those of females, $1 {}^f(x)$, one has

$$l(x) = \frac{SR \, l^m(x) + l^f(x)}{1 + SR}$$

where

SR is the sex ratio at birth (assumed to be 1.03).

In order to obtain values for either $1^m(x)$ or $1^f(x)$ when only $1(x)$ is known, an assumption has to be made about *SR* and the relationship between $1^m(x)$ and $1^f(x)$. For this, the ratio $1^m(x)/1^f(x)$ was computed for different levels of mortality in the Coale–Demeny West model life tables, and the average was found. For each level of mortality the value of $1^m(x)/1^f(x)$ was almost the same for childhood ages 2, 3, and 5 (the relevant ages). For levels 15, 20, and 25, the average of the $1^m(x)/1^f(x)$ values was 0.987. These values were used in the separation of $1(x)$ values into male and female values.

For adult mortality, tables were extracted from the full 1996 census database, which enabled the calculation of proportion of the respondents who responded about their fathers' survivorship status (for estimating male adult mortality) and those who responded about their mothers' survivorship status (for estimating female adult mortality). Unfortunately, a substantial proportion of respondents did not report their orphanhood status. Work on the 1996 census data has shown that the inclusion or exclusion of those respondents who did not know the survivorship status of their parents (DK), or those who did not state it (NS) made quite a difference in adult mortality estimates. After assessing the plausibility of the different sets of estimates (with and without DK and NS included in the totals), the proportions used in the computation were those for which "not applicable" (NA) was excluded from the totals, but for which DK and NS were included. After obtaining the proportions by five-year age group of respondents, the variant proposed by Timaeus was applied in a straightforward manner.

In the case of estimating provincial and national life tables for 1996, it was clear from the onset that estimation of completeness of death registration would be the major issue. While there are many methods for estimating completeness of death registration, most of them use data from two censuses (or growth rates derived from them), and some need intercensal deaths in addition. If one has to use data from only one census (1996) and deaths for that year, and one does not want to use either intercensal growth rates or intercensal deaths, then options are very limited. One would have to resort to the Brass (1975) method or employ direct methods to estimate the degree of incompleteness of death registration. While the Brass method is more appropriate under conditions of stability, it has been found to work adequately in quasi-stable conditions.

The Brass method starts by making the observation that, in general, for any closed population, the following equation applies:

$$r_{x+}^T = b_{x+}^T - d_{x+}^T$$

where

r_{x+}^T is the true partial growth rate for age x.

b_{x+}^T is the true partial birth rate for age x and is given as:

$$b_{x+}^T = \frac{_5N_x + _5N_{x-5}}{10 * N_{x+}}$$

where

$_5N_x$ is the number of persons recorded in the age interval from x to $x + 5$, and

d_{x+}^T is the true partial death rate for age x.

The growth balance method makes two major assumptions: (a) the assumption of population stability and (b) the assumption that the completeness of death registration is invariant to age within the range specified.

   This means that

$$r_{x+}^T = r^T$$

and

$$d_{x+} = C \, d_{x+}^T$$

where

C is the completeness of death recording, and d_{x+} is the partial death rate for age x based on recorded deaths. Using these two assumptions, the closed population equation could be written as follows:

$$b_{x+}^T = r^T + \frac{1}{C} d_{x+}$$

This is a linear equation with the parameters r^T as intercept and $1/C$ as the slope. The reciprocal of the slope therefore gives the proportion of completeness of death recording.

In order to explicitly take account of the wide differential level of completeness of death registration between urban and nonurban areas within the provinces, the strategy adopted for estimating them is given in what follows. Given that the true number of deaths in South Africa is the sum of the deaths in the urban and nonurban areas, one has the following:

$$D_{RSA}^T = D_{ur}^T + D_{nur}^T$$

where D^T represents the true number of deaths, and the subscripts ur and nur stand for urban and nonurban, respectively.

As the true number of death, D^T, is a multiple of the registered deaths, D:

$$D^T = k\,D, \text{ where } k = \frac{1}{c}$$

Hence,

$$k_{nur} = \frac{k_{RSA}\,D_{RSA} - k_{ur}\,D_{ur}}{D_{nur}}$$

or,

$$k_{nur} = \frac{D_{RSA}}{D_{nur}}\,k_{RSA} - \frac{D_{ur}}{D_{nur}}\,k_{ur}$$

In short, having obtained the more reliable correction factors for South Africa as a whole and for the urban population, the additive relationship between the number of the deaths in the subcomponents and the whole allows one to estimate the correction factors for less reliable or suspect nonurban data (Stats SA 2000).

Similarly, for any given province, i, the total number of deaths in the province is a sum of the deaths in the urban and nonurban areas of that province:

$$D_i^T = D_{ur,i}^T + D_{nur,i}^T$$

Hence, in terms of reported deaths, one has

$$k_i * D_i = k_{ur,i} * D_{ur,i} + k_{nur,i} * D_{nur,i}$$

or

$$k_i = \left(\frac{D_{ur,i}}{D_i}\right) * k_{ur,i} + \left(\frac{D_{nur,i}}{D_i}\right) * k_{nur,i}$$

Assuming that $k_{ur,i} = k_{ur}$ and that $k_{nur,i} = k_{nur}$, one has

$$k_i = \alpha_i * k_{ur} + (1 - \alpha_i) * k_{nur}$$

where

$$\alpha_i = \frac{D_{ur,i}}{D_i}$$

(Stats SA 2000).

Results

After applying all the methods outlined above, official life tables were produced for different periods. Tables 7.1 and 7.2 give a summary of the life
expectancies at four selected ages, 0, 5, 30, and 60, for the four population
groups for males and females, respectively. An alternative way of studying
the trend in the life table values is to plot the life table survivorship function
$l(x)$ obtained from those life tables. Figures 7.1 and 7.2 show the trend over
time in the life table survivorship function $l(x)$ against age, for White males
and females, respectively. Figures 7.3 and 7.4 show similar curves for Colored males and females, respectively, and Figures 7.5 and 7.6 show the similar curves for Indian/Asian males and females, respectively.

One would expect that as health and living conditions improved over
time, the improvement in life expectancy would occur across almost all
ages. In some ages, the improvement would be relatively more than in others. This is what one observes when one looks at published U.S. life tables
for Whites. In Table 7.1, however, with regard to the pre-1985 South African life tables, one sees that the life expectancy at birth for White males
stayed virtually the same—around 64 years from 1946 to 1970. Similarly,
the life expectancy at age 5 stayed around 62 years from 1946 to 1980. For
the same period, 1946 to 1980, the life expectancy at 30 stayed around 39
years. Lastly, for all the life tables, from 1921 to 1985, the life expectancy
at 60 years for White males stayed around 15 years. For females, a similar

Table 7.1

Trends in Published Life Expectancy at Selected Ages, Among the Different Population Groups, Males, South Africa, 1921–94

	Whites				Coloreds				Indians/Asians				Africans/Blacks			
	e(0)	e(5)	e(30)	e(60)	e(0)	e(5)	e(30)	e(60)	e(0)	e(5)	e(30)	e(60)	e(0)	e(5)	e(30)	e(60)
1921	55.61	58.34	37.08	15.14												
1926	57.78	59.51	37.87	15.31												
1936	58.95	59.86	37.93	14.97	40.18	50.27	32.10	14.08								
1946	63.78	62.32	39.29	15.34	41.70	48.84	30.29	13.16	50.70	53.05	32.72	11.97				
1951	64.57	62.77	39.60	15.53	44.82	52.18	32.31	13.60	55.77	57.59	34.49	12.19				
1960	64.73	62.33	39.11	15.01	49.62	56.67	34.79	13.83	57.70	58.49	33.36	12.53				
1970	64.74	61.69	38.48	14.61	48.88	54.24	32.47	12.93	59.19	57.48	34.06	11.98				
1980	66.59	62.96	39.80	15.32	54.34	54.92	33.06	12.96	62.26	59.31	35.82	13.57				
1985	68.37	64.37	40.97	15.90	57.92	57.09	34.92	14.09	64.12	60.55	37.21	14.31				
1985–94	65.22	63.06	40.18	14.80	57.36	56.41	34.78	11.91	60.95	58.80	36.37	12.33	52.51	53.53	33.04	11.60

Sources: Central Statistical Service 1987; Statistics South Africa 2000.

Table 7.2

Trends in Published Life Expectancy at Selected Ages, Among the Different Population Groups, Females, South Africa, 1921–94

Year	Whites				Coloreds				Indians/Asians				Africans/Blacks			
	e(0)	e(5)	e(30)	e(60)	e(0)	e(5)	e(30)	e(60)	e(0)	e(5)	e(30)	e(60)	e(0)	e(5)	e(30)	e(60)
1921	59.18	61.38	39.93	16.56												
1926	61.48	62.76	40.77	16.76												
1936	63.06	63.30	40.98	16.82	40.86	49.99	33.41	15.07								
1946	68.31	66.40	43.06	18.04	44.00	50.88	33.50	14.97	49.75	51.62	32.12	11.96				
1951	70.08	67.81	44.10	18.40	47.77	55.06	36.21	15.83	54.75	55.63	34.22	11.84				
1960	71.67	68.90	44.82	18.64	54.28	61.14	38.72	15.89	59.57	60.02	36.87	12.40				
1970	72.36	69.02	44.86	18.76	55.82	61.34	38.36	15.97	63.17	61.16	37.35	12.85				
1980	74.24	70.42	46.22	19.67	62.55	63.17	39.83	16.90	68.39	65.10	40.98	15.57				
1985	75.84	71.63	47.32	20.48	66.52	64.68	41.18	17.89	70.74	67.07	42.97	17.18				
1985–94	73.08	70.10	46.34	19.01	65.02	63.51	40.81	15.51	68.90	66.01	37.98	16.14	64.62	65.71	43.47	18.19

Sources: Central Statistical Service 1987; Statistics South Africa 2000.

197

Figure 7.1   Life Table 1(x) Values for White Males, Republic of South Africa, 1921–85

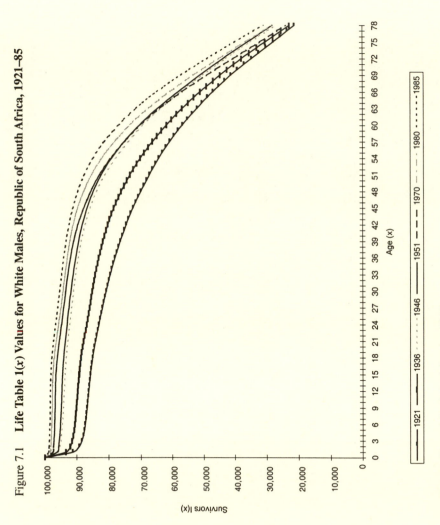

Source: Central Statistical Service 1987.

198

Figure 7.2   Life Table l(x) Values for White Females, Republic of South Africa, 1921–85

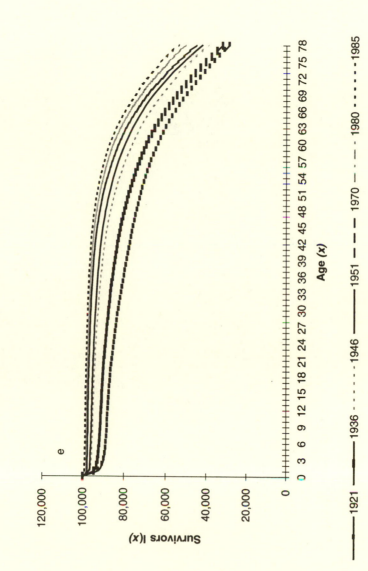

Source: Central Statistical Service 1987.

Figure 7.3   Life Table 1(*x*) Values for Colored Males, Republic of South Africa, 1921–85

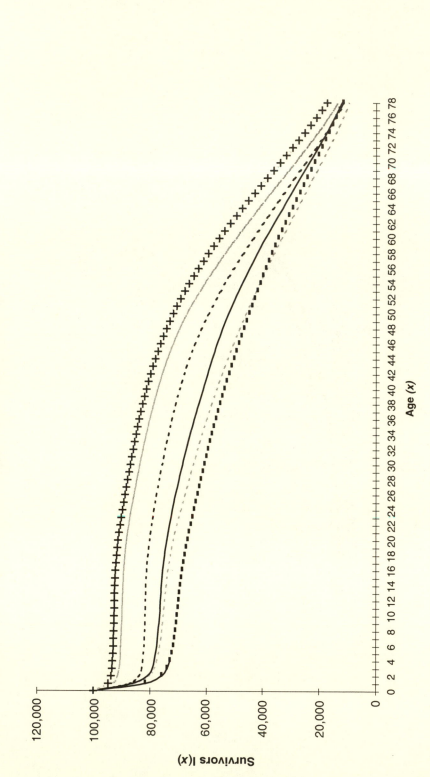

Source: Central Statistical Service 1987.

Figure 7.4   Life Table l(x) Values for Colored Females, Republic of South Africa, 1921–85

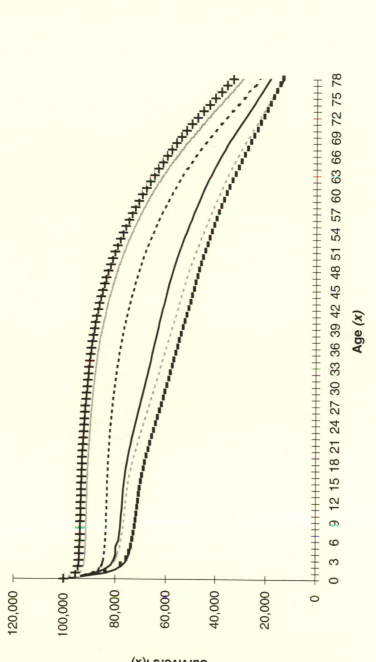

Source: Central Statistical Service 1987.

Figure 7.5   Life Table 1(x) Values for Indian/Asian Males, Republic of South Africa, 1921–85

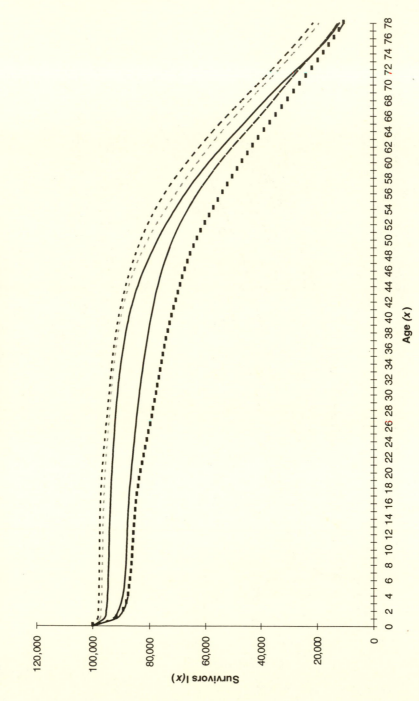

Figure 7.6 Life Table 1(x) Values for Indian/Asian Females, Republic of South Africa, 1921–85

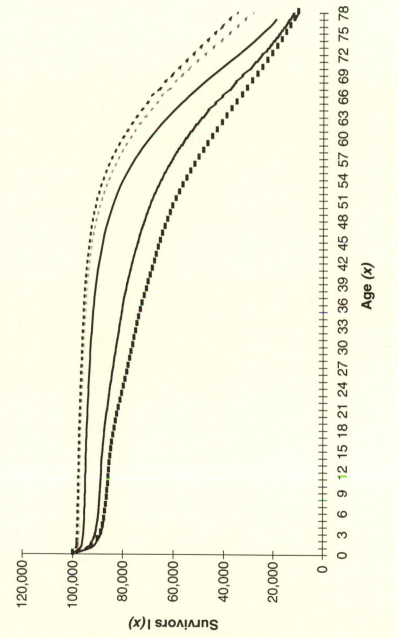

Source: Central Statistical Service 1987.

phenomenon occurs for age 30, with life expectancy staying around 44 years from 1951 to 1970, and, for age 60, with life expectancy staying around 18 years from 1946 to 1970.

Turning to the $l(x)$ curves, one sees in each figure that the trends show some peculiarity. For White males, the peculiarity occurs over the period 1946–70. Survivorship up to age 40 is very high from 1946 onward. Also, the $l(x)$ values for 1946, 1951, and 1970 are very close to each other, with mortality crossover occurring around age 55. After the crossover, mortality in 1970 became higher than mortality in either 1941 or 1951. For White females, no crossovers occur in the $l(x)$ curves, but survivorship up to around age 40 is exceedingly high from 1970 onward. For Colored males, one peculiar feature is the convergence of the $l(x)$ for 1936, 1951, and 1970 in the old ages. Another peculiarity is the crossover of the 1936 and 1946 $l(x)$ curves around age 55. For Colored females, there is convergence of the $l(x)$ curves for 1936 and 1946. Also, an excess gain in survivorship was experienced during the period 1951–70, especially over the age range 30–55. For Indian/Asian males, the $l(x)$ curves are very peculiar. The 1946 $l(x)$ curve has an uneven distribution, and there is convergence between the 1951 and the 1970 $l(x)$ curves, especially in the oldest ages. The survivorship values for 1980 and 1985 are very high and very close for ages less than 40. For Indian/Asian females, again, the survivorship values for 1980 and 1985 are very high and very close for ages less than 40, and they diverge appreciably after age 40. The 1946 $l(x)$ curve has an uneven distribution, and there is convergence between the 1946 and the 1951 $l(x)$ curves, especially in the oldest ages. Further analyses based on these $l(x)$ have been undertaken in Bah (2000).

While the life tables for the period 1985–94 are also broken down by population group, their construction is based on fundamentally different methods from those used in preparing the pre-1985 set. For this reason, results from these life tables are shown on separate graphs. For convenience, the $_nq_x$ values have been used instead of the $l(x)$ values. The values are shown in Table 7.3 and the graphs are shown in Figures 7.7 and 7.8 for males and females, respectively. Similarly, as there are no previous official life tables showing geographic breakdowns as in the 1996 life tables, the results from these life tables are also shown on separate graphs. The $_nq_x$ values are shown in Figures 7.9 and 7.10 for males and females, respectively.

Figure 7.7 shows that male adult mortality is very low among Africans and higher among Coloreds and Indians/Asians. Figure 7.8, however, shows adult mortality below age 70 being highest among African females, followed by Colored females, and then by Indian/Asian females. It seems as if

Table 7.3

Probabilities of Dying Between Age x and $x + n$ by Sex for RSA and Population Group, 1985–94

Age, x	RSA	African	Colored	Indian/Asian	White	Other and unspecified
Males						
0	0.05162	0.05559	0.03359	0.02185	0.02250	0.04969
1	0.04773	0.05242	0.03503	0.02449	0.02050	0.03699
5	0.01350	0.01490	0.01024	0.00731	0.00578	0.00991
10	0.01061	0.01173	0.00814	0.00585	0.00455	0.00768
15	0.01858	0.02054	0.01446	0.01050	0.00803	0.01326
20	0.02661	0.02941	0.02110	0.01553	0.01162	0.01865
25	0.02905	0.03212	0.02350	0.01756	0.01283	0.01999
30	0.03211	0.03548	0.02649	0.02008	0.01436	0.02175
35	0.03809	0.04204	0.03205	0.02468	0.01731	0.02545
40	0.04755	0.05240	0.04088	0.03205	0.02207	0.03140
45	0.06338	0.06963	0.05585	0.04473	0.03026	0.04149
50	0.08838	0.09664	0.08013	0.06594	0.04393	0.05757
55	0.12836	0.13934	0.12029	0.10245	0.06762	0.08389
60	0.19113	0.20523	0.18580	0.16518	0.10957	0.12712
65	0.28546	0.30205	0.28762	0.26867	0.18411	0.19770
70	0.41530	0.43191	0.42966	0.42049	0.30997	0.30809
75	0.57111	0.58451	0.59637	0.60124	0.49178	0.46308
80	0.72919	0.73809	0.75645	0.76870	0.69061	0.64295
Females						
0	0.05206	0.05783	0.02909	0.01599	0.01578	0.04447
1	0.02923	0.03135	0.02342	0.01443	0.01169	0.02677
5	0.00736	0.00784	0.00640	0.00406	0.00313	0.00684
10	0.00560	0.00595	0.00499	0.00320	0.00243	0.00523
15	0.00952	0.01009	0.00871	0.00565	0.00423	0.00893
20	0.01308	0.01381	0.01241	0.00818	0.00600	0.01236
25	0.01368	0.01439	0.01349	0.00905	0.00650	0.01303
30	0.01456	0.01526	0.01489	0.01016	0.00715	0.01396
35	0.01670	0.01744	0.01769	0.01228	0.00849	0.01612
40	0.02021	0.02101	0.02220	0.01573	0.01066	0.01965
45	0.02618	0.02710	0.02994	0.02171	0.01442	0.02566
50	0.03566	0.03671	0.04265	0.03182	0.02070	0.03528
55	0.05114	0.05231	0.06427	0.04976	0.03169	0.05116
60	0.07686	0.07802	0.10182	0.08271	0.05179	0.07788
65	0.12062	0.12131	0.16765	0.14487	0.09044	0.12395
70	0.19589	0.19504	0.27947	0.25979	0.16747	0.20402
75	0.32105	0.31682	0.44796	0.44542	0.31549	0.33708
80	0.50304	0.49439	0.64721	0.66600	0.54494	0.52649

Source: Statistics South Africa 2000.

Table 7.4

Probability of Dying Between Age x and $x + n$, Extracted from the South African Life Tables, 1996, for RSA, Provinces, and Urban/Nonurban Areas, Males

Age, x	Western Cape	Eastern Cape	Northern Cape	Free State	KwaZulu-Natal	North West
0	0.03330	0.02367	0.05777	0.07824	0.05825	0.05513
1	0.00931	0.00768	0.01721	0.02025	0.02049	0.02298
5	0.00558	0.00389	0.00633	0.00688	0.00841	0.00638
10	0.00439	0.00359	0.00449	0.00529	0.00757	0.00618
15	0.01939	0.01224	0.01959	0.01490	0.01954	0.01441
20	0.03608	0.03077	0.04230	0.03121	0.04794	0.03087
25	0.04071	0.04894	0.05090	0.05318	0.07115	0.05222
30	0.04469	0.06591	0.06039	0.06823	0.09181	0.06178
35	0.04980	0.07317	0.06536	0.07195	0.09162	0.07847
40	0.06212	0.09459	0.07431	0.09194	0.11405	0.09363
45	0.07980	0.12179	0.10108	0.11533	0.14430	0.12801
50	0.10928	0.15593	0.13866	0.14225	0.17789	0.15703
55	0.16295	0.18819	0.19782	0.20153	0.23095	0.22139
60	0.20791	0.20936	0.25495	0.25437	0.26559	0.24498
65	0.28041	0.24755	0.31553	0.33205	0.33216	0.34163
70	0.37862	0.31791	0.38693	0.41507	0.40612	0.42618
75	0.47290	0.40083	0.48368	0.51783	0.50385	0.55246

Table 7.5

Probability of Dying Between Age x and $x + n$, Extracted from the South African Life Tables, 1996, for RSA, Provinces, and Urban/Nonurban Areas, Females

Age, x	Western Cape	Eastern Cape	Northern Cape	Free State	KwaZulu-Natal	North west
0	0.02926	0.02301	0.04915	0.07114	0.05255	0.04972
1	0.00832	0.00697	0.01211	0.01955	0.01850	0.01893
5	0.00319	0.00270	0.00364	0.00464	0.00553	0.00563
10	0.00300	0.00240	0.00255	0.00449	0.00504	0.00539
15	0.00703	0.00574	0.00877	0.00991	0.01144	0.01312
20	0.00980	0.01332	0.02041	0.02531	0.02492	0.02687
25	0.01327	0.02226	0.02714	0.03688	0.03717	0.03982
30	0.01686	0.02519	0.03093	0.04312	0.03926	0.04708
35	0.02275	0.03059	0.03842	0.04837	0.03908	0.05207
40	0.03269	0.03819	0.04926	0.05540	0.04662	0.05914
45	0.04492	0.05177	0.06846	0.06719	0.05906	0.07505
50	0.06178	0.06284	0.08620	0.09025	0.07618	0.09031
55	0.08980	0.09298	0.11807	0.12383	0.11833	0.12682
60	0.13099	0.09960	0.15217	0.15932	0.15426	0.15972
65	0.17903	0.14522	0.19565	0.21321	0.22116	0.22129
70	0.23218	0.19910	0.26522	0.26331	0.28116	0.28692
75	0.33608	0.30680	0.35459	0.39967	0.39363	0.41060

Table 7.4 (*continued*)

Gauteng	Mpumalanga	Limpopo	RSA	Urban	Nonurban
0.04477	0.04906	0.01826	0.04425	0.05818	0.02989
0.01329	0.01757	0.00994	0.01439	0.01827	0.01282
0.00548	0.00688	0.00459	0.00583	0.00722	0.00578
0.00474	0.00698	0.00424	0.00524	0.00658	0.00484
0.01821	0.01781	0.00832	0.01579	0.02037	0.01194
0.03385	0.03769	0.02248	0.03605	0.03932	0.03019
0.03832	0.05307	0.04197	0.05073	0.04924	0.05162
0.04550	0.07005	0.06202	0.06331	0.05978	0.07001
0.04799	0.07270	0.06666	0.06776	0.06416	0.07423
0.06184	0.09746	0.09498	0.08637	0.08210	0.09469
0.07994	0.13826	0.13201	0.11288	0.10756	0.12555
0.10647	0.17125	0.17104	0.14426	0.13858	0.15870
0.14458	0.23957	0.21401	0.19344	0.19203	0.20448
0.18662	0.26397	0.22643	0.22903	0.23856	0.21757
0.26025	0.36384	0.28930	0.29470	0.32703	0.27097
0.36483	0.44521	0.38454	0.38132	0.41660	0.35191
0.46844	0.53875	0.46318	0.47293	0.53366	0.43042

Source: Statistics South Africa 2000.

Table 7.5 (*continued*)

Gauteng	Mpumalanga	Limpopo	RSA	Urban	Nonurban
0.03878	0.04530	0.01649	0.04023	0.05054	0.02970
0.01104	0.01505	0.01037	0.01274	0.01525	0.01230
0.00394	0.00539	0.00424	0.00419	0.00494	0.00494
0.00305	0.00563	0.00379	0.00379	0.00439	0.00419
0.00782	0.01189	0.00757	0.00882	0.00976	0.00767
0.01391	0.02315	0.01337	0.01815	0.02090	0.01564
0.01755	0.03322	0.02138	0.02631	0.02357	0.02329
0.02191	0.04379	0.02767	0.03083	0.02621	0.03146
0.02655	0.04455	0.03238	0.03480	0.02830	0.03199
0.03185	0.05704	0.03794	0.04241	0.03262	0.03784
0.04237	0.07466	0.04819	0.05524	0.04179	0.04508
0.05887	0.09923	0.05790	0.07180	0.05570	0.05389
0.09500	0.14021	0.09093	0.10621	0.09225	0.09674
0.12444	0.17247	0.10362	0.13242	0.12797	0.11668
0.18806	0.21602	0.15770	0.18540	0.17396	0.15288
0.24993	0.30928	0.21579	0.24873	0.20268	0.12839
0.36369	0.42868	0.35537	0.35851	0.32285	0.30609

Source: Statistics South Africa 2000.

Figure 7.7   **South African Life Tables for Males by Population Group, 1985–94**

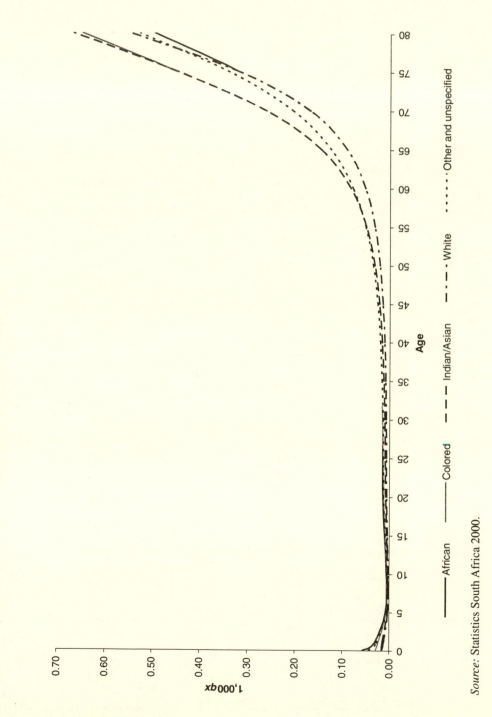

Source: Statistics South Africa 2000.

Figure 7.8   **South African Life Tables for Females by Population Group, 1985–94**

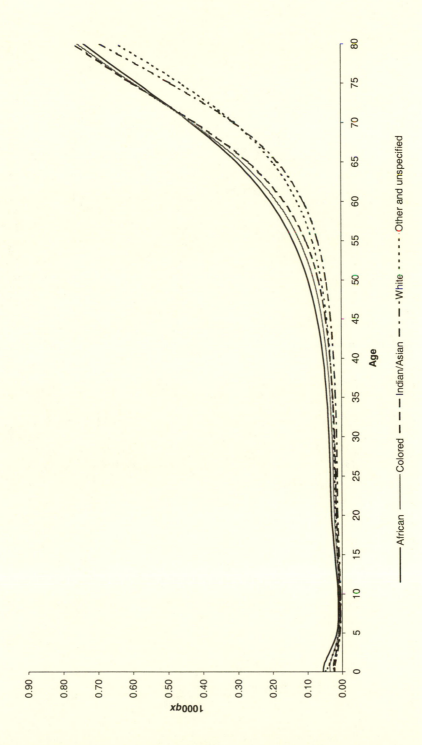

Age

African ———— Colored — — — Indian/Asian — ∙ — ∙ — White ∙ ∙ ∙ ∙ ∙ Other and unspecified

Source: Statistics South Africa 2000.

Figure 7.9 **South African Life Tables for Males by Province, 1996**

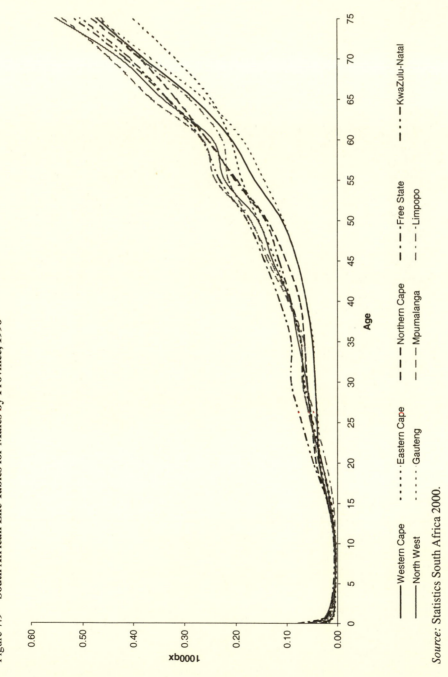

Source: Statistics South Africa 2000.

Figure 7.10 **South African Life Tables for Females by Province, 1996**

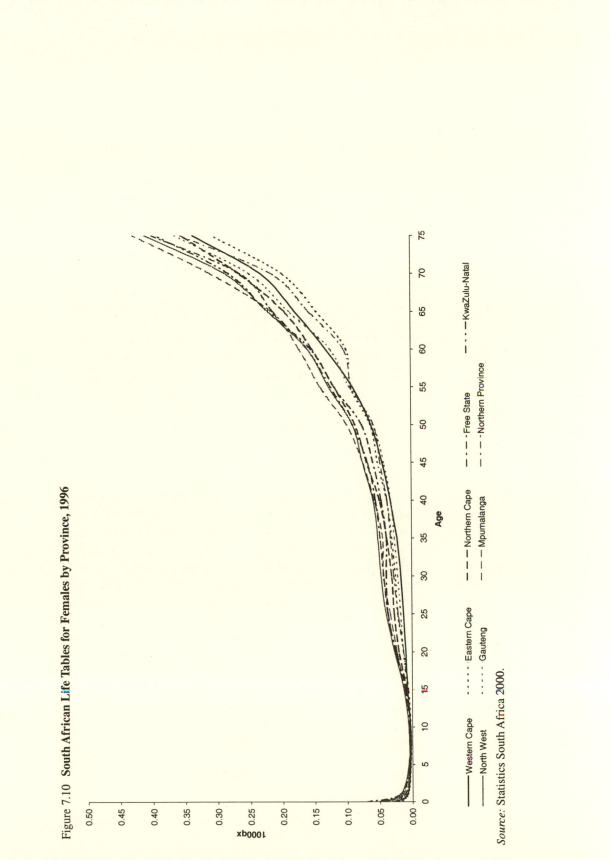

Source: Statistics South Africa 2000.

the female life tables in the 1985–94 set are more plausible than the male ones. For both sets of graphs, the curves are very smooth, showing the effect of the strong smoothing inherent in their generation.

For the 1996 reported deaths, there were two problems present in the data. One was that of underreporting, and the other was that of irregular concentration of deaths at different ages. We are not sure whether this was the effect of age misreporting or not. While the death data were adjusted for underreporting, they were not adjusted for any possible misreporting of ages at death. The values of $_nq_x$ are shown in Tables 7.4 and 7.5 for males and females, respectively, and the graphs are shown in Figures 7.9 and 7.10 for males and females, respectively. The figures show some peculiar features at about the age range of 55–59. For several provinces, there is an abrupt change in mortality around this age group. For males, this phenomenon is found in the data of the following provinces: Mpumalanga, North West, Limpopo Province, and Eastern Cape. For females, the phenomenon is found in the data of Limpopo Province and Eastern Cape. The graphs show that these abrupt changes are most likely due to lower recorded deaths in the older ages beyond 60 years.

Discussion

Methodologically, the pre-1970 South African official life tables followed the best practices of the time. Close attention was paid to the methods used in developing the life tables in England and Wales and in the United States. In general, the methods used were continuously improved as better methods become available. This was the same practice followed in constructing the earlier U.S. life tables. One important aspect included in the construction of those life tables was the regrouping of population and death data into unconventional age groupings to minimize the problem of age misreporting. On the other hand, an important missing dimension in the construction of all the pre-1985 life tables for South Africa was the failure to adequately address the question of the degree of completeness of vital statistics. In the case of the early U.S. life tables, this was addressed, and life tables were adjusted to reflect the values obtained for the completeness of death registration. In South Africa, life tables for different population groups were only calculated and published based on the perception that death registration was either complete among that population subgroup or at least that its vital statistics were usable without needing any adjustment. But this is contradictory when viewed against statements such as the following found in the 1921 life table report:

> It cannot be claimed that the record of the Union in the matter of vital statistics is

satisfactory. . . . From 1910 to 1917 the vital statistics were still neglected, and it was only upon the constitution of the Union Statistics Office in the latter year that an attempt was made to place this branch of statistics of the Union on a more satisfactory basis. (Union Office of Census and Statistics 1923: 99)

In addition, uniformity in birth and death registration throughout the Union of South Africa was only achieved after the passing of Act 17 of 1923. As such, the life table of 1921 could not have been representative of all Whites in the Union of South Africa. When this is viewed in light of the observation that the published life expectancies at birth for White males stayed around 64 years over a twenty-year period, 1951–70, a clear picture emerges. The picture one sees is that the 1921 life tables underestimated mortality and, over the years, as death registration was improving, the life tables became closer to reality but could not reflect improvement in health and living conditions (by showing increases in life expectancy for ages other than zero). The U.S. life tables for the 1920s indicated about the same life expectancy at birth for Whites as did the tables for South Africa, but as they were based on more complete vital statistics, they were able to reflect the improvements in health and living standards. By 1985, Whites in the United States had about three to four years higher life expectancies at birth than Whites in South Africa.

In a similar manner, when life tables for Coloreds were first published for the 1936 census year, the following remarks were made:

It was not possible to calculate the mortality rates for young Colored children with the same degree of accuracy as in the case of Europeans as complete vital statistics were not tabulated before the year 1935. (Census and Statistics Office 1939: iii)

For subsequent years, one observes fluctuations in the life expectancies at the different years. As the implied increase in mortality was not sustained, these cannot be manifestations of reversals of mortality. For populations that are not experiencing mortality reversals, fluctuations such as those exhibited by the life tables for Coloreds are not plausible features and can only suggest errors in the life tables. The source of these errors is largely in the faulty assumption of death registration being complete from 1936 onward. The issue of the convergence of the $l(x)$ curves for the life tables for 1936, 1951, and 1970 is possibly the result of faulty handling of the closing of those life tables rather than a lack of improvement in old-age survivorship.

For these reasons, the life tables for post-1985 were not compared to the pre-1985 ones. However, the fact that there were problems with the survivorship of kin data emphasizes the need for further efforts to verify the plausibility of those life tables. Similarly, the fact that there was constraint in the choice of method used for estimating the level of coverage of death registration in 1996 also means that those life tables need to be further verified. With the availability of census results for 2001, one would now have two comparable censuses to use for mortality estimation. These two censuses, with or without death data, offer many possibilities for applying "variable-r" methods for obtaining life tables and estimating level of completeness of death registration (Bennett and Horiuchi 1981, 1984; Preston and Coale 1982; Preston and Bennett 1983). If these methods are to be applied to obtain subnational life tables, care has to be taken with respect to the inclusion of migration in the estimation procedure. For example, if we assume that Free State remained largely geographically intact between 1991 and 1996 (with the exception of small homeland areas such as Thab'Nchu), one can reason that it would be possible to apply variable-r methods to such a province. This was attempted, using the two censuses and the intercensal deaths. The results show fairly plausible estimates for males but implausible ones for females. For males, the median percentage of completeness of death registration is 69.8 percent, but for females it is 259.1 percent. It would seem as if the issue of internal migration is playing a bigger role among females than males in Free State. Theoretically, it could also possibly mean that deaths are "overregistered" relative to completeness of census enumeration, but this does not seem plausible. The point is that the availability of two compatible censuses does not automatically guarantee good subnational life tables if due care is not taken to address issues of net migration and other possible sources of error.

The Way Forward for Producing South African Life Tables for 1996–2001 and Beyond

In the case of a typical African country with a poor vital registration system and in the non-AIDS era, census-based national life tables were possibly adequate for research and national planning needs. However, South Africa is an atypical African country, with a fairly well-developed vital registration system. In addition, the country is squarely in the AIDS era and is still undergoing various forms of geopolitical transformations. Under such circumstances, the call is for a dynamic life table program to be put in place. The proposed life table program should include the following elements:

- Life tables should be constructed for metropolitan areas. As local government is now being reorganized to include metropolitan areas, it would be useful for population projections to be published showing breakdown by metropolitan area. This would be in line with what was done in the United States in constructing life tables based on the 1960 census. It would also fit with the urban/nonurban approach used in constructing the 1996 life tables for provinces.

- Stats SA should consider publishing one set of life tables referring to the intercensal period and based on variable-r methods. These life tables would make use of the two censuses and registered deaths in order to obtain national and subnational life tables. The plausibility of these life tables should be assessed in comparison to the plausibility of using the traditional method of constructing life tables, which involves using (adjusted) deaths centered on census year and those based on survivorship of kin.

- For life tables for population groups, Stats SA should also consider publishing one set of life tables referring to the intercensal period and based on variable-r methods. In this case, such life tables would primarily make use of the two censuses, as there are no registered deaths by population group. The plausibility of these life tables should be assessed against life tables constructed using data on survivorship of kin.

- For the regional and provincial life tables, Stats SA should consider updating them yearly by publishing provisional life tables based on adjustment of the timely population register data. This would help in monitoring the impact of deaths due to HIV/AIDS.

- The practice used in preparing the old South African life tables, wherein population and death data were regrouped into unconventional ages to avoid the problem of digit preference before the interpolation starts, should be revived.

- After constructing abridged life tables, adjusted for underregistration, the practice of using interpolation and graduation for obtaining complete life tables should be revived. A literature review is needed to see if improvements have been made on interpolation and graduation formulas previously used. More research is needed to see how the Heligman and Pollard (1980) model fares as compared to the older methods of graduation, when the age pattern of mortality has been distorted by HIV/AIDS.

- The practice adopted in life tables between 1970 and 1985 in which the Beers formula was mechanically applied to the oldest age groups should not be used. Other methods for handling mortality at the old ages should be explored.

- The practice of continuously refining life tables as better methods become established should be maintained. Methods could be applied as they are or could be modified as necessary.

- Stats SA should put more resources into the construction of life tables. In particular, skilled manpower resources are needed.

In conclusion, it may be folly to adopt an iconoclastic approach for putting into place a dynamic life table approach for South Africa. The excellent work that was done in developing earlier life tables should be built upon. At the same time, new techniques for estimating completeness of death registration should be put to use, and meaningful strategic decisions should be made to suit South Africa's needs, just as the National Center for Health Statistics made such decisions to suit the needs of the United States.

References

Bah, S. 2000. "Critical review of South African life tables." *Canadian Studies in Population* 27(2): 283–306.

Bennett, N., and S. Horiuchi. 1981. "Estimating the completeness of death registration in a closed population." *Population Index* 47(2): 207–21.

_____. 1984. "Mortality estimation from registered deaths in less developed countries." *Demography* 21(2): 217–33.

Brass, W. 1975. *Methods for Estimating Fertility and Mortality from Limited and Defective Data.* Chapel Hill, NC: Laboratories for Population Statistics.

Bureau of the Census. 1943. *United States Abridged Life Tables, 1939: Urban and Rural by Regions, Color and Sex.* Washington, DC: Bureau of the Census.

Census and Statistics Office. 1939. *Sixth Census of the Population of the Union of South Africa, Enumerated 5th May, 1936, Volume XI, South African Life Tables, No. 3 (Europeans) and C.1. (Colored Persons).* Pretoria: The Government Printer.

Central Statistical Service. 1987. *South African Life Tables, 1984–1986.* Report No. 02–06–04. Pretoria: The Government Printer.

Coale, A., and N. Rives. 1973. "A statistical reconstruction of the Black population of the United States 1880–1970: Estimates of true numbers by age and sex, birth rates and total fertility." *Population Index* 39(1): 3–36.

Foudray, E. 1923. *United States Abridged Life Tables: 1991–1920.* Washington, DC: Bureau of the Census.

Glover, J. 1921. *United States Life Tables 1890, 1901, 1910 and 1901–1910.* Washington, DC: Bureau of the Census, U.S. Department of Commerce, Government Printing Office.

Greville, T. 1967. *Methodology of the National, Regional and State Life Tables for the United States: 1959–61.* Washington, DC: NCHS.

Heligman, L., and J. Pollard. 1980. "The age pattern of mortality." *Journal of the Institute of Actuaries* 107: 49–80.

Himes, C., and C. Clogg. 1992. "An overview of demographic analysis as a method for evaluating census coverage in the United States." *Population Index* (58)4: 587–607.

London, D. 1988. *Survival Models and Their Estimation.* Winsted and New Britain, CT: Actex Publications.

Lunde, A. 1980. *The Organization of the Civil Registration System of the United States.* IIVRS Technical Papers, No. 8, May.

National Center for Health Statistics (NCHS). 1967. *Life Tables for Metropolitan and Nonmetropolitan Areas of the United States: 1959–61,* Vol. 1, No. 5. Washington, DC: U.S. Government Printing Office.

_____. 1975. *Methodology of the National and State Life Tables for the United States: 1969–71,* Vol. 1, No. 3. Washington, DC: U.S. Government Printing Office.

_____. 1992. *Vital Statistics of the United States, 1989.* Volume II-Section 6. Washington, DC: U.S. Government Printing Office.

National Office of Vital Statistics. 1950. *Vital Statistics of the United States, 1950.* Volume I. Washington, DC: Government Printing Office.

_____. 1963. *Vital Statistics of the United States, 1963.* Volume II-Section 2. Washington, DC: Government Printing Office.

_____. 1964. *Vital Statistics of the United States, 1963.* Volume II-Section 5, Washington, DC: Government Printing Office.

Preston, S., and N. Bennett. 1983. "A census based method for estimating adult mortality." *Population Studies* 37(1): 91–104.

Preston, S., and A. Coale. 1982. "Age structure, growth, attrition and accession: A new synthesis." *Population Index* 48(2): 217–59.

Preston, S., I. Elo, A. Foster, and H. Fu. 1998. "Reconstructing the size of the African American population by age and sex, 1930–1990." *Demography* 35(1): 1–21.

Robinson, J., B. Ahmed, P. Das Gupta, and K. Woodrow. 1993. "Estimation of population coverage in the 1990 United States census based on demographic analysis." *Journal of the American Statistical Association* 88(423): 1061–71.

Sirken, M., and G. Carlson. 1954. *United States Life Tables: 1949–51.* Vital Statistics-Special Reports. Vol. 41 , November 23. Washington, DC: National Office of Vital Statistics.

Statistics South Africa (Stats SA). 2000. *South African Life Tables, 1985–1994 and 1996.* Report No. 092–06–04. Pretoria: Statistics South Africa.

Timaeus, I. 1992. "Estimation of adult mortality from paternal orphanhood: A reassessment and a new approach." *Population Bulletin of the United Nations,* No. 33: 47–63.

Union Office of Census and Statistics. 1923. *South African Life Table No. 1.* Pretoria: The Government Printer.

United Nations. 1983. *Manual X: Indirect Techniques for Demographic Estimation.* New York: United Nations.

Whelpton, P. 1950. *Births and Birth Rates in the Entire United States, 1909–1948.* Vital Statistics-Special Reports. Vol. 33(8), September 29. Washington, DC: National Office of Vital Statistics.

8. Racial Differences in Household Structure

Eliya Msiyaphazi Zulu and Amson Sibanda

Many African sociocultural institutions have been experiencing considerable structural changes over the past few decades. The African family is one such institution where profound changes have taken place in its various features, including family formation, strength of family ties and relationships, and the nature of residential and living arrangements in which people coexist (Adepoju and Mbugua 1997; Isiugo-Abanihe and Obono 1999; Murray 1981). The residential and livelihood arrangements in which family and nonfamily members coexist (households) are an important indicator of social systems and family welfare, since household structure is responsive to social, cultural, economic, political, and demographic changes. For instance, changes in fertility, mortality, and migration are bound to affect household size and composition. Changes in people's livelihood and subsistence mechanisms may affect the nature of familial support that they provide to each other, and hence, the composition and structure of their residential and livelihood arrangements. The sharp increase in the cost of living, increasing importance of education, decline in farm sizes, and increasing unemployment have led to changes in the options for and patterns of young people's transition to adulthood, which are traditionally marked by landmark events such as marriage, parenthood, family formation, employment, and household formation. The increase in marital instability and incidence of widowhood are also likely to affect household composition (Aryee 1997).

Various census and national survey data collected in sub-Saharan Africa over the past three decades have shown that age at first marriage and first birth have increased, the proportion of people who are married at any given point in time has declined, and the incidence of divorce and separation has increased (Bledsoe and Cohen 1993; Gage and Meekers 1994; Sibanda et al. 2003, van de Walle 1993), while the downward trend in the proportion of children living apart from their mothers (McDaniel and Zulu 1996) is being reversed by the HIV/AIDS crisis. The escalating AIDS scourge is exerting enormous pressure on the capacity of household members to stay together and provide for each other's well-being because of the disease's disproportionate effect on economically active people. Consequently, the proportion of households headed by single parents and the elderly (mostly women) and the number of orphaned children are growing rapidly (Case et al. 2002; Mbugua 1997; Oppong 1997).

While many localized studies have examined various aspects of household structure (Singh 1996; Siqwana-Ndulo 1998), little is known about trends and variations in family and household structures across population subgroups differentiated by social, cultural, and geographical factors (Aryee 1997; Ocholla-Ayayo 1997). For instance, although it is widely believed that forms of extended households are widespread in sub-Saharan Africa, the extent of this feature, as well as geographical and cultural variations in its occurrence, are not well demonstrated in the literature. It has been argued that with increasing modernization, African families are bound to be more nuclear and less extended (see Amoateng 1997, 1998; Koen 1998; and Russel 1998 for a debate on this issue in South Africa). However, it is not clear how much family and household nucleation is actually taking place, if at all, with rapidly increasing modernization and urbanization.

This study uses census data to analyze racial differentials in household structure in South Africa. South African households are not only a product of existing cultural and socioeconomic conditions, but their form and structure have been affected by the unique apartheid political system and the associated mining-based industrial capitalist system that imposed strict residence and mobility controls on non-White groups beginning at the end of the nineteenth century. The analysis focuses on differentials in household size, composition (extendedness), headship, and mother–child co-residence among the country's four major racial groups (Africans, Coloreds, Indians/Asians, and Whites) using data from the 1991 and 1996 population censuses. We also examine living arrangements of children and female household headship, as these two indicators of household structure are very sensitive to economic, social, demographic, and cultural differences between population groups (McDaniel 1994; Morgan et al. 1993). The two censuses allow us to examine changes in household structure from 1991, when the apartheid system had just started crumbling, to 1996, when all segregation rules were abolished and majority democratic rule was instituted. Although the 1991–96 period is too short to depict the full impact of the socioeconomic and political changes on household structure, one would expect the relaxation of such strong restrictions on movement and residence to have an immediate and profound effect on household structure.

South Africa's Sociopolitical Background

Although the first Whites settled in South Africa in 1652, the beginning of the country's unique sociopolitical history is linked to the discovery of diamonds and gold in 1886 (Lucas 1985; Massey 1983). The growth of the mining industry was accompanied by the development of a modern industrial infrastructure that was not found elsewhere on the African continent. The mining and industrial economy ignited rapid urbanization and attracted and exploited cheap labor from the impoverished African population within the country and other countries in southern Africa (Packard 1989). In order to keep labor costs low, the mining and industrial companies targeted and relied on poor temporary and circular migrant workers who were accommodated in single-sex hostels in the mushrooming mining towns and cities. The economic and political strategy was aimed at exerting full control over Africans' productivity and labor resources and culminated in the institution of racially motivated discriminatory laws in 1948. Many of the segregation policies and strategies that were institutionalized and legalized in 1948, including restriction of human settlement patterns along racial lines and the exclusion of African people from the prime parts of urban areas, took root between 1900 and the 1930s (National Development and Planning Commission 1999).

In the 1950s, the apartheid government passed a number of laws to restrict mobility and residence for Africans and other non-White populations. For instance, the Population Registration Act of 1950 officially categorized the country's population into three racial groups: Whites, Africans, and Coloreds, and later added the fourth category Indians/Asians. The Group Areas Act of 1950 assigned racial groups to different residential and business parts of urban areas, and the Land Acts of 1954 and 1955 restricted non-White residence to specific areas (Africana Encyclopedia 2001). In pursuance of the policy of "separate development" for the country's racial groups, the apartheid government created ten African homelands through the Bantu Self-Government Act of 1959. By making every black South African a citizen of the homeland states, the 1970 Bantu Homelands Citizenship Act precluded Africans from being citizens of the Republic of South Africa. This policy restricted movement of Africans into the "Republic," or what was referred to as the "Common Areas," and any African person found outside the homelands was required to have a visitor's pass. The pass laws placed limits on the movement of Africans and prevented spouses, children, and the elderly from staying in White neighborhoods (Appolis 1996; Moerdijk 1981; Murray 1980, 1987). Consequently, most men and women who worked in White neighborhoods in urban centers were forced to stay apart from their spouses and children, who mostly remained in rural areas. Such forced separation of African families and households invariably led to changes in family roles and household structure. Additionally, the single-sex hostels and institutional residential arrangements that most mining, industrial, and commercial farming employers set up did not encourage workers to live with their families. Even in situations where workers were provided housing, the houses were too small to accommodate families. These residential environments and restrictions discouraged most families from living together, resulting in a marked absence of extended families in urban settings (Nhlapho 1986; Ramphele 1989). The whole economic system was, thus, set up to deliberately create unstable jobs, families, and households among the African population. The high level of migration of male workers from the neighboring countries to work in South Africa's mining industry also affected household structure in the wider southern African region. This contributed to a greater proportion of single males living in South Africa's major economic centers (Davis and Head 1995, Lucas 1987).

The official end of apartheid began in 1986 with the abolishment of the pass laws (the Group Areas Act). The relaxation of apartheid restrictions on residence and movement of people of different races accelerated after 1990, following the release of Nelson Mandela, the most prominent African leader of the anti-apartheid movement, from prison, where he had spent twenty-seven years. Mandela led the country in negotiations that led to the birth of a new multiracial and multiparty democratic South Africa in 1994, thereby marking the official end of apartheid and associated restrictions on residence, movement, and association.

Adequate understanding of the evolution and state of household structures across South Africa's four major racial groups needs to take into account these socioeconomic and political developments that have affected the country. The mining industry, manufacturing industries, segregation laws, and reliance on a migrant labor system have all influenced household structure for Africans as well as Colored and Indian/Asian households (Amoateng 1997, 1998; Appolis 1996; Russel 1998; Singh 1996; Siqwana-Ndulo 1998). Based on the 1996 census, Africans make up 77 percent of South Africa's 40.6 million population. Whites, Coloreds, and Indians/Asians make up 11 percent, 9 percent, and 3 percent, respectively. This paper analyzes data collected around the time the segregation laws were being relaxed to establish whether, and to what extent, the political revolution and associated socioeconomic changes affected racial differences in household structure in the immediate period following the demise of apartheid.

Data and Methods

A unique data source that has traditionally been used to analyze household structure around the world is the census. However, there has been little research devoted to household structure in Africa on the basis of census data, or survey data, for that matter, in comparison to the studies on European household relationships based on historical censuses (van de Walle 1999a). This study examines racial differentials in household structure in South Africa using data from the 1991 and 1996 censuses. We use a full count for the 1991 census and a 30 percent sample of the 1996 census. The 1996 census was carried out two years after the end of apartheid and was the first to cover all racial groups of the population equally and comprehensively. Censuses were highly politicized during the apartheid era (see Khalfani et al., chapter 1 in this volume). While Whites were canvassed entirely, the African population was mostly estimated through samples and analysis of air photography (Statistics South Africa 1998). Although the 1991 census presented the first effort by the apartheid government to enumerate the majority African population, the effort was characterized by substantial inconsistencies and shortcuts that should be taken into account when comparing the 1991 and 1996 census results. For instance, while all enumerations were done through direct interviews in 1996, the 1991 census mostly involved self-administered questionnaires, which could affect the quality of the data for the less literate African population (Statistics South Africa 1998). Additionally, four self-administered homeland areas (Transkei, Bophuthatswana, Venda, and Ciskei) were not covered in the 1991 census because they were considered independent states. Thus, the 1991 population census did not successfully enumerate the population. A large proportion of the African population was not enumerated because the population in inaccessible African areas was estimated using a combination of sample surveys and aerial photographs (Central Statistical Service 1991). While the limitations of the 1991 census data potentially compromise comparability with the 1996 results (see Ziehl 2001), the two data sets are more comparable if the 1996 results are restricted to the same geographical area covered by the 1996 census (i.e., excluding the four self-administered homelands). By comparing changes in racial differences separately for rural and urban areas in all the tables, we also minimize the comparability problems (for urban areas), because the problems with incomplete canvassing of the African population were more prevalent in rural than urban areas.

Statistics South Africa defines a household as consisting

> of a person or a group of persons, who occupy a common dwelling (or part of it) for at least four days a week and who provide themselves jointly with food and other essentials for living. In other words, they live together as a unit. People who occupy the same dwelling unit, but who do not share food or other essentials, were enumerated

> as separate households. Visitors, both foreign and South African, as well as board-
> ers, who stayed with a household on census night, were counted as part of that
> household. Live-in domestic workers and live-in employees were regarded as sepa-
> rate households. (Lestrade-Jefferis 2000: 85)

In the 1991 census, a slightly different concept of household was used. For instance, the 1991 census included domestic servants in their employers' households if they were living on the property of their employers. In contrast, the 1996 census separated the households of domestic servants from those of their employers (Ziehl 2001). However, in both censuses, a head of household was identified in each household, and his or her relationship with each household member was recorded. Thus, the household head is used as a focal point for defining the nature of relationships in the household. This presents a major limitation of using census data to examine the extent of relationships among household members, because relationships among other household members can only be inferred by each individual's relationship to the head.

Using the headship and relationship-to-household-head variables, we generated four measures of household structure: size, extendedness of households, mother–child co-residence, and female household headship. We examined extendedness of households to establish the extent of racial differences in co-residence of people who were not members of the nuclear family. The residential restrictions that the apartheid system imposed on the African population forced many people to live with relatives and nonrelatives, and in some cases on their own, in order to comply with the prevailing laws and living conditions. While there are some cultural roots to the practice of child fosterage, the extent of the practice is obviously exacerbated by socioeconomic factors (McDaniel and Zulu 1996), including the nature of residential restrictions that the apartheid system imposed on the African population in South Africa. Mother–child co-residence has critical ramifications on child health, schooling opportunities, and other demographic outcomes such as fertility (Ainsworth 1992; Bledsoe et al. 1988; Isiugo-Abanihe 1985; Page 1989). The examination of racial differences in female household headship is important because of the large gender variations in access to resources both at family and community levels (including government services) that continue to exist in the patriarchal African societies and the male-biased economic system built in South Africa. The disappearance of traditional family-support structures in most African countries is pushing many households, particularly female-headed households, into poverty (National Research Council 1993). Apartheid also affected household headship by restricting husband–wife co-residence, especially if the husband was living in one of the single-sex residential compounds that were provided by mining companies.

We used descriptive analysis to demonstrate the extent of racial differences in the four measures of household structure, and went on to utilize multivariate logistic regression to examine racial differentials in female headship net of other demographic and socioeconomic factors. Logistic regression is used, because the dependent variable, household headship, is a binary variable, coded 1 if a female was the head and 0 otherwise. We first estimate a general model that describes the difference in the likelihood of heading a household, and then estimate a model controlling for background characteristics that various studies have shown to affect household headship. For example, female headship is mostly dependent on marital status (in that most married women tend to declare their husband as the head of the household), and there are large racial differentials in the proportions of women who are currently married. For instance, among women ages 15 and above, about 35 percent of African women were currently married, as compared to 59 percent of White women in 1996. Among Coloreds and Indians/Asians, the percentages were about 40 and 57, respectively. In 1991, the percentages of women who were currently married among Africans, Coloreds, Indians/Asians, and Whites were about 35, 41, 57, and 59 percent, respectively. Thus, we conduct the same analysis only for married women in order to determine other factors that affect household headship among currently married women.

Results

Household Size and Composition

Table 8.1 shows the average household size for the four racial groups and by place of residence (rural or urban). The average number of people living in a household decreased from 4.4 to 4.1 between 1991 and 1996, which indicates that many new households were created, because the total population count increased between the two censuses. The decline in household size is even greater if we compare the 1991 and 1996 censuses without the homelands, whereby the 1996 average household size was 3.6. The decrease in household size occurred in both rural and urban areas, and also across all four racial groups. For all races, household sizes fell by 18 percent nationally, 15 percent in rural areas, and 19 percent in urban areas. The reduction in household size was greatest for Africans: in rural areas it fell by 23 percent, while in urban areas it fell by 31 percent. For the other three races, however, there were larger declines in household size in rural compared to urban areas.

Figures 8.1 and 8.2 show the distribution of households of different sizes for Africans and Whites. Both Africans and Whites were more likely to be found in smaller households in 1996 than they were in 1991, but the differences

Table 8.1

Average Household Size by Race, Place of Residence, and Year

Racial group	All areas			Rural areas			Urban areas			Percentage range (1991–96 net)		
	1991	1996 net	1996 total	1991	1996 net	1996 total	1991	1996 net	1996 total	All areas	Rural	Urban
Indian/Asian	4.50	4.17	4.17	4.62	4.03	4.16	4.34	4.18	4.17	−7.3	−12.8	−3.7
African	5.13	3.69	4.27	4.97	3.83	4.78	5.27	3.65	3.74	−28.1	−22.9	−30.7
Colored	4.82	4.42	4.42	4.92	3.90	3.92	4.69	4.54	4.53	−8.3	−20.7	−3.2
White	3.22	2.89	2.90	3.43	2.99	2.99	2.99	2.89	2.89	−10.2	−12.8	−3.3
All races	4.40	3.60	4.05	4.40	3.72	4.68	4.40	3.57	3.63	−18.2	−15.5	−18.9

Source: Computed from the 1991 and 1996 South African Population Census micro-data.

225

Figure 8.1   **Household Size for Blacks: Percentage of Households by Size and Year**

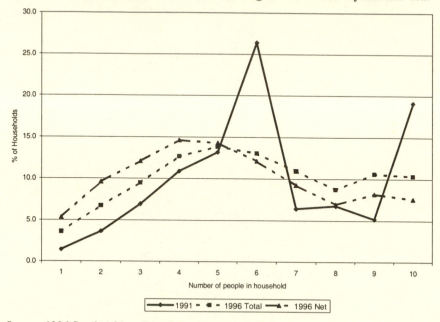

Source: 1996 South African Population Census micro-data.

Figure 8.2   **Household Size for Whites: Percentage of Households by Size and Year**

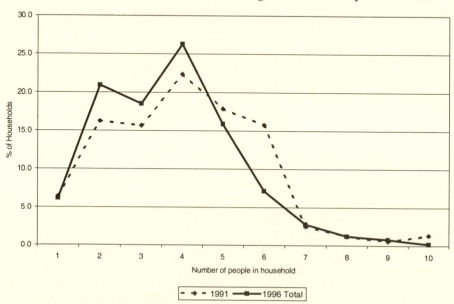

Source: 1996 South African African Population Census micro-data.

were starker for Africans. As noted earlier, we present data for all of South Africa for 1996 (1996 total) as well as data that excludes the four homelands not covered in 1991 (1996 net only for Africans). Since the 1991 census covered all Whites, Indians/Asians, and Coloreds, irrespective of their place of residence, the exclusion of the homelands does not affect the data for these groups. The decline in household size could be a consequence of people moving from bigger to smaller households and/or the creation of new households. The big differences between the proportion of one-person and two-person households between the two censuses shows that many new households were generated during this period. The huge drop in the proportion of six-member households for Africans may be reflective of a decline in shared residential arrangements.

We used the question on relationship of each household member to household head to determine the structure and composition of households across the four major racial groups. Relationships among household members present key indicators of household structure and also allow us to understand the linkage between family and household and the extent to which people who are related or not make economic provisions jointly. The 1996 census listed nine such relationships, as follows: 1) head/acting head, 2) husband/wife/partner, 3) son/daughter/stepchild/adopted child, 4) brother/sister, 5) father/mother, 6) grandparent, 7) grandchild, 8) other relative (e.g., in-laws), and 9) nonrelated person. While all these relationships would be of interest in their own right, this study grouped all categories of relatives into one group ("other relative"), because our interest was in establishing the extent of co-residence between relatives and nonrelatives. This recategorization gives us the following five types of relationships: 1) head, 2) wife/husband, 3) son/daughter/stepchild, 4) other relative, and 5) nonrelative.

Table 8.2 shows the distribution of South Africans by relationship to head of household in the 1991 and 1996 censuses. The data show that South Africans are more likely to be found in households headed by their parents (42 percent in 1991, 40 percent in 1996, and 38 percent in the 1996 areas excluding homelands) than in any other type of household. This pattern is the same for all racial groups except Whites, where the proportion of people living in households where they are heads was the same or slightly higher than those living in their parents' households. This pattern is most likely a reflection of the relatively high level of fertility among the non-White populations. Whites and Africans are generally on the opposite ends of the spectrum for all measures of household structure, with the Coloreds and Indians/Asians in between and closer to Africans than Whites.

In 1996, 35 percent of Whites were household heads, while between 22 and 24 percent of people in the other three races were heads. Africans were

Table 8.2

Distribution of Household Members by Relationship to Household Head by Race and Year

Relationship to household head	Indian/Asian			African			Colored		
	1991	1996 total	1996 net	1991	1996 total	1996 net	1991	1996 total	1996 net
Head	22.6	24.1	24.1	17.3	22.7	26.1	20.0	22.2	22.2
Spouse	18.0	18.8	18.8	8.1	9.8	12.8	14.1	15.2	15.3
Child	47.0	42.1	42.1	45.2	41.1	37.8	44.5	41.2	41.3
Other relative	9.7	13.7	13.7	14.0	22.9	19.3	12.0	17.5	17.4
Non-relative	2.7	1.3	1.3	15.4	3.6	4.0	9.5	3.9	3.9
Total	100.0	100.0	100.0	100.0	100.0	100.0	100.0	100.0	100.0

considerably more likely to live in households headed by relatives (23 percent), compared to Whites (5 percent). Africans have the lowest proportion of people classified as spouses of household heads, which is a reflection of both low levels of marriage and a high proportion of spouses living apart from each other in this group. Africans have the highest percentage of people who are staying in households where the head is a relative in both rural and urban areas. While the other racial groups have more relatives in urban than in rural areas, for Africans, the proportion of relatives is higher in rural than in urban areas. This may be a reflection of the cultural value of extended family support networks among Africans in rural areas. The proportion of people who are nonrelatives is very low for all the racial groups, indicating that when people share a household with others, they mostly live with relatives.

Comparison of the 1991 and 1996 data shows that Africans registered the largest changes in four of the five categories of relationship to household head. The proportion of Africans who were household heads and spouses to household heads increased by about 50 percent, while the proportion living in households headed by nonrelatives declined by 74 percent, and those in households headed by a parent declined by 16 percent. Whites registered the biggest change (51 percent) in the proportion of people living in households headed by other relatives. The trends for Africans are consistent with the hypothesis that free movement and unrestricted residential patterns that followed the demise of apartheid would lead to an increase in the proportion of family members living together and in the number of new households, as individuals

Table 8.2 (*continued*)

	White			All races		Percentage change (1991–96 net)				
1991	1996 total	1996 net	1991	1996 total	1996 net	Indian/ Asian	African	Colored	White	All
32.6	35.0	35.0	21.4	24.0	27.0	7	51	11	7	27
22.7	24.7	24.7	12.7	12.2	15.8	4	57	9	9	25
32.8	32.2	32.2	42.4	40.1	37.5	–10	–16	–7	–2	–12
3.4	5.2	5.2	11.2	20.2	15.9	41	38	45	51	43
8.5	2.9	2.9	12.4	3.6	3.7	–54	–74	–59	–66	–70
100.0	100.0	100.0	100.0	100.0	100.0					

Source: Computed from the 1991 and 1996 South African Population Census micro-data.

who were living with relatives and nonrelatives went on to create their own households.

Further examination of the trends, after breaking down the "other relatives category" (results not shown), suggests that the increase in the proportion of people who were household heads came about because more siblings and parents who were cohabiting with their brothers/sisters and children in 1991 managed to establish their own households by 1996. The big increase in the *s:

- Nuclear households—couple and children only
- Single-parent households
- Extended-direct—nuclear plus relatives only
- Extended-composed—with both related and unrelated people
- Unrelated members only
- One-person households

Tables 8.3, 8.4, and 8.5 show the distribution of the different types of South African households by race. The 1996 data show that the nuclear household was the most common form of household for all racial groups combined. However, the extended household was more common than nuclear households among Africans. More than half of White and Indian/Asian households were nuclear, while 44 percent and 27 percent of Colored and African households, respectively, fell in the same category. There were big changes in the distribution of households between 1991 and 1996. For all races combined,

Table 8.3

Type of Household by Race and Year, Whole Country, 1991 (Unweighted) Full Census and 1996 (weighted) 30 Percent Sample

Household type	Indian/Asian			African			Colored		
	1991	1996 net	1996 total	1991	1996 net	1996 total	1991	1996 net	1996 total
Nuclear	55.9	54.7	54.7	32.6	34.4	27.4	45.5	44.3	44.2
One-person	3.3	4.7	4.8	7.3	20.2	15.6	5.0	7.6	7.6
Single-parent	7.6	7.5	7.5	23.2	10.8	14.9	9.6	8.8	8.8
Extended	22.1	26.5	26.5	27.9	27.5	33.6	23.3	28.6	28.7
Composed	10.3	5.9	5.9	5.6	5.3	7.1	13.3	9.5	9.5
Unrelated	0.9	0.7	0.7	3.4	1.9	1.4	2.3	1.2	1.3
Total	100.0	100.0	100.0	100.0	100.0	100.0	100.0	100.0	100.0

one-person households experienced the biggest change (an increase of 70 percent), followed by a decrease of about 46 percent for composed and unrelated households, and a decline of 37 percent for single-parent households. The proportion of nuclear households did not change much overall or for each race, except among Whites, for whom a sizable increase, 21 percent, took place.

The big overall increase in the prevalence of one-person households mostly reflects the nearly threefold increase among Africans (177 percent). The prevalence of one-person households also increased by sizable rates among Coloreds (50 percent) and Indians/Asians (44 percent), but only marginally among Whites (5 percent). The increase in the proportion of one-person households is further testimony that the removal of residential restrictions allowed more non-Whites, particularly Africans, to start their own households. The high level of marital dissolution and out-of-wedlock childbearing among Africans in the southern African region (Sibanda and Zuberi 1999; van de Walle 1999b) is reflected by the relatively high percentage of single-parent households among Africans. Although the prevalence of these households decreased by almost half between the two censuses (from 23 percent to 11 percent), Africans still exhibited relatively high levels of single-parent households (15 percent for the total 1996 census, compared to less than 10 percent for the other groups).

All racial groups recorded increases in the prevalence of extended (direct)

White			All races			Percentage change (1991–96 net)				
1991	1996 net	1996 total	1991	1996 net	1996 total	Indian/ Asian	African	Colored	White	All
47.6	57.4	57.4	40.7	42.6	34.4	–2	5	–5	21	5
16.8	17.6	17.6	10.1	17.2	15.0	44	177	50	5	70
4.4	5.3	5.3	14.2	9.0	12.6	–1	–54	–9	22	–37
5.8	8.9	8.9	19.4	22.8	29.1	20	–1	23	54	18
20.6	7.8	7.8	12.0	6.5	7.4	–43	–6	–29	–62	–46
4.9	2.9	2.9	3.7	2.0	1.6	–25	–45	–45	–41	–45
100.0	100.0	100.0	100.0	100.0	100.0					

Source: Computed from the 1991 and 1996 South African Population Census micro-data.

households, except Africans, among whom a small decrease was observed. Contrary to what one would expect, Whites registered the biggest increase (54 percent) in prevalence of extended households (Table 8.3). While the rate of increase was very high for Whites in both rural and urban areas, the decrease in prevalence of extended households took place mostly in rural areas for Africans (Tables 8.4 and 8.5). There was a decrease among all racial groups in prevalence of extended households, with Whites registering the biggest change (62 percent), compared to only 6 percent for Africans. So, while the tendency for relatives and nonrelatives to share residential and livelihood arrangements decreased across the board, there was an increase in co-existence of nonnuclear relatives among Whites, Indians/Asians, and Coloreds. All the four racial groups experienced declines in the prevalence of households consisting of unrelated people, ranging from 25 percent for Indians/Asians to 45 percent among Africans and Coloreds.

Whites had the highest occurrence of extended composed households in 1991 (21 percent), but the drop in the occurrence of these households in 1996 (to 8 percent) was the major cause of the big increase in the occurrence of nuclear households. In 1991, close to 34 percent of all African households were either extended-direct or extended-composed, while 37 percent, 32 percent, and 26 percent of Colored, Indians/Asian, and White households fell into these two categories. By 1996, however, the pattern changed dramatically, for Whites

Table 8.4

Type of Household by Race and Year, Rural Areas, 1991 (unweighted) **Full Census and 1996** (weighted) **30 Percent Sample**

Household type	Indian/Asian			African			Colored		
	1991	1996 net	1996 total	1991	1996 net	1996 total	1991	1996 net	1996 total
Nuclear	57.1	61.7	58.1	31.8	36.8	22.6	47.4	49.6	48.7
Single	0.3	5.8	6.4	9.7	22.6	12.2	3.0	12.3	12.4
Single-parent	7.7	6.6	7.2	22.4	9.6	18.0	10.1	5.6	5.8
Extended	23.3	22.0	23.2	27.5	22.8	37.7	24.1	23.7	24.0
Composed	10.5	3.3	4.4	5.5	5.7	8.4	13.2	7.2	7.3
Unrelated	1.1	0.6	0.8	3.1	2.6	1.2	2.3	1.6	1.6
Total	100.0	100.0	100.0	100.0	100.0	100.0	100.0	100.0	100.0

(*continued*)

Table 8.5

Type of Household by Race and Year, Urban Areas, 1991 (unweighted) **Full Census and 1996** (weighted) **30 Percent Sample**

Household type	Indian/Asian			Black			Colored		
	1991	1996 net	1996 total	1991	1996 net	1996 total	1991	1996 net	1996 total
Nuclear	54.5	54.6	54.6	33.4	33.8	32.5	45.6	43.2	43.2
Single	7.0	4.7	4.8	5.3	19.7	19.3	7.4	6.6	6.6
Single-parent	7.4	7.5	7.5	23.9	11.0	11.5	9.1	9.4	9.4
Extended	20.6	26.6	26.5	28.1	28.6	29.3	22.3	29.7	29.7
Composed	9.9	5.9	5.9	5.8	5.2	5.7	13.5	10.0	10.0
Unrelated	0.6	0.7	0.7	3.7	1.7	1.7	2.2	1.2	1.2
Total	100.0	100.0	100.0	100.0	100.0	100.0	100.0	100.0	100.0

(*continued*)

Table 8.4 (*continued*)

White			All races			Percentage change (1991–96 net)				
1991	1996 net	1996 total	1991	1996 net	1996 total	Indian/ Asian	African	Colored	White	All
59.5	69.0	68.7	45.2	43.5	25.1	8	16	5	16	−4
2.0	12.5	12.6	5.5	19.5	12.2	2,216	133	312	539	254
5.5	3.3	3.3	13.9	8.1	17.1	−15	−57	−45	−40	−42
6.1	8.7	8.9	19.2	20.9	36.2	−5	−17	−1	43	9
20.0	5.1	5.1	12.0	5.8	8.2	−69	4	−45	−75	−52
7.0	1.5	1.5	4.3	2.3	1.2	−42	−18	−29	−79	−47
100.0	100.0	100.0	100.0	100.0	100.0					

Source: Computed from the 1991 and 1996 South African Population Census micro-data.

Table 8.5 (*continued*)

White			All races			Percentage change (1991–96 net)				
1991	1996 net	1996 total	1991	1996 net	1996 total	Indian/ Asian	African	Colored	White	All
35.1	56.3	56.3	36.3	42.4	40.6	0	1	−5	60	17
32.3	18.1	18.1	14.6	16.8	16.9	−32	275	−11	−44	15
3.2	5.5	5.5	14.5	9.1	9.6	1	−54	4	73	−37
5.5	8.9	8.9	19.6	23.1	24.2	30	2	33	63	18
21.2	8.1	8.1	12.0	6.7	6.8	−40	−10	−26	−62	−45
2.8	3.0	3.1	3.1	2.0	1.9	5	−53	−48	10	−36
100.0	100.0	100.0	100.0	100.0	100.0					

Source: Computed from the 1991 and 1996 South African Population Census micro-data.

only (from 26 percent to 17 percent). The other racial groups experienced an increase in the combined proportion of extended households. While the comparison of the two data sets may be undermined by the problems already noted, the fact that household structures for all racial groups (even for Whites, who are likely to be least affected by the data problems) underwent substantial changes suggests that monumental changes did take place in the country during this short period.

The results also show that there was a huge increase in one-person households among Africans. This increase was associated with declines in single-parent and unrelated households. For Coloreds, Whites, and Indians/Asians, the increase in the proportion of one-person and extended households was accompanied by decreases in extended-composed and unrelated households. The key changes that distinguish Africans from the rest of the population groups relate to the huge increase in the prevalence of one-person households and the huge decrease in the proportion of single-parent households. These patterns are consistent with the data presented in Table 8.2, where we observe considerable increases in the proportion of Africans who are heads of households and spouses of heads of households over the five-year period.

Household Headship

According to Statistics South Africa, the head of the household is "the person that the household regards as such, and is usually the person who assumes responsibility for decision-making in the household" (Statistics South Africa 1998). The relevance of the concept of household headship has received increasing scrutiny, because the person who is designated as the head of the household may not always be the chief economic provider or decision maker. Many respondents in surveys and censuses typically designate the oldest man or woman as the head of the household, even when there is no clear hierarchy in authority and decision making in a given household. The importance of household headship has mostly been predicated on the assumption that characteristics of the household head are indicative of the household's ability to make economic provisions for its members. Of particular interest is the difference between male- and female-headed households, where households headed by women are more likely to be economically deprived than male-headed households. The economic deprivation associated with female-headed households is even more acute in rural areas, where there are larger proportions of households headed by women (May 1998). In agricultural settings, female-headed households may not have as much access to agricultural credit facilities as their male-headed counterparts, especially where membership to credit societies is restricted to men. A household headed by a woman in a strict patrilineal society may be disadvantaged if the woman does not have rights to inherit land and other productive resources from her husband or her family. Age and marital status of the household head may also affect the nature of resources that household members have.

Nevertheless, female headship is not an automatic indicator of poverty, because many single women are becoming economically active, and emerging evidence demonstrates that women's hard-earned income is usually used for family well-being and less often wasted on things like alcohol and drugs, compared to men's earnings. "One hypothesis is that women can implement their priorities more easily and hence direct resources more efficiently to children when they are fully in charge of the household" (Bruce and Lloyd 1997: 216). For instance, while male-headed households have higher incomes than female-headed households, it was found in some sub-Saharan African countries that children in female-headed households had better nutritional and schooling measures than those in male-headed households (Kennedy and Peters 1992; Lloyd and Blanc 1996). In settings where female headship was a consequence of temporal spousal migration to areas with better employment opportunities, as in the cases of Lesotho and Malawi, where many men were working in the mines in South Africa, some female-headed households actually had higher incomes than average male-headed households (O'Laughlin 1996). Changes in characteristics of household heads may be a reflection of changes in economic circumstances, marital stability, power relationships, and growing incidence and acceptability of out-of-wedlock childbearing among women.

Table 8.6 shows that while female headship among Africans was higher overall in urban compared to rural areas in 1991, the opposite pattern emerged in 1996. In rural South Africa, 47 percent of all household heads were female, as compared to 32 percent in urban areas in 1996. This differential reflects the high level of male migration to the country's urban and mining centers for employment opportunities (Siqwana-Ndulo 1998).

Female household headship varied markedly by racial background, with Africans showing the highest level of female headship of all the four major racial groups in the country. About 43 percent of African households were headed by females, compared to 29 percent, 22 percent, and 19 percent among Coloreds, Whites, and Indians/Asians, respectively. The prevalence of female-headed households increased from about 30 percent in 1991 to 35 percent in the comparable geographical area in 1996. The increase was much more pronounced in rural areas, probably due to a combination of data problems (because the aerial photography counting was mostly applied in rural areas) and an increase in male mobility as a result of the greater economic opportunities that came with the new political atmosphere following the end of apartheid.

Table 8.6

Percentage of Female-Headed Households by Race, Residence, and Year

| Residence | Indian/Asian | | | African | | | Colored | | |
	1991	1996 net	1996 total	1991	1996 net	1996 total	1991	1996 net	1996 total
Rural	15.1	14.0	15.0	40.6	46.1	49.7	24.1	16.3	16.8
Urban	15.7	18.8	18.7	42.4	36.1	36.7	23.3	31.4	31.4
Total	15.4	18.7	18.6	41.53	40.3	43.3	23.7	28.7	28.7

Residential Arrangements for Children

A key aspect of household structure relates to the extent to which children live with their parents, particularly their mothers. When children are not staying with their mothers, they are more likely to be staying with their fathers or next of kin such as grandparents or other relatives. However, in the case of South Africa, children born out of wedlock or from dissolved marriages are even less likely to live with their biological fathers than with their mothers. This is primarily because the Child Care Act of 1983, the Births and Deaths Registration Act of 1992, and the Natural Fathers of Children Born Out of Wedlock Act of 1997 allowed only limited child custody rights to natural fathers (Republic of South Africa 1997, 1998; Department of Welfare 1998). The practice of allowing children to be reared by people other than their parents is very old in sub-Saharan Africa. In part, these practices stem from institutional arrangements and customs with origins that are deeply embedded in African cultural history (Adegboyega et al. 1997). Racial differences in mother–child living arrangements could be a product of many factors, including differences in cultural histories. The fertility of mothers and the competing roles of parenthood and work force some women to let their children live with their relatives. Divorce, widowhood, parental death, and illegitimacy can also influence the living arrangements of children (McDaniel 1994; van de Walle 1999b).

Figure 8.3 shows the proportion of children who were living with their mothers in 1996. We determined the proportion of children living with their mothers by linking enumerated co-resident children to their mothers within households using a computer algorithm that exploited information on relationship to head of household, age, age at first birth, children ever born, children living at home, sex, and marital status. We did not do similar analysis for

White			All races			Percentage change (1991–96 net)				
1991	1996 net	1996 total	1991	1996 net	1996 total	Indian/ Asian	African	Colored	White	All
13.4	10.1	10.2	28.5	42.4	47.0	–7	14	–32	–25	49
24.8	23.0	23.0	32.4	31.3	31.9	20	–15	35	–7	–3
19.93	21.9	21.9	30.5	34.9	37.9	21	–3	78	10	14

Source: Computed from the 1991 and 1996 South African Population Census micro-data.

the 1991 data because no information on children ever born was collected. Information on children ever born is required in matching mother and children (Cho et al. 1986; Morgan et al. 1993; Sibanda and Zuberi 1999). The data show that, in general, most young children live with their mothers, while an increasing proportion of older children do not, for a variety of reasons. Morgan et al. attributed this pattern to the fact that "at older ages the exigencies of schooling and employment necessitates leaving the parental home. Also, the proportion of mothers who die increases with the children's ages: children clearly cannot be linked to deceased mothers" 1993: 812).

African children were considerably less likely to be living with their mothers at all ages below fifteen years compared to other racial groups. Coloreds exhibited the second lowest mother–child co-residence levels, while Whites and Indians/Asians did not differ much in this age range. Apart from actual child fosterage, high levels of underenumeration of children and misstatement of ages among Africans could partly explain these racial differences. However, the consistencies of the variations suggest that the differentials may not simply be an artifact of data problems. The separation of children from their parents was exacerbated by apartheid policies that prevented children of African domestic servants working in homes of Whites from living in the backyard domestic cottages that were provided by the employers (Preston-Whyte 1978, 1991). This arrangement put excessive pressure on African grandmothers and other relatives, who had to absorb the parental responsibilities of their children who were employed and accommodated by Whites (Appolis 1996; Nhlapho 1986).

An equally intriguing aspect of the living arrangements of children is the marital status of the mother. Figures 8.4a through 8.4d show the living arrangements of children by mother's marital status. To get these proportions, we only took the cases in Figure 8.3 where we managed to link mothers and

Figure 8.3   **Percentage of Children Living with Mothers, South Africa, 1996**

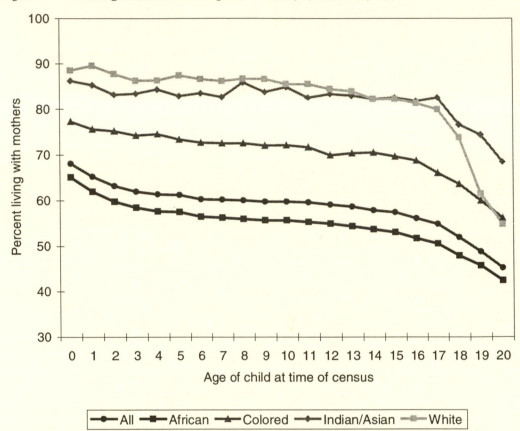

Source: 1996 South African Population Census micro-data.

children. We then split these proportions by mother's marital status. As we can see from these graphs, there are important racial differences in the living arrangements of children when we control for mother's marital status as well. Two basic patterns emerge: the proportion of young children living with unwed mothers is very high among Africans and Coloreds. In contrast, Whites and Indians/Asians do not exhibit high levels of out-of-wedlock births and, of all the children we linked in these population groups, over 90 percent were living with their mothers at the time of the census. What these results seem to indicate is that among Africans, and to some extent among Coloreds, there is greater diversity in children's living arrangements. There is probably a heavy reliance on other family members (particularly grandmothers) when it comes to raising children. Given the HIV/AIDS epidemic in South Africa today, there is no doubt that the role of the next of kin in raising children will con-

Figure 8.4a Children's Living Arrangements by Mothers' Marital Status: Africans

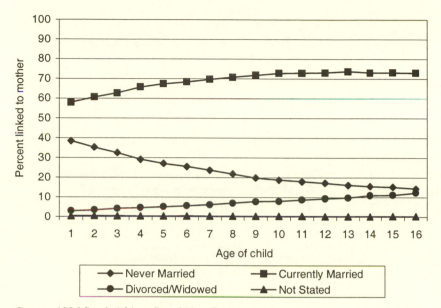

Source: 1996 South African Population Census micro-data.

Figure 8.4b Children's Living Arrangements by Mothers' Marital Status: Coloreds

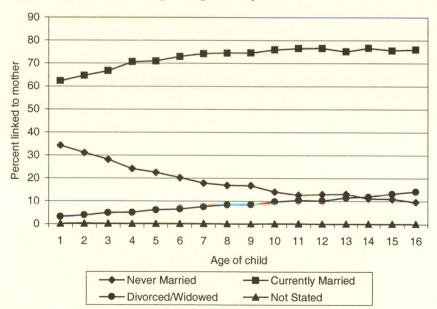

Source: 1996 South African Population Census micro-data.

Figure 8.4c   Children's Living Arrangements by Mothers' Marital Status: Indians/Asians

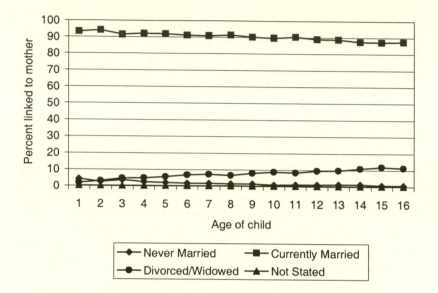

Source: 1996 South African Population Census micro-data.

Figure 8.4d   Children's Living Arrangements by Mothers' Marital Status: Whites

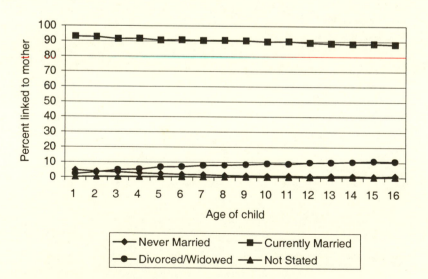

Source: 1996 South African Population Census micro-data.

tinue to play a critical role in the country. However, the HIV/AIDS epidemic seems not to have shaped the patterns of children's living arrangements we see in 1996, simply because HIV/AIDS had not yet taken its toll on South African families at that time. We contend that the effects of AIDS mortality were still minimal in 1996 in South Africa; hence, there was independence between the mortality risks of children and their biological mothers. In other words, we argue that there was a low intergenerational correlation in death that could have produced the living arrangements we see in Figures 8.4a through 8.4d.

Determinants of Female Headship

Table 8.7 shows the effects of race and other independent variables on female household headship. Our choice of logistic regression was dictated by the dichotomous nature of our dependent variable. We estimated logistic regressions of the odds of female household headship in a baseline model (Model 1), with only race as the covariate, and in a full model, including all covariates (Model 2). The odds of female headship were computed relative to African women, the omitted category. The other covariates were included as dummy variables. The odds ratios of these covariates are expressed relative to their omitted complements. Two baseline models and two full models are presented in Table 8.7. The first two models (Models 1 and 2) include all women ages 15 and above, while the last two models (Models 3 and 4) represent the same equation estimated for currently married women only.

The results in the baseline equation (Model 1) indicate that race is a strong predictor of female headship. White, Colored, or Indian/Asian women were significantly less likely to be heads of households as compared to African women. In Model 2, a series of covariates was added to the baseline equation to determine if the strong association between race and female headship might be explained by differences in individual and household-level attributes, such as a woman's level of education, household size, place of residence, and household wealth. The results continued to show statistically strong associations between race and female headship. Race differences in female headship fail to disappear after introducing several control variables in Model 2. The covariates in Model 2 show interesting effects on female headship. Age and marital status differences were large and statistically significant, with never-married and widowed/divorced/separated women significantly more likely to be heads of households. Highly educated women were significantly less likely to be heads of households, while women who were homemakers, unemployed, or students had significantly higher odds of heading households as compared to employed women. Another indicator of socioeconomic status, the

Table 8.7

Logistic Results (Odds Ratios) Predicting the Likelihood That a Woman Is a Head of Household: South Africa, 1996

	All women		Married women	
Variables	Model 1	Model 2	Model 3	Model 4
Racial group				
African (ref)	1.00	1.00	1.00	1.00
Colored	0.51***	0.72***	0.30***	0.58***
Indian/Asian	0.27***	0.46***	0.20***	0.41***
White	0.25***	0.42***	0.09***	0.23***
Age group				
45–54 (ref)		1.00		1.00
15-24		0.79***		1.55***
25–34		0.89***		1.38***
35–44		0.95***		1.17***
55+		1.28***		0.94***
Marital status				
Married (ref)		1.00		—
Never married		2.96***		—
Living with a partner		0.87***		—
Widowed/divorced/separated		5.66***		—
Education				
None (ref)		1.00		1.00
Primary		1.03***		0.94***
Secondary		0.99		0.86***
Postsecondary		0.91***		0.75***
Employment status				
Employed (ref)		1.00		1.00
Unemployed		1.46***		1.60***
Homemaker		1.91***		2.10***
Student		1.21***		2.22***
Migrant workers absent from household				
No migrant worker absent (ref)		1.00		1.00
Migrant worker absent		2.54***		3.55***
Migration status				
Nonimmigrant		1.00		1.00
Recent migrant		0.85***		1.17***
Long-term migrant		0.81***		0.92***
Gender of household member with highest income				
Male (ref)		1.00		1.00
Female		8.47***		6.26***
Household size				
5+ (ref)		1.00		1.00
1–2		0.90***		1.03***
3–4		1.02***		0.94***
Household's standard of living				
High (ref)		1.00		1.00
Low		1.32***		1.35***
Medium		1.14***		1.16***

(continued)

Residence				
Urban (ref)		1.00		1.00
Rural		1.06***		0.82***
Province				
Gauteng (ref)		1.00		1.00
Western Cape		1.01		0.89***
Eastern Cape		1.35***		1.48***
Northern Cape		0.97***		0.90***
Free State		0.89***		0.82***
KwaZulu-Natal		1.04***		1.13***
North West		1.00		1.00
Mpumalanga		1.03***		1.09***
Limpopo		1.44***		1.40***
−2ln	8,206,802.2	6,612,978.2	2248759.0	1,880,455.3
d.f	3	33	3	30
N	6,486,279		2,531,151	

Source: Computed from the 1996 South African Population Census micro-data.
Notes: d.f. = degrees of freedom; *p* < 0.05; **p* < 0.01; ***p* < 0.001

household's standard of living, further showed that female headship in South Africa is closely linked to low socioeconomic status. Women whose household standard of living was classified as low or medium had significantly higher odds of heading households as compared to women from well-off households. However, when we examined the association between household headship and the gender of the person with the highest income in a household, we observed that those women who had the highest incomes in households were about 8.5 times more likely to be heads as compared to men. This finding could be linked to either the "chief earner" or the "power/authority" notion that is often captured by the concept of household headship (Vu 1996; Youssef and Hetler 1983).

An equally important determinant of female headship in South Africa is male labor migration, particularly among Africans. Since the creation of homelands, many African women were forced to live apart from their husbands, who were forced to migrate to urban areas and mining towns. The residential settings in some of these areas prohibited men from staying with their families. Although apartheid collapsed in 1994, male labor migration to the mines and towns has not slowed. During the 1996 South African Population Census, each household was asked whether there were any persons who were usually members of the household, but who were away for a month or more because they were migrant workers. The following definition of a migrant worker was provided: "A migrant worker is someone who is absent from home for more than a month each year to work or to seek work." If the respondent answered that there were migrant workers who were usually members of the household, further details were requested, for up to four migrant workers per household.

Given this unique set of data, we decided to examine if the absence of migrant workers was a strong predictor of female household headship in South Africa. The results presented in Model 2 clearly show that females were more likely to be household heads if they were living in households that reported that there were migrant workers who were absent. Tied to the labor migration issue is place of residence. The results in Model 2 show that women who resided in rural areas were significantly more likely to be heads than urban women. An equally intriguing finding in Model 2 is that females who were recent or long-term migrants were significantly less likely to be heads of households as compared to women who were nonmigrants. Recent migrants were those women who changed their magisterial districts of residence between 1994–96, while long-term migrants were those women who changed their magisterial districts of residence prior to 1994, the year South Africa became independent. Lastly, living in provinces that have historically been affected by out-migration of males, like the Eastern Cape, Kwazulu-Natal, and Limpopo, significantly increased a woman's chances of heading a household.

Because being married is negatively associated with female household headship, and there are substantial differences in the proportion of women who are currently married across the main racial groups in South Africa, we did the same analysis for married women only (Models 3 and 4). This was done to isolate the effect of spousal separation (living in different areas) on racial differentials in headship, as most married women generally tend to declare their husband as the head of the household when the two are living together. The differences in female household headship between White and African women were much bigger when the analysis was restricted to married women. The baseline model (Model 3) shows that currently married White women were 0.09 times less likely to be household heads than African women. Coloreds and Indians/Asians also had significantly lower odds of being heads— 0.3 and 0.2, respectively. The inclusion of the control variables in Models 4 slightly reduced the differences in headship between African women and women from the other racial groups. In general, more educated, married women were less likely to be heads than women with no schooling. Married women who were homemakers, unemployed, or students were also more likely to be heads. If there were migrant workers absent from a household, married women were almost 3.6 times more likely to be household heads than women living in households without migrant workers. However, the results for some covariates in Model 4 slightly differed from those we observed in the full model for all women (Model 2). For instance, there was a statistically significant higher likelihood of headship for married women who were recent migrants, while married women living in rural areas had significantly lower odds of being heads. The association between household size and female headship was also mixed. Married women residing in households with fewer than two members were significantly more likely to be heads than women residing in households with more than five members.

Given the very high proportion of African women who headed households (41.5 percent and 43.3 percent in 1991 and 1996, respectively), we further analyzed the determinants of household headship among Africans only. By restricting our analysis to Africans only, we were also able to control for a woman's ethnic background. The correlates of household headship among Africans are presented in Table 8.8. Results from the baseline model (Model 1) show a clear tendency for Southern Sotho, Swazi, and Tsonga women to be less likely to head households as compared to Zulu women, while women from other ethnic backgrounds were significantly more likely to be heads than Zulu women. However, when we added a set of background variables (Model 2), Southern Sotho women had significantly higher odds of household headship than Zulu women. In contrast, the advantage experienced by Venda women in the baseline model disappears with the addition of several background variables in Model 2.

The full model also showed that age and marital status were very strong predictors of household headship. Younger women were significantly less likely to be heads, while the never married and the widowed/divorced/separated had significantly higher odds of heading households, other things being equal. For women with postsecondary education, the chances of household headship were much lower than those for uneducated women. The odds of becoming the head were also higher for African women who were unemployed, home-makers, or students. Model 2 also shows that the odds of becoming a house-hold head for women residing in households that reported that migrant workers were absent were almost 2.5 times higher than the odds for women living in households without migrant workers. With regard to migration status, both recent and long-term migrants had significantly lower odds of heading house-holds as compared to nonmigrants. Results from Model 2 further reveal that females were almost eight times more likely to be heads if they had the high-est income in the household.

When we run the same equation for married women only (Models 3 and 4), we continue to note significant ethnic differences in female headship. Model 4 reveals interesting age effects. Married women below age 45 were more likely to head households than older women. When we looked at all women (Model 2), younger women had significantly lower chances of being house-hold heads than women ages 45–54. The results in Model 4 also show that the odds of being the household head decreased significantly with an increase in level of education. The importance of socioeconomic status is further highlighted by the higher odds of household headship associated with low household standard of living. Married women whose household standard of living was classified as low were 1.34 times more likely to be heads than married women from households with a high standard of living. The odds of being the household head for married women living in households with migrant workers absent were 3.4 times that of married women living in households without migrant workers. The gender of the person with the highest income in the household was also a very strong predictor of household headship among married women. With regard to place of residence, married women residing in rural areas were significantly less likely to head households as compared to married urban women. Lastly, married women living in major migrant-sending provinces (Eastern Cape, KwaZulu-Natal, Mpumalanga, and Limpopo) had very high odds of heading households compared with married women from other provinces. Overall, these results demonstrate the significant role of ethnicity in explaining female headship among Africans in South Africa. Other significant predictors of female headship were personal characteristics such as age, marital status, employment status, as well as household characteristics like the presence or absence of migrant workers, household size, and place of residence.

Conclusion

Racial and ethnic differences in household structure in South Africa appear to have been shaped by the interaction of social, cultural, economic, and political factors that the country's major racial groups have experienced. Africans in South Africa are more likely to live in single-parent households and extended households than Whites, Indians/Asians, and Coloreds. Additionally, compared with Whites, Indians/Asians, and to some extent Coloreds, African children ages birth through 14 are less likely to be living with their mothers. African women are also substantially more likely to head households than women in the other racial groups. The differences in headship are even greater when the analysis is restricted to married women.

While extended family settings are not a unique characteristic of South Africa's African population, the extreme segregation that the country's African population endured under apartheid has undoubtedly exacerbated the racial differences in household structure in the country. The mobility, residential, and occupational restrictions that the apartheid system imposed on the African population since the beginning of the twentieth century and legalized in 1948 forced the Africans to live apart from fellow family members. For example, the apartheid system restricted migration of Africans, particularly females and children, into urban areas to join their parents and

Table 8.8

Logistic Results (Odds Ratios) Predicting the Likelihood That an African Woman Is a Head of Household: South Africa, 1996

	All women		Married women	
	Model 1	Model 2	Model 3	Model 4
Ethnic group				
Zulu (ref)	1.00	1.00	1.00	1.00
Ndebele	1.03***	1.04***	1.08***	1.16***
Xhosa	1.33***	1.12***	1.47***	1.06***
Northern Sotho	1.31***	1.01	1.48***	1.13***
Southern Sotho	0.89***	1.16***	0.75***	1.16***
Tswana	1.03***	1.21***	0.93***	1.32***
Swazi	0.91***	0.95***	0.88***	0.86***
Venda	1.21***	0.93***	1.28***	0.95***
Tsonga	0.96***	0.89***	1.14***	0.92***
Age group				
45–54 (ref)		1.00		1.00
15–24		0.79***		1.38***
25–34		0.89***		1.32***
35–44		0.97***		1.17***
55+		1.17***		0.94***
Marital status				—
Married (ref)		1.00		
Never married		2.69***		—
Living with a partner		0.78***		—
Widowed/divorced/separated		4.30***		—
Education				
None (ref)		1.00		1.00
Primary		1.00		0.95***
Secondary		0.99		0.89***
Postsecondary		0.90***		0.77***
Employment status				
Employed (ref)		1.00		1.00
Unemployed		1.47***		1.70***
Homemaker		2.19***		2.47***
Student		1.30***		2.47***
Migrant workers absent from household				
No migrant worker absent (ref)		1.00		1.00
Migrant worker absent		2.45***		3.44***
Migration status				
Nonimmigrant (ref)		1.00		1.00
Recent migrant		0.68***		1.01
Long–term migrant		0.77***		0.92***
Gender of household member with highest income				
Male (ref)		1.00		1.00
Female		8.11***		6.65***
Household size				
5+ (ref)		1.00		1.00
1–2		0.75***		1.06***
3–4		1.11***		1.02**

(continued)

Table 8.8 *(continued)*

Variables	All women		Married women	
	Model 1	Model 2	Model 3	Model 4
Household's standard of living				
High (ref)		1.00		1.00
Low		1.29***		1.34***
Medium		1.16***		1.18***
Place of residence				
Urban (ref)		1.00		1.00
Rural		1.02***		0.81***
Province				
Gauteng (ref)		1.00		1.00
Western Cape		0.92***		0.74***
Eastern Cape		1.28***		1.55***
Northern Cape		0.87***		0.86***
Free State		0.81***		0.78***
KwaZulu–Natal		1.07***		1.20***
North West		0.90***		0.87***
Mpumalanga		1.08***		1.17***
Limpopo		1.51***		1.47***
−2 ln	6,533,799.7	5,312,921.5	1,863,645.8	1,530,901.2
d.f	8	38	8	35
N	4,815,640	1,641,070		

Source: Computed from the 1996 South African Population Census micro-data.
Notes: d.f. = degrees of freedom; $*p < 0.05$; $**p < 0.01$; $***p < 0.001$.

spouses. Men and women who were working as domestic workers for Whites and were housed within the White residential areas were restricted from bringing their spouses and children to live with them. These policies also substantially impacted the household structures and living arrangements of Coloreds and Indians/Asians. Comparison of the 1991 and 1996 census data shows that the socioeconomic and political changes that took place during this period have affected household structures for all four racial groups. While the other racial groups registered significant increases in the proportion of nuclear households, the biggest change for Africans was a large increase in the proportion of one-person households. This pattern suggests that one of the immediate effects of the changes for the African population was an increased capacity to form their own households. The results show that a clear understanding of contemporary household structures among South Africa's racial groups can be gained by paying close attention to the genesis of household and family fragmentation that began with the nature of industrialization and a mining-based economy that encouraged use of migrant labor, and culminated in the legalization of mobility and residential restrictions on the majority African population through the apartheid system.

References

Adegboyega, Oluwole, J.P. Ntozi, and J.B. Ssekamatte-Ssebuliba. 1997. "The African family: Data, concepts and methodology." In *Family, Population and Development in Africa*, ed. Aderanti Adepoju, 25–40. London: Zed Books Ltd.

Adepoju, Aderanti, and Wariara Mbugua. 1997. "The African family: An overview of changing forms." In *Family, Population and Development in Africa*, ed. Aderanti Adepoju, 41–59. London: Zed Books Ltd.

Africana Encyclopedia. 2001. "Apartheid, social and political policy of racial segregation and discrimination enforced by White minority governments in South Africa from 1948 to 1994." Available at www.africanaencyclopedia.com/apartheid/apartheid.html; last accessed on 11/08/2001.

Ainsworth, Martha. 1992. "Economic aspects of child fostering in Côte d'Ivoire." Living Standards Measurement Studies (LSMS) Working Papers, No. 92. Washington, DC: The World Bank.

Amoateng, A.Y. 1997. "The structure of urban Black households: New survey evidence from a Colored and an African community on the Cape Flats in the Western Cape of South Africa." *African Sociological Review* 1(2): 22–40.

———. 1998. "Comments on the structure of urban households: A reply to Koen and Russell." *African Sociological Review* 2(2): 108–21.

Appolis, Keith U.C. 1996. *From Fragmentation to Wholeness: The Black South African Family Under Siege*. New York: University Press of America.

Aryee, A.F. 1997. "The African family and changing nuptiality patterns." In *Family, Population and Development in Africa*, ed. Aderanti Adepoju, 78–96. London: Zed Books Ltd.

Bledsoe, Caroline H., and Barney Cohen. 1993. *Social Dynamics of Adolescent Fertility in Sub-Saharan Africa*. Washington, DC: National Research Council, National Academy Press.

Bledsoe, Caroline H., Douglas Ewbank, and Uche Isiugo-Abanihe. 1988. "The effect of child fostering on feeding practices and access to health services in rural Sierra Leone." *Social Science and Medicine* 27(6): 627–36.

Bruce, Judith, and Cynthia B. Lloyd. 1997. "Finding the ties that bind: Beyond headship and household." In *Intrahousehold Resource Allocation in Developing Countries: Models, Methods, and Policy*, ed. L. Haddad, J. Hoddinott, and H. Alderman, 213–28. Baltimore, MD: Johns Hopkins University Press.

Caldwell, J.C. 2000. "Rethinking the African AIDS epidemic." *Population and Development Review* 26(1): 117–35.

Caldwell, J.C., and Pat Caldwell. 1993. "The nature and limits of the sub-Saharan African AIDS epidemic: Evidence from geographic and other patterns." *Population and Development Review* 19(4): 817–48.

Case, A., C. Paxson, and J. Ableidinger. 2002. "Orphans in Africa." Working Paper 9213. Cambridge, MA: National Bureau Economic Research (NBER), Working Paper Series.

Central Statistical Service. 1991. *Population Census 1991 Adjustment for Undercount*. CSS Report No. 03–01–26. Pretoria: Central Statistical Service.

Cho, Lee-Jay, Robert D. Retherford, and. M.K. Choe. 1986. *The Own-Children Method of Fertility Estimation*. Honolulu: East-West Center.

Davis, R., and J. Head. 1995. "The future of mine migracy in the context of broader trends in migration in Southern Africa." *Journal of Southern Africa Studies* 21(3): 439–50.

Department of Welfare (Republic of South Africa). 1998. *Annual Report 1997/8*. Pretoria: National Population Unit (NPU).

Gage, A.J., and D. Meekers. 1994. "Sexual activity before marriage in sub-Saharan Africa." *Social Biology* 41(1–2): 44–60.

Isiugo-Abanihe, Uche C. 1985. "Child fosterage in West Africa." *Population and Development Review* 11(1): 53–73.

Isiugo-Abanihe, U.C., and O.M. Obono. 1999. "Family structure in sub-Saharan Africa: Tradition and transition." In *Third African Population Conference, Durban, South Africa, 6–10 December 1999. The African Population in the 21st Century. Volume III,* 237–66. Dakar: Union for African Population Studies.

Jithoo, Sabita. 1978. "Complex households and joint families amongst Indians in Durban." In *Social System and Tradition in Southern Africa: Essays in Honour of Eileen Krige,* ed. John Argyle and Eleanor Preston-Whyte, 86–100. Cape Town: Oxford University Press.

Kahn, K., S. Tollman, M. Garenne, and J.S.S. Gear. 1999. "Who dies from what? Determining cause of death in South Africa's rural north-east." *Tropical Medicine and International Health* 4(6): 433–41.

Kennedy, E., and P. Peters. 1992. "Household food security and child nutrition: The interaction of income and gender of household head." *World Development* 20(8): 1077–85.

Koen, Charton. 1998. "The structure of urban African households: New survey evidence from a Colored and an African community on the Cape Flats in the Western Cape of South Africa: A comment on Amoateng's methods and findings." *African Sociological Review* 2(1): 165–73.

Laslett, Peter. 1972. "Introduction: The history of the family." In *Household and Family in Past Time,* ed. Peter Laslett and Richard Wall, 1–90. Cambridge: Cambridge University Press.

Lestrade-Jefferis, Joyce. 2000. "Housing, and household access to services and facilities." In *The People of South Africa Population Census, 1996 Summary Report,* Report No. 03–01–12, ed. Eric O. Udjo and Ros Hirschowitz, 85–96. Pretoria: Statistics South Africa.

Lloyd, Cynthia B., and A.K. Blanc. 1996. "Children's schooling in sub-Saharan Africa: The role of fathers, mothers, and others." *Population and Development Review* 22(2): 265–98.

Lloyd, Cynthia B., and S. Desai. 1992. "Children's living arrangements in developing countries." *Population Research and Policy Review* 11: 193–216.

Lucas, R. 1985. "Mines and migrants in South Africa." *American Economic Review* 75(5): 1094–1108.

———. 1987. "Emigration to South Africa's mine." *American Economic Review* 77(3): 313–30.

Massey, D. 1983. "Class struggle and migrant labor in South African gold mines." *Canadian Journal of African Studies* 17(3): 429–48.

May, Julian, ed. 1998. *Poverty and Inequality in South Africa, Summary Report.* Durban: Praxis Publishing.

Mbugua, Wariara. 1997. "The African family and the status of women's health." In *Family, Population and Development in Africa,* ed. Aderanti Adepoju, 139–57. London: Zed Books Ltd.

McDaniel, Antonio. 1994. "Historical racial differences in living arrangements of children," *Journal of Family History* 19(1): 57–77.

McDaniel, Antonio, and E.M. Zulu. 1996. "Fathers, mothers and children: Patterns in child–parent living arrangements in sub-Saharan Africa." *African Population Studies* (December): 1–30.

Moerdijk, Donald. 1981. *Anti-Development: South Africa and its Bantustans.* Paris: UNESCO Press.

Morgan, S.P., A. McDaniel, A. Miller, and S. Preston. 1993. "Racial differences in household and family structure at the turn of the century." *American Journal of Sociology* 98(4): 799–828.

Mturi, A.J., T. Makatjane, and N. Molise. 1999. "Gender differentials in housing characteristics and household possession in Lesotho urban areas." *Genus* LV (1–2): 121–33.

Murray, C. 1980. "Migrant labour and changing family structure in the rural periphery of Southern Africa," *Journal of Southern African Studies* 6(2): 139–55.

———. 1981. *Families Divided: The Impact of Migrant Labour in Lesotho.* London: Cambridge University Press.

———. 1987. "Class, gender and the household: The developmental cycle in southern Africa." *Development and Change* 18(2): 235–49.

National Development and Planning Commission (Republic of South Africa). 1999. "Draft green paper on development and planning." Document No. DPC 4/99.

National Research Council. 1993. *Demographic Effects of Economic Reversals in Sub-Saharan Africa.* Washington, DC: National Academy Press.

Nhlapho, Margaret. 1986. "Domestic workers in South Africa." *Migration World* XIV(1/2): 21–24.

O'Laughlin, B. 1996. *Missing Men? The Debate over Rural Poverty and Women-Headed Households in Southern Africa.* The Hague: The Institute of Social Studies.

Ocholla-Ayayo, A.B.C. 1997. "The African family between tradition and modernity." In *Family, Population and Development in Africa*, ed. Aderanti Adepoju, 60–77. London: Zed Books Ltd.

Oppong, Christine. 1997. "The African family and the status of women's health." In *Family, Population and Development in Africa*, ed. Aderanti Adepoju, 158–82. London: Zed Books Ltd.

Packard, Randall M. 1989. *White Plague, African Labor: Tuberculosis and the Political Economy of Health and Disease in South Africa.* Berkeley: University of California Press.

Page, Hilary J. 1989. "Childbearing versus childrearing: Co-residence of mother and child in sub-Saharan Africa." In *Reproduction and Social Organization in Sub-Saharan Africa*, ed. Ron J. Lesthaeghe, chapter 9. Berkeley: University of California Press.

Preston-Whyte, E. 1978. "Families without marriage: A Zulu case study." In *Social System and Tradition in Southern Africa*, ed. J. Argyle and E. Preston-Whyte, 55–85. Cape Town: Oxford University Press.

———. 1991. "Invisible workers: Domestic service and the informal economy." In *South Africa's Informal Economy*, ed. E. Preston-Whyte and C. Rogerson, 34–53. Cape Town: Oxford University Press.

Ramphele, Mamphela. 1989. "The dynamics of gender politics in the hostels of Cape Town: Another legacy of the South African migrant labour system." *Journal of Southern African Studies* 15(3): 393–414.

Republic of South Africa (RSA). 1997. *Government Gazette* Vol. 18502. Cape Town, December 12.

———. 1998. *Government Gazette* Vol. 19513. Cape Town, November 27.

Russel, Margo. 1998. "African sociological review." *African Urban Households in South Africa* 2(1): 174–80.

Sibanda, A., and T. Zuberi. 1999. "Contemporary fertility levels and trends in South Africa: Evidence from reconstructed census birth histories." In *The African Population in the 21st Century: Third African Population Conference,* Vol. 1, 79–108. Durban: Union of African Population Studies.

Sibanda, A., Z. Woubalem, D.P. Hogan, and D.P. Lindstrom. 2003. "The proximate determinants of the decline to below-replacement fertility in Addis Ababa, Ethiopia." *Studies in Family Planning* 34(1): 1–7.

Singh, Anand. 1996. "Variation and fluidity in household composition in Phoenix, Durban." *Journal of Comparative Family Studies* XXVII (3): 467–84.

Siqwana-Ndulo, Nombulelo. 1998. "Rural African family structure in the Eastern Cape Province, South Africa." *Journal of Comparative Family Studies* XXIX (2): 407–17.

Statistics South Africa. 1998. *The People of South Africa: Population Census, 1996.* Pretoria: Statistics South Africa.

UNAIDS. 2000. *Report on the Global HIV/AIDS Epidemic—June 2000.* Geneva: UNAIDS.

van de Walle, E. 1993. "Recent trends in marriage changes." In *Demographic Change in Sub-Saharan Africa*, ed. K.A. Foote, K.H.H. Hill, and L.G. Martin, 117–52. Washington, DC: National Academy Press.

———. 1999a. "A first look at household data in a census: Botswana 1981." African Census Analysis Project Working Papers, no. 3. Philadelphia: Population Studies Center, University of Pennsylvania.

———. 1999b. "Where are the children of Botswana?" Unpublished manuscript. Philadelphia: Population Studies Center, University of Pennsylvania.

Vu, Manh Loi. 1996. *Female-Headed Households in Vietnam.* Working Paper No. 96–11. Seattle Population Research Center.

Youssef, N., and C.B. Hetler. 1983. "Establishing the economic condition of woman-headed households in the third world: A new approach." In *Women and Poverty in the Third World,* ed. M. Buvinic, M.A. Lycette, and W.P. McGreevey, 216–43. Baltimore, MD: Johns Hopkins University Press.

Ziehl, S.C. 2001. "Documenting changing family patterns in South Africa: Are census data of any value." *African Sociological Review* 5(2): 36–62.

Zuberi, Tukufu, and Amson Sibanda. Forthcoming. "Fertility estimation in sub-Saharan Africa: Applying own-children methods to African censuses." *Reproductive Change in Sub-Saharan Africa, IUSSP.* Oxford: Oxford University Press.

9. Race and Gender Gaps in Education

Amson Sibanda and Gwendoline Lehloenya

Narrowing societal and intragroup differences in educational attainment has been a major goal of most developing countries and international organizations such as the World Bank and the United Nations. Gaps in education between countries or between boys and girls have been shaped by a myriad of factors that range from differential government expenditures on education to gender-specific stratification processes in particular societies (Hyde 1993; Lloyd and Blanc 1996; Sibanda 2004). In line with the body of research that has investigated gaps in various aspects of educational achievement, our objectives in this chapter are very modest. We provide a descriptive analysis of gender, race, and regional gaps in school enrollment and attainment in South Africa. Specifically, we address the following questions: Is there a female disadvantage in education across and within racial groups? How large is the African disadvantage vis-à-vis Whites, Coloreds, and Indians/Asians? Are there marked regional inequalities in school enrollment and attainment?

Studying disparities in education is important for several reasons. First, addressing gender, race, and regional gaps in education contributes in many important ways to alleviating social inequalities that impede overall improvements in the quality of life in a society (Hill and King 1993; Schultz 1993; Sen 1992). These issues are particularly important in the context of South Africa, where access to schools and enrollment, attendance, and school completion rates have been historically very low among Africans because of apartheid policies of separate and unequal development. Second, a major social policy goal of the new South Africa is to close the gaps in employment, housing, health, and other important facets of life that were created by decades of apartheid policies. One route that has been effectively used in many societies has been to narrow the existing gender, race/ethnic, and regional gaps in education (Barrera 1990; Caldwell 1979; Hill and King 1993).

The desire to improve various aspects of educational participation, such as enrollment, attendance, and completion, at all levels and across all population groups, is a major goal of the South African government because it recognizes that disparities in the distribution of educational resources are a major social and economic concern. The unequal provision of educational resources across race has contributed to inequalities in labor-market earnings, housing, and health, and they have also played a critical role in the transmission of inequality across generations (Lam 1999; Thomas 1996).

The analysis of gender, race, and regional gaps in education is based on a 10 percent sample of the 1996 South African Population Census. Individuals aged 5 years and above were asked a series of education questions. The drawback of these data is that no information about contextual-level variables, such as the existence of schools in communities, is provided. This is particularly important, because the presence of schools in an area has an important effect on whether children enroll in school or not. Nevertheless, an analysis of the gaps in education that does not include such contextual-level variables still gives us an opportunity to see if there are any groups that are particularly disadvantaged.

This chapter follows the analytical strategy used by Filmer (1999) and Hill and King (1993) to examine the structure of social disparities in education in developing countries. We calculate gender and race gaps in education because they yield a very clear picture of the magnitude of any differences across or within groups. For instance, male–female gaps in primary school enrollment refer to the size of the difference in the level of enrollment between males and females. In addition to reporting a White–African enrollment gap or a male–female completion gap, we also present the ratios of these outcomes. The male–female difference gives us the absolute gap in a particular outcome, while the male–female ratio (M/F) gives us an idea of the magnitude of the gender difference in the outcome in percentage terms. A ratio of 1.0 indicates parity between the male and female enrollment or graduation rates. According to Filmer, "it is important to consider both the gap and the ratio as these highlight different aspects of the potential disparity. Although the two measures tend to track each other relatively closely, both concepts are independently relevant"(1999: 10).

Results

Gender and Regional Gaps in School Enrollment

In many developing-country settings, educational gaps between boys and girls have been one of the most enduring forms of inequality defining the life chances of both groups. Girls are less likely to be enrolled in school and are also more likely to drop out or repeat (Hyde 1993). We examine here whether gender gaps in enrollment in South Africa fit the general pattern that has been found in most parts of the developing world. Table 9.1 displays the gender gaps in primary-school enrollment rates, by race, for children ages 7 through 18, at the national level and in each province. The results indicate that, at the primary-school level, enrollment rates are near universal across all racial groups. More importantly, the results indicate that there is a very small gender gap in enrollment across all racial groups. In almost all provinces, the absolute gender gap in enrollment is less than 2 percent, and the ratios of the outcomes are equally small. The regional similarities are strong. Among Africans, the enrollment rate of girls is slightly higher in the Northern Cape and KwaZulu-Natal, while in provinces like the Western Cape, the enrollment rate of boys is 98 percent that of girls. For the other population groups, the only noticeable difference in primary-school enrollment is among Indians/Asians living in the North West. In this province, girls have an 8 percent advantage over boys.

These findings contrast sharply with findings from other developing countries. For instance, Filmer (1999) observed that boys had a 58 and 53 percentage point advantage in primary school enrollment in Niger and Benin, respectively. Hyde (1993) and Lloyd and Blanc (1996) also found large female disadvantages in several African countries. However, Hyde also noted that the enrollment rates of girls in most southern African countries, such as Botswana, Lesotho, and Swaziland, were equal to or higher than enrollment rates of boys. Hyde attributes this female advantage to the fact that the majority of males in these countries are drained out of the school system by South Africa's labor markets.

At the secondary-school level, Table 9.2 shows relatively similar enrollment rates across population groups. However, there is a slightly wider gender gap favoring males in secondary-school enrollment among Africans, Coloreds, and Whites. The male–female gap jumps to over 3 percent in some provinces. We also see some interesting gender gaps across race. For instance, among Africans, there is a male advantage in all provinces of about 2 percent. In contrast, the secondary-school enrollment of Indian/Asian boys is lower than that of girls in most provinces with the exception of the Eastern Cape, North West, and Limpopo.

Gender Gaps in School Completion

Tables 9.3 and 9.4 present the gender gaps in school completion at the primary- and secondary-school levels, respectively. Overall, the results show wider differences by race as compared to gender differences. Across all popu-

Table 9.1

Gender Gaps in Primary-School Enrollment: Children Ages 7–18

	Africans			Coloreds			Indians/Asians			Whites		
	Females percent enrolled	Male–female gap	Male/female ratio	Females percent enrolled	Male–female gap	Male/female ratio	Females percent enrolled	Male–female gap	Male/female ratio	Females percent enrolled	Male–female gap	Male/female ratio
Western Cape	94.97	–1.72	0.98	96.11	–1.14	0.99	97.52	1.83	1.02	99.26	–0.02	0.99
Eastern Cape	95.75	–0.77	0.99	95.38	–0.18	0.99	100	–1.30	0.99	98.20	0.25	1.00
Northern Cape	92.25	1.48	1.02	93.14	–0.49	0.99	100	0.00	1.00	99.51	0.02	1.00
Free State	96.40	0.27	1.00	93.82	0.31	1.00	100	–9.09	0.91	98.70	0.42	1.00
KwaZulu–Natal	94.56	0.64	1.01	98.69	–1.46	0.98	99.05	–0.29	0.99	99.09	–0.11	0.99
North West	95.29	–0.08	0.99	95.65	0.36	1.00	92.68	7.32	1.08	99.18	–0.63	0.99
Gauteng	96.84	–0.68	0.99	98.11	–0.14	0.99	98.47	0.23	1.00	98.38	0.04	1.00
Mpumalanga	96.62	–0.28	0.99	98.44	–1.09	0.99	98.28	1.72	1.02	98.27	0.18	1.00
Limpopo	97.48	–0.01	0.99	100	0.00	1.00	100	0.00	1.00	98.44	–0.78	0.99
All	95.92	–0.11	0.99	95.8	–0.83	0.99	98.89	–0.10	0.99	98.70	0.01	1.00

Source: Computed from the 1996 South African Population Census micro-data.

Table 9.2

Gender Gaps in Secondary-School Enrollment: Children Ages 13–24

	Africans			Coloreds			Indians/Asians			Whites		
	Females percent enrolled	Male–female gap	Male/female ratio	Females percent enrolled	Male–female gap	Male/female ratio	Females percent enrolled	Male–female gap	Male/female ratio	Females percent enrolled	Male–female gap	Male/female ratio
Western Cape	82.49	1.80	1.02	78.14	2.59	1.03	90.58	−7.13	0.92	90.65	−1.99	0.98
Eastern Cape	94.27	2.09	1.02	80.97	2.86	1.03	87.50	0.38	1.00	84.74	−0.50	0.99
Northern Cape	88.60	1.89	1.02	83.44	3.21	1.04	86.67	−11.67	0.86	88.99	−2.78	0.97
Free State	91.33	2.56	1.03	84.42	3.25	1.04	94.12	−20.79	0.78	84.39	−0.80	0.99
KwaZulu–Natal	88.33	3.44	1.04	81.63	1.08	1.01	81.69	−1.27	0.98	89.00	−1.05	0.99
North West	91.30	1.62	1.02	82.93	−1.03	0.99	86.49	1.75	1.02	84.05	3.00	1.04
Gauteng	80.70	1.80	1.02	80.44	−1.40	0.98	84.65	−0.63	0.99	85.15	−0.70	0.99
Mpumalanga	90.62	2.42	1.03	88.24	−4.70	0.95	87.10	−3.43	0.96	85.36	3.43	1.04
Limpopo	92.46	3.89	1.04	91.67	−7.95	0.91	82.76	10.10	1.12	85.59	3.85	1.04
All	89.72	2.64	1.03	79.70	2.16	1.03	82.67	−1.51	0.98	86.45	−0.39	0.99

Source: Computed from the 1996 South African Population Census micro-data.

257

lation groups, a slightly higher percentage of girls completed primary school relative to boys. The most disadvantaged groups in terms of primary-school completion are African children. At the national level, only 63 percent of African females, ages 13 to 20 completed primary school, as compared to 82 percent among Indian/Asian females. The primary-school completion rate was even lower among African males living in the Western Cape, at 54.8 percent (i.e., 65.94 minus 11.16), and in the Eastern Cape, at 49.9 percent (i.e., 58.05 minus 8.11).

When we examine the gender gaps in school completion, the patterns we observe at both the primary- and secondary-school levels are quite different from the school-enrollment patterns we observed above (in Tables 9.1 and 9.2). The gender gaps are much wider, reflecting gender differences that existed under apartheid, because the majority of these children were expected to have graduated before the end of the apartheid era in 1994. The male–female gaps reached over 11 percent among Africans residing in the Western Cape. In this province, the primary-school completion rate of boys is 83 percent that of girls. In fact, the gender gap in school completion tips in favor of boys in only one province, the Northern Cape. Among Coloreds, there is no male advantage at all. The largest intragroup disparities are exhibited by Indians/Asians. The primary-school completion rate is highest (11 percent higher) among Indian/Asian boys living in the Northern Cape. But in North West province, the male advantage disappears—their completion rate is just 76 percent that of girls.

Table 9.4 presents race and gender gaps in secondary-school completion among children ages 18 to 25. The clear conclusion evident from this table is that differences across population groups are very wide, particularly between Africans and Whites. The percentage of Whites who completed school is almost three times larger than the African percentage and almost twice that of Coloreds. This racial gap is associated with past underinvestment in the education of African and Colored children. When we look at gender gaps, we see that differences between African boys and girls are small compared to differences across racial groups. However, provincial disparities are quite remarkable. Among Africans, school-completion rates range from just over 20 percent among boys in the Eastern Cape to a high of about 37 percent in Gauteng. In contrast, the lowest completion rate among White girls is about 71 percent in Limpopo Province and reaches a high of about 83 percent in the Western Cape. Indians/Asians also have very high completion rates in all provinces, with the exception of Limpopo where their completion rates are below 50 percent. Coloreds also have low completion rates.

Table 9.4 also shows that the largest intragroup provincial disparities are

Table 9.3 .

Gender Gaps in Primary-School Completion: Children Ages 13–20

Province	Africans			Coloreds			Indians/Asians			Whites		
	Females percent completing	Male–female gap	Male/female ratio	Females percent completing	Male–female gap	Male/female ratio	Females percent completing	Male–female gap	Male/female ratio	Females percent completing	Male–female gap	Male/female ratio
Western Cape	65.94	−11.16	0.83	69.14	−5.78	0.92	86.42	−4.88	0.94	72.26	−1.50	0.98
Eastern Cape	58.05	−8.11	0.86	68.14	−6.06	0.91	82.35	−5.43	0.93	70.95	−2.83	0.96
Northern Cape	58.25	0.89	1.01	60.04	−2.25	0.96	80.00	8.89	1.11	71.68	−2.49	0.96
Free State	61.17	−4.38	0.93	64.11	−8.38	0.87	87.50	−7.50	0.91	74.31	−2.37	0.97
KwaZulu-Natal	61.20	−4.99	0.92	71.74	−1.37	0.98	82.13	−1.10	0.99	83.57	−4.45	0.95
North West	60.78	−4.91	0.92	54.48	−0.68	0.99	87.50	−20.83	0.76	76.54	−3.37	0.96
Gauteng	68.07	−6.55	0.90	77.14	−3.08	0.96	83.16	4.20	1.05	78.15	−1.97	0.97
Mpumalanga	62.82	−6.38	0.89	60.00	−6.03	0.90	78.26	1.74	1.02	80.31	−1.45	0.98
Limpopo	69.24	−7.74	0.89	88.24	−5.89	0.93	81.82	7.07	1.09	77.62	1.14	1.01
All	62.72	−6.21	0.90	67.97	−4.97	0.93	82.44	−0.73	0.99	76.51	−2.14	0.97

Source: Computed from the 1996 South African Population Census micro-data.

Table 9.4

Gender Gaps in Secondary-School Completion: Children Ages 18–25

Province	Africans			Coloreds			Indians/Asians			Whites		
	Females percent completing	Male–female gap	Male/female ratio	Females percent completing	Male–female gap	Male/female ratio	Females percent completing	Male–female gap	Male/female ratio	Females percent completing	Male–female gap	Male/female ratio
Western Cape	28.90	−0.89	0.97	40.62	−3.61	0.91	75.32	−6.09	0.92	82.73	−4.66	0.94
Eastern Cape	21.22	−1.95	0.91	36.83	−3.97	0.89	78.65	−8.12	0.90	75.96	−4.27	0.94
Northern Cape	27.66	−0.42	0.98	29.45	−0.06	0.99	60.00	−10.00	0.83	73.51	−8.98	0.88
Free State	22.39	2.84	1.13	37.39	−0.62	0.98	57.14	−7.14	0.87	75.33	−3.13	0.96
KwaZulu–Natal	27.48	−1.20	0.96	55.20	−7.26	0.87	73.21	−5.61	0.92	82.01	−4.54	0.94
North West	30.06	−0.51	0.98	37.97	−7.31	0.81	77.78	3.47	1.04	73.04	0.62	1.01
Gauteng	37.43	−0.31	0.99	47.55	−2.47	0.95	74.92	−1.76	0.98	79.39	−4.40	0.94
Mpumalanga	27.63	1.25	1.04	45.35	−2.14	0.95	61.64	−0.70	0.99	73.22	−1.96	0.97
Limpopo	27.39	−1.28	0.95	63.16	−30.55	0.52	40.00	36.92	1.92	71.18	−0.036	0.99
All	28.22	−0.26	0.99	40.28	−3.31	0.92	73.38	−4.85	0.93	78.78	−3.94	0.95

Source: Computed from the 1996 South African Population Census micro-data.

among Indians/Asians. For instance, the school-completion rate of Indian/Asian males living in the Northern Cape is just 83 percent that of females, while Indian/Asian boys living in the Limpopo have a 37 percent advantage over girls. Another interesting finding is that Colored males have no advantage over females in all provinces.

Racial Gaps in School Enrollment and Completion

The following analysis focuses only on racial differences in educational attainment, without disaggregating the results by gender. By simply restricting the analysis to population groups, we are interested in uncovering the magnitude of the racial disadvantage in a country that was legally, socially, and economically stratified by race. The creation of the Bantu Education Act in 1953, and similar acts for Coloreds and Indians/Asians in 1963 and 1965, respectively, cemented the unequal distribution of resources across race (Behr 1978). African students received less than a quarter of the funding that was spent on White students. According to Thomas (1996), patterns of educational attainment by race paralleled these unequal patterns in the distribution of resources. Thus, the results displayed in Tables 9.5 through 9.8 give us an opportunity to examine what impact a previously segregated educational system has had on patterns of current school enrollment and completion.

The results in Tables 9.5 through 9.8 are presented in a slightly different way than in the earlier tables. We only display the enrollment or graduation rates of African children. To derive the enrollment rates for the other population groups, one can simply add or subtract the difference in the level of the outcome of a particular racial group to the enrollment of African children. Thus, the enrollment rate of Coloreds residing in the Western Cape is equal to 95.52 (94.10 plus 1.42), and the ratio is equal to 1.01 (95.52 divided by 94.10).

The racial gaps displayed in Table 9.5 indicate that the primary-school enrollment rates of African children fall below the enrollment rates of Whites and Indians/Asians by as much as 6.5 percent (Northern Cape). At the secondary-school level (Table 9.6), the enrollment ratios of African children are surprisingly higher than those of other population groups. At the national level, the gap between African and Colored children is more than 10 percent, in favor of Africans. The White and Indian/Asian deficit is also substantial, at −5 and −9 percent, respectively. These results indicate that Africans made substantial progress barely two years after South Africa attained independence. However, this does not mean that the educational disadvantage of Africans is over. School completion, particularly at the secondary-school level, is a better indicator of educational progress.

Tables 9.7 and 9.8 show that older cohorts of African children are educa-

Table 9.5

Racial Gaps in Primary-School Enrollment: Children Ages 7–18

Province	Africans percent enrolled	Colored– African gap	Colored/ African ratio	Indian/ Asian– African gap	Indian/ Asian/ African ratio	White– African gap	White/ African ratio
Western Cape	94.10	1.42	1.01	4.32	1.05	5.15	1.05
Eastern Cape	95.36	–0.08	0.99	3.98	1.04	2.97	1.03
Northern Cape	93.00	–0.11	0.99	7.00	1.07	6.52	1.07
Free State	96.54	–2.56	0.97	–0.54	0.99	2.37	1.02
KwaZulu-Natal	94.88	3.08	1.03	4.03	1.04	4.15	1.04
North West	95.25	0.58	1.01	1.38	1.01	3.61	1.04
Gauteng	96.50	1.54	1.01	2.09	1.02	1.90	1.02
Mpumalanga	96.48	1.45	1.01	2.64	1.03	1.88	1.02
Limpopo	97.48	2.52	1.02	2.52	1.03	0.57	1.01
All	95.87	–0.50	0.99	2.97	1.03	2.83	1.03

Source: Computed from the 1996 South African Population Census micro-data.

Table 9.6

Racial Gaps in Secondary-School Enrollment: Children Ages 13–24

Province	Africans percent enrolled	Colored– African gap	Colored/ African ratio	Indian/ Asian– African gap	Indian/ Asian/ African ratio	White– African gap	White/ African ratio
Western Cape	83.24	–3.86	0.95	4.26	1.05	6.40	1.08
Eastern Cape	95.16	–12.83	0.86	–7.48	0.92	–10.68	0.89
Northern Cape	89.49	–4.55	0.95	–8.84	0.90	–1.93	0.98
Free State	92.53	–6.51	0.93	–8.15	0.91	–8.54	0.91
KwaZulu-Natal	89.91	–7.74	0.91	–8.87	0.90	–1.44	0.98
North West	92.05	–9.64	0.89	–4.73	0.95	–6.51	0.93
Gauteng	81.53	–1.75	0.98	2.80	1.03	3.27	1.04
Mpumalanga	91.72	–5.53	0.94	–6.13	0.93	–4.62	0.95
Limpopo	94.27	–7.70	0.92	–8.22	0.91	–6.70	0.93
All	90.92	–10.18	0.89	–9.01	0.90	–4.66	0.95

Source: Computed from the 1996 South African Population Census micro-data.

tionally disadvantaged compared to all population groups. Table 9.7 shows that the primary-school completion rate of Whites residing in KwaZulu-Natal is 38 percent higher than that of African children, while the primary-school completion rate of Indians/Asians living in the Eastern Cape, Northern Cape, and Free State is over 40 percent that of Africans. The racial differences are even more astounding at the secondary-school level (Table 9.8). At the na-

Table 9.7

Racial Gaps in Primary-School Completion: Children Ages 13–20

Province	Africans percent completing	Colored– African gap	Colored/ African ratio	Indian/ Asian– African gap	Indian/ Asian/ African ratio	White– African gap	White/ African ratio
Western Cape	60.56	5.59	1.09	23.69	1.39	10.94	1.18
Eastern Cape	54.20	10.87	1.20	25.25	1.47	15.28	1.28
Northern Cape	58.68	0.25	1.00	25.53	1.43	11.71	1.20
Free State	59.05	0.83	1.01	25.57	1.43	14.03	1.24
KwaZulu-Natal	58.74	12.23	1.21	22.83	1.39	22.39	1.38
North West	58.37	–4.26	0.93	19.05	1.33	16.42	1.28
Gauteng	64.72	10.82	1.17	20.46	1.32	12.43	1.19
Mpumalanga	59.65	–2.74	0.95	19.60	1.33	19.89	1.33
Limpopo	65.29	20.00	1.31	19.71	1.30	12.98	1.20
All	59.66	5.76	1.10	22.42	1.38	15.75	1.26

Source: Computed from the 1996 South African Population Census micro-data.

Table 9.8

Racial Gaps in Secondary-School Completion: Children Ages 18–25

Province	Africans percent completing	Colored– African gap	Colored/ African ratio	Indian/ Asian– African gap	Indian/ Asian/ African ratio	White– African gap	White/ African ratio
Western Cape	28.52	10.4	1.36	43.74	2.53	51.83	2.82
Eastern Cape	20.41	14.57	1.71	54.05	3.65	53.40	3.62
Northern Cape	27.48	1.95	1.07	27.52	2.00	41.79	2.52
Free State	23.70	13.40	1.56	30.15	2.27	50.12	3.11
KwaZulu-Natal	26.95	24.75	1.92	43.46	2.61	52.78	2.96
North West	29.82	4.70	1.16	49.75	2.67	43.52	2.46
Gauteng	37.28	9.08	1.24	36.75	1.99	39.96	2.07
Mpumalanga	28.20	16.11	1.57	33.11	2.17	44.05	2.56
Limpopo	26.81	19.62	1.73	36.60	2.36	44.20	2.65
All	28.10	10.62	1.38	42.85	2.52	48.74	2.73

Source: Computed from the 1996 South African Population Census micro-data.

tional level, the school-completion rate of Whites is 173 percent higher than that of Africans. The rate for Indians/Asians is nearly as high, at 152 percent that of Africans. The huge differences in educational attainment that we see at the provincial level could be the result of regional disparities in the quality and quantity of schools that were available to each population group.

To summarize, the results clearly show that the differences in educational attainment are much larger across racial groups than they are between boys and girls within the same group. These results are consistent with patterns of unequal provision of educational resources that were practiced by various apartheid-era governments (Lam 1999; Thomas 1996).

Conclusion

Results from this study show that the racial gap in education is much wider than the gender gap. Although Indians/Asians have educational attainment levels similar to Whites, the gaps between Whites and Indians/Asians and Africans and Coloreds are very large, particularly when it comes to secondary-school completion. These racial disparities are rooted in the unequal distribution of economic and educational resources in South Africa. The effect of decades of unequal distribution of educational expenditures is still being felt at the most critical stages in South Africa's postapartheid educational system. In terms of primary- and secondary-school enrollment, the overall racial gaps are almost indistinguishable, although there are some inequalities at the provincial level. Within-race gender gaps are also very small. This is certainly encouraging news, and it suggests that postapartheid educational policies have led to a dramatic increase in school enrollment among previously disadvantaged communities. However, the biggest challenge is whether these gains in enrollment will be translated into higher levels of completion among Africans and Coloreds. From a policy perspective, it is more urgent that postapartheid educational policies focus on closing the greater differences across population groups in secondary-school completion that we observed. Continuation of these wide racial gaps at the secondary-school level will continue to lead to intergenerational transfers of inequalities in income and living standards among previously disadvantaged groups.

References

Barrera, A. 1990. "The role of maternal schooling and its interaction with public health programs in child health production." *Journal of Development Economics* 32: 69–91.

Behr, A. 1978. *New Perspectives in South Africa Education.* Durban: Butterworth.

Caldwell, J.C. 1979. "Education as a factor in mortality decline." *Population Studies* 33: 395–413.

Filmer, D. 1999. "The structure of social disparities in education: Gender and wealth." World Bank Policy Report. Washington, DC: World Bank, November.

Gomes, M. 1984. "Family size and educational attainment in Kenya." *Population and Development Review* 10(4): 647–60.

Hill, M.A., and E.M. King. 1993. "Women's education in developing countries: An overview." In *Women's Education in Developing Countries: Barriers, Benefits, and Policies*, ed. E.M. King and M.A. Hill, 1–50. Baltimore, MD: Johns Hopkins University Press.

Hyde, K.A.L. 1993. "Sub-Saharan Africa." In *Women's Education in Developing Countries:*

Barriers, Benefits, and Policies, ed. E.M. King and M.A. Hill, 100–35. Baltimore, MD: Johns Hopkins University Press.

Lam, D. 1999. "Generating extreme inequality: Schooling, earnings, and intergenerational transmission of human capital in South Africa and Brazil." PSC Research Report No. 99–439, University of Michigan.

Lloyd, C.B., and A.K. Blanc. 1996. "Children's schooling in sub-Saharan Africa: The role of fathers, mothers, and others." *Population and Development Review* 22(2): 265–98.

Schultz, T.W. 1993. *The Economics of Being Poor.* Oxford: Blackwell.

Sen, A. 1992. *Inequality Reexamined.* Cambridge, MA: Harvard University Press.

Sibanda, A. 2001. "Racial differences in educational attainment in South Africa." Paper presented at the XXIV General Population Conference, International Union for the Scientific Study of Population (IUSSP), Salvador, Brazil, August 18–24.

Sibanda, A. 2004. "Who drops out of school in South Africa: The Influence of individual and household characteristics." *African Population Studies* 19(1): 99–117.

Thomas, D. 1996. "Education across generations in South Africa." *American Economic Review* 86(2): 330–34.

10. Migration and Employment

Tukufu Zuberi and Amson Sibanda

In contrast to Western Europe and North America, there is a lack of research on the social and economic incorporation of immigrants in sub-Saharan Africa. This omission hides the role of internal and international migrations in social and demographic change in sub-Saharan Africa (Russell et al. 1990; Zuberi et al. 2003). In Western societies, considerable research has focused on analyzing immigrant incorporation and the employment and earning opportunities of immigrants in relation to those of nonimmigrants (Bloom and Gunderson 1990; Chiswick 1982; Jasso and Rosenweig 1990; Semyonov et al. 2001; Winkelmann 2000). This body of research has documented wide differences in labor force and socioeconomic outcomes between immigrants and nonimmigrants. For example, studies in Australia and Canada found that immigrants from southern Europe or of Mediterranean origin had poorer socioeconomic outcomes compared to other immigrants and nonmigrants (Chiswick and Miller 1988; Evans and Kelley 1991). In European Organisation for Economic Cooperation and Development (OECD) countries like the Netherlands, Denmark, and Sweden, the gap between the unemployment rates of nationals and of immigrants has been widening, with foreigners being exposed to unemployment rates that are considerably higher than the proportion of the labor force for which they account (OECD 1998). Caribbean Blacks and Bangladesh/Pakistani immigrants in the United Kingdom also have higher rates of unemployment than similarly qualified UK-born Whites (Modood 1997). Mexican immigrants in the United States and northern African immigrants in Israel were also observed to have lower socioeconomic success rates compared to native groups (Borjas and Tienda 1993; Semyonov 1996). In a comparison of the earning attributes of blacks in the United States, Dodoo (1997) compared male African immigrants to Caribbean-born Blacks and U.S.-born Blacks. He found that Caribbean-born immigrants had the highest earnings and that African immigrants fared worst, even though they had considerably higher levels of schooling. Our study adds to this growing literature by comparing the labor force outcomes of male and female immigrants, internal migrants, and nonmigrants in postapartheid South Africa.

In 1996, South Africa had a total of 39,806,598 noninstitutionalized persons. About 2.1 percent of these persons were foreign born (Statistics South Africa 1996). However, this percent was 3.9 among noninstitutionalized foreign-born individuals ages 20 to 55. Among South African-born persons ages 20 to 55, about 59 percent have migrated to their current magisterial district of residence (Table 10.1). Although foreign-born immigrants make up less than 3 percent of the total population of South Africa, the labor force participation of these immigrants in the South African labor market has emerged as a contentious policy issue. With unemployment rates above 30 percent among South African blacks, ongoing debates concern the costs and benefits of immigration in the new South Africa, particularly whether immigrants undermine the job prospects of South African nationals or make important contributions to the economy. Fueled by strong xenophobic feelings, stories of immigrant success are often used to illustrate that immigrants are a threat to the social and economic fabric of the nation (Crush 1999; McDonald et al. 1998). The foreign born are sometimes viewed as competitors for scarce resources who prevent the transition to a new economy in South Africa. The urban absorption of the rural population has also posed complementary policy issues. These concerns predate the new Republic of South Africa. Internal migration, particularly of Blacks, was a major preoccupation of the apartheid government. Apartheid attempted to regulate the movement of the African population in order to enhance the economic opportunities of the White minority and to control African urbanization (Evans 1997).

At the core of this debate are three positions. First, there are those who believe in opening South Africa's doors to skilled migrants and investors who can make substantial contributions to the country's development. Second, there are those who oppose immigration because foreign migrants take away jobs from South African nationals. It is argued that immigration is an obstacle to economic integration for the African majority who are awaiting the gains in employment and living standards anticipated with the end of apartheid. Finally, there are those who oppose immigration, particularly African immigration, because they believe that large numbers of illegal immigrants bring all sorts of diseases and crime into the country (Kotze and Hill 1997; McDonald et al. 2000; Sinclair 1999). These beliefs are so strongly held by some South Africans that violence has often been unleashed on unsuspecting groups of foreign-born workers, particularly street vendors in cities like Johannesburg (Crush 1999).

Because of the very high public interest in immigration and jobs, in particular, and in illegal immigration and its impact on other aspects of South African society in general, this study examines the relationship between migration status, nativity, and labor force outcomes in a postapartheid South Africa. We focus on labor force participation, because it is the main route through which immigrants improve their socioeconomic status. The study also seeks to determine the extent to which duration of residence, human capital, age, marital status, and place of residence contribute to differential labor force statuses in the labor market between various immigrant groups and South African nationals. Besides these factors, there are also unobservable endowments, such as ambition and determination, that often contribute to the success of migrants (Chiswick 1999). In order to adequately assess how migration improves individuals' labor force outcomes in South Africa, we begin by discussing labor migration in the context of the Southern African Migration System (SAMS). This section is then followed by a discussion of the data and methods employed in the study. Our analytic strategy begins with a comparison of the South Africa-born population to the foreign-born immigrants. In the second part of the analysis, we exclude all foreign-born individuals and then compare the labor force circumstances of internal migrants with those of nonmigrants.

South Africa and the Southern African Migration System

Prior to South Africa adopting new immigration laws in 1994, migration policies for most of the twentieth century were designed to attract Whites. People of African descent were only permitted to enter the country under stringent conditions, often to work as contract workers in the mining and agricultural sectors of the apartheid economy (Kotze and Hill 1997; Peberdy and Crush 1998). South Africa's current immigration laws are designed to ease the country's chronic shortage of skilled labor by making it easier to attract skilled foreign workers (*The Economist* 2002). However, despite the stricter Aliens Control Amendment Act of 1995, South Africa is reportedly besieged by waves of both legal and illegal immigrants from many parts of the African continent (Minaar and Hough 1996). An estimated 3.5 million people were residing in the country illegally in 1997. It is also estimated that 3,000 illegal immigrants are deported from the country each month (South Africa, Ministry of Home Affairs 1999). The fact that thousands of undocumented immigrants are believed to be working in the country implies that legal status does not necessarily place constraints on a person's ability to get a job.

The patterns and processes of migration within the SAMS, particularly the flows between regional and local labor markets, represent a major socioeconomic force (Wilson 1976). The dynamic and self-sustaining labor migrations in southern Africa can only be clearly understood when they are studied in the context of the SAMS and its development over time (Mabogunje 1970; Massey et al. 1998). The SAMS exists among countries that have close historical, political, cultural, and economic ties. This migration system primarily covers a subset of the Southern Africa Development Community (SADC) countries: Botswana, Lesotho, Malawi, Mozambique, South Africa, Swaziland, Zambia, and Zimbabwe. SADC is a fourteen-member regional grouping of countries in southern and eastern Africa.

The circular migration of labor within the SAMS has been in existence since the late-nineteenth century. The discovery of gold and diamond mines in South Africa in 1886 led to a huge demand for cheap labor, which could not be met locally. By the mid-1890s, there were over 100,000 immigrants from neighboring countries working in South Africa's mining industry (Lucas 1985, 1987; Massey 1983; Moller 1985). These migrant workers were recruited primarily from Lesotho, Mozambique, and Malawi (McDonald et al. 2000; Wilson 1976). The South African Chamber of Mines, through the Employment Bureau of Africa (TEBA) and its predecessor, the Witwatersrand Native Labour Organization (WENELA), was responsible for recruiting these foreign workers (Chirwa 1997; Davis and Head 1995). At its peak, TEBA operated in ten countries, and in the 1970s, it supplied over 500,000 contract laborers annually to the South African mining industry (Massey 1983). In 1975, about 74 percent of the immigrants working in mines owned by the South African Chamber of Mines came from the SADC (Davis and Head 1995). Although a depressed world gold price in the 1980s forced TEBA to stop its recruitment program in labor-supplier countries like Malawi, the flow of legal and illegal immigrants within the SAMS did not change dramatically. Because of continued regional disparities in incomes, employment, and other related opportunities in southern Africa, the South African economy continues to be a magnetic force to a wide array of skilled and unskilled immigrants. According to neoclassical migration theory, labor migration is likely to occur in such an environment as a result of differences in location-specific employment opportunities or wages (Massey et al. 1998).

Within South Africa, Black Africans were forced to participate in the migrant labor system as a result of the creation of underdeveloped homelands. A range of institutional measures, such as the Group Areas Act and Influx Control legislation were put in place by apartheid governments to tightly control the urbanization and migration patterns of Africans. As a result, Black South Africans were forced to rely on a pattern of oscillating migration that connected them to their rural communities and places of work. The collapse of apartheid in 1994 ended the formal restrictions on African mobility and urbanization. As a result, the migrant labor system was transformed, as highlighted by the sharp increase in female labor migration from rural communities (Posel and Casale 2002). Because of this complicated history of labor migrations in South Africa, we first compare the labor force circumstances of foreign-born immigrants to those of South African-born persons before turning our attention to the labor force circumstances of South African-born internal migrants and nonmigrants.

Data and Methods

We analyze the stock of immigrants and internal migrants from the 30 percent sample of the 1996 South African Population Census. These data provide individual-level demographic and social variables. Although the census is the best source of information to use to examine immigrants, internal migrants, and labor force outcomes without the restrictions of small sample size, the data are limited by capturing individual attributes only at the time of enumeration. There is no information on these attributes at the time when individuals migrated (Oropesa and Landale 2000). For example, we only know the individual's level of education, place of residence, and duration of residence at the time of the census. This is particularly problematic for long-term migrants. However, in the case of recent migrants (i.e., those who moved two years before the census), we assume that some of their characteristics did not change much within the two-year window.

In addition, the census does not provide data on why people move or give us an accurate estimate of the number of illegal immigrants in the country. The cross-sectional nature of the data also means that it is not possible to examine patterns of immigrant progress over time. The census also misses persons who died or returned to their countries of origin before the enumeration. The migration experiences of illegal immigrants or internal migrants who were not enumerated or who refused to answer questions are also not included. It is very possible that illegal immigrants dodged census enumerators or lied about their migration status (McDonald et al. 1999). These issues are important for our analysis. If the composition of immigrants who died or returned to their countries of origin before the enumeration is different from the composition of immigrants who were captured by the census, this could bias the results, because the immigrants who provided information would not be representative. Although these issues are important, there is no way to resolve them. In addition, it is not always clear in what direction the effects of these biases would be on labor force outcomes. Thus, given the lack of vital registration data and the inability of migration surveys to yield reliable estimates of the total number of migrants, censuses are an adequate source of data that can be used to paint a picture of internal and international population movements in African societies.

Because our goal is to examine labor force outcomes, we focus on males

and females between the ages of 20 and 55. Although it is usually recom-
mended to include persons from age 15 to 17 in labor force studies, we exclude the 15 to 19 year olds from our analyses because most of this age group
had not completed their formal education (Sibanda 2001). Also, there are not
many foreign-born Indian/Asian and Colored immigrants; hence our analysis
of labor force outcomes among the foreign-born is restricted to Africans and
Whites. However, South African-born Indians/Asians and Coloreds will be
included in the analysis of the association between internal migration and
labor force outcomes.

To analyze the relationship between migration/nativity status and labor
force outcomes, we estimate regression models for two dependent variables:
labor force participation and employment. These dependent variables are dichotomous in nature; hence, persons were coded 1 if they were in the labor
force and 0 otherwise. Individuals were also coded 1 if they were employed and
0 if they were unemployed and looking for work. Logistic regression is used to
examine the effects of the predictor variables on the probability of being in the
labor force or being employed. We use the logistic regression model, because
the dependent variables are dichotomous and have skewed distributions (Long
1997; Aldrich and Nelson 1984). Our logistic model takes the form:

$$\ln\left[\frac{\Pr(y=1\,|\,x)}{1-\Pr(y=1\,|\,x)}\right]=\sum b_k x_{ik}$$

where the left-hand side of the equation is the logged odds of being employed
or in the labor force, y is a function of the x_{ik} predictor variables with coefficients b_k. This model transforms the probabilities into odds.

An odds refers to how often something occurs relative to how often it does
not occur in the data. Odds ratios can be interpreted like betting odds—an
odds ratio of 2.0 to 1.0, for example, signifies a certain outcome will occur
two times out of three. Thus, an odds ratio of 1.00 implies no difference
between categories in the odds of participating in the labor force, while an
odds ratio greater than 1.00 indicates a higher likelihood of participating in
the labor force associated with a particular characteristic. Lastly, odds ratios
below 1.00 indicate lower odds relative to the reference category.

We test two models. Model 1 uses only nativity and migration as independent variables to predict the likelihood of being in the labor force or employed. Model 2 (the full model) adds individual characteristics (age, schooling,
and martial status) and contextual factors (type of place and province of residence). This full model gives us the leverage to assess the effects of migration
status and nativity on labor force and employment outcomes net of the
individual's other background characteristics. The results of these two models

are given in Tables 10.2 through 6. Tables 10.2 and 3 focus on immigrants and Tables 10.4 and, 10.6 focus on internal migrants as discussed above.

Labor Force Participation and Employment

During the 1996 population census, persons were considered to be participating in the labor force if they were employed or were unemployed but looking for work. The following activities were defined as work: formal work for a salary or wage; informal work such as making and selling things like crafts or rendering a service; and working on a farm, whether for a wage or as part of the household's farming activities. All persons not falling into one of these categories were defined as not working. Of these, only persons who were "unemployed and looking for work" were considered part of the labor force.

Migration Status

The South African census provides information on place of birth and the duration of time elapsed since individuals migrated to their current usual place of residence. We use this information to compare the labor force outcomes of different migrant groups with indigenous nonmigrants. Our basic unit of analysis for migration status is duration of residence in South Africa in the case of foreign-born immigrants and duration of residence in a magisterial district in the case of indigenous internal migrants.

To facilitate the comparison of foreign-born immigrants and South African nationals, migration status and nativity were combined and coded into the following categories: South African-born nonmigrants, South African-born recent and long-term internal migrants, SADC-born recent and long-term immigrants, and other foreign-born recent and long-term immigrants. The dummy variables, long-term and recent migrants, use 1994 as a cutoff date. This allows us to capture the period effects resulting from political transformation in the country. It is possible that political change in South Africa could have fueled expectations of a more accommodating labor market. However, it is important to note that these period effects may be confounded with age effects. Thus, SADC-born and other foreign-born recent immigrants refer to those persons who migrated to South Africa between 1994 and 1996, while SADC-born and other foreign-born long-term immigrants refer to those individuals who migrated to South Africa before the country attained political independence in 1994. Table 10.1 presents the distribution of the male and female populations in each of these categories. The table shows that SADC-born long-term immigrants constitute the largest proportion of immigrants in 1996.

Table 10.1

Sample Distribution of Males Ages 20–55 by Nativity and Migration Status: South Africa 1996

Nativity and migration status	Male		Female	
	Number	Percent	Number	Percent
South African-born nonmigrants	604,451	38.81	816,800	38.71
South African-born recent migrants	288,213	18.51	400,109	18.96
South African-born long-term migrants	625,319	40.15	856,617	40.59
SADC*-born recent immigrants	11,209	0.72	9,111	0.43
SADC-born long-term immigrants	13,551	0.87	11,873	0.56
Other foreign-born recent immigrants	6,136	0.39	6,345	0.30
Other foreign-born long-term immigrants	8,630	0.55	9,323	0.44
Total	1,557,509	100	2,110,178	100

Source: Computed from the 1996 South African Population Census micro-data.
Note: * SADC member states include Angola, Botswana, DR Congo, Lesotho, Malawi, Mauritius, Mozambique, Namibia, Seychelles, South Africa, Swaziland, Tanzania, Zambia, and Zimbabwe.

As a contrast to the foreign-born immigrant versus South African-born comparison, we also examine employment outcomes by looking at the South-African-born male and female population only. We consider only moves across magisterial districts of residence. South Africa is made up of nine provinces, which have been further divided into 354 magisterial districts. Using these magisterial districts allows us to capture inter- and intraprovincial movements. The census recorded whether each person had migrated and, if so, in what year they last migrated. In addition, if the person had ever moved, they were asked for the location (magisterial district and place name) of the previous residence. Although information on place names was collected, the only piece of information we have access to in the 30 percent public use sample is magisterial district of previous residence. This information does not allow us to determine if the previous place of residence was an urban or rural area. All we know is whether someone was living in an urban or rural area at the time of the census, because we have an additional variable that classifies type of current residence using the rural–urban dichotomy. The lack of information on the type of previous residence (rural or urban) prevents us from examining the association between labor force outcomes and various forms of internal migration like rural–urban, urban–urban, or rural–rural.

Thus, we divide the South African-born population into three groups (nonmigrants, recent internal migrants, and long-term internal migrants). The first group is made up of South African nationals who never changed their magisterial district of residence. The second group is made up of South African nationals who changed districts of residence between 1994 and 1996, and the last group is made up of South African nationals who changed districts of residence prior to the end of apartheid in 1994. The recent migration coincides with the independence euphoria and the freedom of movement accorded Africans. Thus, the contexts of reception for pre-1994 and post-1994 migrants were different.

This breakdown gives us the leverage to examine the potential impact of duration of residence and migration status on labor force outcomes. We are also able to examine whether South African-born migrants and foreign-born immigrants have similar labor force outcomes. Differences in labor force outcomes between foreign-born immigrants and South African nationals may reflect differences in access to jobs or selectivity in terms of who is allowed or who chooses to migrate. Access to jobs is further determined by the legal status of immigrants and possible discrimination against immigrants.

Education

Because it is difficult to measure skills using census data, we use the highest level of education completed as a proxy for skills. Highest level of schooling completed was coded into the following categories: no schooling, primary school, some secondary school, and completed secondary or higher. The last category includes all persons with postsecondary certificates and college diplomas.

Results

Who Migrates?

In many societies, migration is known to be age and sex selective, and South Africa is no exception to this observation. Figures 10.1 and 10.2 show the age distributions of males and females ages 20 to 55 by place of birth and migration status. Consistent with the selective nature of the migration process, Figure 10.1 shows substantial variations in the age composition of male migrants. Recent and long-term internal migrants and SADC-born recent immigrants have a disproportionately large percentage of individuals in the youngest age group (20–29). In contrast, long-term SADC-born and other foreign-born immigrants have a much older age composition. In a way, this is expected because individuals who migrated to South Africa prior to 1994 probably did so when they were young; hence, Figure 10.1 simply shows the result of the aging process among these long-term immigrants. When we look at the age composition of females ages 20 to 55 (Figure 10.2), we see somewhat similar age compositions. Recent South African-born and SADC-born female migrants have a similar age composition to that found among South African-born nonmigrants. All three populations are much younger than the other categories.

Labor Force Participation, Employment, and Schooling Distributions

Although migration is a very selective process, not all migrants end up participating in the labor force. Figures 10.3 and 10.4 show the percentage of men and women age 20 to 55 who were in the labor force and employed in 1996 by nativity and migration status. Among men, labor force participation as well as employment percentages were highest for both groups of foreign-born individuals as compared to South African-born males. In fact, Figure 10.3 shows that area of origin and duration of residence do not lead to any major differences in the proportion of foreign-born recent and long-term immigrants in the labor force. In contrast, South African-born nonmigrants have the lowest labor force and employment rates when compared to indigenous recent and long-term migrants. Among South African-born males, recent internal migrants have a slightly higher proportion employed. Figure 10.4 shows much lower labor force participation and employment rates among females in general as compared with the rates among males shown in Figure 10.3. In contrast to their male counterparts, South Africa-born recent and long-term migrants exhibit relatively higher labor force and employment rates than some foreign-born immigrant groups. However, South Africa-born nonmigrants have the lowest percentage of women in the labor force or employed.

The results are interesting in many respects considering the current immigration debate in South Africa, particularly the debate on whether immigrants are out-competing nationals for scarce job opportunities at a time when the country is grappling with a high domestic unemployment rate. These findings are not only unique to South Africa. Recent research in New Zealand suggests that it is not unusual for native-born populations to have lower labor force and employment rates than immigrants (Winkelmann 2000).

On the other hand, the higher employment rates among recent immigrants in South Africa contrast sharply with findings from other countries. For instance, research has consistently shown that recent immigrants tend to have lower employment rates than native groups in immigrant societies such as the United States, Canada, Australia, and Israel (Bailey 1987; Chiswick and Miller 1988; Evans and Kelly 1991; Jasso and Rosenweig 1990; Meisenheimer 1992; Semyonov et al. 2001). This finding is often attributed to recent immigrants' low levels of host-country-specific human capital and lack of language skills. Country-specific human capital is generally measured by taking the time elapsed since immigrants entered the host country (Reagan and Olsen 2000). The number of years since immigration serves as a good proxy for familiarity with the intricacies of the host country's labor market. It is assumed that immigrants use this time to accumulate work experience that is recognized and rewarded in the host country.

Figure 10.1 **Age Distributions of Males Aged 20–55 by Nativity and Migration Status: South Africa, 1996**

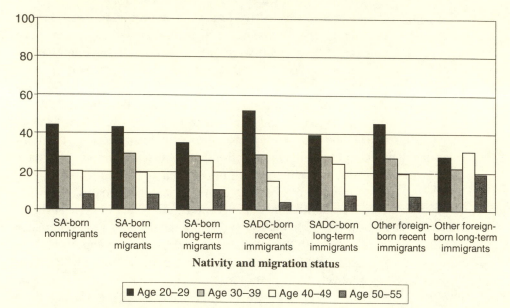

Source: Computed from the 1996 South African Population Census micro-data.

Figure 10.2 **Age Distributions of Females Aged 20–55 by Nativity and Migration Status: South Africa, 1996**

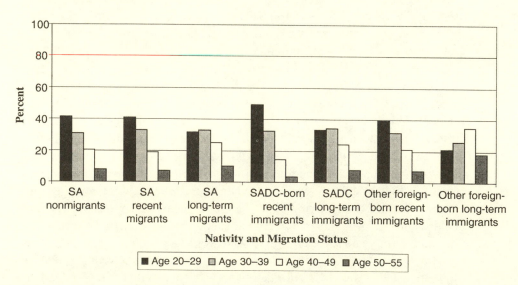

Source: Computed from the 1996 South African Population Census micro-data.

Figure 10.3 **Labor Force Participation Rates and Employment Rates for Males Aged 20–55 by Migration Status and Nativity: South Africa, 1996**

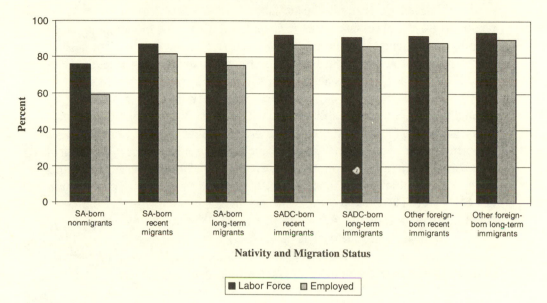

Nativity and Migration Status

■ Labor Force □ Employed

Source: Computed from the 1996 South Africa Population Census micro-data.

Figure 10.4 **Labor Force Participation Rates and Employment Rates for Females Aged 20–55 by Migration Status and Nativity: South Africa, 1996**

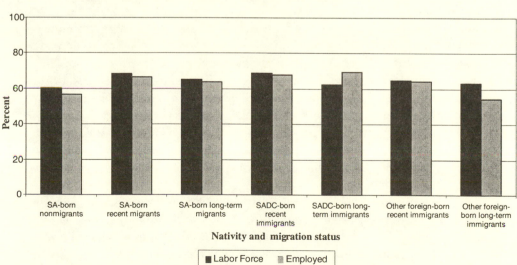

Nativity and migration status

■ Labor Force ▨ Employed

Source: Computed from the 1996 South Africa Population Census micro-data.

In the case of South Africa, our results suggest that immigrants get jobs without accumulating experience in the South African labor market. We should expect this scenario if the domestic labor market has a critical shortage of persons with the necessary skills to meet the demands of the economy. Recruiting immigrants with the right skills can satisfy the demand for skilled workers. U.S. companies, in their recruitment of technology workers, followed this strategy from Asia at the peak of the "dot-com" economy (Martin 2000). The situation might be very different for unskilled workers and illegal immigrants. These groups still have to establish economic contacts through social networks (Sinclair 1999). These groups might also find employment opportunities in the informal sector, which does not require any work permits, or they could be self-employed. Efforts were made in the 1996 South African Population Census to capture informal sector activities. Because such activities were classified as work, one can reasonably assume that the labor force participation of individuals in the informal sector of the economy is adequately reflected in the census data.

Are foreign immigrants in South Africa more educated and professional than the native-born population? Figures 10.5 and 10.6 suggest a partial yes. The graphs show that other foreign-born recent and long-term male and female immigrants have higher levels of education than all South African-born groups. However, SADC-born immigrants do not have higher proportions of highly educated individuals than South African-born recent and long-term migrants. Figure 10.5 also shows that, unlike male immigrants from other regions, immigrants from the surrounding SADC region have slightly higher proportions of individuals with no schooling and with primary schooling. This educational composition of immigrants from the SADC region is indicative of the demand for both low-skilled and very skilled workers—a demand that was historically met by special migrant labor agreements between various South African governments and SADC countries like Lesotho, Mozambique, and Malawi. In other words, the high proportions of SADC-born male immigrants with less than secondary education is reflective of South Africa's long history of relying on both low-skilled and highly skilled foreign workers, primarily in its mining and agricultural sectors. Keeping wages low was the motivation behind the demand for large numbers of workers with low levels of schooling.

An equally important determinant of the schooling distributions among immigrants from the SADC region is proximity to South Africa. One would expect to find fairly large proportions of SADC-born immigrants with low levels of education simply because they face lower costs of traveling to South Africa and of returning home. Within this group are possibly the majority of undocumented immigrants. Jasso and Rosenweig (1990) found a similar situ-

Figure 10.5 **Schooling Distributions for Males Aged 20–55 by Migration Status and Nativity: South Africa, 1996**

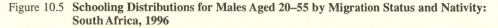
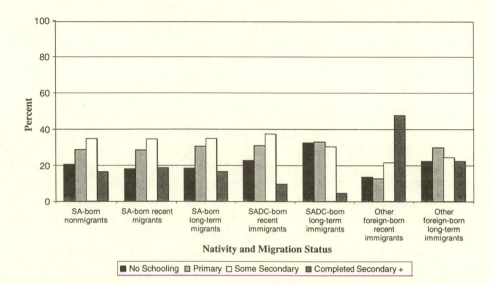

Source: Computed from the 1996 South Africa Population Census micro-data.

Figure 10.6 **Schooling Distributions for Females Aged 20–55 by Migration Status and Nativity: South Africa, 1996**

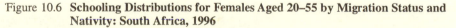
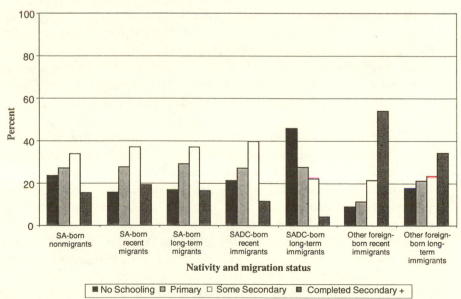

Source: Computed from the 1996 South Africa Population Census micro-data.

ation in the United States with regard to Mexican immigrants. Among women (Figure 10.6), we see very skewed educational distributions among other foreign-born recent and long-term immigrants, with almost 60 percent of them having completed secondary education. Increased migration costs probably account for the educational differences among the foreign born. In other words, a country's distance from South Africa can act to screen for highly educated individuals. It is also possible that women from other regions are more risk aversive; hence, they are probably more likely to migrate to South Africa only after securing a job and having received their immigration documents. SADC-born recent migrants also appear to be more well educated than their long-term counterparts.

Among the South African-born population, recent and long-term internal migrants are more educated than nonmigrants. The higher levels of education among migrants seems to suggest that education (which is a good proxy for skills) is generally well rewarded, and hence, individuals with a certain level of education may be more likely to migrate because of the potential net gains associated with migration. These schooling distributions are also evidence of the selective nature of the migration process.

Multivariate Analysis

Foreign-Born Immigrants Versus South African-Born Males

Table 10.2 shows odds ratios from logistic regression models of employment for males for the two main racial groups that have a significant number of foreign-born individuals in South Africa. For each racial group, we ran a baseline and a full model specification (Models 1 and 2). The baseline model only includes the nativity and migration variable. Controls for age, marital status, education, type of place, and province of residence are added to Model 2. Odds ratios can be interpreted like betting odds—an odds ratio of 2.0 to 1.0, for example, signifies that a certain outcome will occur two times out of three. Thus, an odds ratio of 1.00 implies no difference between categories in the odds of participating in the labor force, while an odds ratio greater than 1.00 indicates a higher likelihood of participating in the labor force associated with a particular characteristic. Lastly, odds ratios below 1.00 indicate lower odds relative to the reference category.

In the baseline specification (Model 1) for Africans, the odds of being employed are significantly higher for all groups of male immigrants as compared to South African-born African males (reference group). For instance, other foreign-born long-term immigrants and recent African male immigrants from the SADC region are 3.67 and 3.4 times more likely to be employed as

Table 10.2

Odds Ratios from Logistic Regression Models of Employment for Separate Racial Groups: Foreign-Born Immigrants and South African-Born Males, 1996

Independent variables	African		White	
	Model 1	Model 2	Model 1	Model 2
Nativity and migration status				
South African born (ref)	1.00	1.00	1.00	1.00
SADC-born recent immigrants	3.44***	3.55***	1.39**	1.42**
SADC-born long-term immigrants	3.08***	2.79***	1.57**	1.41***
Other foreign-born recent immigrants	2.51***	2.45***	1.27**	1.19*
Other foreign-born long-term immigrants	3.67***	2.78***	1.79***	1.40***
Age Group				
20–29 (ref)		1.00		1.00
30–39		1.45***		1.04
40–49		1.35***		1.11**
50–55		1.33***		0.98
Education				
No schooling (ref)		1.00		1.00
Primary		1.01		0.97
Some secondary		1.10***		0.46***
Completed secondary +		1.41***		0.94
Marital status				
Single (ref)		1.00		1.00
Married		4.22***		3.90***
Living together		3.67***		1.85***
Widowed		2.49***		1.48**
Divorced		1.55***		0.99
Type of place				
Rural (ref)		1.00		1.00
Urban		0.67***		1.03
Province of residence				
Gauteng (ref)		1.00		1.00
Western Cape		1.36***		1.12***
Eastern Cape		0.48***		1.01
Northern Cape		1.35***		1.20*
Free State		0.97***		1.12*
KwaZulu-Natal		0.84***		1.00
North West		1.16***		1.03
Mpumalanga		1.40***		1.22***
Limpopo		0.70***		1.28**
Number of cases	803,729		186,191	
−2 log-likelihood	1080341.6	953759.94	64064.6	59877.19

Source: Computed from the 1996 South African Population Census micro-data.
Notes: *p < .05; ** p < .01; ***p < .001.

compared to South African-born males, respectively. When we add a series of background characteristics in Model 2, the odds of being employed remain statistically significant among all immigrant groups. SADC-born recent immigrants are now 3.6 times more likely to have jobs than South African-born Blacks. The odds for other foreign-born long-term immigrants are slightly reduced, from 3.7 to 2.8, suggesting that other background characteristics account for the differences in labor force participation between immigrants and their South African-born counterparts. For instance, African males ages 30–39, 40–49, and 50–55 all have odds of being employed that are over 30 percent greater than those of males ages 20–29.

The odds for education are somewhat surprising. White men with some secondary education comprise the only group with some education whose odds of being employed are significantly lower than those of males without any schooling. Marital status also strongly influences one's chances of being employed. African males who are married or cohabiting have odds of employment about 4.2 and 3.7 times as great as those of single men, respectively. The fact that the odds ratios for married and cohabiting men are significant probably reflects the importance of marriage as a stabilizing force. Men are typically the heads of households in South Africa (see Zulu and Sibanda, chapter 8 of this volume), and are therefore expected to be economically active if they are married. Widowed and divorced males are also significantly more likely to have jobs than single men (reference group).

When we turn to variables that may reflect the influence of variation in labor market conditions across space, we see that African males residing in urban areas have significantly lower odds of being employed as compared to males living in rural areas. The provincial effects are also very strong. African males living in the Western Cape, Northern Cape, North West, and Mpumalanga have statistically significantly higher chances of being employed than African males living in Gauteng province (reference). However, African males living in South Africa's poorest provinces, Limpopo and Eastern Cape, have the lowest odds of being employed (0.70 and 0.48, respectively). Because differences in individual-level attributes are already controlled for in Model 2, it is more likely that some of the provincial effects may be due to historical differences in development and employment creation inputs. Because of its huge mining and industrial infrastructural base, Gauteng Province, which includes the cities of Johannesburg and Pretoria, is the wealthiest province in South Africa. It also has the largest labor market in the country. The other large labor markets are Western Cape Province and KwaZulu-Natal, where the cities of Cape Town and Durban are located, respectively (Hall and Whiteford 1998). Because of South Africa's long history of separate development that resulted in the creation of impoverished Bantustans, the provincial labor markets differ in size and complexity and also in the distribution of wealth and resources (May 1998). Provinces that absorbed most of these former homelands like Eastern Cape and Limpopo Province are characterized by a limited industrial base, and hence, a tighter labor market, especially for Africans. Thus, part of the labor market disparities between immigrant and nonmigrant groups can be attributed to the provincial employment opportunity structure.

In the specification for Whites, Model 1 shows that all immigrant groups have statistically significantly higher odds of employment than South African-born White males (reference). All immigrant groups continue to exhibit higher odds of employment even after we add controls for various background characteristics in Model 2. Some of the background characteristics have similar effects for Whites as well. For instance, the odds of having a job are significantly high for married and cohabiting White males as compared to single men (reference). However, with regard to age, only White males ages 40–49 have statistically significantly higher odds of being employed than White males ages 20–29. The other age groups show no statistically significant difference. Whites with some secondary education are significantly less likely to be employed than those with no education (the reference category), while those with primary education or who completed secondary education show no significant difference in employment. The type of place of residence is not a strong predictor of employment among White males, because the rural–urban differences are not significant. With regard to provincial effects, White males living in the Free State, Western Cape, Northern Cape, Mpumalanga, and Limpopo provinces have odds of being employed that are statistically significantly higher than those of White males residing in Gauteng province.

Foreign-Born Immigrants Versus South African-Born Females

Does the employment advantage enjoyed by male immigrants we saw above hold when we compare foreign-born female immigrants to South African-born females? Table 10.3 presents odds ratios from separate models for African and White females. The first model specification for Africans shows that only other foreign-born recent and long-term female immigrants have odds of employment that are significantly higher than those of South African-born black females. Female immigrants from the SADC region show no difference. For instance, compared with South African-born black females, recent and long-term African female immigrants from outside the SADC regions have odds of employment that are 2.7 and 2.2 times as great. However, African female immigrants from the SADC region have significantly higher odds of being employed than South African-born females when we control for individual and other background characteristics (Model 2). African females born outside the SADC region are also statistically significantly more likely to be employed than South African-born Black females, suggesting that migration status and nativity are not negatively associated with employment outcomes among African females in South Africa. One possible reason for this finding is that immigrants have better human capital attributes than South African-born females. Alternatively, it is possible that those immigrants who could not find jobs in South Africa simply returned to their countries of origin. In contrast, South African-born African females are at home, and therefore, they are more likely to live with unemployment. Among White females, Models 1 and 2 show that long-term female immigrants from the SADC region and from other countries have statistically significantly higher odds of employment than South African–born White females (reference).

There are also strong age effects for both African and White women, and the likelihood of having a job increases with age for both population groups. The effect of education on employment is surprising. The effect of education operates differently for the population groups. Among White women, education is not significant for those who completed secondary school. However, among those with some secondary schooling, the odds of being employed are significantly lower than those with no schooling, the reference category. However, education increases the odds of African women being employed compared to those without any schooling. Being married, cohabiting, and being widowed or divorced are all associated with being more likely to be employed among African women. Whereas, among White women, being married or cohabiting is positively related to employment, while being widowed or divorced has no significant effect on the likelihood of being employed. Both African and White women living in urban areas are significantly less likely to have a job than those in rural areas. There is also evidence that province of residence is associated with employment prospects. White women living in the Western and Eastern Cape provinces have significantly higher odds of being employed than White women living in Gauteng province, the reference category, while women living in KwaZulu-Natal, North West, and Mpumalanga are significantly less likely to have a job than White women in Gauteng province. African women living in the Western Cape, the Northern Cape, Free State, KwaZulu-Natal, North West, and Mpumalanga provinces have significantly higher odds of being employed than African women living in Gauteng province, the reference category, while African women living in the Eastern Cape and Limpopo are significantly less likely to have a job than African women in Gauteng province.

The above findings raise an interesting question. Are South African employers more inclined to hire foreign-born men and women than South African-born individuals even though there is a high domestic unemployment rate?

Table 10.3

Odds Ratios from Logistic Regression Models of Employment for Separate Racial Groups: Foreign-Born Immigrants and South African-Born Females, 1996

Independent variables	African		White	
	Model 1	Model 2	Model 1	Model 2
Nativity and migration status				
South African born (ref)	1.00	1.00	1.00	1.00
SADC-born recent immigrants	0.98	1.17***	1.05	1.08
SADC-born long-term immigrants	1.03	1.21***	1.50***	1.34**
Other foreign-born recent immigrants	2.72***	2.37***	1.02	0.95
Other foreign-born long-term immigrants	2.22***	1.76**	1.78***	1.41***
Age Group				
20–29 (ref)		1.00		1.00
30–39		2.42***		1.42***
40–49		3.42***		1.91***
50–55		3.83***		1.80***
Education				
No schooling (ref)		1.00		1.00
Primary		1.04***		0.86
Some secondary		1.08***		0.36***
Completed secondary +		2.02***		1.02
Marital status				
Single (ref)		1.00		1.00
Married		1.16***		1.79***
Living together		1.15***		1.38***
Widowed		1.60***		1.13
Divorced		2.05***		1.03
Type of place				
Rural (ref)		1.00		1.00
Urban		0.72***		0.73***
Province of residence				
Gauteng (ref)		1.00		1.00
Western Cape		1.29***		1.19***
Eastern Cape		0.73***		1.14**
Northern Cape		1.23***		0.99
Free State		1.17***		1.03
KwaZulu-Natal		1.02***		0.91**
North West		1.04***		0.80***
Mpumalanga		1.90***		0.79***
Limpopo		0.82***		0.90
Number of cases	906,725		173,155	
-2 Log-Likelihood	1249192.4	1165956.0	66238.6	63434.24

Source: Computed from the 1996 South African Population Census micro-data
Notes: *p < .05; **p < .01; ***p < .001.

Some researchers have suggested that this is the case. For instance, Crush contends that "the usual advantages of irregular employment (low wages, vulnerability, exploitative conditions) may be at the core of this preference. Employers also speak of their preference for the work habits of non-South Africans, their higher basic skills and the absence of workplace militancy" (1999: 131).

Besides this preference argument, SADC-born immigrants also tend to do well in the South African labor market because they have long-standing social capital. In a study of emerging immigrant communities in South Africa, Sinclair (1999) found that immigrant communities in cities like Johannesburg and Cape Town provided valuable social capital to friends and relatives by offering information about job opportunities, housing, and the process of migration. Emerging research conducted by the Southern African Migration Project and other ethnographers also seems to highlight the importance of social capital. For instance, McDonald et al. (1998) have shown that a marked presence of either close family members or friends in South Africa resulted in a well-developed migrant network between Lesotho, Mozambique, and Zimbabwe and South Africa. The quality and quantity of these social networks has also been found to be important. The utility of social capital in South Africa is not only confined to international migration. Indeed, social ties between urban migrant communities and their rural communities have helped fuel internal labor migration (Posel and Casale 2002; Sinclair 1999). Relatives and friends are more likely to provide new migrants with information on job opportunities as well as housing, food, and financial assistance. Although we are not able to measure social capital using census data, there is no doubt that international and internal population movements within the SAMS will continue to rely to some extent on the depth and width of one's social capital.

South African-Born Internal Migrants and Nonmigrants

Another objective of our study was to examine if the labor force outcomes of internal migrants are different from those of nonmigrants. To accomplish this, we restricted our analysis to South African-born males and females only. By restricting our analysis to these groups, we were able to examine the labor force outcomes of the four main racial groups in South Africa: Africans, Whites, Coloreds, and Indians/Asians. In Tables 10.4 and 10.5, we present baseline and full model specifications for employment for men and women for those four racial groups. This strategy gives us the leverage to examine intragroup differences in labor force outcomes that are associated with the migration process. This approach is justifiable, given the legacy of state-controlled race-specific population movements in South Africa. We were interested in finding out if African South Africans who changed their magisterial district of residence prior to or soon after independence had better employment outcomes than individuals who did not change their magisterial district of residence.

In the preceding analysis, we showed that foreign-born immigrants are advantaged in South Africa's labor market relative to South African-born men and women. The results presented in Tables 10.4 and 10.5 confirm that the migrant advantage carries over to South Africa-born internal migrants. Baseline and full model specifications consistently show that South African-born recent and long-term internal migrants have significantly higher odds of being employed than South African-born nonmigrant males and females. This finding is maintained across all racial groups except Whites, with recent migrants tending to do even better than long-term migrants. Individual attributes also remain strong predictors of employment outcomes among South African-born nationals (Table 10.4). The effects of schooling are somewhat inconsistent across the four racial groups. Highly educated African, Colored, and Indian/Asian males are significantly more likely to be employed than their counterparts with no schooling. In contrast, the education effect is not strong and significant among Whites. Males who are married or cohabiting are more likely to have jobs than those who are single. African males age 30 and above are significantly more likely to be employed than those between the ages 20 and 29. Among Whites, age has no effect on employment prospects. Residing in an urban area is significantly associated with lower odds of participating in the labor force among South African-born African males. On the other hand, urban residence significantly improves the labor force participation of Colored and Indians/Asians males as compared to their rural counterparts. The results are mixed for South Africa's major labor market (Gauteng province), being significantly associated with higher odds of participating in the labor force among South African-born Africans, Indians/Asians, and Coloreds; however, among Whites, the provincial effects suggest no advantage from living in the Gauteng province.

These patterns generally continue to persist when we look at odds ratios for employment among females (Table 10.5). The baseline models for all racial groups show that South African-born recent and long-term internal female migrants have statistically significantly higher odds of employment as compared to their nonmigrant counterparts. With controls for the full set of covariates (Model 2 for each racial group), the odds of employment are significantly higher among South African-born females who changed their magisterial districts.

The results for the other explanatory variables also appear to be generally consistent with the patterns we saw among males in Table 10.4. The educational payoffs are consistently significantly higher for African females. For Coloreds, having completed at least some secondary education is the only consistent

Table 10.4

Odds Ratios from Logistic Regression Models of Employment for South African-Born Internal Migrants and Nonmigrants: Males, 1996

Independent variables	Africans		Coloreds		Indians/Asians		Whites	
	Model 1	Model 2	Model 1	Model 2	Model 1	Model 2	Model 1	Model 2
Migration status								
SA-born nonmigrants (ref)	1.00	1.00	1.00	1.00	1.00	1.00	1.00	1.00
SA-born recent migrants	3.29***	2.58***	2.29***	1.76***	1.61***	1.25***	1.24***	1.16***
SA-born long-term migrants	2.30***	1.71***	1.51***	1.23***	1.37***	1.15***	1.61***	1.31***
Age Group								
20–29 (ref)		1.00		1.00		1.00		1.00
30–39		1.50***		1.11***		1.12**		1.03
40–49		1.41***		1.05*		1.07		1.06
50–55		1.41***		0.96		0.89		0.98
Education								
No schooling (ref)		1.00		1.00		1.00		1.00
Primary		1.01		0.76***		0.84**		0.96
Some secondary		1.11***		0.83***		0.62***		0.44***
Completed secondary +		1.47***		1.50***		1.23***		0.93
Marital status								
Single (ref)		1.00		1.00		1.00		1.00
Married		3.99***		3.57***		3.14***		3.94***
Living together		3.21***		2.20***		1.41**		1.84***
Widowed		2.44***		1.79***		2.09***		1.50**
Divorced		1.51***		1.23***		0.89		1.00

Type of place							
Rural (ref)		1.00	1.00		1.00		1.00
Urban		0.83***	4.10***		1.47***		1.08
Province of residence							
Gauteng (ref)		1.00	1.00		1.00		1.00
Western Cape		1.25***	2.11***		1.04		1.15***
Eastern Cape		0.51***	1.08**		0.64***		1.01
Northern Cape		1.39***	0.80***		0.98		1.19*
Free State		0.95***	0.81***		1.33		1.12*
KwaZulu-Natal		0.93***	1.01		0.89**		1.01
North West		1.19***	0.84**		1.80**		1.03
Mpumalanga		1.39***	1.08		1.31		1.19**
Limpopo		0.79***	0.77		1.56		1.36**
Number of cases	85,407	133,971		49,376		167,521	
–2 log-likelihood	1019637.8	128636.19	115708.63	34179.04	32415.90	58,970.21	55058.89

Source: Computed from the 1996 South African Population Census micro-data.
Notes: *$p < .05$; ** $p < .01$; ***$p < .001$.

Table 10.5

Odds Ratios from Logistic Regression Models of Employment for South African-Born Internal Migrants and Nonmigrants: Females, 1996

Independent variables	Africans		Coloreds		Indians/Asians		Whites	
	Model 1	Model 2	Model 1	Model 2	Model 1	Model 2	Model 1	Model 2
Migration status								
SA-born nonmigrants (ref)	1.00	1.00	1.00	1.00	1.00	1.00	1.00	1.00
SA-born recent migrants	1.91***	1.91***	1.82***	1.49***	1.61***	1.27***	1.36***	1.29***
SA-born long-term migrants	1.92***	1.57***	1.71***	1.31***	1.57***	1.20***	2.08***	1.73***
Age group								
20–29 (ref)		1.00		1.00		1.00		1.00
30–39		2.48***		1.93***		2.09***		1.37***
40–49		3.55***		2.64***		2.80***		1.79***
50–55		4.02***		2.91***		3.12***		1.73***
Education								
No schooling (ref)		1.00		1.00		1.00		1.00
Primary		1.04***		0.87***		0.63***		0.82*
Some secondary		1.10***		1.13***		0.73***		0.35***
Completed secondary +		2.09***		2.70***		1.49***		1.00
Marital status								
Single (ref)		1.00		1.00		1.00		1.00
Married		1.08***		2.04***		1.78***		1.77***
Living together		1.03***		1.14***		0.95		1.43***
Widowed		1.53***		1.53***		1.02		1.14
Divorced		1.95***		1.67***		1.03		1.04

	(1)	(2)	(3)	(4)
Type of place				
Rural (ref)	1.00	1.00	1.00	1.00
Urban	0.85***	3.13***	0.69**	0.75***
Province of residence				
Gauteng (ref)	1.00	1.00	1.00	1.00
Western Cape	1.22***	1.92***	1.08	1.18***
Eastern Cape	0.75***	0.89***	0.86	1.13**
Northern Cape	1.27***	0.59***	0.64	1.00
Free State	1.16***	0.58***	0.48*	1.04
KwaZulu-Natal	1.09***	1.30***	0.89*	0.88***
North West	1.06***	0.65***	0.88	0.81***
Mpumalanga	1.17***	0.65***	0.97	0.80***
Limpopo	0.89***	0.54***	0.85	0.99
Number of cases	898,350	141,149	34,670	157,174
−2 log-likelihood	1215412.5	147498.6	25819.3	60672.6
	1143315.8	132096.1	24628.7	58157.2

Source: Computed from the 1996 South African Population Census micro-data.

Notes: *$p < .05$; ** $p < .01$; *** $p < .001$.

Table 10.6

Odds Ratios from Logistic Regression Models of Employment for All Racial Groups: South African-Born Internal Migrants and Nonmigrants, 1996

| | Males | | Females | |
Independent variables	Model 1	Model 2	Model 1	Model 2
Migration status				
SA-born nonmigrants (ref)	1.00	1.00	1.00	1.00
SA-born recent migrants	4.15***	2.40***	2.85***	1.86***
SA-born long-term migrants	2.90***	1.66***	2.55***	1.56***
Population group				
African (ref)		1.00		1.00
White		7.96***		12.99***
Colored		2.20***		3.44***
Indian/Asian		3.67***		6.05***
Age group				
20–29 (ref)		1.00		1.00
30–39		1.42***		2.36***
40–49		1.35***		3.34***
50–55		1.31***		3.75***
Education				
No schooling (ref)		1.00		1.00
Primary		0.98**		1.02**
Some secondary		1.04***		1.07***
Completed secondary +		1.49***		2.14***
Marital status				
Single (ref)		1.00		1.00
Married		3.87***		1.17***
Living together		3.15***		1.08***
Widowed		2.28***		1.53***
Divorced		1.28***		1.78***
Type of place				
Rural (ref)		1.00		1.00
Urban		0.90***		0.91***
Province of residence				
Gauteng (ref)		1.00		1.00
Western Cape		1.47***		1.62***
Eastern Cape		0.54***		0.75***
Northern Cape		1.02		0.88***
Free State		0.95***		1.11***
KwaZulu-Natal		0.89***		1.05***
North West		1.13***		1.00
Mpumalanga		1.33***		1.10***
Limpopo		0.75***		0.82***
Number of cases	1,145,554	1,241,332		
−2 log-likelihood	1346522.3	1141597.9	1633857.1	1379714.9

Source: Computed from the 1996 South African Population Census micro-data.
Notes: *p < .05; ** p < .01; ***p < .001.

predictor of better employment outcomes. However, Model 2 for Whites shows that primary and some secondary education are negatively associated with employment prospects. White females with some secondary education are only 35 percent as likely to have a job than women with no schooling. Compared with single females, married or cohabiting females have odds of employment that are significantly larger across all racial groups. Widowed or divorced African and Colored females also have significantly higher odds of being employed than single women. The results are not as significant for the Indians/Asians and Whites as they are for Africans and Coloreds. With the exception of Coloreds, women living in urban areas are less likely to have jobs than women living in rural areas. Lastly, the odds ratios for the province covariate show considerable variation in provincial effects across racial groups. For instance, South African-born African, Colored, and White females living in the second-wealthiest province in the country (Western Cape) are statistically significantly more likely to be employed than females living in Gauteng, the wealthiest province. On the other hand, living in some of South Africa's poorest provinces, such as the Eastern Cape and Limpopo, significantly reduces the likelihood of being employed among African, Colored, and Indian/Asian women.

Conclusion

We began by discussing the state of the immigration debate in South Africa and the country's long history of relying on foreign labor reserves. The continued movement of people from neighboring SADC countries and even as far away as West Africa and Asia has led to a huge debate on whether South Africa should close its doors to immigrants, because these migrants are "taking away jobs" from South African nationals, leaving a high domestic unemployment rate. As the policy debate on African immigration continues, it has become increasingly important to examine not only the impact of immigration on the postapartheid South African labor market, but also its fiscal implications, because immigrants use social and health services.

This study has attempted to provide partial insights into the politically and emotionally charged issue of immigration and labor force participation in South Africa. Our primary objective was to determine whether foreign immigrants and internal migrants fare better or worse than nonmigrants in a postapartheid South African labor market and to account for any observed differences in labor force outcomes by migration status after controlling for covariates that are thought to affect employment. By first comparing foreign-born immigrants to South African-born males and females and then comparing South African-born internal migrants and nonmigrants, this study has provided an interesting portrait of the labor force fortunes enjoyed by both immigrants and internal migrants.

Our results suggest that immigrants and internal migrants are more likely to be employed than nonmigrants, with immigrants from other countries and the SADC region having the highest employment rates. Unlike migrants from countries outside the SADC region, most SADC-born migrants face significantly lower fixed costs of migrating to South Africa, because SADC countries like Botswana, Lesotho, Mozambique, Namibia, and Zimbabwe share a common border with South Africa. In addition, some of the SADC immigrants do not require visas to enter South Africa, and many of them have social networks in South Africa that they continue to use if they want to enter the country legally or illegally. It is likely that some SADC citizens take advantage of these conditions to migrate and search for work in South Africa, even if they are undocumented.

Our results are also consistent with the perception that immigrants and internal migrants with higher levels of education and probably a stronger will to succeed are indeed successful in sub-Saharan Africa's strongest economy. The success enjoyed by recent immigrants, particularly those from the SADC region, could be because these immigrants are drawn disproportionately from a pool that was already successful in their home countries. This finding contrasts with recent findings in developed countries, where it has been observed that recent immigrants are generally less likely to have; Jasso and Rosenzweig 1990; OECD 1998; Semyonov 1996). It is probably this success, coupled with the perceived "huge influx" of illegal immigrants and high unemployment among South African nationals that could be the underlying basis of current tensions between immigrants and local South Africans.

References

Aldrich, J.H., and F.D. Nelson. 1984. *Linear Probability, Logit, and Probit Models.* Beverly Hills, CA: Sage.

Bailey, T. 1987. *Immigrants and Native Workers: Contrasts and Competition.* Boulder, CO: Westview.

Bloom, D.E., and M. Gunderson. 1990. "An analysis of the earnings of Canadian immigrants." In *Immigration, Trade and Labour Market*, ed. R. Freeman and J.M. Abowd, 321–42. Chicago: University of Chicago Press.

Borjas, G., and M. Tienda. 1993. "The employment of male Hispanic immigrants in the United States." *International Migration Review* 27: 712–48.

Chirwa, W.C. 1997. "No TEBA . . . forget TEBA: The plight of Malawian ex-migrant workers to South Africa, 1988–1994." *International Migration Review* 31(3): 628–54.

Chiswick, B. 1982. *The Employment of Immigrants in the United States.* Washington, DC: American Enterprise Institute.

———. 1999. "Are immigrants favorably self-selected?" *American Economic Review* 89: 181–85.

Chiswick, B., and P. Miller. 1988. "Earnings in Canada: the roles of immigrant generation, French ethnicity and language." *Research in Population Economics* 6: 183–224.

Crush, J. 1999. "The discourse and dimensions of irregularity in post-apartheid South Africa." *International Migration* 37(1): 125–51.

Davis, R., and J. Head. 1995. "The future of mine migrancy in the context of broader trends in migration in Southern Africa." *Journal of Southern Africa Studies* 21(3): 439–50.

Dodoo, F.N. 1997. "Assimilation differences among Africans in America." *Social Forces* 76(2): 527–46.

Evans, Ivan, 1997. *Bureaucracy and Race.* Berkeley: University of California.

Evans, M.D., and J. Kelley. 1991. "Prejudice, discrimination, and the labour market: Attainment of immigrants in Australia." *American Journal of Sociology* 97: 721–59.

Hall, P., and A. Whiteford. 1998. "Poverty gap." In *Service Needs and Provision in Gauteng,* ed. B.M. O'Leary, V. Govind, C.A. Schwabe, and J.M. Taylor, 25–28. Pretoria: Human Sciences Research Council.

Jasso, G., and M. Rosenweig. 1990. *The New Chosen People: Immigrants in the United States.* New York: Russell Sage Foundation.

Kotze, H., and L. Hill. 1997. "Emergent migration policy in a democratic South Africa." *International Migration* 35(1): 5–36.

Long, J. Scott. 1997. *Regression Models for Categorical and Limited Dependent Variables.* Thousand Oaks CA: Sage.

Lucas, R. 1985. "Mines and migrants in South Africa." *American Economic Review* 75(5): 1094–1108.

———. 1987. "Emigration to South Africa's mine." *American Economic Review* 77(3): 313–30.

Mabogunje, A.L. 1970. "Systems approach to a theory of rural–urban migration." *Geographical Analysis* 2: 1–17.

MacDonald, J.S., and L.D. MacDonald. 1974. "Chain migration, ethnic neighborhood formation, and social networks." In *An Urban World,* ed. C. Tilly, 226–36. Boston: Little, Brown.

Martin, P. 2000. "North America, Central America, and the Caribbean." In *World Migration Report 2000.* Geneva: International Organization for Migration and United Nations.

Massey, D. 1983. "Class struggle and migrant labor in South African gold mines." *Canadian Journal of African Studies* 17(3): 429–48.

Massey, D., J. Arango, G. Hugo, A. Kouaouci, A. Pellegrino, and J.E. Taylor. 1998. *Worlds in Motion: Understanding International Migration at the End of the Millennium.* New York: Oxford University Press.

Massey, D.S., and F. Garcia Espana. 1987. "The social process of international migration." *Science* 237: 733–38.

May, J., ed. 1998. *Poverty and Inequality in South Africa, Summary Report.* Durban: Praxis.

McDonald, D., J. Gay, L. Zinyama, R. Mattes, and F. de Vletter. 1998. *Challenging Xenophobia: Myths and Realities about Cross-Border Migration in Southern Africa.* SAMP Migration Policy Series, No. 7. Cape Town.

McDonald, D.A., L. Mashike, and C. Golden. 1999. *The Lives and Times of African Migrants and Immigrants in Post-Apartheid South Africa.* SAMP Migration Policy Series, No. 13. Cape Town.

McDonald, D.A., L. Zinyama, J. Gay, F. de Vletter, and R. Matters. 2000. "Guess who's coming to dinner: Migration from Lesotho, Mozambique and Zimbabwe to South Africa." *International Migration Review* 34(3): 813–41.

Meisenheimer, J.R. 1992. "How do immigrants fare in the U.S. labor market?" *Monthly Labor Review* (December): 3–19.

Minaar, A., and M. Hough. 1996. *Who Goes There? Perspectives on Clandestine Migration and Illegal Aliens in Southern Africa.* Pretoria: HSRC Publishers.

Modood, T. 1997. "Employment." In *Ethnic Minorities in Britain: Diversity and Disadvantage,* ed. T. Modood and R. Berthoud with J. Lakey, J. Nazroo, P. Smith, S. Virdee, and S. Beishon, 83–149. London: Policy Studies Institute.

Moller, V. 1985. "Change in the South African labour migration system: A phase model." In *Up Against the Fences: Poverty, Passes, and Privilege in South Africa,* ed. H. Giliomee and L. Schlemmer, 28–38. New York: St. Martin's Press.

Organisation for Economic Co-operation and Development (OECD). 1998. *Trends in International Migration Annual Report.* Paris: OECD Publications.

Oropesa, R.S., and N.S. Landale. 2000. "From austerity to prosperity? Migration and child poverty among Mainland and Island Puerto Ricans." *Demography* 37(3): 323–38.

Peberdy, S., and J. Crush. 1998. "Rooted in racism: The origins of the Aliens Control Act." In *Beyond Control: Immigration and Human Rights in a Democratic South Africa,* ed. J. Crush, 18–36. Cape Town: IDASA.

Posel, D., and D. Casale. 2002. "What has been happening to internal labour migration in South Africa, 1993–1999?" Unpublished manuscript. Durban: University of Natal.

Reagan, P.B., and R.J. Olsen. 2000. "You can go home again: Evidence from longitudinal data." *Demography* 37(3): 339–50.

Russell, S.S., K. Jacobsen, and W.D. Stanley. 1990. *International Migration and Development in Sub-Saharan Africa.* Vol. I, Papers, Africa Technical Series No. 101. Washington, DC: World Bank.

Semyonov, M. 1996. "On the cost of being an immigrant in Israel: the effect of tenure, ethnicity and gender." *Research in Social Stratification and Mobility* 15: 115–31.

Semyonov, M., N. Lewin-Epstein, and A. Yom-Tov. 2001. "Metropolitan labour markets, peripheral labour markets and socio-economic outcomes among immigrants to Israel." *International Migration* 39(3): 99–119.

Sibanda, Amson. 2001. "Racial differences in educational attainment in South Africa." Presentation at the XXIV General Population Conference, International Union for the Scientific Study of Population (IUSSP), Salvador, Brazil, August 18–24.

Sinclair, M.R. 1999. "I know a place that is softer than this . . .emerging migrant communities in South Africa." *International Migration* 37(2): 465–81.

South Africa. Ministry of Home Affairs, Task Team on International Migration. 1999. White Paper on International Migration. Available at www.gov.za/whitepaper/1999/migrate.htm.(Accessed March 5, 2003.

Statistics South Africa. 1996. *The People of South Africa Population Census, 1996.* Report Number 03–01–11. Pretoria: Statistics South Africa.

———. 1987. "Undocumented Mexico–U.S. Migration and the returns to households in rural Mexico." *American Journal of Agricultural Economics* 69: 626–38.

The Economist. 2002. "South African immigration: Want them, throw them out" June 8: 43.

Wilson, F. 1976. "International migration in Southern Africa." *International Migration Review* 10: 451–88.

Winkelmann, R. 2000. "The labor market performance of European immigrants in New Zealand in the 1980s and 1990s." *International Migration Review* 34(1): 33–58.

Zuberi, T., A. Sibanda, A. Bawah, and A. Noumbissi. 2003. "Population and African society." *Annual Review of Sociology* 29: 465–86.

About the Editors and Contributors

Tukufu Zuberi is Lasry Family Professor of Race Relations and the director of the African Census Analysis Project (ACAP) at the University of Pennsylvania. His recent books include *Thicker Than Blood: How Racial Statistics Lie* (2001) and *Swing Low, Sweet Chariot: The Mortality Cost of Colonizing Liberia in the 19th Century* (1995). He has published numerous articles in peer-reviewed journals and as book chapters. Professor Zuberi is currently working on a book and documentary film on African development, and he is the series editor of *A General Demography of Africa.*

Amson Sibanda, formerly a research associate with the African Census Analysis Project, is Population Affairs officer at the United Nations Economic Commission for Africa (UNECA). His research focuses on HIV/AIDS, children's schooling, migration and labor force outcomes, reproductive health and food security, sustainable development issues, and the general demography of Africa. He has published several articles in peer-reviewed journals and as book chapters. He is currently writing a paper on HIV/AIDS in Africa.

Eric O. Udjo, formerly a staff member of Statistics South Africa, is senior manager at the Human Sciences Research Council (HSRC) and research director in the Epidemiology and Demography Unit in the Social Aspects of HIV/AIDS and Health Programme. Dr. Udjo has published several articles in peer-reviewed journals. His current research interests include demographic modeling and HIV/AIDS impact.

Pali J. Lehohla is the first statistician-general for the Republic of South Africa. He is the head of Statistics South Africa and a vice president of the International Association for Official Statistics (IAOS).

Akil Kokayi Khalfani is president and CEO of ATIRA Corporation. He is also a research associate with the African Census Analysis Project at the University of Pennsylvania. Dr. Khalfani has written articles and book chapters on racial classification in South Africa, Pan Africanism, and population statistics. He is currently editing a special volume on critical sociology and a book that examines the use of racial data in statistical analysis.

Amadou Noumbissi was a research associate with the African Census Analysis Project at the University of Pennsylvania. His research focuses on demographic methods and the living arrangements and well-being of vulnerable populations. He was the author of *Méthodologies d'analyse de la mortalité des enfants, Applications au Cameroun* (1996), and articles and book chapters on African demography. Dr. Noumbissi died before the publication of this volume; however, his work was essential for the realization of the volume and the work of the African Census Analysis Project.

Ayaga A. Bawah is Population Council Mellon Postdoctoral Fellow and head of the Navrongo Demographic Surveillance System at the Navrongo Health Research Centre in Ghana. He is also a research associate with the African Census Analysis Project at the University of Pennsylvania. His research interests are mainly in the areas of mortality and fertility. He has published several peer-reviewed articles and book chapters. His latest contribution is in the development of *Model Life Tables for Sub-Saharan Africa.*

Sulaiman Bah, formerly a staff member of Statistics South Africa, is senior lecturer in epidemiology at the National School of Public Health, Medical University of Southern Africa. His research interests are very broad and include vital statistics, improvement in vital registration systems, causes of death, migration, population projections, and the epidemiology of historical Islamic populations. He has published numerous papers on these subject areas in peer-reviewed journals and book chapters.

Eliya Msiyaphazi Zulu is the deputy director of research at the African Population and Health Research Center and vice president of the Union of African Population Studies. He has published articles on fertility control, sociocultural factors affecting reproductive behavior, sexual networking, maternal health, and child fosterage and household structure. His current research mostly focuses on investigating interlinkages between rapid urbanization, poverty, and health in sub-Saharan Africa.

Gwendoline Lehloenya is currently provincial manager of the Gauteng Provincial Office for Statistics South Africa. She holds a master's degree in development economics from Williams College in Massachusetts and a second master's degree in demography from the University of Pennsylvania. Mrs. Lehloenya has worked for the South African government since 1977.

Index

Adegboyega, Wole, 13, 236
Adepoju, Aderanti, 218
Adopted children, 172, 173
African Independent Churches, age at first
    birth, **74**, 75, 77, **78**, 83, **84**
African National Congress (ANC), census
    and, 15, 32
Africans/Blacks
  age at first birth, **72**, 73, **74**, 76–77,
    78–79
  under apartheid, 220–221, 223, 246, 248
  birth registration, 42
  children's living arrangements, 237, **238**,
    238, **239**
  fertility rate of, 46, **47**, **49**, 49, **50**, 51–52,
    53, 55, 57–58, **58**, 66, **71**
  household headship (female), 223, 235,
    236–237, 241, **242**, 244, **247**
  household size and composition, **174**,
    174, 221, 224, **225**, **226**, 227–231,
    228–233, 234
  labor force participation, **281**, 283, 284,
    285, 287, **288**, **290**, **292**, 293
  life expectancy of, **196**, **197**
  life tables, **208**, **209**
  migrant workers, 220, 221, 269
  mortality, **117**
    child, 94, **95**, 96, **97**, 110, **114**, **117**
    female, **99**, **101**, 101, **105**, **107**, 114

Africans/Blacks
  mortality *(continued)*
    male, 103, **104**, **116**, **205**
  out-of-wedlock births, 238, **239**
  parental survival status, **163**, 164, **165**,
    166, **167**, 167, **179**, **180**
  in population, **12**, 15, 221
  in poverty, 66–67
  racial classification, **11**, 13–14
  resettlement policy, 18–19, 86
  school completion, 258, **259**, **260**,
    261–264, **263**
  school enrollment, 255, **256**, **257**, 261,
    262
  underenumeration of, 15–16, 16–17, **20**
  vital statistics among, 21–22
Afrikaans Language Movement, 30
Afrikaners
  age at first birth, 80, **81**, 82
  fertility rate of, 80
  hegemony of, 8–9
  See also Whites/Europeans
Age
  fertility rate and, **44**, **50**, 51, 52–53
  household headship (female) and, **242**,
    245, **247**
  labor force participation and, **281**, 283,
    285, **288**, **290**, **292**
  life expectancy and, **196**, **197**, **205**, **206**

Page numbers in **bold** refer to figures and tables

Age *(continued)*
  maternal, at first birth, 65–86
  migration and, 274, **276**
  mortality and, 130, **131**, 132, **133–144**,
    145
    HIV/AIDS, 129–130, 145–146,
      147–150, 151, 160
  parental survivor status and, 164, **165**
Ahmad, W.I.U., 68
AIDS. *See* HIV/AIDS
Ainsworth, Martha, 223
Allison, D. Paul, 163
Amoateng, A.Y., 219
Apartheid
  censuses under, 9–19
  household structure under, 168, 219–220,
    223, 246, 248
  legislative basis for, 9, 12, 18, 66
  racial classification of, 31–32, 66, 68
  state partition policy, 18, 86, 220
Appolis, Keith U.C., 221, 237
Arriaga, E.E., 43, 57
Aryee, A.F., 218, 219
Asians. *See* Indians/Asians

Bah, Sulaiman, 3–39, 120–159, 161,
  181–216, 204
Bailey, T., 275
Bamgboye, E.A., 94
Bangha, Martin W., xi–xiv
Bantu Education Act of 1953, 261
Bantu Homelands Citizenship Act of 1970,
  18, 220
Barrera, A., 254
Barringer, Herbert, 7
Bawah, Ayaga A., 160–180
Beers, M., 123
Beers formula, 189, 215
Behr, A., 261
Beinart, W., 86
Bélec, L., 123
Bennett, N., 214
Berkow, R., 123
Birth. *See* Childbearing
Birth rate. *See* Fertility rate
Birth registration, **38**, **39**, 42, 183, 213
Births, Deaths and Marriages Registration
  of of 1923, 21

Births and Deaths Registration Act
  of 1963, 24–25
  of 1992, 23, 25, 126, 236
Blacker, J., 98, 104
Blanc, C.B., 253
Bledsoe, C., 65, 68, 75
Bledsoe, Caroline H., 223, 249
Bloom, D.E., 266, 294
Bongaarts, J., 43, 52, 65
Booth, H., 43
Borjas, G., 266
Bradshaw, D., 26
Brass, W., 41, 43, 45, 92–93, 94, 105, 161,
  162, 191, 192–193
Bruce, Judith, 235
Burgard, S., 96, 176

Caldwell, J.C., 65, 68, 80, 175, 254
Caldwell, P., 65, 68, 80
Calves, A.E., 68
Campbell, C., 68
Casale, D., 270, 286
Case, A., 67, 219
Catholics, age at first birth, **74**, 75, 77,
  78, **81**, 82, 83, **84**
Cell, John W., 8
Census
  in Black (TBVC) states, 17–19
  education data, 254
  fertility data, 40, 42, 67
  household structure data, 169, 222–223
  immigration/migration data, 270, 272,
    273
  mortality data, 90, 92, 161
  postapartheid, 19–20, 32
  racial classification in, 4, 9–14, **11**, **12**,
    31, 32
  sex composition in, **16**, 16–17, **17**
  underenumeration of, 14–16, **20**, 57,
    222
Center for Disease Control and Prevention
  (CDC), definition of HIV/AIDS,
  123–124
Central Reference Bureau (CRB), 22, 24
Central Statistical Service (CSS), 10, 13,
  14, 15, 16, 17, 18–19, 32
  See also Statistics South Africa
Cherlin, A., 65

Childbearing
  age at first birth, 65–86
  birth registration, **38**, **39**, 42
  location/timing of, 51–52, 65
  out-of-wedlock, 168, 230, 235,
      237–238, **239**, **240**
  vital statistics, 21, 23, 24–25
  See also Fertility rate
Child Care Act of 1983, 236
Child mortality, 75, 90
  data collection, 91–92
  estimates of, 92–93
  female, 105–106, **107**, **108**
  HIV/AIDS, 97, 111
  infant, 75, 108, **109**, 111
  life tables, 187–188, 190–192
  race/ethnicity, 94–96, **95**, 110,
      114–115
  trends in, 96–98, **97**
Children, education of. *See* School
    completion; School enrollment
Children, living arrangements of,
    236–238, **238**, **239**, **240**, 241
  fosterage, 172, 173
  in institutions, 162
  parental survival and, 168–170, **171**,
      172, 172–175, **173**, **174**
Chimere-Dan, O., 57, 66, 67, 70
Chirwa, W.C., 269
Chiswick, B., 266, 268, 275
Cho, Lee-Jay, 237
Christians, age at first birth, **74**, 75, 77,
    78, **81**, 82, 83, **84**
Christopher, A.J., 7, 14, 18
Civil registration system, 23–24, 33, 181
  See also Life tables
Classification Board, 5, 6
Clogg, C., 183
Coale, A., 183, 214
Coale-Demeney West model life tables, 192
Cobley, A.G., 75
Cohen, B., 65, 68, 75
Cohen, Barney, 219
Coloreds
  age at first birth, **72**, 73, **74**, 82–83, **84**
  census of, **12**, 15, **20**
  children's living arrangements, 237, **238**,
      238, **239**

Coloreds *(continued)*
  fertility rate of, **47**, 48, **50**, 51, 52, **53**, 55,
      58, 67, **71**
  household headship (female), 235,
      236–237, 241, **242**, **242–243**, 244
  household size and composition, **174**,
      174, **225**, 227–231, **228–233**, 234
  labor force participation, 287, **288**, **290**,
      292, 293
  life expectancy of, **196**, **197**
  life tables, **200**, **201**, 204, **208**, **209**, 213
  mortality, **117**
    child, 94, **95**, 96, **97**, **114**, **117**
    female, 98, **99**, **101**, 101–102, **105**,
        107, **114**
    male, 103, **104**, 204, **205**
  out-of-wedlock births, 238, **239**
  parental survival status, **163**, 164, **165**,
      166, **167**, **179**, **180**
  racial classification, 7, **11**, 13
  school completion, 258, **259**, **260**, 261,
      263
  school enrollment, 255, **256**, **257**, 261,
      262
  vital statistics, 24
Cooper, R.S., 68
Cousins, C.W., 5, 31
Cox, Oliver C., 31
Crush, J., 267, 286
Crush, J.S., 76

Davenport, T.R.H., 6, 23
David, R., 68
Davies, G., 124
Davis, R., 221, 269
Death. *See* Mortality
Death registration, 121, 123, 151, 154, 181,
    183, 190, 213
Deaton, A., 67
Decennial life tables, 185–186
de Graft-Johnson, K.T., 32
Demographic Health Survey (DHS), 169
Desai, S., 161
Diamond, I., 65, 73
Diseases
  causes of death, **152–153**, **158**, **159**
  HIV/AIDS-related, **157**, **158**, **159**
Dodoo, F.N., 266

Dorrington, R., 57
Dubow, Saul, 5, 11
du Plessis, G.E., 70

Educational attainment
  age at first birth and, 69, **72**, 73, **74**, 77,
    78, **81**, 82, 83, **84**, **85**
  analysis of social disparities, 253–254
  gender and, 254–255, **256**, **257**, 258, **259**,
    260, 261
  household headship (female) and, 241,
    242, 243, 245, **247**
  of immgrants/migrants, 278, **279**, 280
  labor force participation and, **281**, 282,
    284, **285**, 287, **288**, **290**, **292**, 293
  race and, 261–264, **262**, **263**
Elo, I.T., 164

Employment
  household headship (female) and, 241,
    242, 243–244, **247**
  immigrant studies, 266–267
  self-employed, 278
  See also Labor force participation
Employment Bureau of Africa (TEBA), 269
Ethnic identity, 8–9
  See also Africans/Blacks; Coloreds;
    Indians/Asians; Whites/Europeans
Evans, I., 21, 22
Evans, Ivan, 267
Evans, M.D., 266, 275
Extended households, 169–170, **172**, **173**,
  174, 174–175, **230**, 230–231, **232–233**,
  234

Family structure. *See* Households
Fathers
  deaths of, **166**, 166, **167**, 167–168
  natural, 236
  survival status of. *See* Parental survival
    status
Feeney, G., 52
Females. *See* Childbearing; Fertility rate;
  Women
Fernandez, C.R.E., 93
Fertility rate, 40–64
  Afrikaner, 80
  age pattern of, **44**, **50**, 51, 52–53

Fertility rate *(continued)*
  data sources on, 41–42
  decline in, 52, 55–56, 67
  methods of analysis, 42–43
    Gompertz relational model, 43–44, 46,
      48–52, **49**, **50**, 54, 61, **62–64**
    P/F ratio, 43, 44, **45**, 46, **47**
  overestimation of, 57–58
  by race, 70–71, **71**
  regional pattern of, 53–55, **55**
  religion and, 75
  total (TFR), 52, **53**, **55**, 56–58, **58**, 67
Filmer, D., 254
Forste, R., 66
Foster, G., 160
Frederickson, H., 102
Futures Group International, 125

Gage, A.J., 65, 69, 163, 169, 219
Gardner, Robert W., 7
Gender
  population, composition , **16**, 16–17, **17**
  school completion and, 255, **257**, 258,
    259, **260**, 261
  school enrollment and, 254–255, **256**, **257**
  See also Males; Women
Gerhart, Gail M., 8
Giliomee, H., 80
Giliomee, Hermann, 30
Glover, J., 182, 184, 185
Gompertz relational model, 43–44, 46,
  48–52, **49**, **50**, 54, 61, **62–64**
Grandparent-headed households, 170, **172**
Gray, R.H., 102
Gregson, S., 70, 75
Greville, T., 183, 184, 189
Group Areas Act of 1950, 220, 221, 269
Gunderson, M., 266, 294

Hakulinen, T., 122
Hall, P., 76, 282
Hamad, A.M., 44, 47
Hanchard, Michael George, 7
Head, J., 221, 269
Heligman, L., 215
Hetler, C.B., 243
Hill, K., 94, 161
Hill, L., 267, 268

Hill, M.A., 253, 254
Himes, C., 183
Hindus, age at first birth, **85**
Hirschowitz, R., 92
HIV/AIDS
  deaths related to, 130, 132, **134**, **159**
    age-specific, 129–130, 146, **147–150**,
      151, 160
    child, 97, 111
    from complications and related
      conditions, **158**, **159**
    estimating, 122–126, 151, 154–155
    by gender, 103, **134**, 146, **147–150**,
      151
    projections, 126–128
    vital statistics, 27–28
  defined by CDC, 123–124
  family, impact on, 160, 238, 241
  growth rate, 125
  health conditions related to, **157**
  household structure and, 219
  prevalence, **109**, **119**
Horiuchi, S., 214
Hough, M., 268
Households
  under apartheid, 168, 219–220, 246,
    248
  children's living arrangements, 236–238,
    238, **239**, **240**, 241
    parental survival and, 168–170, **171**,
      172, 172–175, **173**, **174**
  defined, 169, 222–223
  headship, 170, **171**, **172**, 172, 282
    female, 223, 224, 234–235, **236**, 241,
      242–243, 243–246
  size and composition, 46, 224, **225**, **226**,
    227–231, **228–233**, 234
  sociocultural changes and, 218–219
  types of, 163, 169–170, **172**, 172–175,
    174, 229
Hull, T.H., 122
Human Sciences Research Council
  (HSRC), 15
Hunter, S., 160
Hyde, K.A.L., 253, 255

Identity cards, 21–22
Ignatiev, Noel, 7

Immigrants
  census data on, 270, 272
  educational attainment and, 278, **279**,
    280
  employment research on, 266–267
  illegal, 268, 270, 278
  labor force participation of, 267, 268,
    275, **277**, 278, **281**, 282, 283, 294
  in migrant labor system, 269
  See also Migration, internal
Immigration policy, 267, 268
Indians/Asians
  age at first birth, **72**, 73, **74**, **85**
  census of, **12**, 14, **20**
  children's living arrangements, **240**
  fertility rate of, 46, **47**, 48, **49**, 49, **50**, 51,
    52, **53**, 56, **58**, 67, **71**
  household headship (female), 235,
    236–237, 241, 244
  household size and composition, **174**,
    174, **225**, 227–231, **228–233**
  labor force participation, 287, **288**, **290**,
    292, 293
  life expectancy of, **196**, **197**
  life tables, **202**, **203**, 204, **208**, **209**
  mortality, **118**
    child, 94–96, **95**, **97**, **115**, **118**
    female, 98, **99–100**, **101**, 102, **105**,
      107, **115**
    male, **104**, 204, **205**
    parental survival status, **163**, 164, **165**,
      166, **167**, **179**, **180**
  racial classification, 14
  school completion, 258, **259**, **260**, 261,
    262, **263**
  school enrollment, 255, **256**, **257**, 261,
    262
  vital statistics, 24
Infant mortality, 75, 108, **109**, 111, **119**,
  187, 188, 190–191
Institutional residence, 162, **179**
Isiugo-Abanihe, U.C., 218, 223

Jackson, Fatimah L.C., 5
Jasso, G., 266, 275, 280, 294
Jenkins formula, 189
Jewkes, R., 28
Jones, J., 124

Karup-King formula, 189
Kaufman, C.E., 67, 70
Kelly, J., 266, 275
Kennedy, E., 235
Khalfani, Akil Konayi, 3–39, 4, 19, 20, 30, 32, 222
Kiernan, K., 65, 73
King, E.M., 253, 254
Kington, R., 164
Kleinschmidt, I., 124
Knodel, J., 70
Koen, Charton, 219
Kotze, H., 267, 268
Krieger, N., 68
Krige, E.J., 69
Kuper, A., 69
Kuper, L., 57–58

Labor force participation, 271–272, **292**
    educational attainment and, **281**, 282, 284, **285**, 287, **288**, **290**, **292**, 293
    female, 275, **277**, 283–284, **285**, 286, **290–291**, 293
    immigrants, 267, 268, 275, **277**, 278, **281**, 282, 283, **285**, 286, 294
    migrants (internal), 168, 220, **277**, 286–287, **288–291**, 294
    by region/province, **281**, 282–283, 284, **285**, 287, **289**, **291**, **292**
    social networks and, 286
Lam, D., 254
Lamb, W.H., 102
Landale, N.S., 270
Lands Acts, 220
LaVeist, T.A., 68
Lehloenya, Gwendoline, 253–264
Lehohla, Pali J., 3–39
Lesthaeghe, R.J., 69, 70
Levin, Michael J., 7
Life expectancy
    female, 106, 195, **197**
    male, 195, **196**, 213
    See also Life tables
Life tables, 181–216
    female, 104–106, **105**, **199**, **200**, **203**, **209**
    male, **198**, **200**, **202**, 204, **208**, **210**
    post-1985, 186–189, 213–214

Life tables (*continued*)
    pre-1985, 186–189, **198–203**, 204, 212–213
    proposed program, 214–216
    by race, 195, **198–203**, 204, **208**, **209**, 213, 215
    by region/province, **206–207**, 212, 215
    two-parameter, 94
    in U.S., 182–186
Linder, F., 28
Linguistic differences, 69
Lloyd, A.K., 253
Lloyd, C., 77
Lloyd, Cynthia B., 161, 235
London, D., 187
Long, J. Scott, 163
Lopez, A., 122
Lopez, A.D., 122
Lucas, R., 76, 220, 221, 269

Mabogunje, A.L., 269
Magubane, Bernard Makhosezwe, 14
Magubane, P., 69
Malan, D.F., 18
Males
    educational attainment of, 278, **279**
    labor force participation by, 275, **277**, 280, **281**, 282
    life expectancy of, 195, **196**, 213
    life tables, **198**, **200**, **202**, 204, **208**, **210**
    migrant labor, 168, 220, 221, **242**, 243–244
    migration status, 274, **276**
    mortality, 102–104, **104**, **116**, 175, 212
        age-specific, 130, **131**, **133–140**, **142–143**
        causes of death, **152**
        HIV/AIDS-related, 103, **134**, 146, **147–150**, 151
        by race, 204, **205**
        by region/province, **206**, 212
    underenumeration of, 16–17
    See also Parental survivor status
Mamdani, M., 21, 22
Mandela, Nelson, 221
Mandela, N.R., 103

Marital status
  household headship (female) and,
      237–238, **238**, **239**, 244, 245, **247**
  labor force participation and, **281**, 282,
      284, **285**, **288**, **290**, **292**
Marriage patterns, 168, 218–219, 224
Martin, P., 278
Marwick, M., 69
Massey, D., 220, 269
May, J., 66, 76, 283
May, Julian, 234
Mbugua, Wariara, 218, 219
McDaniel, A., 7, 65, 66, 86, 169, 219, 223
McDaniel, Antonio, 160, 163, 219
McDonald, D.A., 267, 269, 286
Meegama, S.A., 102
Meekers, D., 75, 219
Meisenheimer, J.R., 275
Men. *See* Males
Menken, J., 65
Migration, internal
  age distribution and, 275, **276**
  census data on, 270, 272, 273
  educational attainment and, 278, **279**, 280
  household headship (female) and, **242**,
      243–244, 244, 245, **247**
  labor force participation and, 168, 220,
      286–287, **288–291**, 294
  population groups, **273**, 273–274
  See also Immigrants
Miller, P., 266, 275
Minaar, A., 268
Modood, T., 266
Moerdijk, Donald, 176, 221
Moffat, J.B., 10
Moller, V., 269
Morgan, S. Philip, 66, 163, 169, 219, 237
Mortality
  age-specific data, 130, 131, 132,
      133–144, 145–146
  cause-of-death data, 28–29, **29**, 121–122,
      126, 151, **152–153**, 155
  data collection, 90–91, 154, 192
  estimates of, 93–94
  by gender. *See* Males, mortality; Women,
      mortality
  by race, **117–118**, 204, **205**
  by region/province, **206–207**, 212

Mortality *(continued)*
  underreporting/misreporting, 212
  vital statistics system, 21, 23, 24–25,
      27–28, **38**, **39**
  See also Child mortality; HIV/AIDS,
      deaths related to; Life tables;
      Parental survival status
Mothers
  child living arrangements, 236–238, **237**,
      238
  deaths of, 164, **165**, 166–168, **167**, 173
  marital status of, 237–238, **238**, **239**
  survival status of. *See* Parental survival
      status
  See also Childbearing; Fertility rate
Murray, C., 122, 218, 221
Muslims, age at first birth, **74**, 75, 77, **78**,
      83, **84**, **85**

Nascimento, Abdias do, 31
Nascimento, Elisa Larkin, 31
National Health Information System for
      South Africa (NHIS/SA), 26–27
Native Laws Amendment Act of 1952, 22
Natural Fathers of Children Born Out of
      Wedlock Act of 1997, 236
Newman, P., 102
Newton-Sheppart formula, 189
Ngom, P., 68
Nhlapho, Margaret, 221, 237
Noumbissi, Amadou, 160–180
Nuclear households, 169, **172**, 172–173,
      173, 175, 229, **230**, **232–233**

Obono, O.M., 218
Ocholla-Ayayo, A.B.C., 219
October Household Surveys (OHS), 40,
      41–42, 54, 90, 91–92
O'Laughlin, B., 235
Olson, R.J., 275
One-person household, **230**, 230
Oppong, Christine, 219
Orkin, M., 92
Oropesa, R.S., 270
Orphanhood. *See* Parental survival status
Orphanhood reports, 93–94
Out-of-wedlock childbearing, 168, 230,
      235, **238**, **239**

Page, Hilary J., 223
Palloni, A., 122
Parental survival status, 162–163, 175–176, 219
    by age and gender, 164, **165**, **166**, 166–168, 175
    data collection, 161–162, 190, 192
    HIV/AIDS epidemic and, 160
    misreporting of, 103–104
    by race, **163**, 163, 164, **165**, **166**, **167**, **179**, **180**
    regional differences in, **167**, 167–168, 176
    residential patterns and, 160–161, 168–170, **171**, **172**, 172–176, **173**, **174**
Patterson, Sheila, 8
Pebley, A.R., 70
Peires, J.B., 86
Peters, P., 235
P/F ratio method, 43, 44, **45**, 46, **47**
Piani, Andrea L., 169
Pickel, B., 68, 70
Pictet, G., 154
Pogrund, Benjamin, 6
Pollard, J., 215
Polygynous households, 169
Population groups. *See* Africans/Blacks; Coloreds; Indians/Asians; Whites
Population register, 21–24, 33, 122, 130, 154
Population Registration Act of 1950, 12, 21, 220
Population Registration Act Repeal Act of 1991, 13, 23, 25, 181
Population statistics, 3–4, 32–33
    See also Census; Life tables; Vital statistics system
Posel, D., 270, 286
Preston, S.H., 66, 68, 104, 122, 162, 164, 183, 214
Preston-Whyte, E., 69
Provinces. *See* Region/province

Quinn, C. Thomas, 160

Race, defined, 4–8
Racial classification
    apartheid and, 31–32, 66, 68

Racial classification *(continued)*
    census, 4, 9–14, **11**, **12**, 32
    ethnicity and, 7, 8–9
    impact of, 31
    legitimate, 29–30
    vital statistics, 21–22, 24, 25
    See also Africans/Blacks; Coloreds; Indians/Asians; Whites/Europeans
Ramphele, Mamphela, 221
Reagan, P.B., 275
Reconstruction and Development Programme (RDP), 26
Region/province
    age at first birth, 70, **72**, **74**, 75–76, 77, **78–79**, **81**, 82, **84**, **85**
    HIV/AIDS deaths, 124
    household headship (female), **243**, **248**
    household type, **174**, 175
    labor force participation, **281**, 282–283, 284, **285**, 287, **289**, **291**, **292**
    life tables, **210**, **211**, 215
    mortality
        female, 106–108, **108**, **110**, **206–207**, 212
        male, **206**, 212
    parental survivor status, **167**, 167–168, 176
    school completion, 258, **259**, **260**, **263**
    school enrollment, 255, **256**, **257**, **262**
Religion, age at first birth and, 70, 73, **74**, 75, **77**, **78**, **81**, 82, 83, **84**, **85**
Residential patterns. *See* Households
Riley, N., 65
Rindfuss, R.R., 65, 68, 69, 73
Rives, N., 183
Rosenweig, M., 266, 275, 280, 294
Ross, Roberts, 8
Rural areas
    age at first birth in, **72**, **74**, 75, **78**, **81**, 82
    household headship (female) in, 235, **236–237**, **248**
    household structure in, 175, 231, **232–233**
    labor force participation in, **281**, **285**, **288**, **290**, **292**, 293
    life tables, **206–207**
    parental survival in, **167**, 167–168

Russel, Margo, 219, 221, 266
Rutstein, S.O., 92

Sadie, J.L., 30–31, 40, 57, 66
St. John, C., 65, 68
Schapera, I., 69
School completion
  gender gap, 255, 258, **259**, **260**, 261
  racial gap, 261–264, **263**
School enrollment
  gender gap, 254–255, **256**, **257**
  racial gap, 261, **262**
Schultz, T.W., 253
Self-employed, 278
Self-Governing Territories (SGT), 18
Semyonov, M., 266, 294
Shisana, O., 97
Sibanda, Amson, xi-xiv, 56, 65–89, 67, 70,
    75, 168, 218–248, 219, 230, 237, 253,
    253–264, 266–294, 271, 282
Simbayi, L., 97
Simkins, C., 40
Sinclair, M.R., 267, 286
Singh, Anand, 219, 221
Single-parent households, 169, 219, **230**,
    230, **232–233**
Siqwana-Ndulo, Nombulelo, 219, 221, 235
Smith, J., 164
Social networks, 286
Socioeconomic status
  age at first birth and, 69–70
  household headship (female) and, 241,
    242, 243, 245–246, **248**
Sommerfelt, A. Elisabeth, 163, 169
South Africa Demographic and Health
    Survey (SADHS), 56
South African Law Commission (SALC),
    27
South African Migration System (SAMS),
    268–269, 269
South African Native Trust Lands, 18
Southern Africa Development Community
    (SADC), 269
Starr, Paul, 30, 31
Statistics South Africa, 19–20, 24, 33, 42,
    56, 90, 91, 121, 125, 162, 234
  cause of death statistics, 28–29, **29**
  household defined by, 169, 222–223

Statistics South Africa *(continued)*
  life tables, 181–182
Stillbirths, 97
Stolley, P.D., 68

TBVC states, 18–19
Thomas, D., 254, 261
Thompson, Leonard, 8, 18
Tienda, M., 66, 266
Timaeus, I., 103, 161, 191, 192
Tobias, Phillip V., 4, 5, 11
Trussell, J., 161

Udjo, Eric O., xi-xiv, 40–64, 56, 70,
    90–111, 94, 96, 103
Underenumeration, census, 14–16, **20**, 222
United States, life tables in, 182–186
Urban areas
  age at first birth in, **72**, **74**, 75, **78**, **81**, 82
  household headship (female) in, 235,
    236–237, **248**
  household structure in, 175, 231,
    232–233
  labor force participation in, **281**, **285**,
    287, **288**, **290**, **292**, 293
  life tables, **206–207**
  parental survival in, **167**
Urban Areas Act of 1923, 21

van de Walle, E., 65, 67, 70, 219, 222
van Wyk, D.H., 5, 6
*Villages and Townships Vital Statistics
    Network* (VTVSN), 28
Vital statistics system, 20–29
  among Africans, 21–22
  completeness of, 212, 213
  development of, 24–28
  future of, 28–29, 33
  origins of, 20–21
  population register and, 22–24
  See also Life tables
Vu, Manh Loi, 243

Wade, Peter, 7, 31
Watson, Graham, 7
Westoff, C.J., 68, 69, 82
Whelpton, P., 183
Whiteford, A., 76, 282

Whites/Europeans
  age at first birth, **72**, 73, **74**, 80, **81**
  census of, **12**, 15, **20**
  children's living arrangements, **240**
  ethnic identity, 7, 8–9
  fertility rate, **47**, 48–49, **49**, **50**, 51, 52,
    53, 56, **58**, 67, **71**
  household headship (female), 241, **242**,
    244
  household size and composition, **174**,
    174, 224, **225**, **226**, 227–231, **229**,
    231, **233**, 234
  labor force participation, 281, 283, 284,
    285, 287, **288**, **290**, **292**, 293
  language and, 30–31
  life expectancy, 195, **196**, **197**, 213
  life tables, **198**, **199**, 204, **208**, **209**
  mortality, **118**
    child, **95**, 95–96, **97**, **115**, **118**
    female, 98, **100**, **101**, 102, **105**, **107**,
      115
    male, 104, 204, **205**
  parental survival status, **163**, **165**, **166**,
    167, 167, **179**, **180**
  racial classification, 6–7, **11**, 12–13
  school completion, 258, **259**, **260**, 262,
    263
  school enrollment, 255, **256**, **257**, 261,
    262
  vital statistics, 24
Wilkinson, D., 124
Williams, D.R., 68
Williamson, J., 160
Wilson, F., 268, 269
Winkelmann, R., 266, 275
Women
  educational attainment of, **279**, 280
  HIV/AIDS prevalence among, **109**

Women *(continued)*
  household headship by, 223, 224,
    234–235, **236–237**, 241, **242–243**,
    243–246
  immigrants/migrants, 270, 274, **276**,
    283–284, **285**
  labor force participation of, 275, **277**,
    283–284, **285**, 286, **290–291**, 293
  life expectancy, 106, 195, **197**
  life tables, 104–106, **105**, **199**, **200**, **203**,
    209
  marital status, 237–238, **238**, **239**, 244
  mortality, 98, **99–100**, **101**, 101–102,
    105, 106–108, **107**, **110**, **114**, **115**,
    212
    age-specific, **132**, 132, **133–138**,
      140–142, **143–144**, 145
    causes of, **153**
    HIV/AIDS-related, **134**, 145–146,
      147–150, 151
    by race, 204, **205**
    by region/province, **206–207**
  in population, **16**, 16–17, **17**
  See also Childbearing; Fertility rate;
    Mothers; Parental survivor status
Wood, K., 28
Wyrick, R., 122

Youssef, N., 243

Zaba, B., 43
Ziehl, S.C., 222, 223
Zuberi, Tukufu, xi-xiv, 3–39, 4, 7, 17, 19,
  20, 30, 31, 32, 33, 56, 65–89, 67, 68,
  70, 160–180, 168, 230, 237, 266,
  266–294
Zulu, Eliya Msiyaphazi, 160, 168,
  218–248, 219, 223, 282